POST-VICTORIAN POETRY

HERBERT PALMER

POST-VICTORIAN POETRY

∘O∘

Herbert Palmer

London

J. M. DENT & SONS LTD

PREFACE

SEVERAL of the chapters in this book have already been published—in the *Cornhill Magazine, Bookman, Dublin Magazine*. Scraps and parts of some other chapters have appeared in the *New Statesman, Irish Statesman, Adelphi Magazine, Dublin Magazine, John o' London's Weekly, Everyman, Bookman, New Britain, Country Life, Listener.* But there has, of course, of many of the published portions been much revision, because press criticism of single books generally gave a very incomplete survey of a poet's real quality, while even when it was a case of reviewing collected works or writing a short study of a poet as a whole, some things were oversaid or said incompletely.

Professor W. Macneile Dixon has written in the preface of twenty-one 'Maxims' to his book of verse, *In Arcadia* (1933), 'The poet who has not a critic in him is no poet; the critic who has not a poet in him is no critic,' which is true enough, though in some instances of criticism likely to introduce rather too much of the personal element; for when I recently asked a critic and prominent poet of one of the older schools why he hadn't thought of writing a book of this kind, he very humanly answered me: 'Because I didn't want to leave myself out.' . . . Perhaps I have been too conscious of my own shadow, and in two or three instances I have not entirely avoided it, though, generally speaking, I think I have sufficiently dodged its contact. But in what chapter, if I were able to write in sufficient detachment, would I have specially placed myself? . . . I think it would have been in the chapter on Narrative Poetry. For were some angel to descend out of heaven telling me it was decreed that no more than 150 pages of my verse should be preserved, but with the pleasing information that stress would be put upon my own preferences, I think I should leave short space for odes and lyrics by making first choice of all those longer poems of from three to sixteen pages which directly or indirectly tell some sort of a tale.

As regards my special fitness for this kind of criticism it is perhaps just as well to inform readers that my springs are far-seated—for as far back as the end of the last century I published verse (in a northern weekly); and even in those adolescent days I was by no means oblivious of what was going on in the post-Tennyson world, though it was not till the age of thirty-eight, during the final year of the Great War, that I issued my first book, an attempt at a tiny matured selection (but with topical implications) which allowed entrance of none of those very early ineffective lyrics. I have lived and written through the hostilities and clashes of many vogues and fashions, always interested, sometimes irritated, sometimes enchanted, yet never, even when envious, quite able to put their characteristics into my own fiddle; and in the end I see no very overwhelming difference between verse of the different schools and personalities once it can pass the test of Poetry. All that is essential is that it should be genuine, that it should be 'sensuous and impassioned,' that it should make experience completely alive, that it should be capable of giving pleasure to a listening ear; and because I pride myself nearly as much on my capacity for reading verse to an audience as for writing it and writing about it, I feel that I have not erred in the selections of poems and stanzas which struck me as specially good. 'Poems should be statues in sound, to be remembered as one remembers the Delphian Charioteer, or Nike fastening her sandal,' says Macneile Dixon in his 'Maxims,' and though this chiefly applies to lyrical verse, it clearly functions throughout every long poem of consequence.

I have tried to get into the book and write something about every poet of consequence (especially those who have published more than one brochure or volume), but I am aware that I have not fully succeeded. Omniscience might have included another fifty, and blotted out a score of those listed and discussed—for even some of my supposed blackbirds and thrushes may turn out to be little better than sparrows. But as in most instances some part of twentieth-century criticism coincides with my own, I think I have not too frequently erred.

As a moderate conservative outlook in a book of this kind is unavoidable, the main stress has been laid on the poets who published their first volume before 1930; but as regards the space allotted to them (especially some of the women poets) this must not in a number of instances be taken as the exact measure of their quality and importance, particularly as the verse which the future may prize is unlikely to coincide always with present- and recent-day preferences.

The title of the book has been difficult to fix, for though I have sought to write almost entirely of the creative output following the death of Queen Victoria, several of my important twentieth-century poets, especially Newbolt, Kipling, and Watson, wrote a large proportion of their best verse before that date. It is unfortunate that the title partially crosses that of Sir Arthur Quiller-Couch's fine anthology, *The Oxford Book of Victorian Verse*, which included some of the best lyrical verse of the reign of King Edward VII. But to-day we realize that so many of the poems having the appearance of a Victorian overflow, really belonged to a quite new period—the Georgian. Then as time went on some of its traditional elements changed into what might be termed 'Neo-Georgian,' while others, antagonistic to both, developed into what might be termed 'Sub-Georgian.' I have dealt, as far as space would allow, with all these three types, and since the book is about the poetry of the British Isles, I have naturally avoided the discussion of American and Colonial poets, save where, as in the case of H. D., they sailed very obviously in one of the strong currents. And because of the amount of space that has been taken up by the verse dating from 1900 (more than three-quarters of the book), the subject-matter seems to justify the selection of the title, *Post-Victorian Poetry*.

H. E. P.

February 1938.

ACKNOWLEDGMENTS

For whole short poems and half poems or more, and certain long passages, I thank Lascelles Abercrombie, Richard Aldington, J. Redwood Anderson, J. D. Beazley, Laurence Binyon and Messrs Macmillan & Co., Gerald Bullett and Messrs J. M. Dent & Sons, W. R. Childe, Richard Church, Austin Clarke, Mrs Daryush, Oxford University Press and Messrs Macmillan & Co., Walter de la Mare, Lord Alfred Douglas, Helen Friedlaender, the Hon. Robert Gathorne-Hardy, W. W. Gibson and Messrs Macmillan & Co., Douglas Goldring, Lord Gorell, Philip Henderson, Frank Kendon and Messrs J. M. Dent & Sons for an extract from *Tristram*, Everest Lewin (Mrs E. H. G. Macdonald), James Mackereth, Sir Henry Newbolt, Max Plowman, Edgell Rickword, Lady Margaret Sackville, Siegfried Sassoon, Edward Shanks and Messrs Macmillan & Co., Sir John Squire and Messrs William Heinemann, Jan Struther (Mrs Joyce Maxtone Graham), Gilbert Thomas and Messrs Allen & Unwin for the lyric from *Mary of Huntington*, Edward Thompson, Sherard Vines and Messrs Cobden-Sanderson Ltd, and the Hon. V. Sackville-West and Seumas O'Sullivan; and Sir Edward Marsh for prose extracts from two short prefaces, and Morley Roberts for long prose extracts from a short article.

Thanks are also due to Messrs Allen & Unwin for *Evening* by Richard Aldington and *The Lost Heifer* by Austin Clarke; Messrs Ernest Benn and Humbert Wolfe for the epitaph on G. K. Chesterton from *Lampoons*; Messrs Basil Blackwell and W. R. Childe for 'Song of the Folk in the Industrial Cities'; Messrs William Blackwood and J. Redwood Anderson for the lines from 'The Goat' from *Haunted Islands*; Messrs Blackwood and Hugh MacDiarmid for half the poem entitled *The Watergaw*; Messrs Jonathan Cape for the poems from W. H. Davies and the poem from Mary Webb's short story *The Name Tree*; Messrs Chatto & Windus for lines from Swinburne and Wilfred Owen; Messrs Cobden-Sanderson for half a poem by Lazarus Aaronson; the Clarendon and the Oxford University Press for extracts from Robert Bridges,

xi

the Oxford University Press for extracts from J. Redwood Anderson; Messrs Constable and Rose Macaulay for 'Farmer's Boy' from *Three Days*; Mrs G. M. P. Welby Everard for the lines from Maurice Hewlett; Messrs Faber & Faber for extracts from *Poems* by T. S. Eliot and *One Way Song* by Wyndham Lewis; Messrs Victor Gollancz and Humbert Wolfe for 'This Blind Rose' from the book of that title and 'The Immortal Hour' from *Snow*; Messrs Gollancz and J. Redwood Anderson for the lines from 'Headpiece: the Whirlwind,' from *Vortex*; Messrs George G. Harrap for extracts from *The Poems of Sir William Watson*; Messrs William Heinemann and Mrs Flecker for extracts from James Elroy Flecker, and Messrs Heinemann for the lines from Arthur Symons's 'Bianca'; Messrs John Lane, the Bodley Head, Ltd, for poems by Ernest Dowson, and passages from 'The Sphinx' by Oscar Wilde and Stephen Phillips's 'Nero' and two poems by Frank Kendon; Mr Grant Richards and Messrs John Lane for lines from John Davidson; Mrs Kipling, Messrs Macmillan, and Messrs Methuen for extracts from Kipling's poems; Messrs Macmillan for extracts from James Stephens; Mr Yeats and Messrs Macmillan for 'I made my song a coat' and lines from 'Down by the Sally Gardens' and 'Wanderings of Oisin' from *The Collected Poems of W. B. Yeats*; Messrs Macmillan and the author's executors for extracts from A.E.; Messrs Methuen and the author's executors for extracts from G. K. Chesterton's *Collected Poems*; Mrs Monro, the Poetry Bookshop, for extracts from her husband's work, the poem from M. M. Webster's *Alien Guest*, lines from Hueffer's 'Antwerp,' and half a poem by Frances Cornford; Messrs John Murray for the poem by W. N. Hodgson; the Richards Press and the executors for half a poem by the late A. E. Housman; Messrs Elkin Mathews and Marrot for 'I know you: solitary griefs' by Lionel Johnson; a sonnet by Everest Lewin, and half a poem by Nancy Cunard; Messrs Martin Secker & Warburg, Ltd, for the poem by T. W. H. Crosland; Mr Masefield and the Society of Authors for extracts and Mr Masefield and Messrs Sidgwick & Jackson and the Macmillan Co. of New York for the lines from 'The Everlasting Mercy'; Messrs Sidgwick & Jackson for 'Reciprocity' by John Drinkwater and lines from F. W. Harvey; and Mrs Helen Thomas for an extract from Edward Thomas.

CONTENTS

xiii

CHAPTER I

THREE great poetry ages have adorned the pages of English history and thrust their glamour and optimism or stimulating disillusion into the cultural life of a people which since the invention of the printed page has always tended to look askance upon any kind of art not directly utilitarian or made for light entertainment and amusement. If the antithesis is not quite true concerning the first, the Elizabethan, it is profoundly true of the second, the Romantic Revolt of the time of George III, and the third, the Victorian Age.

Of poetry preceding the Tudor times, so much has been lost, and so little of it was dependent on the written page, that it is difficult to write with any assurance save to remark that poetry entered more fully into the life of the common people than it does now, and the bard, save where he caused clashes with the priesthood, was honoured and revered above the common run of men.

But with the advance of a machine civilization the poet was thrust more and more upon himself, more and more did he tend to cultivate faith in art as a means to an end in itself, or as in this last decade, made defeatist decisions which were to lead him into barren obscurity and muddled intellectualism. But this last is not yet the characteristic poetry of this century, nor perhaps is its opposite the 'Georgian,' which, though it has taken its name from a king who reigned more than twenty years, has only partially dominated the period.

The end of the Victorian Age, though it saw no wide reactions against its characteristic poets, Tennyson and Robert Browning, was marked by the rise of verse rhetoricians and rhapsodists, as well as the less popular poets of the aesthetic school who were affected by the philosophy of Walter Pater.

Swinburne and Kipling and William Watson, and in the last three years Henry Newbolt, rather than George Meredith, or William Morris, or D. G. Rossetti, were the best known, or the most cultivated and influential, of the later stars; and though of Swinburne, like D. G. Rossetti, it might be truer to say that he belonged to the middle period rather than the late, it was towards the end of his life (which continued into the twentieth century) that he was the most approved and his influence most strongly felt. But Swinburne's special admirers, if somewhat hesitant disciples, Ernest Dowson, Arthur Symons, Oscar Wilde, and some others, set a restraint upon their emotions which was not exactly characteristic of their rhapsodical prophet, though a magnificent lapse of Ernest Dowson's was good enough to put much of his more Parnassian work into the shade, bringing him into closer contact not only with Swinburne but all those popular poets whose orthodox fervours and ardours were generally so approved by the man in the street:

Before my light goes out for ever if God should give me a choice
    of graces,
I would not reck of length of days, nor crave for things to be;
But cry: 'One day of the great lost days, one face of all the faces,
Grant me to see and touch once more and nothing more to see.

'For, Lord, I was free of all Thy flowers, but I chose the world's
    sad roses,
And that is why my feet are torn and mine eyes are blind with sweat,
But at Thy terrible judgment-seat, when this my tired life closes,
I am ready to reap whereof I sowed, and pay my righteous debt.

'But once before the sand is run and the silver thread is broken,
Give me a grace and cast aside the veil of dolorous years,
Grant me one hour of all mine hours, and let it see for a token
Her pure and pitiful eyes shine out, and bathe her feet with tears.'

Her pitiful hands should calm, and her hair stream down and blind me,
Out of the sight of night, and out of the reach of fear,
And her eyes should be my light whilst the sun went out behind me,
And the viols in her voice be the last sound in mine ear.

Before the ruining waters fall and my life be carried under,
And Thine anger cleave me through as a child cuts down a flower,
I will praise Thee, Lord, in Hell, while my limbs are racked
    asunder,
For the last sad sight of her face and the little grace of an hour.

The poem, a very pomegranate of 'pity and terror,' in which
the pity, though self-pity, is transmuted and sublimated into
something far beyond the individual, does really seem to be
one of the memorable poems of the period. One of the
highest tributes possible to pay to it comes, strange to say,
from Lawrence of Arabia, in *The Seven Pillars of Wisdom*, who
found himself reciting part of it on the battlefield:

I was torn completely from the saddle, sailed grandly through the
air for a great distance, and landed with a crash which seemed to
drive all the power and feeling out of me. I lay there, passively
waiting for the Turks to kill me, continuing to hum over the verses
of a half-forgotten poem, whose rhythm something, perhaps the
prolonged stride of the camel, had brought back to my memory as
we leaped down the hillside:

'For Lord I was free of all Thy flowers, but I chose the world's
    sad roses,
And that is why my feet are torn and mine eyes are blind with
    sweat.'

While another part of my mind thought what a squashed thing I
should look when all that cataract of men and camels had passed over
me.

The poem, however, contains other than popular elements
of form and feeling and Biblical theology,—notes of disillusion,
pessimism, and despair which for some time had been creeping
into English verse. Also, it makes plain references to Dowson's disintegrating life in the tentacles of drink and women,
though we have to go to his most popular lyric, *Cynara*, for a
plainer statement:

All night upon mine heart I felt her warm heart beat,
Night-long within mine arms in love and sleep she lay;
Surely the kisses of her bought red mouth were sweet.

Indeed, besides pessimism and despair, the recurrent theme of much of the latest Victorian poetry, or at least the new movement by the apostles of Art for Art's sake, was a crude contemplation of sex (how different from its subtle analysis in Meredith's magnificent sonnet sequence,[1] *Modern Love* !) coupled with exceptionally strong sympathy for harlots and women of easy virtue. Poems like Arthur Symons's fleshly *Bianca* and his less decadent *Emmy* are only instances of many lyrics of a type unfamiliar to the early and middle Victorians:

> There with the women, haggard, painted and old,
> One fresh bud in a garland wither'd and stale,
> She, with her innocent voice and her clear eyes, told
> Tale after shameless tale.

Which completes with the doubtfully pious hope, 'And I think the soul of a man shall answer for yours in hell. . . .' The poem, however, is beautiful, and lifted from morbidity by a strain of noble simplicity. But sentimentality, though deftly covered over, steals out of it, for we can't quite credit the innocence and freshness of women living in brothels, any more than we can believe with Oscar Wilde that 'all men kill the thing they love' and that the murderer is an extremely amiable creature (i.e. 'the kindest use a knife'). But it is very different from the aggressively sensuous and supersensual *Bianca* poem, where stanza after stanza breathes the heavy aroma of Baudelaire's *Fleurs du Mal*, and where virginity almost becomes a theme for ignominy and reproach:

> Her cheeks are hot, her cheeks are white;
> The white girl hardly breathes to-night,
> So faint the pulses come and go,
> That waken to a smouldering glow
> The morbid faintness of her white.

What drowsing heats of sense, desire
Longing and languorous, the fire
Of what white ashes, subtly mesh
The fascinations of her flesh
Into a breathing web of fire?

Only her eyes, only her mouth,
Live in the agony of drouth,
Athirst for that which may not be:
The desert of virginity
Aches in the hotness of her mouth.

There is a touch of D. G. Rossetti in it, no doubt, and slight reminiscences of Villon—translations of whom by Rossetti, Swinburne, and John Payne had attracted many of the moths of English poetry to the searing candle of the latest French verse. But the healthy sensuality and barbarous robustiousness of Villon had really little in common with the work of his admirers on either side of the Channel; only it was partly through Villon that English Victorian poets cast their eyes upon the latest French school, though how uneasily that medieval gallows-bird and vagabond walked hand in hand with Baudelaire and Verlaine is best apparent when you compare his poetry with Shakespeare's, with whom he had considerably more in common. The symbolist side of Baudelaire and Verlaine was to find few cultivators till after the first decade of this century, but their Parnassian work (directly or indirectly) dominated a small crowd of clique and coterie poets who exhibited their wares in half a dozen exclusive journals and anthologies, and, from the yellow-cover characteristics of the age, might be not inaptly nicknamed 'the Yellow Poets.' There is no intention to attack or strongly disparage them, for some of their work, particularly Dowson's, is very beautiful, and they were, perhaps, necessary reactions against a Victorian attitude which tended to judge a poem by its moral content rather than by its significance as a work of art. But the bedroom-tavern content was sometimes overdone, and the sinner was not merely forgiven (a perfectly

Christian activity) but he was sentimentalized over, to say nothing of the background of beautiful corpses and cypress-shadowed tombstones.

But Swinburne had a vaster side to him; his Venus was the Greek Aphrodite rather than the Roman Venus, an open-air goddess rising out of the joyous sea-foam rather than a languorous creature stretched on a dubious couch beneath the heavy scents of hot-house roses and lilies. Moreover, a great cleansing wind blew through so many of his exuberant periods, a wind from the prophets of the Old Testament and from the high peaks of Wordsworth's heather-scented lakelands. Though he sang of the sea rather than the hills he does preserve something of the Wordsworthian feeling, and his rhapsodies of dawn and doom are of the open air rather than the tavern or the study:

The sea is awake, and the sound of the song of the joy of her waking is rolled
From afar to the star that recedes, from anear to the wastes of the wild wide shore.
Her call is a trumpet compelling us homeward: if dawn in her east be acold,
From the sea shall we crave not her grace to rekindle the life that it kindled before,
Her breath to requicken, her bosom to rock us, her kisses to bless as of yore?
For the wind, with his wings half open, at pause in the sky, neither fettered nor free,
Leans waveward and flutters the ripple to laughter: and fain would the twain of us be
Where lightly the wave yearns forward from under the curve of the deep dawn's dome,
And, full of the morning and fired with the pride of the glory thereof and the glee,
Strike out from the shore as the heart in us bids and beseeches, athirst for the foam.

Though there was little of that kind of thing in the work of the poets of the Decadents and their aesthetic kin, Swinburne quite as much as Rossetti was the English planet around which they circled, though they were selective in their admirations, and bound his rhapsodical voice into hoops of silk and silver. His 'maximum of sound' with its 'minimum of sense' rarely had place in their fascinating, if at times rather morbid or too-sentimental, orchestra.

The place of meeting of some of these young poets was 'The Cheshire Cheese,' a tavern now as famous for its literary associations as for its good cheer. They called themselves the 'Rhymers' Club,' and the foundation of it is claimed by W. B. Yeats and that exceptional bookman Ernest Rhys, though there was little of the character of 'Everyman' about it. The most prominent of its twelve or thirteen members as regards poetry were, I suppose, W. B. Yeats, Arthur Symons, Ernest Dowson, and Lionel Johnson; while prominent associates included that luckless megalomaniac John Davidson. Some of its 'goings-on' can be well imagined, though it has had its biographers of chapter and fact, among them Morley Roberts the novelist and Exmoor trout-angler,[1] who recently (September 1933) published some very interesting, if scathing reminiscences in *John o' London's Weekly* of an encounter in one of the member's private rooms:

Plarr, the mildest but soundest minded of them all, told me that when I came into the room it was as though a blast of air from the prairie had blown the door open. Can it be wondered at when I found some four of them sitting hand in hand before the fire? Shall I put down what that savage, myself, said to them? I asked: 'What the hell are you fellows holding each other's hands for?' This was a sad beginning, but somehow it passed over and we talked for hours. During these hours Lionel Johnson got drunk three times with absinthe. Perhaps the rapidity with which the effect of absinthe passes off, so that it can be renewed, is one of its deadly charms. Having tried it and admired its opalescence I soon ceased to take it, but for some of these men it meant slavery. What we talked of I cannot remember, but on the whole, in spite of my

---

[1] One of his most interesting books is *A Humble Angler*, a volume of angling experiences on Exmoor and elsewhere.

entrance, the afternoon was a literary Bohemian success. So successful was it that when we broke up Plarr and Dowson, both smoking
cigarettes, embraced on the landing and then fell downstairs, in
company, emitting sparks like a Catherine wheel, but luckily
landing unharmed.

'Plarr, the mildest but soundest-minded of them all' and
'blast of air from the prairie' sound like hard knocks at
W. B. Yeats and Ernest Rhys. But Yeats has publicly declared that he was at that time a 'convinced ascetic' living
on milk and buns; and Ernest Rhys is obviously undeserving
of hard knocks; for his Muse had no tavern or graveyard spots
on it, as is testified by the contents of his early book of the
period, *A London Rose*. (Yet how symbolic in its title of much
of the verse of the nineties!) Nor did he take to suicide or
drink as was the appalling fate of several of his colleagues
and associates, the poet merging into the critic and editor;
while as a fine reciter of other poets' work he was to become
during this century a mainstay of Harold Monro's Poetry
Bookshop, and at his own house in Hampstead a generous
shepherd of much budding talent. He has published several
volumes of verse during this century, and, indeed, has continued
his romantic, bardic, and somewhat rustic note into the present
day. Among his best-known lyrics is that quaint derivation
from Anglo-Saxon verse, *The Leaf-Burners*, and his entirely
durable autobiography lines:

Wales England wed; so I was bred. 'Twas merry London gave me
breath.
I dreamt of love, and fame: I strove. But Ireland taught me love
was best:
And Irish eyes, and London cries, and streams of Wales may tell
the rest.
What more than these I asked of life I am content to have from
Death.

But it was Rhys's Celtic fellow-founder, the elastic Yeats,
who was to win the great fame. The Yeats of to-day and
those early years has told us that he was studiously 'wringing
the neck of rhetoric' (and I dare say getting across John

Davidson while he was doing it), and from evidences of the printed page we know that he was effectively transmuting his Swinburne, and nodding over Ronsard and Verlaine, particularly Verlaine, and by aid of Irish legend and ballad creating the dim opalescent colours of the 'Celtic Twilight.' And if his grasp of French was insufficient, he was being dominated by the hypnotic scholarship of Arthur Symons, who was the most learned member of the group. He had something in common with Dowson, and though the general level of his nineteenth-century work is much higher, it is doubtful if half a dozen of his best lyrics are superior to an equal number of the best of Dowson's. But even on the basis of a narrow selection there is greater metrical originality in Yeats, for Dowson was quite traditional, and though the latter's ideal of a line of verse was Poe's 'the viol, the violet, and the vine,' he did not always remember it, and dropped too frequently into a cloying sweetness, or quite ordinary charm and morbid prettiness. The technical excellence of Dowson's few exceedingly good poems, among them *Cynara* and the lyric beginning:

> Why am I sorry, Chloe? Because the moon is far:
> And who am I to be straitened in a little earthly star?

must not blind us to his lack of technical achievement in general.

Probably Yeats had a bigger following than Dowson. I am not quite sure of this; but, at any rate, the average reader of poetry, outside Ireland, had not got hold of Yeats, and it was not till the beginning of this century that he became a name of great importance, with certain striking lyrics dangling from his twilight banner, particularly *The Lake Isle of Innisfree*, which were to be frequently read and remembered.

Standing partially away from Yeats at the end of the nineties, but perhaps closer to Swinburne, and yet right away from any kind of sentimental deterioration or decadence, was the Irish mystic A.E. (George Russell). He hardly comes into the general current of English poetry as a known force till the

* B

beginning of this century, but before 1900 he had evidently left his mark upon Irish thought and lyrical activity, for writing in *The Dome* magazine in 1898, the delightful Yeats of those early years says of him:

The only two powers that trouble the deeps are religion and love, the others make a little trouble upon the surface. When I have written of literature in Ireland, I have had to write again and again about a company of Irish mystics, who have taught for some years a religious philosophy which has changed many ordinary people into ecstatics and visionaries. Young men, who were, I think, apprentices or clerks, have told me how they lay awake at night hearing miraculous music, or seeing forms that made the most beautiful painted or marble forms seem dead and shadowy. This philosophy has changed its symbolism from time to time, being now a little Christian, now very Indian, now altogether Celtic and mythological; but it has never ceased to take a great part of its colour and character from one lofty imagination. I do not believe I could easily exaggerate the direct and indirect influences which A.E. [George Russell], the most subtle and spiritual poet of his generation, and a visionary who may find room beside Swedenborg and Blake, has had in shaping to a definite conviction the vague spirituality of young Irish men and women of letters.

But Yeats was more widely known in English literary circles than A.E.; for his unique 'lofty imagination' does not seem to have penetrated to the English intelligence till a little before the War. And less known than Yeats and probably even less than A.E. was the late Poet Laureate Robert Bridges, who, however, had published much of his best poetry before 1900. Very few of his lyrics had been anthologized, and he was rarely, if ever, mentioned in the press or in books of criticism or on the lecture-platform, and the eager devourer of the modern poetry of that time was frequently ignorant of his existence. One of our most prominent literary weeklies even boycotted his review copies, and his sudden spring to fame when he was elected poet laureate in 1913 was one of the greatest literary surprises of a century. He was really very much of a Victorian, almost a middle Victorian, for an anthology entitled

Latter-Day Lyrics (1878) and sub-titled 'Poems of Sentiment and Reflection by Living Writers' makes him an active contemporary with such poets as Tennyson, Browning, Longfellow, Matthew Arnold, Coventry Patmore, Lord Lytton, Palgrave, D. G. Rossetti, Christina Rossetti, Jean Ingelow, Professor Edward Dowden, Austin Dobson, Edmund Gosse, Arthur O'Shaughnessy, and the light-footed Frederick Locker (this last the father of Commander Oliver Locker-Lampson), who was the chief inspirer and influencer of Austin Dobson. And it is interesting to note that though the two Rossettis are represented by fourteen lyrics, and Edward Dowden by five, Swinburne is represented by only two; and so classed among the minor poets (many of whose names are too insignificant to mention). The anthology contains over seventy contributors, and claims to be the first anthology of modern Victorian poetry—that is, poetry by living Victorian authors. Robert Bridges figures as an experimenter with the French forms of the rondeau and triolet, which is amusing, for his influences were ultimately to be entirely non-French. Milton and the Greeks, and perhaps the Italian Dante, were to dominate his horizon, out of which were to come not only some of the most chastely finished of modern lyrics, but also some of the most original and convincing experiments in new forms. Probably his strong, though comparatively silent, opposition to Swinburne and the poets who were close to him, his detestation of Verlaine and the whole absinthe-drinking crew (French as well as English) of the Yellow Nineties, was one of the causes of his uncertain position at the end of last century. He was, moreover, not too favourably inclined to some others of his contemporaries; and as poets and their critic friends are rarely good Christians, and therefore not always fair to those who ignore them or are unsympathetic in their judgments, it is not so very strange, after all, that he was not widely known. At any rate he was an aloof scholarly figure, unrecognized and unheeded save by a comparatively small public. His very gradual, stealthy ascent, and final burst into fame near the age of seventy, helped to prove that pure poetry has really no need of advertisement or press assistance, and is bound to conquer its essential public sooner or later. But he was free from the trammels of literature and poetry as a means towards livelihood. As a physician till the age of thirty-seven he had the care and healing of the human body to think about, and, in addition he was not quite without private means. He wrote with no very eager eye on either the public or his purse, and the 'unendurable calamity' of unrecognition or rejection with a wife and children to support out of literary work, which battered John Davidson to death, brushed him only with a teasing finger. Until two or three years before the death of Tennyson, he seemed, according to W. B. Yeats, 'a small Victorian poet, whose poetry, published in expensive hand-printed books, one could find behind glass cases in the houses of wealthy friends.'

How different was Bridges in his private life as well as the manner of his art from some of the poets preferred to him! And yet poetry is not necessarily related to virtue, and great technique may even spring out of a dunghill. Oscar Wilde would be passed over with a shrug of the shoulders were it not for his claim on our attention as a technician, though this applies chiefly to one poem, a rather long poem, *The Sphinx*. Indeed, it is not merely a very ingenious achievement, but one of the chief technical feats of the last sixty years. And it is strange that it should come from Wilde rather than Swinburne, for with the added exception of two or three beautiful lyrics and some snatches of the *Ballad of Reading Gaol*, Oscar Wilde's poetry is chiefly flowery pastiche. But in *The Sphinx* he generally transmutes his derivations very cunningly. It is not merely that he took Tennyson's *In Memoriam* stanza and wrote it out as two lines instead of four, but he has very operatively proved that Tennyson's rhymes are much more effective as internal and cross rhymes than as end rhymes, sign-pointing, too, to a more flexible stanza and greater speed and resonance in the metrical beat. Though the rhyme arrangement and metrical form have been borrowed from Tennyson, and the theme suggested by Poe's *Raven,* the outstanding literary background is deftly fused Baudelaire and Swinburne, while the *Rubáiyát* of Omar Khayyám has helped to create his Eastern atmosphere:

Upon the mat she lies and leers and on the tawny throat of her
Flutters the soft and silky fur or ripples to her pointed ears.

Come forth, my lovely seneschal! So somnolent, so statuesque!
Come forth you exquisite grotesque! half woman and half animal!

Come forth my lovely languorous Sphinx! and put your head upon
    my knee!
And let me stroke your throat and see your body spotted like the lynx!

And let me touch those curving claws of yellow ivory, and grasp
The tail that like a monstrous Asp coils round your heavy velvet paws!

.   .   .   .   .   .

Wild ass or trotting jackal comes and crouches in the mouldering
    gates:
Wild satyrs call unto their mates across the fallen fluted drums.

And on the summit of the pile the blue-faced ape of Horus sits
And gibbers while the fig-tree splits the pillars of the peristyle.

.   .   .   .   .   .

Follow some roving lion's spoor across the copper-coloured plain,
Reach out and hale him by the mane and bid him be your paramour!

Couch by his side upon the grass and set your white teeth in his
    throat
And when you hear his dying note lash your long flanks of polished
    brass.

And take a tiger for your mate, whose amber sides are flecked with
    black,
And ride upon his gilded back in triumph through the Theban gate,

And toy with him in amorous jests, and when he turns, and snarls,
    and gnaws,
O smite him with your jasper claws! and bruise him with your
    agate breasts!

Only examples from the best parts of the poem have been chosen, for it is not entirely even, marred in several places by excessive violence and crude sensuality, while its technical exactions sometimes produce nonsense, as in 'whose amber sides are flecked with black,' which suggests that some tigers are not striped. But, otherwise it is an astounding performance of disciplined vigour and ingenuity and outlandish learning, and very much more original than *The Ballad of Reading Gaol* which sends you questioningly back to Coleridge's *Ancient Mariner* rather than the ancient anonymous Border ballad (despite some very obvious old ballad tags) from which *The Ancient Mariner* was so splendidly derived.

The notes of pessimism and despair which so bespattered the work of the decadents, were, strangely enough, to change into downright saturation in the work of certain poets who were otherwise directly contrary to them. In the poems of A. E. Housman and Thomas Hardy their tears of morbidity and hopelessness were to be crystallized into what Sir Richard Rees has called 'black, vicious melancholy,' and their grave-yard yearnings into a stratum of uncompromising bitterness. Heralded by the second James Thomson, especially in his long poem *The City of Dreadful Night*, Housman and Hardy were to capture a far more extensive public, and exert an influence where James Thomson had only been regarded as a melancholy oddity.

But perhaps FitzGerald's rendering of the *Rubáiyát* of Omar Khayyám had exerted an influence where James Thomson had failed; for it was eminent in technique, in word-magic, that complete fusion of sound and sense, of form and content which rarely characterizes the work of the author of *The City of Dreadful Night*, whose chief pitfalls were dullness and prosaic-ness, and whose spontaneous *naïveté* when he attained to rapture insufficiently came under the restraining and purifying file.

Thomas Hardy, however, save for a few occasional publi-cations, was keeping his poems locked away in his desk; but A. E. Housman published his *Shropshire Lad* in 1896, and though it was at first little thought of, and ran through only five editions in the space of nine years,[1] after 1906 it was to prove one of the strongest abiding influences of the new century. Here were none of the hothouse obsessions of the Yellow Poets and the most dissipated members of the Rhymers' Club, but pessimism and despairs which were rooted in ancient stoicism, in an austere paganism. Austere, chaste, frugal, and economical in form, *A Shropshire Lad* touched hands with the short poems of Horace, with the lyrics of Heinrich Heine (that magical transformer of common speech), and even with some of the verse of Charles Kingsley. The religious content of Charles Kingsley is, of course, entirely absent; but when Kingsley wrote:

> For men must work, and women must weep,
> And the sooner it's over, the sooner to sleep;
> And good-bye to the bar and its moaning,

he did strike a note which was the recurrent theme of Housman's lyrics, crystallized into such a stanza as:

> Lovers lying two and two
> Ask not whom they sleep beside,
> And the bridegroom all night through
> Never turns him to the bride.

And when Kingsley wrote:

> When all the world is young, lad,
> And all the trees are green;
> And every goose a swan, lad,
> And every lass a queen;
> Then hey for boot and horse, lad,
> And round the world away;
> Young blood must have its course, lad,
> And every dog his day.
>
> When all the world is old, lad,
> And all the trees are brown;
> And all the sport is stale, lad,
> And all the wheels run down;

---

[1] In 1905 *A Shropshire Lad* was still only in its fifth edition, but in the same year Newbolt issued the twenty-first edition of *Admirals All*, a little book which had been published later than *A Shropshire Lad*.

> Creep home, and take your place there,
>   The spent and maimed among:
> God grant you find one face there,
>   You loved when all was young,

his utterance forestalled something of Housman's greater art in:

> When I was one-and-twenty
>   I heard a wise man say,
> 'Give crowns and pounds and guineas
>   But not your heart away;
> Give pearls away and rubies
>   But keep your fancy free.'
> But I was one-and-twenty,
>   No use to talk to me.

And perhaps more manifestly in such stanzas as:

> Leave your home behind, lad,
>   And reach your friends your hand,
> And go, and luck go with you
>   While Ludlow tower shall stand,

particularly in their recurrent use of 'lad,' and a colloquial simplicity and *naïveté* of language which in both instances is not characteristic of poets of high academic attainments. Kingsley was more approved for his prose than for his verse, but some of his lyrics have an enduring stamp upon them, and common justice demands that a connecting-link which, I believe, has never been pointed out, should be shown its existence in the chain of English poetry.

But very few of the later Victorians knew of the existence of A. E. Housman; for his light at the beginning was overshadowed by Kipling and Watson, and Swinburne and his disciples. Though Francis Thompson in 1898 and 1899 was probably even less known, his personality was to overflow strongly into the new century. His *Hound of Heaven* was to be frequently quoted in Sunday sermons, and though his influence has never been very definite, spasmodic rather than taking upon itself the form of any current, it might be possible to prove that next to Housman he did affect the poetry of the

new century up to 1930 more than any other Victorian.   But
though read and frequently anthologized, he was little referred
to and acknowledged in current criticism, save as a unique
Roman Catholic poet with a predilection for diffuse and difficult language and crowded symbolism, a sort of metaphysical
Keats running rampant in the granary of William Blake.   As
regards the creative efforts of a spiritual kinsman, the Jesuit
priest Gerard Manley Hopkins, his poems were still in manuscript, unknown save to Robert Bridges and some of his most
intimate friends.   But when of recent years they were published and his strange bizarre genius received rather more than
its due of recognition, his coupling with Francis Thompson
was to escape entirely the eye of his admirers, though some
of Francis Thompson's passages show resemblances of manner
which the Catholic mysticism of both will in no wise explain
—as in the following:

> Hearken my chant, 'tis
> As a Bacchante's,
> A grape-spurt, a vine-splash, a tossed tress, flown vaunt 'tis!
> Suffer my singing,
> Gypsy of Seasons, ere thou go winging; . . .
>
> .   .   .   .
>
> Tanned maiden! with cheeks like apples russet,
> And breast a brown agaric faint-flushing at tip,
> And a mouth too red for the moon to buss it
> But her cheek unvow its vestalship. . . .

There was no contact between the two that is known of, but
the manner of both is at times no high hills apart, though in
Francis Thompson there is richer sensuousness and more
grammatical and prosodical discipline.   But Gerard Manley
Hopkins was an austere ascetic, and across that contrary background how much of Francis Thompson's ecstatic exuberance
was due to drugs and drink will never be accurately known,
for, curiously enough, intemperance does not seem to have
injured him in the way that it injured Dowson and Lionel
Johnson.

As aloof from current movements as Francis Thompson, that other individualist, John Davidson, puzzled contemporary opinion, and then went out into the night of obscurity and neglect. Though John Davidson belongs almost entirely to the last century, he lived through nine years of this before he committed suicide in despair. Necessity forced him to overwrite himself, and an overbearing pride and arrogance estranged him from his fellow-poets. Few poets of such strong imaginative and verbal powers have committed themselves to quite so much unevenness of diction, nor, indeed, to so many contradictions of vision. Pessimist and optimist, and though atheist and rationalist still a believer in some sort of immortality, and both accepting and rejecting the Christian vision of heaven and hell he could write:

> He doubted; but God said 'Even so;
>   Nothing is lost that's wrought with tears;
> The music that you made below
>   Is now the music of the spheres,'

and yet continually commit himself to a pessimism of unbelief that seems to sing through the lips of the author of *The City of Dreadful Night*. And the tremendous, if arrogant dignity of *Holiday* (his assertion of his various reincarnations) makes the disparity with his scoffing lyric *The Outcast* only the more plainly obvious. There is only space to quote a few stanzas of *Holiday*, but how every line holds the attention, and how great is the power of:

> First, a woman broke my heart,
>   As a careless woman can,
> Ere the aureoles depart
>   From the woman and the man.
>
>   .   .   .   .
>
> All the brilliances of Hell
>   Crushed by me, with honeyed breath
> Fawned upon me till I fell,
>   By pretenders done to death.
>
>   .   .   .   .

But my essence and intent
　Ripened in the smelting fire:
Flame became my element;
　Agony, my soul's desire.

Twenty centuries of Pain,
　Mightier than Love or Art,
Woke the meaning in my brain
　And the purpose of my heart.

Straightway then aloft I swam
　Through the mountain's sulphurous sty:
Not eternal death could damn
　Such a hardy soul as I.

The complete poetical contrary of all that is the aggressively satirical lyric *The Outcast*—which seems to place its author upon a pinnacle of blameless sociability and convention. We can understand his writing the poem in one of those sombre backstair moments that came to him so frequently, but why he should so admire it as to allow it to go into a special volume of *Selected Poems* is a question to be answered only by the angels. Knowing what we do of John Davidson, it is difficult to avoid pinning *The Outcast* (at any rate the title) upon his own back, and, if we renounce all the strong sympathy which is due to his thwarted and misapprehended genius, feel that the lines:

Scowl, and be rude
　Should love entice;
Call gratitude
　The costliest vice.

Deride the ill
　By fortune sent;
Be scornful still
　If foes repent . . .

might almost be made to apply to his own case; though he was probably hammering at some of the members of the Rhymers' Club, especially when he wrote:

Laugh wisdom down;
Abandon fate;
Shame the renown
Of all the great.

Dethrone the past;
Deed, vision—naught
Avails at last
Save your own thought.

To quote further from Morley Roberts, he says of one of
his encounters with John Davidson on a night when he visited
the Rhymers' Club:

What Davidson read I cannot now remember, but it was certainly
the best piece given us that night: perhaps this, proved to me by
its scanty and grudging reception, was the cause of the next news
I heard of the Rhymers' Club, which was that immediately on our
departure those left behind resolved themselves into a committee
and passed a resolution that there should be no more members
elected. It was to be a sacred and forbidden place of resort and
consolation for pure poets. This was told me by Davidson, not
without laughter. His humour might be scanty, but what there was
resounded to such a smack. He might have resented it save for
his deep consciousness that all of them together would not make a
man of his calibre. . . . But for Davidson, with a wife and children
to support, failure was an unendurable calamity. And failure was
his inescapable fate, a fate which at last so broke him that he turned
back into himself and became a paranoiac, or something that suggests
it. . . . It seems to me that it might indeed be better for a poet
to soak absinthe and die than to live the passionate resentful life of
John Davidson. . . . Little things wrought him to fury. I shall
not criticize his work, nor even say here how those of the Rhymers'
Club, so much less men than he, criticized it. They were mostly
foolish young fellows, occasionally stumbling into beauty and then
going half crazy because they could not pursue it. . . . I left John
Davidson one day to visit the rooms of one of these poets, for he
would not come with me. His contempt for them was vast and
explicable. Davidson, for all his savage self-assertion, his denial
of religion and accepted morality, was a sober and clean-living man.

There is no doubt of all that. The members of the Rhymers' Club were not willing to admit the intellectual and imaginative excellence of one who was at least the equal of the best of them, and John Davidson's spiritual life was of too flickering and self-contained a nature to allow him to get away from his reactions intact. The ill-will, I suppose, spread to the public and the press, and so this country lost a 'people's poet' with greater possibilities for speaking to the masses than any between Tennyson and John Masefield. The combination of apocalyptic force and moving simplicity of his metrical tales (which he wrongly called 'ballads') helps to prove this, and the content of some of his other work suggests a man speaking to the Communists of to-day with a fuller voice than any poet of this age. Indeed, our so-called Communist poets show not only a complete ignorance of the working-man, but also a strange irrationality as regards the tastes and emotions of the variegated rebellious masses in general—who ask for plain English and straightforward thinking; even the most sensitive of them demanding an art which is as far removed from the preferences of an Eliot or a Pound as an ox is different from a bat. Unfortunately, however, at his worst John Davidson sank alienatingly deep into the slough of doggerel and verbal cheapness, the fault often of the poet who trusts his self-dictated message before his God or his Muse, the fault, too, of the poet who overrates his message in the superlative way that John Davidson did, for he even seemed to set himself up by the side of Shakespeare, nowhere more evident than in this strange extract, taken from his will:

No word except of my writing is ever to appear in any book of mine as long as the copyright endures.

No one is to write my life now or at any time; but let all men study and discuss in private and in public my poems and plays, especially my Testaments and Tragedies.

But he was a good enough lyrist to have ascended by now into the serenity of paradise, and to-day our combined pity and admiration is probably shot through with bursts of his own accusing laughter as he sits uncomfortably between the cherubim pelting Dowson with asphodels, and reciting that dissipated poet's exquisite homage to Despair:

> They are not long, the weeping and the laughter,
>   Love and desire and hate:
> I think they have no portion in us after
>   We pass the gate.
>
> They are not long, the days of wine and roses;
>   Out of a misty dream
> Our path emerges for a while, then closes
>   Within a dream.

Davidson himself might have achieved such miracles of unalloyed loveliness; but resentment drove him into the arms of fervours which can neither reconcile nor forgive. Always thinking of himself he even seems to identify himself with the fairies of his unusually beautiful, though very uneven, *All Hallows' Eve*:

> In Elfland is no rest,
> But rumour and stir and endless woe
>   Of the unfulfilled behest—
> The doleful yoke of the Elfin folk
>   Since first the sun went west.
>
>   .   .   .   .
>
> One planet is all their poor estate,
>   Though a million systems roll;
> They are dogged and worried, early and late,
>   As the demons nag a soul,
> By the moon and the sun, for they never can shun
>   Time's tyrannous control.
>
> The haughty delicate style they keep
>   Only the blind can see:
> On holynights in the forest deep,
>   When they make high revelry
> Under the moon, the dancing tune
>   Is the wind in a cypress tree.

'The haughty delicate style they keep only the blind can see' gives the show away as nothing else does. The haughty delicate style of John Davidson when he really got going on his winged horse was no doubt only apparent to the blind, those peculiarly sensitive, independent critics who could not see such superior merit in his rivals, but it was there right enough if you looked for it carefully. His influence was almost nil on his contemporaries, and though his voice does sound pretty clearly throughout Lionel Johnson's *Dark Angel*—which also has a sombre glitter of Oscar Wilde's *Sphinx* in it—it was reserved for a later poet, James Elroy Flecker (and perhaps G. K. Chesterton), to appreciate him more fully and bind something of his plangent voice into his own magical 'numbers.'

Of the fortunate poets who ended up as distinguished university professors only A. E. Housman ever captured a public for verse alone. Arthur Quiller-Couch was devoting to criticism and prose romance an imaginative impulse which he might nearly as successfully have put into a larger output of verse; and W. Macneile Dixon (not to be confused with Robert Bridges's protégé, the neglected Richard Watson Dixon), a disciple of Tennyson and Professor Edward Dowden, who was to become professor of English language and literature at the university of Birmingham and afterwards at Glasgow, regarded his Muse as a special minister of private pleasure and the expression of himself in verse as a sheer luxury. But occasional lyrics of his stole into print, and a recent book, *In Arcadia* (1933), in which he seems to show himself under the classical influence of Matthew Arnold, is prefaced by some of the wisest maxims about poets and poetry ever uttered.

A few years after Tennyson died in 1892, to the astonishment of every one a comparatively minor figure was made Laureate. It is understandable that Bridges should be pushed on one side, for very few people knew of his existence. It was natural, too, that such a violent rebel and effusive singer of Liberty as Swinburne should be proved unsuitable. Out of the running, too, was William Morris, for was he not a declared Socialist! As to Coventry Patmore, the poet of

domestic love and erotic mysticism, though he was alive in
1892 and did not die till 1896 he seems to have been very
much underrated save by a small band of devoted admirers,
for when Professor George Saintsbury published his crowded
History of Nineteenth-Century Literature in 1896 he did not so
much as mention his name; and when Clement Shorter
published his little handbook *Victorian Literature* in the year
following, he depreciated Patmore as 'not always sincere' and
declared that his 'admirers spoilt him by adulation,' spitefully
adding, 'He probably looked forward with the same keen
assurance to the verdict of posterity as did Southey; and
posterity, it is all but certain, will be as ruthless in the one
case as the other'—a judgment which has certainly not established Clement Shorter among the prophets.

Kipling, a far more promising laureate, had not yet established his position, for *Barrack-Room Ballads* was first published
in book form in 1892 (the year of Tennyson's death). And
as for George Meredith, he was more generally known as a
novelist than as a poet in verse. Equally likely as the author
of *Modern Love* he was deemed too analysing and destructive a critic of the revered national edifice of marriage, even
the tremendous sermon embedded in the final sonnet insufficiently atoning for the disturbing and unpeaceful microscope
set upon it in the other forty-nine.

> Thus piteously Love closed what he begat:
> The union of this ever-diverse pair!
> These two were rapid falcons in a snare,
> Condemned to do the flitting of the bat.
> Lovers beneath the singing sky of May
> They wandered once; clear as the dew on flowers:
> But they fed not on the advancing hours:
> Their hearts held cravings for the buried day.
> Then each applied to each that fatal knife,
> Deep questioning, which probes to endless dole

Moreover he was sometimes rather obscure, and, comp red
with Tennyson, very rough in his consonants and vowels, a
Robert Browning without his popularity. Probably his fine

accidental music was generally missed, and too infrequent
were such wonderful snatches of song as:

> She can be as wise as we,
>   And wiser when she wishes;
> She can knit with cunning wit,
>   And dress the homely dishes.
> She can flourish staff or pen,
>   And deal a wound that lingers;
> She can talk the talk of men,
>   And touch with thrilling fingers.

And even the great charm of *Love in the Valley* could not atone
for everything. No! the occasional gorgeous Elizabethan and
fine moralist in Meredith had escaped notice as far as the
general public was concerned. He was an extremely difficult and
involved novelist, a wounding modern intellectual, a romantic
psychologist who seemed to be continually shooting arrows
of destruction into the honest thews of bourgeois morality.
That last in particular must have been the parliamentary and
royalist feeling about Meredith. So he was passed over, and
the laureateship kept vacant for some years. One can understand it all; but it is much more difficult to grasp the reason
for the rejection of William Watson, for he had already published *Wordsworth's Grave,* and here was a poet who fulfilled
the demands of respectability and assertive loyalty to the
Crown, united to a really fine and individual gift of poetry.
But such were the decrees of Fate and the gods, and to the
surprise of nearly everybody a newspaper journalist, Alfred
Austin, was made poet laureate. But the honour did not
fit him, for he deteriorated instead of getting better; the
following stanza a by no means unusual example of his mar-
vellous contributions to the worst verse of the age:

> High up, on larch and cypress, merle and mavis
>   Vociferated love-lays sweet as strong,
> And the bird dear to Homer and to Hafiz
>   Proclaimed the joy of sadness all night long;
> Vowed each new Spring more Spring-like than the last,
> And triumphed over Time, futile iconoclast.

It is almost comical in its splay-footed lyricism, though it is necessary to point out that the Alfred Austin of the earlier pre-laureate days was not wholly bad. In addition to some striking sonnets and pleasant lyrics he had written one good rustic narrative poem, *In the Month when sings the Cuckoo* (of very melancholy content), which would not, in time to come, have disgraced the pages of Thomas Hardy, and in another poem at least one memorable stanza:

> Where have you been through the long sweet hours
>   That follow the fragrant feet of June?
> By the banks and the hedgerows gathering flowers,
>   Ere the dew of the dawn is sipped by noon.

So perhaps they made him poet laureate on the strength of *that*. At any rate he was in the Wordsworthian current of tradition, his national outlook impeccable, and at his best he wrote pleasantly and musically of the country; though perhaps prone to miss the centre of some rural verity, as, for instance, when he forgot that English cypresses are short trees and not specially selected by singing birds. He was without dispute the weakest of all the lesser poets of fame.

Others with some claim to more even respect and admiration were Alice Meynell, Wilfrid Scawen Blunt, R. L. Stevenson, and W. E. Henley. But Stevenson, though he was to have much influence on the open-road poetry of the twentieth century, to say nothing of the verse of childhood, was a little too lacking in depth and muscular power, while his stature as a poet was completely overshadowed by his importance as an essayist and romantic novelist. His friend Henley, the John Silver of his *Treasure Island*, despite a Pegasus with one of its legs of wood and a hop of uncertainty in his development (due somewhat to his passion for experimentalism), was really more dynamic and original, though his most accepted poems have something of the rhetorical flavour of Kipling, and such lines as

> When I was a King in Babylon
> And you were a Christian slave

are sometimes ascribed to Kipling. But Henley would have

been a greater poet if he had not been such a giant among the journalists.

A less read poet was Wilfrid Scawen Blunt, chiefly known to Victorians through William Sharp's one-time widely distributed anthology, *Sonnets of this Century*, for he was a sonneteer of skill and power. But poetry to him was only a starry incident in an active life of hunting, travelling, and politics, which not only included some flag-waving for Ireland and a consequent season in jail, but also much vocal indignation in the cause of Egypt. His *Wind and the Whirlwind* was the forerunner of much of that bitter poetry of national indignation and inquiry of which Siegfried Sassoon was to become the chosen prophet. It is strange that a Sussex squire and rearer of stud-horses should trouble himself so strongly about affairs beyond the Mediterranean; but in *The Wind and the Whirlwind*, a poem of over a hundred loud clanging stanzas, he not only strongly espouses the cause of Egypt, but violently curses and denounces the interloping England, prophesying her downfall and the severance of her colonial empire.

> Oh insolence of strength! Oh boast of wisdom!
> Oh poverty in all things truly wise!
> Thinkest thou, England, God can be outwitted
> For ever thus by him who sells and buys?

A more alive present-day Government might possibly assert its respect for poetry by publicly burning the thing in Trafalgar Square, for in the light of the present Italian threat to Egypt, Scawen Blunt sounds like becoming an exact prophet. Some of the poem is almost unprintable in its indignation and fierceness; and therefore it is not at all surprising that the imperialistic Victorians unduly cold-shouldered its too passionate author. But he was an uncertain artist, as a fault in the otherwise perfect ultimate stanza ('must' in the place of 'not') testifies.

> Therefore I do not grieve. Oh hear me, Egypt!
> Even in death thou art not wholly dead.
> And hear me, England! Nay, thou needs must hear me.
> I had a thing to say. And it is said.

But if an uncertain artist, he was a very exploring one, and, in his fine paraphrases from the Arabic, he copiously attempted and often successfully achieved a rare English technique of rhyming by assonance (sighs, night; heel, thee; below, homes, etc.), which though it had been used by the old Gaelic poets of Ireland (and something like it recently taken over by both Austin Clarke and Frank Kendon) as also by Matthew Arnold in his lyric *Philomela*, had little established precedence to justify it as a popular intrusion.

As regards Alice Meynell, she was finally overshadowed by her protégé, Francis Thompson. George Meredith wrote flatteringly of her 'princely journalism' and Francis Thompson said of her verse: 'The footfalls of her muse waken not sounds, but silences.' Perhaps she was too much of an exquisite journalist (though journalism did not in the least enter into her verse) and too fragile as a poet. Though her verse escapes the anaemic it is full of boudoir whiteness; and perhaps the unsympathetic might be tempted to call her 'a shepherdess of sheep.' At any rate the bulk of her verse lacks colour and passion, though some of it was highly rated by Ruskin and D. G. Rossetti, and her sonnet *Renouncement* is unlikely to be ever forgotten. Though a hypersensitive poet she was a very ladylike one, and as such failed to leave her mark upon any save the later Georgian pastorals. She overflowed into this century, and when she published her *Collected Poems* in 1913 she was a 'best seller.'

Such were the chief of the later nineteenth-century poets, among whom the Decadents and border-line Aesthetics created a peculiar interest. But when the terrible twentieth century dawned they were ceasing to cause disturbance, though Swinburne stood unshaken and foursquare. Swinburne, Kipling, Watson, and Henry Newbolt were the burning stars on the horizon. Others were only twinkling, or demanding that the clouds which obscured the full light of their genius should be swept away.

CHAPTER II

WHEN, recently, his late Majesty King George V, acting more or less under the advice of the late Labour Prime Minister, Mr Ramsay MacDonald, appointed Mr John Masefield to the Laureateship, many people felt that excellent as was the choice, it was nevertheless not a perfect expression of national justice. Among the middle-aged poets none deserved the honour so plainly; but it was also felt that perhaps length of years and labour ought to count in some degree, and the older men considered first—Sir William Watson, Rudyard Kipling, and Sir Henry Newbolt in the first running.

Sir William Watson had already been twice overlooked (though this is not to say that he ever, by divine right of pure poetry, deserved the honour more than Robert Bridges), and the ridiculous Victorian judgment which put Alfred Austin in his place was crying out for some sort of eleventh-hour gesture of obliteration and restitution. The knighthood which he had been awarded for his poetry during the first decade of this century emphasized his importance, though it may indeed have been regarded as sufficient recognition in itself, for there was no getting away from the evidence that Masefield on an assembly of quantity combined with quality had won hands down. But ignoring Sir William Watson's many dead and merely competent pages and the alienating bombast and rhetoric (eloquence that was not always noble or magical) and selecting only his long elegy, *Wordsworth's Grave*, and a bare score of lyrics and odes, and half as many of those short four- to six-lined poems which he generally terms 'epigrams,' it did almost seem as if he might perhaps be the better poet. Even A. E. Housman, after you have made such an enormous pruning, seems to yield fewer pieces of white and glowing marble, and the thrifty Gray to offer considerably less in the way of terse and memorable articulation. For William Watson at his pinnacle is a poet in the finest classical tradition, so inevitable and exact in utterance that the mind retains him intact. To weed him is to remember him, and in remembering there seems little need of further reference to the printed page, save to re-con what the pencil here and there has marked for remembrance. It was, perhaps, his misfortune that he has always been too easy to weed, and not very exciting nor deeply interesting in mass unless the reader's mind is concentrated for purposes of weeding. After middle age he did not seem to grow, so that by the outbreak of the War he had been quite assessed and all curiosity about him had vanished. So down went his sales, and he was left in a backwash among the poets who were not worth quarrelling over. He was very good indeed, and also rather bad; though it is true that much of the bad was just verbal competence, and, if some of it roused interest and a flicker of pleasure, that might have been because, as in *The Ballad of Semmerwater*, the specialized reader was already familiar with the legend or countryside of the theme, and found in the poem some streak of thought or feeling to heighten his knowledge. Only a few of his poems had a completely independent existence, for their music had to be very rich and felicitous to survive the conventional phrasing. The good in the man seemed to be well known, the bad was getting more frequent and self-evident; and as he was a rather pompous egoist (almost as bad a megalomaniac as John Davidson) and believed in himself beyond the confines of normality, all you could do was to shrug your shoulders and leave him alone. He could not develop. Unlike Robert Bridges he had no powers of late growth in him. He was a back number, and on the shelf.

To the Imagists and some of the 'Georgians' he may, indeed, have seemed little better than a worm not worth treading on. But that didn't prevent the worm from turning occasionally, with a sort of iridescent twist in its expostulations. To verse which he immensely disliked, but which was

considerably less crude and defeatist than the monthly fare
of editors and reviewers nowadays, he somewhat ungraciously
snapped:

> The method is simple. With care and with pains
> Conceal, if you have them, all semblance of brains.
>
> .   .   .   .
>
> Let Metre eternally jump, jolt, and lurch;
> For infinite crudeness make infinite search.
>
> .   .   .   .
>
> And always, as pattern and paradigm, take
> The stagger of Donne or the stammer of Blake.

What followed must have hastened his death. For we have
got much further than that—neither staggering nor stammering,
but lying down flat and gibbering to the jackals. And the
concealment of brains has developed into an intensity of
cerebral advertisement that suggests there are sometimes no
brains there to conceal—only a windy cavity of inarticulate
despair. What, short of old age, killed Sir William Watson?
The answer is not another sphere away:

> There are in Painting, Sculpture, Song,
> A few new ways of being wrong;
> But it is plain to most men's sight
> There's no new way of being right.

Such unqualified truth almost sounds like a lie; but the
rabid conservative in Watson rejected even a glimmer of
compromise, and it was this whole-hog way of looking at
things which after middle age nearly destroyed the poet in the
man, and pushed him during the War years into publishing a
book of verse (*The Man who saw*) that would have disgraced
the Muse of many lesser men. William Watson, like many
another, now and in those days, continually wrote when the
fit was not on him, when he could not shake with vision and
divine madness, when he was flat and barren of inspiration.
For though inspiration when it came to him had none of the
flame of Swinburne or immense vitality of Blake, it was

sufficiently a real force to justify all the trouble he took upon its shapings. Perhaps inspiration is the wrong term of definition, perhaps it would be better to speak of emotion or vision—yet rarely flung down white-hot, and only in his finest work successfully recollected in tranquillity. His annoyance with his contemporaries always seems to have been a clog upon his feet, so that even in his finest long poem, *Wordsworth's Grave*, he could not quite leave them alone:

> I hear it vouched the Muse is with us still;—
>   If less divinely frenzied than of yore,
> In lieu of feelings she has wondrous skill
>   To simulate emotion felt no more.
>
> .   .   .   .   .   .
>
> And idly tuneful, the loquacious throng
>   Flutter and twitter, prodigal of time,
> And little masters make a toy of song
>   Till grave men weary of the sound of rhyme.
>
> And some go prankt in faded antique dress,
>   Abhorring to be hale and glad and free;
> And some parade a conscious naturalness,
>   The scholar's not the child's simplicity.

To those of us who are so critical of these abandoned crowcawing days, that description of the current poetry in vogue a little before the death of Tennyson may seem rather too scathing. Moreover, its epigrammatic power and occasional fidelity to fact are weakened by violence and spitefulness. Much firmer and more veracious was his touch when he describes the beginning of the age of Dryden and Pope:

> A hundred years ere he to manhood came,
>   Song from celestial heights had wandered down,
> Put off her robe of sunlight, dew and flame,
>   And donned a modish dress to charm the Town.
>
> Thenceforth she but festooned the porch of things;
>   Apt at life's lore, incurious what life meant.
> Dextrous of hand, she struck her lute's few strings,
>   Ignobly perfect, barrenly content.

Unflushed with ardour and unblanched with awe,
  Her lips in profitless derision curled,
She saw with dull emotion—if she saw—
  The vision of the glory of the world.

How penetratingly apt!   And yet there was always rather more than a faint touch of Dryden and Pope, particularly of Pope, in the verse of William Watson.   Too often did his song wander down from 'celestial heights,' too often was it 'ignobly perfect,' and he himself 'barrenly content' with an emotion insufficiently fused.   Too often his 'lips in profitless derision curled'; but not too often did he don the vesture of the epigram, 'a modish dress,' indeed, 'to charm the Town,' but at its best well done, excellently done, Pope pitchforked deftly into the lap of Gray, and reaching its highest culmination in his definition of Poetry:

Song is not Truth, not Wisdom, but the rose
Upon Truth's lips, the light in Wisdom's eyes.

Yet he emulated Wordsworth and felt himself to be Wordsworth's successor; and much of his outlook is clearly Wordsworthian.   He came from the furthest fringe of the Wordsworth country, and there is much of the atmosphere of the glamorous country of the Pennines in his verse.   But the affinity with Wordsworth, beyond mere outlook and some descriptive powers, is more imagined and gloated over than naturally sustained. To what extent he was barrenly intrigued by the double William of the Christian names and the double W of the surnames we can only conjecture, though he could write feelingly and with clear insight of Wordsworth's deepest quality, and as an aside describe with fine felicity the qualities of some of Wordsworth's peers and rivals:

Not Milton's keen, translunar music thine;
  Not Shakespeare's cloudless, boundless human view;
Not Shelley's flush of rose on peaks divine;
  Nor yet the wizard twilight Coleridge knew.

C

What hadst thou that could make so large amends
    For all thou hadst not and thy peers possessed,
Motion and fire, swift means to radiant ends?—
    Thou hadst, for weary feet, the gift of rest.

From Shelley's dazzling glow or thunderous haze,
    From Byron's tempest-anger, tempest-mirth,
Men turned to thee, and found—not blast or blaze,
    Tumult of tottering heavens, but peace on earth.

Not peace that grows by Lethe, scentless flower,
    There in white languors to decline and cease;
But peace whose names are also rapture, power,
    Clear sight, and love; for these are parts of peace.

But there was little of Wordsworth's strong peacefulness in William Watson, partly because he hovered between two platforms, the classical and the bardic, and, apart from his other defects, he has often been unfairly judged and assessed because of that unnatural coupling. But his magnificent *Ode on the Day of the Coronation of King Edward VII* is a triumph of combination, a feat that falls not a thousand miles behind Milton's *Lycidas*, even his vices nearly as much as his virtues helping to produce its power, the two miraculously uniting into a shining sphere of exceptionally fine creation—very little of it falling behind the arresting opening:

Sire, we have looked on many and mighty things
    In these eight hundred summers of renown
Since the Gold Dragon of the Wessex Kings
        On Hastings field went down;
        And slowly in the ambience of this crown
Have many crowns been gathered, till, to-day,
How many peoples crown thee, who shall say?
        Time, and the ocean, and some fostering star
        In high cabal have made us what we are.

Moreover the poem is full of striking images, to say nothing of warnings and prophecies:

And yonder march the nations full of eyes.
Already is doom a-spinning.

He seems to have aspired to be a national bard, almost a people's poet, but he was right away from either the sophisticated or primitive balladist, and with the exception of two or three outstanding pieces, like his great coronation ode and *Ode in May*, insufficiently flexible in regard to his metrical forms. As a people's poet he had nothing of the versatility of Tennyson; and, judged on a lower plane, he lacked swing, music-hall ecstasy, and stampede. Rudyard Kipling and Henry Newbolt have done that kind of thing much better.

As a poet for poets, an aesthete with a special message for the sensitive, his couplet:

> Not peace that grows by Lethe, scentless flower,
> There in white languors to decline and cease,

must have been peculiarly annoying to the Victorian Aesthetes and Decadents who just at that time (1890) were beginning creep into daylight; and with some justice they might have retorted that his verse was not sufficiently idiomatic, his voice too wrapped in dying conventions, his intellectual content too ordinary. He could not always wring the neck of his admirations and transmute as Yeats transmuted; and he rode his hobby-horse of simplicity and clarity almost to death. But his eyes were on the great eternal verities, and sometimes he ascended fully into their light.

His lyric, *The Glimpse*, begins:

> Just for a day you crossed my life's dull track,
> Put my ignobler dreams to sudden shame,
> Went your bright way, and left me to fall back
> On my own world of poorer deed and aim.

And though it tumbles down in a second stanza which shows some of William Watson's faults of diction at their very worst, it movingly saves itself in a final stanza of great power and beauty. Speaking of the jaded city worker's flight into the country, he says:

> In stainless daylight saw the pure seas roll,
> Saw mountains pillaring the perfect sky:
> Then journeyed home, to carry in his soul
> The torment of the difference till he die.

The note has gone right out of English poetry. Nowadays it is a case of the Seven Deadly Virtues and the Seven Vital Sins, with a cannibal dance round the camp-fire ashes of Victorian and Edwardian values. Such is the reaction against excessive didacticism, even where the didacticism was entirely right. And if William Watson was just a little too didactic and sometimes mixed up ethics with ordinary national values he could walk sufficiently frequently into the arena of pure poetry:

> Pass, thou wild light,
> Wild light on peaks that so
> Grieve to let go
> The day;
> Lovely thy tarrying, lovely too is night;
> Pass thou away.

> Pass, thou wild heart,
> Wild heart of youth that still
> Hast half a will
> To stay.
> I grow too old a comrade, let us part,
> Pass thou away.

And I wonder how many young pre-War poets, tongue-tied to their admirations, and yet groping to express themselves through their own lips, found their lines in moments of melancholy re-echoing (or rather distorting) the transparent, and yet elusive magic of:

> In the night, in the night,
> When thou liest alone,
> Ah, the sounds that are blown
> In the freaks of the breeze,
> By the spirit that sends
> The voice of far friends
> With the sigh of the seas
> In the night!

> In the night, in the night,
> When thou liest alone,
> Ah, the ghosts that make moan
> From the days that are sped:

The old dreams, the old deeds,
And the wound that still bleeds,
And the face of the dead
In the night!

It almost sounds as if William Watson had been brushed by
a petal from the purist garden of the gods of Verlaine, for
pin him as you like (as a poet without his own idiom) to
Pope and Gray and Wordsworth, and after that to Horace
and Milton and Matthew Arnold and the poets of the
Greek Anthology, every now and again something quite
indefinable steals through, and you realize that Watson is a
poet in his own right, completely triumphing over derivation and shallow rhetoric, and securely seated among the
immortals.

There is, however, no intention to abuse rhetoric. It is
only when it is used for purposes of fake, for the impression
of unnatural power in places where the content is at variance
with the form, where there is weakness in the emotional
urge, that it becomes a thing to strangle and denounce.
I have written in my recent autobiography of Victorian childhood, *The Mistletoe Child*:

All poetry should be written for the voice. In all poetry that is
valuable there is a touch of something that almost might be defined
as Rhetoric (it is even present in the poems of Keats). It should
excite the listening ear when it is read alone. It should be wholly
or partially understood by a listener; and, though it is true that the
very best poetry more fully expands and communicates when
conned by eye, it is equally true that if it entirely fails the oral test
it fails altogether.

And to that I would add that the whole of Shakespeare, save
some of the weakest of the sonnets, gets right across to a
listening audience, that even the soliloquies in the most meditative of the plays were made right away from the printed
page; and though a listening audience misses much of their
beauty and subtle intellectualism unless it turns immediately
afterwards to the printed page, they were primarily intended

for the vocal chords and the attentive ear. By Rhetoric in heavy emphasis I suppose we mean an effect that can make the spoken words twenty times better than the printed page will ever allow, where the intellectual or spiritual import is deadened by a noisy appeal to crude emotions. At its worst rhetoric is mere platform strumming and strutting and trumpeting, the bounce of a bladder, large in size, but which, being hollow, is at the prick of a pin reduced to nothing much to look at. William Watson wrote rather too much bad and border-line rhetoric, but also some that was not bad, and a still smaller amount, which, if we drastically limit the application of the term, was no rhetoric at all.

Another poet, but one who is still with us, Sir Henry Newbolt, is also a poet of rhetoric, but very little of it is bad rhetoric even when it is indifferent poetry; and, again, judged on the same basis, some of the flower of his work is no rhetoric at all. When Newbolt arose in the firmament of Swinburne and the Decadents and Aesthetes, he was veritably a new bolt, and if not exactly like the lightning, it was just as if a great sea-wind had smitten the drooping lilies and roses and told even the rhapsodical Aphrodite to pack and begone. Here was health! Here was the great music! Here was courage and sinew! Here were all the healing patriotic ardours! Such was its effect upon surfeited readers of the latest vogues. And, strange to say, it was his first volume of lyrics, a little paper-bound brochure of only forty pages called *Admirals All*, which won the popular approval. It was first published in 1897; and by 1912 it had run through thirty editions. To Victorians and Edwardians nearly every page seemed exciting, and though some of the best poems have become hackneyed through too constant repetition, there is still captivating vitality in its buffeted bowels. *Drake's Drum*, I suppose, is the best of the items, though three or four others run it close. The key and frontispiece poem, though indifferent in quality, is intriguing; for Newbolt seems to have quite deliberately remembered that the names of three of his admirals are the names of well-known poets:

Effingham, Grenville, Raleigh, Drake,
   Here's to the bold and free!
Benbow, Collingwood, Byron, Blake,
   Hail to the Kings of the sea!

Leaving that poem to look after itself (which it has difficulty in doing) and pointing out that in another king-of-the-sea lyric he has reminded us of the existence of a Captain Keats, the little book's more characteristic qualities can be better shown by quoting the second and third stanzas of *Hawke*, which terminates with four lines of exceeding pomp and uplift:

'Twas long past noon of a wild November day
   When Hawke came swooping from the West;
He heard the breakers thundering in Quiberon Bay,
   But he flew the flag for battle, line abreast.
Down upon the quicksands roaring out of sight
Fiercely beat the storm-wind, darkly fell the night,
But they took the foe for pilot and the cannon's glare for light
   When Hawke came swooping from the West.

The Frenchmen turned like a covey down the wind
   When Hawke came swooping from the West;
One he sank with all hands, one he caught and pinned,
   And the shallows and the storm took the rest.
The guns that should have conquered us they rusted on the shore,
The men that would have mastered us they drummed and marched
      no more,
For England was England, and a mighty brood she bore
   When Hawke came swooping from the West.

The clamant brass band that had preceded *Admirals All*, Kipling's *Barrack-Room Ballads*, had probably helped to ensure the poem's popularity, though *Admirals All* shows little close affinity with *Barrack-Room Ballads* as a whole. Kipling's derived Moody and Sankey hymn-tunes and rants are not in it, neither are his music-hall jingles. But notes from the old Scotch Border-ballad, popular school songs, and nursery rhymes ramble through the pages. True, the Border-ballad had also got into Kipling, but there seems almost more of it in *Admirals All*. Self-evident also was the note of A. E. Housman, probably the first of the many occasions when his influence upon young poets intruded itself:

> Lad, and can you rest now,
>   There beneath your hill?
> Your hands are on your breast now,
>   But is your heart so still?
> 'Twas the right death to die, lad,
>   A gift without regret,
> But unless truth's a lie, lad,
>   You dream of Devon yet.

The poem is unabashed Housman at his least depressing; and so good that one feels that Housman might have been glad to have taken it over. However that may be, there is less tumpty-tum in *Admirals All* than in *A Shropshire Lad*. Tumpty-tum was Housman's besetting metrical vice, for though he borrowed something of the sentiment and external texture of the Old Ballad, he took from it little of its metre. The Old Ballad was composed in erratically regulated weak and strong stresses, which prevented the tumpty-tum; but Housman seems to have fallen back upon the classical division into regular feet (though, of course, accent took the place of quantity). The lilts of the Old Ballad are dependent upon shifting or rolling stress (nowadays, I think, they call it by the new-fangled term of 'Sprung Rhythm'[1]), but though Housman did not actually count syllables, and introduced much variation of accent, some of his poems reduce themselves to complete unballad-like regularity. One can be excused for suspecting that Housman misunderstood or despised the metre of the Old Ballad, and that occasional lilts and irregularities are due to the introduction of trochees and anapaests into the regular iambic movement. But

[1] Really it should be called 'Springing Rhythm,' though, perhaps, Gerard Manley Hopkins's special use of it requires a less logical name. It is the rhythm which is at the back of nearly all my own poems.

Newbolt from the very beginning, especially in his *Ballad of John Nicholson*, showed that he knew all about it. His verse, therefore, is more characteristically English than Housman's.

Nevertheless, surveying Newbolt's whole career, the proportion of good verse to indifferent is not greater than Housman's. At his best Newbolt is a fine metrical artist, rubbing shoulders with Swinburne and Elroy Flecker; but at his worst, though rarely trivial, he is just a little too ordinary. He has only three sure notes, nothing approaching an octave, and it has not been particularly to his advantage that he has struck certain others, over which (save in less than half a dozen special instances) he has showed insufficient command. The best-known of them is the prime note of Thomas Campbell of *Hohenlinden* and *The Battle of the Baltic*, and it is this which he fingered so glitteringly in *Admirals All*.

The books that followed *Admirals All* were not quite so good, though each contained something striking. He continued his belaurelling of the public school, one of the themes of *Admirals All*, and in *The Best School of All* gave us a very universal school song, with one stanza so infectiously musical that he felt obliged to repeat it:

> We 'll honour yet the School we knew,
>   The best School of all;
> We 'll honour yet the rule we knew,
>   Till the last bell call.
> For, working days or holidays,
> And glad or melancholy days,
> They were great days and jolly days
>   At the best School of all.

He also occasionally struck another note, not sufficiently often, but the best Newbolt of all, one that he had already touched in *He fell among Thieves*, a very haunting note that seems dropped out of the sleeve of some great wind of loneliness, the undertone thrusting upwards and keeping pace with the overtone:

* c

I sat by the granite pillar, and sunlight fell
    Where the sunlight fell of old,
And the hour was the hour my heart remembered well,
    And the sermon rolled and rolled
As it used to roll when the place was still unhaunted,
And the strangest tale in the world was still untold.

Something of the same note, too, runs through the strange
grim ballad of *Gillespie,* and though we can only really get the
poem's flavour as a whole, a few detached stanzas may give
some faint idea of its unusual quality:

'The Devil's abroad in false Vellore,
    The Devil that stabs by night,' he said,
'Women and children, rank and file,
    Dying and dead, dying and dead.

            .   .   .   .   .

Fierce and fain, fierce and fain,
    The troopers rode their reeking flight:
The very stones remember still
    The end of them that stab by night.

They've kept the tale a hundred years,
    They'll keep the tale a hundred more:
Riding at dawn, riding alone,
    Gillespie came to false Vellore.

But it was in *Messmates* that he seemed to reach the high-
water of that kind of thing, though the poem is also important
for another reason, for it is written in a very original metre,[1]
one that seems to have no precedent.

He's there alone with green seas rocking him
    For a thousand miles around;
He's there alone with dumb things mocking him,
    And we're homeward bound.

---

[1] At any rate I have never come across it elsewhere, though I once wrote
something like it myself in a suppressed poem that I have no intention to
revive. I seem to remember that I have sometimes heard that peculiarly
rhythmical beat when I was lying in my passenger bunk at the back of a
steamer and that its basis is a combination of the roll of the steamer and
the beat of the screw.

> It 's a long, lone watch that he 's a-keeping there
> And a dead cold night that lags a-creeping there,
> While the months and the years roll over him
>   And the great ships go by.

During most of the years of the Great War Newbolt's poems were much admired. But shortly after the War his popularity began to decline. The disillusioned soldiers who returned, for the most part civilians who had been torn from their homes, were weary of martial ardours, weary of patriotism, weary of any kind of emotionalism. They wanted escape, retreat, the country, dreaming landscapes, even Socialism, something which Newbolt never or rarely offered. And if they read poetry at all it was the escapist pastoral poetry of Edward Marsh's later 'Georgians,' something that caused no swift beat in the blood. So he was cast aside; but he was less forgotten and cold-shouldered than Sir William Watson.

But during the War, at least during the early period of it, his poems were very popular. Yet his few new creations during that period added little to his fame, and, indeed, one of his reviewers said of his relationship to his public that he was 'in danger of confusing it with a public meeting,' meaning, I suppose, that mere rhetoric was triumphing over song. But two or three of the lyrics had something of the old distinction. And entirely in his old swinging manner was *The Toy Band* (an inspiring song in a tin-can setting), the song about the retreating beaten battalion, the metrical anecdote of:

> Half a thousand dead men marching out to fight,
>   With a little penny drum to lift the feet.

The big dragoon when all hope seemed at an end had entered a toyshop and with a child's drum and some penny whistles had succeeded in lifting the defeated spirits of the lost five hundred:

> As long as there 's an Englishman to ask a tale of me,
>   As long as I can tell the tale aright,
> We 'll not forget the penny whistle's wheedle-deedle-dee
>   And the big dragoon a-beating down the night.

Rubadub! Rubadub! Wake and take the road again,
  Wheedle-deedle-deedle-dee, Come, boys, come!
You that mean to fight it out, wake and take your road again.
  Fall in! Fall in! Follow the fife and drum.

A penny whistle! A drum and fife band! Call Newbolt's poetry that, if you like; but it beats the road to Paradise (the paradise of hope and courage) as well as Valhalla, and there's little of the verse of the last decade that does that. Though it is full of the British Army and Navy, to say nothing of the public school, out of it, every now and again, steals the great symbolism of poetry, so that there is no need to sail in a material ship to be one with Admiral Hawke, and one can take 'the foe for pilot and the cannon's glare for light' in the darkest of everyday ventures against the fleets of destruction and evil. And though it is not yet true that

The guns that should have conquered us they rusted on the shore,
The men that would have mastered us they drummed and marched
   no more,

it may yet become so—of this beleagured English nation, and of the outraged human spirit in the final hour of its uprising. And yet again and again it can happen that the beaten battalion shall spring from the dust and go forward to the sound of the small drum and penny whistle; and Gillespie, supported by nothing save his iron valour and sense of right, come alone to false Vellore and so acquit himself that the very stones bear witness to 'the end of them that stab by night.'

CHAPTER III

RUDYARD KIPLING

THE death of Rudyard Kipling happened strangely — only a few days before the fateful hour that saw the passing of a beloved English king. He himself was more than a Kipling, for he had been a little king, a kingling, in his day the adored voice of the Empire and the English mind—a bugle and a symbol.

As he was such a power in the land and youth hugged him so much to its heart—to which company in his heyday I belonged—I am tempted to write of him almost personally.

I first made acquaintance with his writings in 1898, a few months after I had left school; and during the three years which followed I read him hungrily. I was told that he was the greatest living (or 'modern') creative writer, and though I was a little hypercritical as regards the truth of that, I generally enjoyed him immensely—though in varying degrees of censure and approval.

He was of no very obscure or dingy birth, for he was closely related to Stanley Baldwin and the children of Burne-Jones, the painter; and was, moreover, of sound Nonconformist stock, the grandson of Wesleyan Methodist ministers—on both the mother's and father's side. Manifestly his work would be full of Puritan and Nonconformist elements (which, of course, it was), a peculiarity which has not been sufficiently dwelt on by recent critics. But I remember that the Wesleyan Methodists did not quite accept him. They were shocked by his irreverence and public-house violence; for he used livid raw-hide words where all other Victorian writers used dashes (indeed he was the fathering pioneer of modern outspokenness, though translated into more lurid terms by D. H. Lawrence and his kin) and was much too free with the name of the Deity, whom his soldier heroes generally called 'Gawd.'

There was something, too, about his Christianity which didn't always quite come off. His ethics were too pagan, particularly Roman-pagan. It is true that a great many of our prominent Nonconformists were imperialists, but Rudyard Kipling's imperialism was sometimes just a little too downright and committal for them. But they were proud of him in a sort of back-stairs way, and forgave him when he wrote the hymn *Recessional*. He had some of the right stuff in him, at any rate; and even if he was a black sheep, he had at least half a hoof in the heavenly fold. And, moreover, we were the God-baptized successors of the imperialistic pagan Romans.

His influence on me was not entirely beneficial. He made me despise myself as a physical and social weakling, and I am sure I was not alone. Looking back I know now that his glorification of physical prowess and endurance sometimes weakened his stature as a creative writer. Many of his heroes were too beefy, too often men of great physical activity rather than spiritual activity, while he exalted the machine at the expense of his own romanticism. But the *Spectator* (I feel almost sure it was the *Spectator*) called him 'The Great Interpreter,' and the definition was not entirely ill-fitting. He interpreted India and the British Army; and he voiced the feelings of all sorts of energetic common men—emigrants and Indian civil servants and sailors and explorers and smugglers. His India was scarcely the India of Edward Thompson, for we were not so self-critical in those days, but it was nevertheless one side of the medal. And he adored adventurers and people who roved, so long as they were creatures of 'Progress' and governed by the Law. Yes, that was his great exaction and limitation. He was hag-ridden by the Law, by the rules of the game, the Roman code (if he was quite right, why did the Christians rise up and bruise it?), the public school spirit (it seemed that you could be quite white and preserve the public school spirit even when you were doing wrong); and some of us, quite good and honourable children of the realm, but nursing potentialities for rebellion against humbug and hypocrisy, felt that he was unduly autocratic and severe. But that was certainly the Nonconformist in him, the Methodist preacher half-astray and in profane pulpits.

But some little time after he published his school story *Stalky and Co.*, there was a mild reaction against him. Some avenging wit defined the book as a cad's book. The malicious fellow said that it was 'about cads, by a cad, and for cads'; and something whirled abroad and gathered force and size like a rolling snowball. His attitude to Ireland and the Irish certainly savoured of caddishness, and he deserved all the trouncings he got in reply from that quarter (though he was really quite the opposite of a cad). But his vices were rather too strongly emphasized. Then people enlarged their judgments against him as a jingo imperialist, and even slated him (O perverse and hypocritical public!) for giving expression to their own feelings. After that nearly all the poets deserted him, the 'Georgians' in particular being very 'down' on him, and 'Kiplingese' became a label for the noisiest and slickest stuff a verse-writer with a talent for jingles might be guilty of. As a matter of fact he was a better poet than many of his detractors; and he could strike their own note when he wanted to do so (take for instance the Georgian-*cum*-Celtic-twilight lyric, *The Way through the Woods*). There is something very memorable about his *best* poems; they cling to the mind, they have music, energy, sonority, and are sometimes touched with magic and beauty. His *Barrack-Room Ballads* were the sensation of the year, and tatters of their long-ago stupendous appeal still adhere:

> Kabul town's by Kabul river—
>   Blow the bugle, draw the sword—
> There I lef' my mate for ever,
>   Wet an' drippin' by the ford.
>   Ford, ford, ford o' Kabul river,
>   Ford o' Kabul river in the dark!
>   There's the river up and brimmin', an' there's
>   'arf a squadron swimmin'
>   'Cross the ford o' Kabul river in the dark.

Kabul town 'll go to hell—
  Blow the bugle, draw the sword—
'Fore I see him 'live an' well—
  'Im the best beside the ford.
    Ford, ford, ford o' Kabul river,
      Ford o' Kabul river in the dark!
      Gawd 'elp 'em if they blunder, for their boots 'll
          pull 'em under,
        By the ford o' Kabul river in the dark.

The whole book is crowded with such effective repetitions
of words and phrases, a device recently resorted to by T. S.
Eliot, who must have more than a nodding acquaintance
with the Kipling poems.

The label 'Kiplingese' is something of a misnomer, for
Kipling had few mannerisms outside his particular use of
repetition, and not an intensely individual style—at any rate
not in the same way as Swinburne and the early Yeats, and
perhaps G. K. Chesterton and Humbert Wolfe, have individual styles. He is not quite the first poet who wrote
'Kiplingese,' and the crime of falling into that particular gait
does not necessarily imply any acquaintance with Kipling.
A poet who soaks himself in the old Border ballad, and then
reads Macaulay's *Lays*, imposing on the combination many
music-hall jingles and Moody and Sankey hymns, will, of
course, unless his individuality is very pronounced, write
poems in the Kipling manner—though rarely with such
striking art—for, at his best, Kipling the verse-writer is a
formidable artist (as, for instance, in *The Last Chantey*):

Thus said the Lord in the Vault above the Cherubim,
Calling to the Angels and the Souls in their degree:
  'Lo! Earth has passed away
  On the smoke of Judgment Day.
That Our word may be established shall We gather up the sea?'

Loud sang the souls of the jolly, jolly mariners:
'Plague upon the hurricane that made us furl and flee!

But the war is done between us,
In the deep the Lord hath seen us—
Our bones we 'll leave the barracout', and God may sink the sea!'

.   .   .   .

Loud sang the souls of the jolly, jolly mariners:
Plucking at their harps, and they plucked unhandily:
'Our thumbs are rough and tarred,
And the tune is something hard—
May we lift a Deepsea Chantey such as seamen use at sea?'

Nearly the whole of *The Last Chantey* is rich with fine phrases and unusual words—barracout', picaroon, fulmar, frapp'd, bull-mouth'd breakers, windless glassy floor—for how 'highbrow' the man could be, 'high-brow' and popular at the same moment and in the same breath! His knowledge was enormous; he was a walking encyclopaedia, and yet he could bring himself down to the humblest reader. You may hate poetry or you may love it, but either way, whatever plank of extremity you stand on, you are bound to be excited by some of his melodies, particularly by *Danny Deever*, that wild, macabre, and yet intensely modern ballad—François Villon and the medieval Scotch-border and the public school and the British Army and Moody and Sankey rolled into a single molten bar of grim gold. One cannot do justice to it in fragments, though even a fragment is hypnotic:

They are hangin' Danny Deever, they are marchin' of 'im round,
They 'ave 'alted Danny Deever by 'is coffin on the ground;
An' 'e 'll swing in 'arf a minute for a sneakin' shootin' hound—
O they 're hangin' Danny Deever in the mornin'!

Manifestly Kipling valued *Danny Deever* very highly, for he put it first of his *Barrack-Room Ballads*, but the English mind tends to avoid the grim and terrible (even cautiously rejecting what excites or pleases it) and so the poem has never been estimated at its true literary worth. Nor has Kipling ever been sufficiently estimated as a Teutonic 'scop' or 'skald,' though he was the direct spiritual descendant of those old minstrels who sailed with the northern sea-rovers and stirred the heart to tears and frenzy. The note is sometimes unmistakable, though rarely does he strike it with such directness as in *The Harp Song of the Dane Woman*:

> What is a woman that you forsake her,
> And the hearth-fire and the home-acre,
> To go with the old grey Widow-maker?

A memorable stanza! and it is a pity that none of the others in the poem are quite as good; for too often, much too often, Kipling the verse-writer was occupied with what he wanted to say rather than the manner of saying it, though no man was ever clearer in his mind as to the importance of form—beauty and power arrived at by some strange or super-perfect arrangement of words and syllables. A jingle, and even a very simple one, may be lifted into the atmosphere of poetry—so that the song of the Roman legionaries in *Puck of Pook's Hill* becomes more than a mere commonplace rime:

> And I've tramped Britain, and I've tramped Gaul,
> And the Pontic shore where the snow-flakes fall
>   As white as the neck of Lalage—
>   (As cold as the heart of Lalage!)
> And I've lost Britain, and I've lost Gaul,
> And I've lost Rome, and worst of all,
>   I've lost Lalage!

Like Goldsmith, whatever Kipling touched he adorned. He was a good poet in two or three different manners (that is, when he really chose to be good), a great short-story writer, an impressive recorder of Nature in her simplest and most visible aspects, and an arresting novelist.

I am tempted to step aside and speak of his prose, because his verse and prose are not always quite separable. Perhaps the future will value him highest for his short stories; for things like *The Brushwood Boy* seem to have the aureole of immortality upon them. Moreover, he could be exceedingly strange (even supernatural) and at the same time entirely convincing. And what he put to paper he deleted and rewrote, carefully rejecting the weakest and least necessary passages, and then hammering what remained into firm shapes of colour and form. He is probably the greatest short-story writer of the English language, our Maupassant, though greater than Maupassant, who is limited by his depressing and uncompromising realism. He was as painstaking as he was prolific—at any rate in his prose, for he left his slickness to his verse.

Of recent years he has been a little neglected. Probably this has been due more to his emotionalism than to the rabid imperialist thread which so frequently runs through his work. Emotionalism to-day is not looked upon with favour when it appears on the printed page; and it is too often misnamed 'sentimentalism' when it is simple and homely. Even though it is disciplined and restrained (and Kipling's emotional prose is always that) the new consciousness wants to flee from it.

When Rikki got to the house, Teddy and Teddy's mother (she looked very white still, for she had been fainting) and Teddy's father came out and almost cried over him; and that night he ate all that was given him till he could eat no more, and went to bed on Teddy's shoulder, where Teddy's mother saw him when she came to look late at night.

'He saved our lives and Teddy's life,' she said to her husband. 'Just think, he saved all our lives.'

Rikki-tikki woke up with a jump, for all the mongooses are light sleepers.

'Oh, it's you,' said he. 'What are you bothering for? All the cobras are dead; and if they weren't, I'm here.'

That passage certainly does not sound very striking taken away from its context, but reading the story from beginning to end (it is 'Rikki-Tikki-Tavi' of *The Jungle Book*) it is difficult to refrain from tears when you come to it.

The true estimation of Kipling has, perhaps, not yet begun. When the chaff is swept away from the wheat, what a bulky body of good work will still remain to us! Even some of the apparently superficial (and one has to continually emphasize that Kipling wrote much that is apparently very superficial) is curiously touched with magic; for Kipling had a diamond in one of his finger-nails, which sometimes changed garbage and dust into things of glittering wonder. He was no great teacher, no delver into the abyss, no poet of profundities; but he made a world, indeed many worlds; and as a creator he surely walks in the company of the great, and to-day adorns the tapestries of the Celestial City with images of purple and gold.

CHAPTER IV

ROBERT BRIDGES AND SOME OTHERS

AMONG the poets of this century other than Watson, Kipling, and Newbolt, who originally counted as Victorians, claiming a high position and much of their due of praise in volumes of criticism terminating with the year 1900, the most specially noteworthy are A. E. Housman and Robert Bridges.

As regards their very prolific rival Thomas Hardy, though most of his volumes of verse were published in this century, not all the contents belong to it, being often an overflow from his novels. Hardy is supreme as an imaginative novelist, a giant among prose creators (though his prose is sometimes a little formless), and it is only his constant pessimism which has prevented him from being recognized as the first of all English novelists; but as a poet in verse, his quality and importance have surely been exaggerated. He is too often static and laboured, indeed as a metrical artist he is occasionally execrable, which does not mean that he is not a vital poet— sometimes he is a very good poet—but his perfect lyrics are few, so that out of a very large quantity the anthologists have chosen a comparatively small number, these repeated over and over again. His original and unconventional use of words does not always hide the fact that the poem is little better than rough doggerel. Compare him, for instance, with W. H. Davies, with whom the anecdotal and pastoral realism of much of his lyrical output has affinities, and it will be seen immediately who is really the better lyrical poet.

At first Hardy's poems shocked and annoyed his readers by their emphasis on God as a blind mechanical force who had no action in any benevolent shaping of the universe. God had wound up the clock and then left it to go on or run down as it chose. All this was even more definitely expressed in his verse than in his novels. But as time went on Hardy seemed to imply that some benevolent consciousness was

53

slowly being evolved through mankind, and that the blind force had foreseen a far-away ultimate issue of justice and righteousness. But if Hardy had not originally won a strong reputation as a writer of imaginative prose it is improbable that he would to-day be seated so high upon the slopes of Parnassus. The case is other with A. E. Housman and Robert Bridges (two poets of contraries), both of whom, whatever their fame in other fields, won their position by poetry and have maintained it by poetry alone. It is odd, considering the captiousness of modern criticism, that Housman, who published the greater part of his best work in the last century, should have maintained such an unalterable position as a modern poet of consequence. He had in this century printed only three or four lyrics that have universally been accepted as of high order, including the *Epitaph on an Army of Mercenaries*, and the very impassioned but acrid *The Chestnut casts his Flambeaux*, remembered chiefly from its violent stanza:

> We for a certainty are not the first
>   Have sat in taverns while the tempest hurled
> Their hopeful plans to emptiness, and cursed
>   Whatever brute and blackguard made the world.

But he is unchallenged and is likely to remain so—probably because ere the opening of the War he had been exactly sized up, and his true qualities neither underrated nor exaggerated. An even darker, bitterer poet than Hardy, he was chiefly accepted for the beauty and precision of his form—though much of his later verse shows a certain amount of deterioration.

Neither Hardy nor Housman has been noteworthy as a poet of growth, though some defenders of Hardy may point to his long dramatic poem *The Dynasts* to show that he developed into a poet of much larger dimensions. The case is otherwise with Robert Bridges, who advanced in technique as his age increased, and lost little in poetical content or vision. He is at least the equal of Thomas Hardy as a poet, though the recent new edition of the *Encyclopaedia Britannica* seems to place him some distance behind; while a popular verse anthology published by Methuen in 1921 is dedicated to 'Thomas Hardy, O.M., the greatest of the moderns,' thereby indirectly disparaging Bridges in company with Yeats and some others.

The poems of Bridges's old age are thought by some admirers to be superior to those of his middle age and youth, and though it is improbable that *The Testament of Beauty* is actually his best book, certain it is that this work, written in loose alexandrines, received wider approval than any other of his books, and was the only one to succeed triumphantly as a 'best seller,' though it was composed after his eightieth year. *October and Other Poems*, published in 1920, and *New Verse*, in 1925, are possibly each better than *The Testament of Beauty*, and certainly not inferior to any of his earlier volumes. Both of them make use of entirely new rhythms, not based on Middle English rhythms as was frequently supposed, but developed from a very close study of Milton's syllabic prosody. Of one of the items, *Noel : Christmas Eve, 1913*,[1] Bridges has written:

And on Nov. 28th, when I had been considering whether I would send His Majesty a Christmas Poem to commemorate my appointment in his household, a poem called *Noel* appeared on the scene.

'A frosty Christmas Eve when the stars were shining.'

This was sent to the King at Christmas, and His Majesty sent it to *The Times* for publication. Of that poem I can say that it has won more favour from all classes of people than any other poem that I ever wrote: and since not one of the readers knew how it scanned, it seemed to me that my extension of Milton's rules must be worth something.

It is, of course, not easy to see how the extension of Milton's rules achieved the curious but beautiful lines which caused a learned critic to exclaim: 'What is this lovely new metre?'

> Then sped my thought to keep
>   that first Christmas of all
> When the shepherds watching
>   by their folds ere the dawn

---

[1] To-day published in *The Shorter Poems of Robert Bridges* (Clarendon Press, Oxford, 1931).

Heard music in the fields
  and marveling could not tell
Whether it were angels
  or the bright stars singing.

Now blessed be the tow'rs
  that crown England so fair
That stand up strong in prayer
  unto God for our souls: . . .

But Bridges himself so frequently emphasized the fact that his later metrical work sprang into being through a close study of Milton's prosody, involving not so much what Milton had done already, as what he would have eventually done if he had lived longer and extended his technique. Bridges has not only published a complete book on the subject, but also some independent notes, the most important of which come at the end of his second volume of *Collected Essays* (1933), entitled *Explanation of the Prosody of my Late Syllabic 'Free Verse.'*

Continuously he emphasized the necessity of discovering new rhythms—but which were not to be of the nature of free verse as popularly understood. For in his essay *Harum-Scarum* he has not only chastised F. S. Flint and all his co-workers and followers, but nearly knocked the bottom out of their kettle, so that it seems that his own 'free verse' is most ironically designated, and really nothing of that kidney. If anything, Bridges was inclined to exaggerate the importance of form, and some of his assertions in his essay on Kipling and Wordsworth (two poets whom he much admired), though they cannot be easily denied, seem to lay almost too much stress on newness of rhythm as a means of communicating interest or delight.

It is true in all art that when a great master appears he so exhausts the material at his disposal as to make it impossible for any succeeding artist to be original, unless he can either find new material or invent some new method of handling the old. In painting and music this is almost demonstrable to the uninitiated; in poetry the law may not be so strict, but it still holds; and any one may see that serious rhyme is now exhausted in English verse, or that Milton's blank verse practically ended as an original form with Milton. There are abundant signs that English syllabic verse has long been in the stage of artistic exhaustion of form which follows great artistic achievement.   Now as far as regards the verse-form, Wordsworth was apparently unconscious of this predicament. It never occured to him that he was working with blunted tools.

Nevertheless some of Bridges's best poetry was executed with blunted tools; though he seems to gain in power and passion when he is applying his new metrical theories—as in *The Psalm* (published in *New Verse*, 1925):

A great Huguenot psalm, it trod forth on the air
with full slow notes, moving as a goddess stepping
through the responsive figures of a stately dance
conscious of beauty and of her fair-flowing array
in the severe perfection of an habitual grace,
then stooping to its close, paused to dance forth anew;

To unfold its bud of melody everlastingly
fresh as in springtime when, four centuries agone,
it wing'd the souls of martyrs on their way to heav'n
chain'd at the barbarous stake, mid the burning faggots
standing with tongues cut out, all singing in the flames—
O evermore, sweet psalm, shalt thou break forth anew!

It is, moreover, noteworthy that though his newest verse has had some influence upon the young modernists, it rarely halts, stammers, or becomes harsh. In so much of the new verse later than Bridges the best effects are suddenly lost in a glutinous web of bad prose. This is a violation of the fundamental rules of art; because what has been offered must not be withheld, especially when the ear has been keyed to expectancy.

One of Bridges great advantages over his modernist contemporaries has come from his very intimate knowledge of Greek and Latin prosody. He is possibly the most Greek of all our poets, while it is certain that his experiments in classical prosody have been more successful than those of any other English poet. Nevertheless, he exonerated the ruggedness of Burns and Kipling, whom he greeted as masters of words and revitalizers of language; but he attacks all who by content or form have waylaid the Muse and sought to set her in ugly positions.

> I prop so far my slight fable with argument
> to lay malison and ban on the upstart leprous clan
> who wrong Nature's beauty turning her face about:
> for, certes, hath the goddess also her hinder parts
> which men of all ages have kindly thought to hide.

Such lines pin the enemy without ambiguity, but it is not so plain what he is driving at in his satiric verses, *To Catullus*, dated 1902:

> Would that you were alive to-day, Catullus!
> Truth 'tis, there is a filthy skunk amongst us,
> A rank musk-idiot, the filthiest skunk,
> Of no least sorry use on earth, but only
> Fit in fancy to justify the outlay
> Of your most horrible vocabulary.

He felt very strongly about some things and occasionally expressed himself very strongly. As leonine in spirit and character as he was in appearance, he was swift in attack on all that he considered to be unwholesome or disintegrating. It was not enough for him to be one of the most original and exquisite artists in the English tongue. He was convinced of his mission to guard the foundations. So he devoted a great part of his life to the examination and preservation of English pronunciation. He was emphatic that a good northern pronunciation was the best for preserving the native music of English verse; but recognizing that much current pronunciation had become too corrupted to be ever corrected he devised a scheme of phonetic spelling by means of which the best educated speech should be preserved from further corruption and attention drawn to the disparities between the spoken and written word. Moreover, there was considerable difference between what he and cultured Londoners regarded as educated speech, so his phonetic spelling primers were to function as trained warriors against the destructive influence of Cockneyism. His greatest antagonist was the famous London phonetician Daniel Jones, whose sphere of influence was very wide, and had even been so far extended as to fortify at German universities a system of English pronunciation which could often be challenged as something more than doubtful.

Scotch blood was in his veins, and however unlike Burns he was in manner, he felt a resemblance to him in the spirit of his external matter. For has he not written in the shortest of his appreciative poems addressed to Burns:

> To Burns! brave Scotia's laurel'd son
> Who drove his plough on Helicon—
> Who with his Doric rhyme erewhile
> Taught English bards to bend their style . . .

But actual verbal or metrical influence emanating from Burns is not discernible. The case is otherwise with Burns's brother poet, the German Heine, whose skill in accent-shifting was much admired by Bridges, and seems to have affected some of his early lyrical work.

Of his many lovely pre-Laureate lyrics probably the one beginning 'I never shall love the snow again' is the most popular and moving, none of its seven stanzas falling behind the opening ones:

> I never shall love the snow again
>   Since Maurice died:
> With corniced drift it blocked the lane
> And sheeted in a desolate plain
>   The country side.
>
> The trees with silvery rime bedight
>   Their branches bare.
> By day no sun appeared; by night
> The hidden moon shed thievish light
>   In the misty air.

Though Bridges was a little lacking in lyrical passion, as also in sudden inspiration and fluency, he made up for nearly everything by his intellectual ardour, his vision, his sensitiveness, his diligent concentration, and his metrical learning. Though he was essentially a scholar-poet he was a very good one, and careful never to over-write, he frequently turned to prose for the purpose of expressing himself outside the exacting imaginative margins.

He was a master of lucid, delicate prose, lightly weaponed with irony and unobtrusive wit. His attitude was nearly always sharply critical, but his thrust was the rapier's, and only on very few occasions the glaive's or the broadsword's. He rarely espoused a bad cause. An entirely sincere writer, he was very antagonistic to those who did not write what they fundamentally believed.

He waged war incessantly on modern showiness and vulgarity. But it was no haughty castle of narrow academicism that he guarded, but the walled city of essential culture; something rudimentary and yet highly civilized. Few English poets have more deeply combined imaginative insight with moral integrity and practical common sense.

One of his most characteristic features as Laureate was a sort of gallant independence. When the press clamoured for 'war' odes and 'unknown warrior' odes and suggested that he needed 'stimulating' and was not doing his duty as Poet Laureate he simply said, 'I don't care a damn' (a common defensive remark of his), and got on with his pamphlets, his copious letter-writing, and the sort of verse that pleased him best. Moreover, as an artist he was entirely conscientious, and preferred the reproach of inactivity to publication until there had been thorough application of the file and diamond-cutter. As Laureate he set a very fine example. Though he did occasionally write verse of national significance, he felt that his office of Laureate opened doors on many other issues, and that the moralities he represented went beyond mere patriotic fervours and antagonisms. He refused a knighthood and liked to be known by his bare name without even the appellation of Mr or Dr or Esq. A very old-fashioned Tory, he was nevertheless as democratic as a Saint Francis.

CHAPTER V

PRELUDE TO THE FIRST GEORGIAN REVOLT

THE maiden twentieth century was crowned by William Watson's great coronation ode, in which he reached not only the culmination of his powers as a poet, but donned the mantle of an old Hebrew prophet. But shortly before its appearance, during the year 1900, G. K. Chesterton published his *Wild Knight*, which, though confused by James Douglas with John Davidson's creations, was something of a new note—but to have little influence upon the twentieth-century verse in general. Then in 1902, John Masefield, at that time a young man groping in darkness, published his *Salt Water Ballads*, which chiefly showed him as an admirer of Kipling, Newbolt, and Stevenson, but was really the prelude to a new kind of song, which for a short time was to dominate English poetry. But Wilfrid Gibson, whose name in later years was to be sometimes coupled with Masefield's (chiefly as poets of the back streets), had preceded him during the nineteenth century with several scattered lyrics in the press, one of them a ballad of some grim external power (though little innate force of originality) in the pages of *The Dome* magazine, which placarded him as a disciple of the anonymous minstrels of the Scotch Border country. But it did not reappear in his first book, *Urlyn the Harper* (1902), which chiefly showed him as under the influence of Tennysonian romanticism.

But the new accepted poet of the century was Stephen Phillips; and for rather over a decade, until the Georgians pushed him completely out of the ring, he was to be much read and admired—and listened to. He sprang into prominence right upon the century's threshold, and did so well that he must have made a small fortune out of his verse. Yet, tragical to relate, he died in 1915 in abject poverty—due largely to drink and extravagance. Though for a time he was a 'best seller,' his success was due less to his reading public than his listening public, for his creations for the most part were plays, and very successful plays; and the anthologist can only do him justice by cutting pieces out of these plays.

He had already had much success during the preceding century with poems that pointed no very strong finger to the stage, and these helped to prepare the way for the public's acceptance. The fulsome and exorbitant press praise bestowed upon these poems seems entirely out of touch with the actual performance; but his later work, the dramas which came after *Paolo and Francesca*, was rather more worthy of acclamation. *Paolo and Francesca*, published in 1900 (and played in 1902), despite its great success, is clearly inferior to those plays that followed—at any rate inferior from the poet's and reader's standpoint, for, though Stephen Phillips had completely mastered stage technique, he had not sufficiently risen to the requirements of literary form, and one wonders what was the matter with critics who raved themselves hoarse about work which in verbal texture was little better than the earlier poems, and which was often not only weak verse, but very ordinary poetry. He started his career as an actor (in Benson's company), in which professional capacity he thoroughly acquainted himself with every finesse of the popular stage. In a way his creative feat was remarkable, for he brought back blank verse into English popular drama, and so was unusual among dramatists since the Elizabethans. But it was the blank verse of Marlowe rather than Shakespeare—pompous, gaudy, showy, but sometimes really good, and, when well spoken, astonishingly effective. Rarely did he reach the magnificence of Marlowe's 'mighty line,' at any rate he is less even and sustained than Marlowe, but, save at his worst, he was a very reincarnated Marlowe (at moments almost a parody of him) as dozens of passages will very clearly show:

> But, O the raining of the blooms;
> The cymbals and the roarings and the roses!
> I seemed to drink bright wine and run on flowers,
> Nay, Mariamne, how should I forget thee?

The Aesthetes and Decadents (W. B. Yeats to some extent amongst them) had prepared audiences for the lilies and roses and spilt wine and splashed blood and swooning music and broodings upon Death that riot through his pages. But there was some intrinsic power in the man, and some of his lines are really memorable:

> I 'll recreate her out of endless yearning,
> And flesh shall cleave to bone, and blood shall run.
> Do I not know her, every vein? Can I
> Not imitate in furious ecstasy
> What God hath coldly made?

Very few of the long speeches are sufficiently sustained, or entirely satisfying from beginning to end. On the stage the efficient actor could work across the weaknesses, but they are jarring and unsatisfying to the reader. In snatches, however, how good he could be, especially in pomp; and the threaded brocade and jewellery was not always paste and tinsel to disillusion upon a second encounter:

> I dreamed last night of a dome of beaten gold
> To be a counter-glory to the Sun.
> There shall the eagle blindly dash himself,
> There the first beam shall strike, and there the moon
> Shall aim all night her argent archery.
>
> .   .   .   .   .   .
>
> And I will think in gold and dream in silver.

But it is only the half of Herod's speech, and the rest of it is distinguished by little save vapidity and inconsistency. Very rarely has his blank verse the quiet, effective, sustained power of Yeats's—though Yeats, in spite of the Wordsworth tag in the first line, might not have disowned:

> A sense of something coming on the world,
> A crying of dead prophets from their tombs,
> A singing of dead poets from their graves.

But the blank verse of the poets of the Celtic Twilight rarely creeps into him, for weak or strong, pompous or drivelling,

Elizabethan or Jacobean in texture, the voice is nearly always the voice of Marlowe. But he is so much more effective for the modern stage than Marlowe.

For instance, when Nero, singing and reciting his poems, is confronted by a yawning courtier, the laughter Stephen Phillips evokes is not particularly characteristic of anything promoted by the Elizabethan stage:

Third Spy. [*Creeping forward.*] Sir, Titus Cassius yawned while thou
    didst sing.
Fourth Spy. Nay, Caesar, worse, he slept, and must he live?
Nero. [*Gently.*] No! he must die: there is no hope in sleep.
    Witness, you gods, who sent me on the earth
    To be a joy to men: and witness you
    Who stand around: if ever a small malice
    Hath governed me: what critic have I feared?
    What rival? Have I used this mighty throne
    To baulk opinion or suppress dissent?
    Have I not toiled for art, forsworn food, sleep,
    And laboured day and night to win the crown,
    Lying with weight of lead upon my chest?
    Ye gods, there is no rancour in this soul.   [*Thunder.*
    Silence while I am speaking. He must die,
    Because he is unmindful of our gifts
    And of the golden voice on me bestowed,
    To me no credit; and he shall not die
    Hopeless, for ere he die I 'll sing to him
    This night, that he may pass away in music.
    How foolish will he peer amid the shades
    When Orpheus asks: 'Hast thou heard Nero sing?'
    If he must answer 'No!' I would not have him
    Arrive ridiculous amid the dead.

The theme of Stephen Phillips's dramas is similar to Marlowe's—the monster, or the superman or would-be superman—Nero, Herod, Ulysses, etc. Such characters occur in Shakespeare's plays, but Marlowe concentrated on them, and Stephen Phillips goes on, as it were, at the point where Marlowe left off. For if Marlowe had not so suddenly ended his career, it is quite possible that Tamburlaine, the Jew of

Malta, Faustus and Mephistopheles might have been capped by one or more of Stephen Phillips's *dramatis personae*.

But he followed the Greek drama rather than the Elizabethan. So in most of the plays there was no violence upon the stage, no stabbings or executions before the eyes of the spectator. He did not adhere absolutely to this rule (for instance in *Ulysses* one of Penelope's suitors is shot on the stage by an arrow), and he certainly did not adhere closely to all three Unities of Time, Place, and Circumstance. Nevertheless his plays are Greek in mould, and have more shape, more perfection of form than Marlowe's. They abound in single-lined utterances, and, as in Marlowe, when the speaker ends his say in the middle of the blank-verse line it is continued to the end of the iambic beat by the next speaker. But, unlike the Greek, the action is swift, extremely swift, with many exits and entrances, every stage trick studied and reproduced effectively—Greek, Elizabethan, and modern stage-technique rolled into a co-ordinate whole. Unfortunately his superabundant colour and energy are not always effectively reproduced for the eye and ear of the *reader*. Stephen Phillips had immense gifts; but too frequently is his work fevered and slipshod, though so skilfully shaped to the stage-requirements,—its verbal weaknesses probably largely the fault of his fulsome worshipping critics, whom he too wholeheartedly trusted. Overpraise at the beginning, when a young poet is on the threshold of real performance, is much more difficult to recover from than blame or neglect—so that his friends often become more dangerous to him than his detractors or enemies. To what extent that great actor Beerbohm Tree, who took the leading parts in three of his dramas, is responsible for some of the overrating, can, of course, be guessed at; but certain it is that, though Stephen Phillips improved on *Paolo and Francesca*, he never reached the climax of excellency his more critical public expected him to reach.

Stephen Phillips was in part a throw-off from the Decadent and Aesthetic movement. But other throws-off were Lord

D

Alfred Douglas and Richard Middleton. Of Lord Alfred
Douglas and his work the least we can say is that he is a
sonnet-writer of outstanding distinction. Few poets trouble
to concentrate on that extremely exacting thing called the
Sonnet, and though Alfred Douglas's sonnets are sometimes
a little too stiff and unspontaneous, and would perhaps have
shone with more dynamic gleam if he had used the Shakespearian mould rather than the Petrarchan (for when not too
stiffly tied up by a continually recurrent rhyme how easy and
flowing he can be), they do constitute a small body of beautiful
and effective work. Other verse of his is lyrical and satirical,
while he has written at least one narrative poem of high
excellence. His satirical verse is little known, but many living
people who remember his prose writing in the *Academy* and
Plain English know that he has an extremely biting tongue,
not unmixed with strong wit and uproarious humour. If
some of his victims have writhed (and more than one of them
has made him pay unduly for his recklessness), others less
savagely hit, and immune in a good conscience, must have
nearly split their sides with laughter. Something of his true
self, along with his attitude to life, is very well expressed in
one of his sonnets, *To Olive*:

> I have been profligate of happiness
> And reckless of the world's hostility,
> The blessed part has not been given to me
> Gladly to suffer fools; I do confess
> I have enticed and merited distress,
> By this, that I have never bow'd the knee
> Before the shrine of wise Hypocrisy,
> Nor worn self-righteous anger like a dress.

His religious note (he is a professed Catholic) is best illus-
trated by his short poem, *A Prayer*, which begins:

> Often the western wind has sung to me,
>   There have been voices in the streams and meres,
> And pitiful trees have told me, God, of Thee:
>   And I heard not. Oh! open Thou mine ears.

The lyric is very graceful and finished, and would be entirely satisfying were it not for the somewhat ambiguous 'pitiful,' which in present-day English as an attributive adjective, means 'contemptible' as often as not.

A slight artificiality which makes him sometimes put his simple and clearly arranged words before the idea (an occasional incomplete fusion of substance and form) is his besetting vice. But he is one of the important twentieth-century poets, though fifty per cent of him is in the Victorian age.

As regards Richard Middleton, his is not a name which is much in the public eye to-day; but I remember how between the years 1907 and 1912 he was a figure of some importance, his posthumous prose volume *The Ghost Ship* hoisting him into something approaching real fame, and drawing attention to him as a charming silly fellow who had committed suicide for no adequate reason.

He was the fag-end of the Aesthetic-*cum*-Decadent Movement, an overflow from the *Yellow Books*, his graceful, and at times rather beautiful prose reminiscent of both Oscar Wilde and R. L. Stevenson. Indeed, his best prose (though he wrote rather too much that was mawkish and sloppy) was not only nearly as good as Stevenson's, but easier and more natural. In verse he comes between Dowson and Theodore Wratislaw, considerably better than Wratislaw, but rarely quite as good as Dowson at his summit. In spite of the fact that none of his books were published during his lifetime, he had a following of eager readers—though he did not seem to know it. His work was much admired by some of the readers of the *Academy* (whose editor, Lord Alfred Douglas, claims to have been the first to give him recognition), *Vanity Fair*, and the *English Review*;[1] and his suicide in Brussels at the age of twenty-nine, committed during a fit of acute melancholia and insane impatience, came as a terrible surprise to his admirers.

[1] A collection of Middleton's prose pieces other than those in *The Ghost Ship* has recently been issued in a volume entitled *The Pantomime Man* (Rich & Cowan), with a 'foreword' by John Gawsworth and an 'introduction' by Lord Alfred Douglas.

John Davidson had done a similar thing in 1909, two years earlier, but John Davidson had got to the end of his tether, and for Richard Middleton there seemed no solid excuse of reason. But a sentence from one of his letters, '. . . that I have missed in my passionate search for enjoyment,' and something scattered throughout his writings (particularly in his worst work) give the show away. He was trammelled in the meshes of a very enervating nostalgia, an oppressively strange, almost sickly yearning for something over the border-line, which really expressed a strong dissatisfaction with life. He wanted so much, but he confused the spiritual with the material, and was too weak to take refuge in the strongholds of religion. And added to his many unsatisfying love-affairs was the torture he suffered from neuralgia. And he was impatient and impulsive and galled by his poverty—which, however, was not so very terrible if he had had sufficient back-bone to live more spartanly; for his output was considerable, and his earnings out of literary journalism must have been quite sufficient to keep his head above water. He easily made friends, for he was a man of great charm and amiability, beloved by most who came in contact with him, especially by children. But he was beset by inordinate Desire and lack of Faith. They finally put the cap on everything, driving him into the outer dark of despair and self-annihilation.

I remember walking into the *English Review* offices one day during the War and noticing a striking framed head of Richard Middleton hung alongside Joseph Conrad's. I asked that keen-witted, generous-minded, but extremely candid and rather Ishmaelitish editor Austin Harrison, to explain why such a very promising writer came to commit suicide, and I was startled, and almost annoyed, by his answer (though it showed how completely Middleton was a lyrical child of the nineties): 'He had an awkward luxury vein, you see. He wanted things like caviare for breakfast every morning, and couldn't afford it. He had no backbone. He was just a poet; but weak as a man. . . .' At any rate, he was too easily cast down; while as regards his critical writings he was downright backboneless if he was moving within his subject's shadow. He had little of the independence of the self-convinced artist or critic. His essays on Frank Harris (the literary dictator of those days) are outrageous exhibitions of fatuous adulation, and reveal his lack of self-reliance.

Still, it is necessary to recognize that there is another side to the penny. It was the fashion of those days to beflag your paragraphs with wildly enthusiastic phrases if you only rather liked a writer (a fashion probably set by Swinburne) and to exaggerate your praise still further if you were in any way beholden to him.

But as a poet Middleton is not without importance. Like Dowson he had something in common with Verlaine (the Verlaine of the early period, Verlaine the Parnassian), and indeed Austin Harrison called him 'the carolling boy of English poetry . . . our Verlaine.' He is magical or exquisite at his best, merely sentimental or pretty at his frequent worst. Very many of his poems are no more than fluent emotional exercises; but in others the stanza of enchantment, the gleaming couplet stir the poem into life:

> Oh my belovèd, is not the night our cup,
> Are not the stars our wine?

Two of his most seductive lyrics are about dead children, and the shorter of them (included by Sir Arthur Quiller-Couch in *The Victorian Book of English Verse*) begins with the lovely memorable lines:

> Man proposes, God in His time disposes,
>   And so I wander'd up to where you lay,
> A little rose among the little roses,
>   And no more dead than they.

The longer, quoted in full in R. L. Mégroz's critical study, *Modern English Poetry, 1882–1932*, is rather better as a whole, but not so outstanding in its initial lines. The most striking couplet he ever put to paper is probably:

> I have lit no eternal fire
> To burn my dreams on Judgment Day!

What on earth it exactly means is another matter; but it is hypnotic and communicative, a fragmentary unconscious parent of Modernism.

But Middleton's death in 1911 quite definitely marked the end of a period. Subconsciously he may have felt that his literary manner and outlook would soon be no longer wanted, and that this hastened his decision to put an end to himself.[1]

Another poet loosely connected with the ultimate end of the Aesthetic and Decadent movement was T. W. H. Crosland, a rather wild irregular bird, but very strong-willed, who was continually in trouble of some kind, and for a season Lord Alfred Douglas's assistant editor. He was best known for his venomous and witty prose work *The Unspeakable Scot*, a highly amusing, but unfair book, in which all the folk north of the Tweed were held up to scathing ridicule. As a poet he has possibly not yet been quite fairly assessed, though one lyric of his (if you can call the strange modernist thing a lyric) stuck fast on the horizon and will probably continue to stick there for a long time. Cynical and evasive, yet profoundly suggestive and moving, it is a laurel wreath for the heads of all the damned who are not really damned, and a whip to scourge the back of every successful opportunist and bedizened hypocrite who goes smiling and lying down the primrose path to the everlasting bonfire:

> If ever I should be in England's thought
>   After I die,
> Say, 'There were many things he might have bought
>   And did not buy.
>
> 'Unhonoured by his fellows he grew old
>   And trod the path to hell,
> But there were many things he might have sold
>   And did not sell.'

---

[1] But Middleton was not quite the last poet of the decadent period, for two or three others using the old counters and stock-in-trade of the Yellow Nineties lingered on into the first year of the War, but they are unimportant, and expired of their sensual inefficiency.

But there were dozens of others, for the most part entirely new voices, many of whom were speaking in a different manner from the poets of the preceding century (I am writing of the period till the middle of 1914, till the outbreak of the War), among them—besides the early advance guard, Masefield, Gibson, and Chesterton—Lascelles Abercrombie, Maurice Baring, Anna de Bary, Hilaire Belloc, Laurence Binyon, Gordon Bottomley, Rupert Brooke, Mary Coleridge, W. H. Davies, Walter de la Mare, Charles M. Doughty, John Drinkwater, 'Michael Field,' J. Elroy Flecker, John Freeman, Norman Gale, John Galsworthy, Douglas Goldring, Gerald Gould, Lord Gorell, Ralph Hodgson, Laurence Housman, Ford Madox Hueffer, D. H. Lawrence, Richard Le Gallienne, Patrick Macgill, James Mackereth, Harold Monro, T. Sturge Moore, Alfred Noyes, Sir Ronald Ross, Arthur Salmon, Edmund Beale Sargant, Lady Margaret Sackville, J. C. Squire, W. Force Stead, R. C. Trevelyan, Rachel Annand Taylor, Gilbert Thomas, Edward Thompson, Wilfrid Thorley, E. H. Visiak, Charles Williams, Margaret L. Woods.

But a few of them, such as Robert C. Trevelyan, Sturge Moore, and Laurence Binyon, though no advance guard, had their starts in the preceding century; and Norman Gale, a charming poet of country life with a rather too conservative voice, had a firm foot in each century. Very many of Mary Coleridge's lyrics were also published during the preceding century. The same as regards Richard Le Gallienne (a good poet, soon to be blindly depreciated), who is always associated with the *Yellow Book* and Rhymers' Club rather than this century. And 'Michael Field' is also sometimes put into the same period.

In addition to that aviary, and supplementing and influencing it, there was an extensive Irish School headed by A.E. (George Russell) and W. B. Yeats, with its roots in Dublin, and influencing intellectual and aesthetic thought all over Ireland.

Round about 1910, about four years before the War, it became very evident to the literary public (and there was an extensive literary culture in those halcyon days) that the first decade of the century had exceptionally blossomed and that a crowd of new poets, some of them exceptionally promising, was assaulting the stronghold of the Victorians. Some of them, not necessarily the best, got into the public eye well in front, for they were given special prominence in the weekly press, and as time went on, in such select monthlies and quarterlies as the *English Review* (in those days it took up a similar position as the present-day *London Mercury*), Douglas Goldring's *Tramp*, Harold Monro's *Poetry Review* (which changed into *Poetry and Drama*), and Middleton Murry's *Rhythm*. The names of three of these magazines are well known in literary history, but the most raggedly endowed is little known. The *Tramp* was unique among monthly magazines, and probably no such combination of good literature and ingenuous open-airness has ever got on to the bookstalls. There was a popular, free and easy, touch about it, but in spite of all its fine features, and all the pleasant pictures and photographs which decorated it, it died after a twelve months' run. In its pages appeared many contributions by such people as Flecker, John Freeman, W. H. Davies, F. S. Flint, and John Drinkwater, some of their best poems among them. John Freeman's lovely moon lyric, beginning:

> It was the lovely moon—she lifted
> Slowly her white brow among
> Bronze cloud-waves . . .

came out in it, as also Flecker's *War Song of the Saracens,* and his *Tenebris Interlucentum.* The Housman touch and influence were also rather evident.

But there were enough good lyrics in the twelve numbers to make an agreeable anthology, two or three of the best by poets who have never been heard of since. An unknown poet called Charles Laurence Bewley contributed several— one of them beginning 'There's many a precious thing lies hidden for ever unknown,' very good indeed, and another less even, which brandished the astonishing couplet:

> Ruin is over me now and the black disgrace,
> But I have seen in a dream white Deirdre's face.

But the most original of all was J. D. Beazley's *The Visit*,[1] a lyric which condenses into a few lines the main content of Bürger's long ballad, *Lenore*:

'Sweetheart, is it you? I 've been all night looking out for you,
  But how cold your hands are, and your face is so pale.
Thunder and lightning, and the soldiery about for you:
  But yesterday you promised, and I knew you wouldn't fail.'
'Yes, yes, it 's me, and I 'm sorry I am late for you,
  Dearest, and I 'm sorry that my fingers are so cold:
But you said, "Whatever happens, come to-morrow, and I 'll wait
  for you":
  So I thought I 'd come and see you, though a dead man a day
  old.'

'Lovely sweetheart, quick and come to bed to me,
  For I 'm sick with longing for you, and the night is nearly gone,
We shall easily forget, O sweetheart, what you 've said to me,
  And you 'll soon get warm, and there 's still an hour till dawn.
'Death when the dawn comes will take me and make from me
  A sorry love for women, the worm's delight:
But the pains of death and hell like water I shall shake from me
  For this our last and our wonderfullest night.'

It was enthusiastically admired by Elroy Flecker, and is noteworthy as one of the last good lyrics, if not actually the very last, of the Decadent period. But Beazley, save for one or two other distinguished appearances in the literary press, published no more. One of the young men of the greatest poetical promise, he cast aside poetry for scholarship, and is now professor of archaeology at Oxford University.

But in the centre of all this lyricism there was a community of notes which stood away, which made a world of verbal music to itself, which was a little different or a great deal different from what came before, which had little in common

---

[1] After the War this poem was rescued by W. H. Davies for his very fine anthology *Shorter Lyrics of the Twentieth Century, 1900-1922*. But lines five and six of the first stanza, and line one of the second stanza, should read as above, and not as in Davies's anthology.

with late Victorian poetry or its overflow, the Edwardian poetry, which, constituted a world of revolt, and which at the time seemed very fresh and underived. In fact it was the beginning of what is known as Georgian poetry—it was the first movement of 'the Georgian Revolt.'

Thus commenced a period of literary uniformities and certainties. . . . But for much interesting first-hand information about some of the literary personalities who were active during the staccato period preceding this revolt, particularly the nineties of the last century, I would direct readers to Ernest Rhys's very valuable volume of memoirs, *Everyman Remembers*.

CHAPTER VI

THE FIRST GEORGIAN REVOLT

DURING the years 1911–12 Edward Marsh (now Sir Edward Marsh), a literary connoisseur, began to select from the numerous poets, and at the end of 1912 (soon after the accession of George V to the throne) he published the first anthology of 'Georgian poetry.'

In his prefatory note he wrote:

This volume is issued in the belief that English poetry is now once again putting on a new strength and beauty.

Few readers have the leisure or the zeal to investigate each volume as it appears; and the process of recognition is often slow. This collection, drawn entirely from the publications of the past two years, may if it is fortunate help the lovers of poetry to realize that we are at the beginning of another 'Georgian period' which may take rank in due time with the several great poetic ages of the past.

It has no pretension to cover the field. Every reader will notice the absence of poets whose work would be a necessary ornament to any anthology not limited by a definite aim. Two years ago some of the writers represented had published nothing; and only a very few of the others were known except to the eagerest 'watchers of the skies.' Those few are here because within the chosen period their work seemed to have gained some accession of power.

The anthology was 'limited by a definite aim,' and it chiefly seemed to be this: the revival or preservation of the Wordsworthian tradition, particularly as exemplified or stressed in the writings of those chosen. Thus one feature of this poetry was its open-airness and naturalness. So when Professor G. Bullough in his recent scholarly, but much too condensed, volume *The Trend of Modern Poetry* tells us that Georgian poetry was equivalent to the poetry of the opening century and that, identified with it as one of its significant tendencies, was 'a scholarly tradition going back through Tennyson and Wordsworth to Milton and the Elizabethans, refining on old themes and forms,' I think he is only partially right. This new poetry was not particularly Shakespearian or Elizabethan, though much of Masefield's work (somewhat avoided in the Georgian volumes) constituted an awkward exception.

There also seemed to be a definite attempt to break away from the Tennyson tradition, from Tennysonian influences; and though in more than one poem we can hear some admiration for Milton, his voice is not at all dominant. More dominant is the voice of A. E. Housman, though rarely directly reminiscent of him, with something of Blake (the simpler aspect of Blake) and something of Francis Thompson (the simpler aspect of Francis Thompson). This new poetry constituted a definite break with nearly everything known as 'Victorian'—which meant that the Elizabethan note, which, though transmuted, had been rather strongly cultivated by the Victorian poets, was somewhat in the background.

As a direct result or a corollary, the following certainties and half-certainties steal into evidence:

(1) Very little nostalgia and no wild yearning.

(2) Everywhere restraint in the diction. (Very good, of course, as poetry should be 'impassioned' rather than passionate. But avoidance of the passionate too often ruled out ecstasy, and it is better to be passionate than merely competent, and better to risk the passion becoming hysteria or noisy violence than to put a fence right round it.)

(3) Avoidance of poetic licence. Avoidance of 'thee' and 'thou.' Avoidance of odd grammatical forms like 'hast,' 'doth,' 'methinks.' Avoidance of 'o'er' for 'over.' Avoidance of all subterfuges, especially those unusual in cultured, conversational prose. (These new poets aimed at naturalness, though their naturalness was sometimes too much of the front rooms of the manor-house—of the country-house drawing-room rather than the kitchen or workshop.)

(4) Avoidance of all hackneyed Victorian rhythms of the quick or tumpty-tum type. (So there is nothing reminiscent

of Austin Dobson, Frederick Locker, or Norman Gale—though in stating this I have no intention to disparage the best work of these poets.)

(5) No carnal influences due to French poetry. (Even Flecker's two included lyrics do not show them.)

(6) Avoidance of the queer, the bizarre, the difficult, the obscure, and the vernacular. (So there is scarcely anything reminiscent of Robert Browning, George Meredith, Rudyard Kipling, D. G. Rossetti, or the great odes of Francis Thompson. Though unfortunately for Edward Marsh's aims, Lascelles Abercrombie, the Robert Browning of our days, constituted a curious exception; but he was not represented by his most antagonistic verse.)

(7) Avoidance of the phrase, of any strongly coloured or aggressive group of words, especially those kinds likely to distract from attention to the poem as a whole. (This is downright anti-Shakespearian, and as a result there is not much in the Georgians that is quotable or memorable in half-lines, single lines, or couplets—though in whole stanzas and passages from half a dozen to a dozen lines how very good they sometimes were.)

(8) Avoidance of symbolism, not necessarily the symbolism of the 'French Symbolists,' but the symbolism of such poets as Blake and Francis Thompson and St John of the Apocalypse. (As a result there is something almost anti-Biblical about characteristic Georgian poetry. Strangest of all is the way Blake and Francis Thompson are both present in and entirely absent from the pages. Each of these poets has a double voice, and in each instance only one of them seemed to be approved of.)

(9) Avoidance of strictly Christian themes. (So there is nothing in Edward Marsh's first Georgian anthology—and little in those of the later years—which is relative to the church hymn. And very little indeed which comes under the term 'religious poetry.')

(10) Avoidance of national and patriotic themes. Avoidance, too, of themes that were aggressively ethical or with

Brooke?

quick appeal to the man in the street. (That is, the Georgians had little in common with the old-fashioned bard or his descendants.)

(11) Avoidance of both rhetoric and rhapsody. (This, of course, was related to other avoidances, particularly No. 10 —though it was also an antagonism against the exuberance of Swinburne. And it made clear that Yeats, who from the beginning had been engaged in wringing the neck of rhetoric, had become an influence of great consequence.)

(12) Avoidance of plangent and crashing rhythms. (But the Georgian dislike of noise sometimes led the poet into the thicket of mere whisperings.)

(13) Avoidance of all verbal cheapness and facility. (The Georgian poet in an emergency chose to be aggressively literary rather than commonplace.)

(14) Emphasis upon Nature, upon Country Life. (This was the natural result of the Georgian poet being so much in the Wordsworthian current.)

Such were the main lines of negation upon which the New Revolt of Poetry, or the Georgian Revolt, or whatever you like to call it, was chiefly based. It seemed to establish rules, in some instances openly expressed by the Georgian shepherds and leaders, though a few of these rules were made to be broken, and there was not as regards the first three issues of the Georgian anthologies such a uniform application of them that poets like Flecker, Abercrombie, and Masefield were kept out; while John Drinkwater in at least one of his included poems gets, at moments, very close to rhapsody.

These Georgians aimed at perfection, at pure poetry. They gave the flower, but rarely the root or the leaves. As poets of the middle range they were occasionally remarkably good, and like the contemporary Irish poets (with whom they had some affinities) they seemed to establish a new dimension in verse. Though you might not be able to achieve major poetry, you still could rise to a prominent platform just below it— that is, *pure poetry*, something quite distinct from minor poetry, though it might belong to the lower range. It is true that Ernest Dowson had done something of the same thing; but the Ernest Dowson vogue and influence had branched off into directions not entirely pleasing to the new movement. These new poets did not aspire to be poets of the tavern and garish city, while the theme of sensual love was very nearly taboo.

It may, of course, be affirmed that such poetry constituted the poetry of negations. But this is by no means the case. Though the Georgian poet as time went on began to feel himself hampered by negations and obliged to conform to a new tradition, he was really a poet of strong affirmations. If he was in a hole and corner, how festooned was his hole, and how floral was his corner—a pride to himself, and the envy and admiration of nearly every young poet of the day. If he was an escapist, it was because he felt himself, owing to a miscarrying civilization and the general cheapening of verse, obliged to escape. And in a sense much first-rate Art is Escape, an escape from odious realities into the kingdom of dream, into the kingdom of fairyland, into the light of heaven.

Two prominent Georgians who did not entirely conform as regards modern, naturalistic language were Walter de la Mare and W. H. Davies. Of these, however, Walter de la Mare was the more intrinsically Georgian. Though his verse was sometimes very fragile in texture, of almost too gossamer a quality, it was so original in its wavering movements and at the same time so disciplined and carefully wrought that it became a sort of lodestar for all the best Georgian verbal art. As time went on many comparisons were made with both Coleridge and Edgar Allan Poe. But though there was present much of the fairy-land strangeness of Coleridge, Walter de la Mare had none of his plangency and nothing of his occasional vehemence. He lay closer to Poe, though here again he lacked Poe's intensity, particularly his intensity of madness and sorrow, and he avoided aggressive metrical effects and the catching phrase. More self-conscious than Coleridge, he was a more even craftsman (none of Walter de la Mare's poetry is third-rate, as is a certain amount of Coleridge's), and though less emotional than Poe, he was more balanced and prolific. Elusive and fragile, a maker of moonlit, dew-hung cobwebs rather than rainbows, of delicate silver tissues rather than tiaras of cut diamonds, he gave exquisitely (though very plentifully) rather than royally—a poet of green and silver rather than of purple and gold. He is a poet of childhood as well as of nature and mystery; and since the appearance of the first Georgian anthology, he has grown considerably in strength and music—as also in content:

> My child!—the words like poison ran
> Through her quick mind. 'What!' she began,
> In fuming rage; then stayed; for, lo,
> This visage for all its starven woe,
> That now met calmly her scrutiny,
> Of time's corruption was wholly free.
> The eyes beneath the level brows,
> Though weary for want of sleep, yet shone
> With strange directness, gazing on.
> In her brief life she had never seen
> A face so eager yet serene,
> And, in its deathless courage, none
> To bear with it comparison.
> 'I will begone,' at length he said,
>   'All that I asked was bread.'

From among the poets of the new century Walter de la Mare seems to have been preferred above all others by Robert Bridges, and his technical affinity with Bridges (the Bridges up to 1919) is often obvious enough, though Bridges would never have written such mystery poetry as is exemplified in *The Listeners*:

> 'Is there anybody there?' said the Traveller,
>   Knocking on the moonlit door;
> And his horse in the silence champed the grasses
>   Of the forest's ferny floor.

Nor would Bridges have written anything so technically uncertain, for not all the poem has the excellence of those first four lines. If it is the fashion to judge Walter de la Mare from the stamp of *The Listeners* it must be remembered that his very individual technique rarely fumbles—a thing that is only too apparent in *The Listeners*. His avoidance of regularity and monotony of cadence rarely pushes him into dissonance and awkwardness.

But although Walter de la Mare exemplified so many of the finer peculiarities of the Georgians, he stood a little way from most of them in his predilection for ballad technique (though he avoided the plangency of the most 'swinging' of the anonymous northern ballads) and in his occasional use of the previous centuries' licence of grammar (but occurring even more frequently in the lyrics of William Davies). As, for instance, in these stanzas (though only one of them appeared in the Georgian anthology):

> The bindweed roots pierce down
> Deeper than men do lie,
> Laid in their dark-shut graves
> Their slumbering kinsmen by.

and:

> Not any flower that blows
> But shining watch doth keep;
> Every swift changing chequered hour it knows
> Now to break forth in beauty; now to sleep.

and:

> But of the three around the fire,
> None turned a questioning head to look.
> Still read a clear voice, on and on,
> Still stooped they o'er their book,

and (to a dead sailor):

> Thou mock'd'st at land
> Who now art come
> To such a small
> And shallow home,

and:

> Sweet sounds, begone—
> Whose music on my ear
> Stirs foolish discontent
> Of lingering here;
> When, if I crossed
> The crystal verge of death,
> Him I should see
> Who these sounds murmureth.

In the first and second of these five stanzas (whose quotation is rather unfair, as they rarely show De la Mare at his really best) 'do' and 'doth' are hardly compatible with the Georgian way of saying things. In the first stanza the inversion of 'by' in 'Their slumbering kinsmen by' for 'By their slumbering kinsmen' is also an example of something the new poets sought to avoid (though William Davies is another occasional trespasser). In the other stanzas 'o'er' for 'over' is frankly old-fashioned, hammered and hackneyed out of use by such poets as Felicia Hemans. In the fourth stanza, 'Thou mock'd'st at land' was hardly allowable, as no more was the auxiliary-verb form 'art,' while 'murmureth' in the final quoted stanza is downright anti-Georgian. Robert Bridges, however (to whom the first volume was dedicated, and who would most certainly have found his way into the Georgian anthologies if he had been young enough), was immersed in much of the old-fashioned poetical licence and grammar,[1] and doubtless endorsed Walter de la Mare's occasional oddities.

But Edward Marsh selected for his anthology very carefully, and though some margin was allowed in the first volume, in the later volumes he was more drastic, and rarely admitted old-fashioned grammar or poetic licence. Exceptions, of course, occur all through, even in the work of Harold Monro, who was one of the strongest pioneers of naturalness; but it is noteworthy that while W. H. Davies addressed the kingfisher as 'thou,' Edmund Beale Sargant

---

[1] But, of course, this does not refer to Bridges's rhythms and general vocabulary—which were more or less free from all forms of stereotyped traditionalism.

addressed the cuckoo as 'you,' and that W. H. Davies changed the singular pronoun into the plural in the second stanza of the *Kingfisher*, as if he were in some doubt as to what was permissible.

Before going further it will be interesting to consider half a dozen of the poets who were omitted from the first Georgian anthology, and by means of their excluded peculiarities get a further grip on what it was Edward Marsh specially strove to select.

One necessary qualification for entrance seems to have been youth. The poet had to be young or only mildly middle-aged, not older than about forty, and preferably not older than thirty-five. He had also to be a poet of promise as much as of actual performance, one who showed strong possibilities of development and increase in the years to come. Neglected poets, however good they might be, who had already grown old or too middle-aged were outside the Georgian scope. Which, however, doesn't explain the reason for the exclusion of Alfred Noyes. But probably he had already made himself too popular. And other reasons intrude themselves. His best poems were full of old-fashioned pomp and too obvious colour. His atmosphere was Tennysonian, Victorian, his rhythms somewhat hackneyed and conventional. Moreover he was fervid and rather declamatory, at moments even a little noisy. True, some of his poems and many of his stanzas were good from an old-fashioned Victorian point of view, but that was hardly what was wanted. He belonged to an earlier world like Newbolt, Kipling, and William Watson. And threatening and slaughter were being breathed against him by some of the new poets for capturing a bigger public than he ought. One might have forgiven him for *Sherwood*, for such real enchantment as frolics out of:

> Robin Hood is here again: all his merry thieves
> Hear a ghostly bugle-note shivering through the leaves,
> Calling as he used to call, faint and far away,
> In Sherwood, in Sherwood, about the break of day.

. . . . .

> Oberon, Oberon, rake away the gold,
> Rake away the red leaves, roll away the mould,
> Rake away the gold leaves, roll away the red,
> And wake Will Scarlett from his leafy forest bed.

But even that was rather too obvious, and too old-fashioned in its rhythm. Osbert Sitwell's claim in post-War years that Alfred Noyes's 'position in the great line of English poets would be found somewhere between Tennyson and Horatio Bottomley'[1] was a thrust of professional antagonism, for one could just as truthfully suggest that Edith Sitwell's present position lies somewhere between Mallarmé and Ella Wheeler Wilcox. But it is a fact that while Alfred Noyes has always been accepted by a not very critical public, he has for the most part been rejected by literary connoisseurs, shepherds, and cautious critics. But the public of the future will probably read him less, and the critics of the future give him more serious consideration, especially as he has recently established himself as a narrative poet of real consequence. The turn of the wheel is baffling and troubling and makes the writing of books of criticism of contemporary writers a rather arduous undertaking.

Laurence Binyon was excluded from the first volume for the obvious reason that he had not published any book within the allotted time; but it is not quite so apparent why he was excluded from all the succeeding volumes. It can hardly have been that one of his feet was too deep in the preceding century, for that charge might also have been levelled against Sturge Moore (a poet, too, very little younger), who was actually included. Perhaps it was thought that the dust of the British Museum was clinging to him and that there was too much diffuseness or even vagueness in some of his verse.

The Georgian revolt which strove somewhere between vagueness and rhetoric may not have been always quite fair in its assessments, but it did institute a definite mode of

[1] While in jail Horatio Bottomley (whose name must not to be confused with that of the dramatic poet Gordon Bottomley) wrote a number of doggerel rhymes which he published when he was set at liberty.

inquiry and procedure. Laurence Binyon is a very sensitive, intellectual, and cultured poet, standing, in his technique, closer to Bridges and Walter de la Mare than most other poets on the English side of the Irish Sea, but he communicates slowly, for he lacks intensity, and his content is often at variance with his physical form. He has always been a considerable nature poet, a careful and imaginative recorder of natural phenomena, seen in wide landscapes as well as through the fogs of London, seeming, too, to exercise a good deal of influence upon the Georgian pastoral poets (particularly on John Freeman) as time went on. A little out of date, perhaps, a little close to Matthew Arnold in his impelling moments, his right place in modern poetry has always been something of a puzzle, for, though often wordy, he is a master of words; and some readers place him very high.

A good poet, omitted from the first volume, who was to be included in later volumes was John Freeman. He was pre-eminently a Georgian and helped to set the seal and signature upon their envelope, and it is rather odd that his first books were overlooked.

A more naturally excluded poet was James Mackereth. He had already made a strong push for recognition, and published volumes in 1907, 1910, 1912, and though he was to issue several more, no Georgian anthology was to include him. But although he was largely a pastoral poet, and had some affinity with John Drinkwater, he was much too free with the old poetic stock-in-trade and facilities of rhyme and rhythm, though occasionally he could be sufficiently successful:

> He sang the hymn in which the stars have joy,
>   That tunes the turbulent laughter of the sea
> Whose cosmic chorus doth the gods destroy,
>   And bids the gods to be.
>
> He stung to pain the temperate lips of art;
>   He loved, and mocked, and, laughing, died the while;
> A tortured spirit with the yearner's heart
>   Beneath the cynic's smile.

That rather good and quite memorable poem on Heinrich Heine illustrates Mackereth's defects as well as his virtues. A true-green Georgian could be expected to run ten times round the table at the mere ring of 'cosmic chorus,' and turn somersaults to the sound of such a taboo substantive as 'yearner,' to say nothing of the unnecessary insertion of the obsolete 'doth' where 'does' would do just as well. Moreover there is a glimmer of strained passion in the stanzas linked to hyperbole and assertive symbolism; and though the poem in its odd way really does succeed, it illustrates more or less what the Georgian did *not* write and what was not in his armoury of revolt.

Since the War years Mackereth's fluent fervours have grown in power and depth, though still frequently reminiscent of the period of the Romantic Revolt that preceded and immediately followed the battle of Waterloo. He is a poet of the Pennines; and at his best in such lines as:

> There mourn the waters of the ghylls;
>   In the mist sighs the rain;
> The raven in the homeless hills
>   Croaks; and the winds complain.

For rather similar reasons Edward Thompson (a poet of strange loneliness) must have been excluded—if Edward Marsh knew of him at all. His inspiration was old-fashioned, and where it was literary, came from the Carolines and Jacobeans, such as Vaughan, John Fletcher, and Marvell. Though he was partly a nature poet (note, for instance, his fine descriptive lyric, *The Eden*), he was also very strongly a religious poet; and religious poetry did not come into the Georgian corridor. But several of his lyrics, particularly *The Knight Mystic*, or a part of it, would be assets to any anthology of religious and mystical verse:

> Kneeling in spirit, but in limb
>   Steadfast, unquivering, unafraid,
> With unveiled eyes I stood by Him,
>   Pavilioned with obsequious shade.

One was I with that Living Light
    Whereof all stars and spirits be,
Whose tabernacle is cloud and night,
    Whose ways are firmament and sea.

Then from that height I wandered down,
    And sought the common steps of men;
With hamlet and imperial town
    My thoughts grew conversant again.

But folk, that marked my mien and eyes
    Unlike the man's they knew so well,
Questioned me, and in earnest wise
    I opened all I had to tell.

I have walked and talked with God indeed,
    Nearer than any saint, and I,
Though known a weak and worthless reed
    (Marvel of marvels!) did not die!

Such stanzas, though freer than most of his early poetry from old-fashionedness, give a good idea of Edward Thompson's quality at its best. 'Nearer than any saint' is perhaps a defect, though it does state how the poet in ecstatic moments occasionally passes beyond those bounds of vision which are denied to many a so-called 'saint.' Edward Thompson (Dr) was originally connected with the Wesleyan Methodist Church in India, a minister and educational missionary, and much of his verse is stamped with his religious and social experiences.

The Knight Mystic was published in 1907, but a later book of 1911, John in Prison, came within Mr Marsh's date; but it was not quite the kind of thing that was wanted. Edward Thompson, though he published during and after the War many other books of verse, chiefly 'found' himself as a novelist, as an authority on India, as a writer of very striking and original prose (in which he is sometimes a very scathing and even bitter satirist). He also, like Edward Marsh, donned shepherd garb, for he became the chief editor and originator of the sixpenny Augustan Books of Poetry, which included many of the moderns.

The journalist Gerald Gould was also distinguished among

the absentees, though he had published his second book in
1911. Nor was he to be included in any of the later volumes.
Here was a poet whose language seemed to be in line with
many of Mr Marsh's aims, and a careful study of his numerous
lyrics does not reveal any very emphatic reason for his omis-
sion—unless it is that he was deemed too ecstatic and visionary, and therefore too close to the Victorians. He is a very
real poet—naturalistic, mystical, religious, emotional, careful,
and very musical in his technique, rarely descending to cheapness, though lacking somewhat in individual idiom. His
promise at the beginning was considerable, and when the first
Georgian volume was published he was very young. If he
relates to any one at all it is to Stevenson, or perhaps more
intimately to Masefield; though he has been rather more
occupied with the theme of erotic passion. As regards his
outdoor verse his *Wander-Thirst* is one of the most popular
short poems of the century, and one can say without hesitation that in its swinging, triumphing, lilting movement
no other poem of the same kind is quite so successful. If
some people do not like it, that is because they have read or
heard it too often and are therefore tired of it. But I wonder
how many have really absorbed the moving beauty of the
end, the lovely, suggestive, spiritual content of the final stanza:

Yonder the long horizon lies, and there by night and day
The old ships draw to home again, the young ships sail away;
And come I may, but go I must, and if men ask you why,
You may put the blame on the stars and the sun, and the white
    road and the sky.

Among his later work there is a sonnet series of very masculine
content (and here quite manifestly non-Georgian) which yields
some striking passages, among them the somewhat startling:

For God's sake, if you sin, take pleasure in it,
    And do it for the pleasure. Do not say:
'Behold the Spirit's liberty! a minute
    Will see the earthly vesture break away
And God shine through.' Say: 'Here's a sin—I'll sin it;
    And there's the price of sinning—and I'll pay.'

Another exclusion was Douglas Goldring. He had already made some slender appearances, and looked like a poet with an unusually promising future. His pleasure in A. E. Housman was expressed in the title as well as some of the contents of his first book of verse, *A Country Boy*. Part of this was reprinted with additions in 1912 as *Streets*, where the affinity to Housman drew closer—though from the first he was considerably more sentimental. There was in him, too, an occasional touch of something remindful of Wilfrid Gibson, and even of Seumas O'Sullivan (who had preceded him with some poems about houses and streets), and perhaps still more of Arthur Symons. But the Arthur Symons note was not so strong in Goldring as to obscure the potential Georgian. Also, one or two of the poems had been obviously inspired by some of the early work of his intimate friend Elroy Flecker. But in spite of all this suggested hotch-potch, here was an original and fresh voice:

> Off through the dripping, moonless night,
>   Up West End Lane and Frognal Rise,
> They trace their footsteps by the light
>   Of love that fills their weary eyes.
>
> 'Nellie, though Town's a tiresome place
>   With far less joy in it than tears,
> To set my lips to your warm face
>   Is worth a sight of dismal years!'
>
> .   .   .   .   .   .
>
> Pausing, they gaze across the Heath
>   Submerged in fog—a dim hush'd lake,
> Wherein the wretched might seek death,
>   And lovers drown for dear love's sake.

It was the art of Heine (the popular Heine of the lyrics)—commonplace emotions expressed musically, in the simplest and most felicitous of words used in common speech—magic sought and achieved without oddity, remoteness or strain. Such an art, however, is the most difficult of all—because, before you know where you are, you are dropping into simplicities that are too cheap and easy, or worn threadbare by too frequent and thoughtless repetition, or used without due thought to the state of emotion behind them. Such inconsistencies spoilt half of Goldring's second book and more than two-thirds of the first—though there stand out two or three lyrics which are good literature without 'literary taint,' which would be a decoration to any anthology of plain musical speech. He may not have actually 'stung to pain the temperate lips of art,' but there were evidences that three or four years' application would have put him in the forefront of the new verse writers. But except for an occasional satirical poem he abandoned verse for prose, and became a novelist and distinguished literary journalist, a writer of exceptionally good topographical prose, and an espouser of lost causes—suffering the usual fate of those who refuse to run with the opportunists and the masters of the cliques.

So much for some of the poets who were omitted. But as regards the inclusions they were pretty numerous, in all, seventeen: Lascelles Abercrombie, Gordon Bottomley, Rupert Brooke, Gilbert K. Chesterton, William H. Davies, Walter de la Mare, John Drinkwater, James Elroy Flecker, Wilfrid Wilson Gibson, D. H. Lawrence, John Masefield, Harold Monro, T. Sturge Moore, Sir Ronald Ross, Edmund Beale Sargant, James Stephens, Robert Calverley Trevelyan.

But five of these poets were not to reappear in any of the four succeeding anthologies, and were therefore not in any way to be classed as Georgians by future critics: G. K. Chesterton, Sir Ronald Ross, Edmund Beale Sargant, T. Sturge Moore, Robert Calverley Trevelyan.

G. K. Chesterton definitely did not come into the scope. He was an old-fashioned bard—a Saxon scop, a Danish skald. It might, however, be argued that neither Masefield, Flecker, nor D. H. Lawrence belonged there. Probably they did not. But their notes were varied, and, with the exception of D. H. Lawrence, much of their work fitted very nicely. Flecker, however, was to die about the time of his inclusion in the second Georgian anthology—which strangely enough represented him by a very odd poem, *Gates of Damascus*, a million miles away from the other inclusions, a poem with more affinity to the best verse of the French Symbolists (in spite of its hard glittering form) than anything even in Eliot —and Masefield in coming years was to be attacked and depreciated by his own side.

As regards Chesterton's contribution, it stands right away from everybody else's. It is a selection from his long poem, *The Ballad of the White Horse*, and is full of ancient Border-ballad plangency:

> There is always a thing forgotten
>   When all the world goes well;
> A thing forgotten, as long ago
> When the gods forgot the mistletoe,
> And soundless as an arrow of snow
>   The arrow of anguish fell.

That wasn't the note sought after; and if the selection was used as a reminder that the new Georgian song was the in-danger-to-be-forgotten innocent thing which was to smite and wound the old Victorian and Edwardian rhetoric and tavern love-passion, it must have been nearly as quickly remembered that Chesterton himself was too much like a piece of mistle-toe (the plant that slew Balder), and likely to damage in his turn the new song. No! The Georgians didn't want to incur the risks of any more suicides like Middleton's and Davidson's by floating a Jonah in their ship. He was best left outside, and dangerous enough at that. So he didn't appear any more.

Robert Calverley Trevelyan was represented by one short lyric, which gives no idea of his real quality. He is a scholar poet with a small public and a reputation far behind his actual work and performance. He has been much influenced by classical rhythms, and there is a strength and original movement in some of his work which puts him near the shoulder of Robert Bridges. But he is not a Georgian and never could have fitted comfortably into their company.

T. Sturge Moore (also omitted from the later volumes), though represented by only one poem, got the lion's share as regards length. Here again was another poet who was too free in the old-fashioned manner and address of the subject by 'thee' and 'thou'—a romantic-classical muddle, a wolf in sheep's clothing. Manifestly no Georgian.

Sir Ronald Ross was also represented by only a single short poem; and one which contains the strange archaism 'methinks' and the equally obsolete 'e'en.' Here quite evidently was a poet who was no Georgian; and acute consciousness of this perhaps explains the small room allowed to him, and his non-appearance in the later volumes. He was knighted and received the Nobel Prize, not for literature but for researches in the field of science and medicine. It was he who made the great mosquito discovery, and by his inspired researches made life tolerable for Europeans in so many malaria-ridden countries. But he seems to have rated his literary work on the same level as his scientific—indeed he has intimated that he loved it better—and John Masefield said of one of his books of verse, *In Exile*: 'It is the only poem I ever read which kept me awake half through the night; it is a wonderful work. It is a great loss to the world that it is not more accessible.' His scientific and literary career has been treated in detail by R. L. Mégroz in his volume *Ronald Ross*.

As regards Edmund Beale Sargant's contribution—a nature poem—it combined something of Wordsworth with the mysticism of Blake. Gleams of both Francis Thompson and A. E. Housman also seem to quiver through its rustic lattice-work.

The only real Irishman admitted was James Stephens; and this perhaps is a little odd, for though most of the good Irish poets might be considered too old for a young man's anthology, there were one or two others who also might have fitted in appropriately, especially as the Irish influence upon Georgian verse was exceptionally strong; but to become more evident as time went on.

The most intellectual of the poems were contributed by

Lascelles Abercrombie, T. Sturge Moore, John Drinkwater, and Gordon Bottomley; the most Elizabethan (at any rate in their texture) by Lascelles Abercrombie, T. Sturge Moore, Gordon Bottomley, and John Masefield; the most Wordsworthian by John Drinkwater and Gordon Bottomley. But *In the Poppy Field* by James Stephens was the most ecstatic; and next to it the poems by D. H. Lawrence, Rupert Brooke, and John Drinkwater were the most emotional. But John Drinkwater's emotionalism was not always quite articulate, and Rupert Brooke's emotionalism here, as so frequently, had too much of the external sensuousness and softness of red plush. He is a warm-coloured poet, but something of a hang-over from the nineties, and his ruddiness has more of the drawing-room in its colour and texture than that of raw life. All the same, at that time he was the most approved for consistently combining pure poetry with a popular, embracing note. Though considerably less successful than Masefield just before the War years in capturing a wide public, he had fewer adverse critics or detractors; and though his reputation after the War declined in the estimation of his critics and fellow-poets, it did not seem to lessen his public, so that as late as Christmas 1936 he was a 'best seller' (indeed, I believe he was actually *the best*) among the poets of this century.

In D. H. Lawrence's very uneven poem *Snap-dragon*, there was a note of cruelty, and in Wilfrid Gibson's *Geraniums* and W. H. Davies's *The Heaps of Rags*, notes of deep strong pity. Both the latter poets were frequently concerned with the sufferings of the outcast poor, and their social verse in its pity and resentment was the true prelude (along with some of Masefield's) to much of the later War poetry by disillusioned soldiers, headed by Siegfried Sassoon.

But Wilfrid Gibson was chiefly represented by one of his narrative poems, *The Hare*, which though not the best out of the book from which it was taken, was presumably selected because of its pastoral qualities. The Georgian anthologies from first to last tended to concentrate upon pastoral verse, and upon the Wordsworthian rather than the Shakespearian, or Victorian, or the medieval manner, so the inclusion is quire compatible with Edward Marsh's aims. Edward Marsh has been attacked by many of us, but he is to be extolled for the general consistency of his anthologist plan, in which he has shown himself quite different from W. B. Yeats.[1] Though the verse he chose was in the Romantic current, it was, for the most part, only in the outer stream of that current, and the critic was able quite clearly to see to the bottom of that current. There was no perversity or muddle in Edward Marsh's mind.

Odd inclusions, as I have said, occur throughout, and one of the oddest is D. H. Lawrence's *Snap-dragon*. The general tone of it is not only egoistic and cruel, but it is also in parts very vague and obscure, and the general movement of the verse too staccato. It is the work of a genius (a somewhat destructive genius too) struggling passionately to express himself and not entirely happy in his medium. Flashes of sinister splendour, and stanzas which are more original and forceful than anything else in the whole book, insufficiently atone for the unsatisfactory character of the poem as a whole, which is quite incompatible with the 'good taste' upon which the editor prided himself. The shepherd had let a black sheep into the fold; and as the black sheep had up to date published no book, the inclusion is all the more to be wondered at. But Lawrence, whatever the apparent sincerity of his literary voice, had the knack of worming himself into the good graces of people whom he inwardly despised. He would run with the hounds and hunt the hare until such moment as he chose to baa at them ferociously or rend them with his wolfish teeth. At the beginning of his career he was something of an opportunist, and though I do not wish to intimate that he ever treated Edward Marsh scurvily, the general trend of his character is too well known to invite serious contradictions.

So much for the first Georgian anthology, probably next to Palgrave's the most important and influential anthology ever published, and the herald of four more on the same lines,

[1] See *The Oxford Book of Modern Verse*, edited and selected by W. B. Yeats.

and over two score of others (but not edited by Edward Marsh) directly or indirectly relative to them. For a time these anthologies emphasized the poet's importance and helped to establish him in the public's good graces and increase the sale of his books. But as the anthologies increased in number his individual sales naturally diminished, for the public refused to expend money on expensive single copies when samples of a dozen to half a hundred or more poets' work were procurable for the same money. So the popularizing of the special lyric indirectly helped to depreciate the poet as an important writer with a composite 'message,' and pushed novelist and biographer in front of him.

But a rather better innovation than these specialized anthologies was the institution of Harold Monro's Poetry Bookshop, which was opened in Devonshire Street (London) directly after the publication of Edward Marsh's first volume. Here not only were most new volumes of verse on sale, but once a week an eager audience collected in a large room at the back for the purpose of hearing poets read poetry—often from their own works. Sometimes the readings were by Harold Monro himself, or by Alida Klemantaski (his second wife), or by Ernest Rhys—who had, of course, their own special views about the way in which verse should be read. But Edward Marsh published his anthologies from the Poetry Bookshop, and as for a long time his 'Georgians' got nearly all the cake in the way of recognition and sales, the Poetry Bookshop in the minds of many came to be associated with clique favouritism.

But this was partially rectified by the publication of Harold Monro's 'chapbooks' (officially known as *The Chapbook: a monthly miscellany*), which tended to favour the poets of the Left Wing. His *Poetry and Drama* (preceding the 'chapbooks') was an excellent quarterly which grew out of *The Poetry Review*, originally edited by Harold Monro for 'The Poetry Society,' and to-day under the direction and editorship of Galloway Kyle for the same society.

CHAPTER VII

THE IRISH SCHOOL OF POETS

A FEW months before the War, while I was living in Germany, a distinguished German critic and university professor said to me one day: 'All the best English poetry of to-day is coming from Ireland.' That was in the days when not only Yeats but also A.E. (George Russell), James Stephens, Seumas O'Sullivan, Katharine Tynan, Padraic Colum, Joseph Campbell, and J. M. Synge were so much in the bardic limelight. The first six were purists—whose aim was pure poetry, the flower of song. The last, Synge, more human and brutal, wrote chiefly in prose, expressing his broadly imaginative mind in dramas of an entirely new quality. He has been compared with both Shakespeare and Molière; but he died too soon to take the place he promised—as the second or third dramatist of Europe.

The German professor exaggerated, but there is little doubt that very much of the cream of the best poetry was issuing from Ireland; and its influences upon the Georgian school, as time went on, became very plain.

These Irish poets were revolutionaries, and very considerable revolutionaries, though in pre-War days the fact was not entirely recognized. It is strange that escapists should be revolutionaries and act as strong influences upon the developing political drama, but such was the unfolding reality. They were seeking by means of the creation of a purely Irish literature with its roots in old myth and folk-lore to stir up a strong national consciousness, and there is little doubt that they succeeded nearly as much as the political agitators. But imaginative prose, of course, was nearly as strong an element in determining their position as were their outpourings in verse—for example, those two fantastical, but immensely

96

thrilling novels by James Stephens, *Deirdre* and *The Crock of Gold.*

The most prominent poet of them all, W. B. Yeats, is generally recognized as the greatest poet of the British Isles writing in English to-day—though it is quite possible that Masefield (whom he has influenced) will be preferred to him ere the conclusion of the century, because of his broader human tapestry.

The discovery (imaginatively contemplated) that Ireland had a great past was made in 1872 by Standish O'Grady, who in 1878 published an imaginative and bardic history of Ireland, and this was followed by Douglas Hyde's translations of old Irish stories and love-poems and an attempt to revive the old Gaelic arts and the language for literary purposes.

Then in 1889 W. B. Yeats published *The Wanderings of Oisin,* and began to consider the possibility of creating a literature that would sufficiently reveal the Celtic consciousness in English. He was, of course, not quite a new broom, for in the year 1886, shortly before the publication of his first book of poems, died Sir Samuel Ferguson, who, bracketed with Clarence Mangan, was really the first of the profoundly conscious Gaelic poets to write in English. But neither Mangan nor Ferguson had produced any great effect, and to W. B. Yeats came the great inspiration to take over their mantle and so repair and bedeck it that all might wonder and see. The dominant atmospheric hues which emerged came to be known as 'The Celtic Twilight,' in which moved strangely and suggestively a world between sunset and starry dark, between dream and waking, myth and reality.

The activities of Yeats's followers and men and women with similar aims, continued until some years after the War—almost the last of the strictly Irish poets being Austin Clarke and (rather later) F. R. Higgins, of which company Austin Clarke is a considerable Gaelic scholar, and perhaps the most Gaelic-minded of them all.

In regard to the poets, the division might be made in this manner: Yeats, A.E., James Stephens, and Austin Clarke,

E

saturated with Irish history, myth, and folk-lore; Seumas O'Sullivan, Padraic Colum, Joseph Campbell, F. R. Higgins, Katharine Tynan, concerning themselves less with the romantic background, but nevertheless Irish in their different manners, and frequently Irish in their atmosphere.

The least Irish in manner and feeling of any of them was Katharine Tynan. This is probably because she was a devout orthodox Christian believer, and therefore insufficiently moved by this new national consciousness. Her few essentially Irish poems are overshadowed by her religious poems in the English manner, and though half a dozen of them are distinguished by exceptional charm or natural beauty, nearly fifty per cent of her output is little above the level of facile prettiness. A more fundamentally Irish poet (at any rate in her subject-matter) is Alice Milligan, who by some has been judged to be the best woman poet of Ireland. Some of her poems, such as *Dectora of the Dun*, have much strength of form and perfection of technique.

An Irish poet who stands a little apart, in that he did not come directly into the current or get himself recognized as a member of the Twilight School, is Herbert Trench, who was born in the same year as W. B. Yeats. But his profusely embroidered long narrative poem, *Deirdre Wedded* (an early work), is as Irish as anything that came out of the Revival, and to many an English reader more remotely Gaelic than much of the verse of Yeats. He is actually a better poet than one or two of those discussed, and half a dozen of his lyrics are shot with an imperishable lustre. His *She comes not when the noon is on the roses* is as poignantly beautiful as anything by Dowson; and though uneven, he occasionally yields lines which belong to the really great utterance of English poetry, such lines as 'Come, let us make love deathless, thou and I,' and

> She, who remade a Poland out of nothingness
> And hath created
> Ireland, out of a breath of pride
> In the reed-bed of despair.

Lionel Johnson (who died in 1902), on the other hand, has been definitely put into the movement, though that has been due more to his loyalty to the Irish cause and his friendship with Yeats than to the Celtic atmosphere or content of his verse. He was less than half an Irishman, though he tried to persuade himself that his origins were Irish, while as a prominent Cockney member of the Rhymers' Club he was more under the sway of Dowson than of Yeats. His best lyric, *The Precept of Silence*, fuses the Rhymers' Club atmosphere with the Hibernian:

> I know you: solitary griefs,
>   Desolate passions, aching hours!
> I know you: tremulous beliefs,
>   Agonized hopes, and ashen flowers!
>
> The winds are sometimes sad to me;
>   The starry spaces, full of fear:
> Mine is the sorrow on the sea,
>   And mine the sigh of places drear.
>
> Some players upon plaintive strings
>   Publish their wistfulness abroad:
> I have not spoken of these things,
>   Save to one man, and unto God.

Other writers more definitely attached to the Irish Renaissance movement, such as George Moore and Lord Dunsany, must be classed with the creators who wrote verse as an aside. George Moore, one of the giants of English and Irish letters (if a rather malicious giant), was a very indifferent poet in verse, but Lord Dunsany has given us several lyrics which are memorable. He is a delightful writer of fantastical tales and romantic plays, the creator of a new mythology which cannot be easily identified with anything specifically Irish, though the Irish imagination runs riot through it.

Between the first appearance of Yeats and the year 1930 more than half a hundred good poets and imaginative prose-writers of distinction put in an appearance, creating what is

known as 'The Irish Literary Renaissance.' The Irish War
killed it, and very little of it now remains—the broken ends
kept together by Seumas O'Sullivan in his quarterly, the
Dublin Magazine—the only platform left for the Gaelic
consciousness.

The career of W. B. Yeats as a poet divides itself into the
three periods:

(1) The period in which he was occupied with mythology
and richly embroidered verse, when, though variable in his
technique, he concentrated mainly on wavering rhythms. It
was the period of the Celtic Twilight.

(2) A middle period, which commenced shortly before the
War, when he wrote more intellectually and with greater
austerity. His rhythms harden, and are more in line with
the Elizabethan texture of verse.

(3) A later period which commenced some years after the
War, when affected by the cult of the Modernists he becomes
increasingly cerebral and obscure. He is still Yeats, but
inclined to be academic and sometimes a little sour. The
English poet who seems to have most affected him is John
Donne.

He has never written entirely independently, but though
influenced by cults and movements, and sometimes gesticu-
lating to them, his natural originality sets him apart from
cults and movements. During his earliest years he was not
quite free from the all-pervading spell of Tennyson, and had
manifestly read both Shelley and Edmund Spenser with
pleasure. Then, as he ripened, he came under the influence
of Ernest Dowson and Arthur Symons, passing through them
to Verlaine. To what extent he was proficient in the French
language is not certain, but he seems to have rubbed shoulders
with the French Parnassians and the more restrained of the
Symbolists, while earlier French poets like Ronsard seem also
to have stirred him, one of his most approved early poems
being little more than a translation from Ronsard. To what
extent he borrowed elsewhere only the most widely read can

say with assurance, though he certainly took over one of the Irish folk-lore lyrics, and reproduced it:

Down by the sally gardens my own true love and I did meet,
She passed the sally gardens a-tripping with her snow-white feet,
She bid me take life easy, just as the leaves fall from each tree,
But I being young and foolish with my true love would not agree.

That is not Yeats, but the first stanza of an MS. in the possession of James Cogley, Enniscorthy, of a song well known in South Leinster, rendered by Mr W. B. Yeats thus (in a poem which is generally believed to be entirely his own):

Down by the salley gardens my love and I did meet;
She passed the salley gardens with little snow-white feet.
She bid me take love easy, as the leaves grow on the tree;
But I, being young and foolish, with her would not agree.

But to Irish folk-lore poetry should be added something coming from the anonymous Scottish Border-ballad. Behind that was the ancient world of Standish O'Grady, known to him through the great Irishman's florid prose. Page upon page of the early Yeats seems to prove his debt to Standish O'Grady, a good example of it probably present in the following lines:

Caoilte, and Conan, and Finn were there,
When we followed a deer with our baying hounds,
With Bran, Sceolan and Lomair,
And passing the Firbolgs' burial mounds,
Came to the cairn-heaped grassy hill
Where passionate Maeve is stony still;
And found on the dove-grey edge of the sea
A pearl-pale, high-born lady, who rode
On a horse with a bridle of findrinny;
And like a sunset were her lips,
A stormy sunset on doomed ships;
A citron colour gloomed in her hair,
But down to her feet white vesture flowed,
And with the glimmering crimson glowed
Of many a figured embroidery. . . .

That magnificent and profusely embroidered passage (from *The Wanderings of Oisin*) written in 1895, and revised from an earlier passage written in 1889, gives the main 'motives' of the early Yeats. The effect of Blake (whose genius he was partly instrumental in bringing before the eyes of a lukewarm Victorian public) has always been less strong on him than on A.E. and James Stephens, though Blake (like nearly every English poet of consequence) went into the stuff of which his dream tapestry was woven. Yeats's great strength has always lain in his vast background—one which he had completely assimilated, so that he was really able to tread new ground, and advance with confidence from the already accomplished to the new. But troubled by numerous imitators he gradually changed his style, announcing the new Yeats in this way:

> I made my song a coat
> Covered with embroideries
> Out of old mythologies
> From heel to throat;
> But the fools caught it,
> Wore it in the world's eyes
> As though they'd wrought it.
> Song, let them take it,
> For there's more enterprise
> In walking naked.

Yeats is a great technician. Even when his content baffles or alienates, when it eludes or tantalizes us, he still triumphs by his strangely communicating forms. No living poet better understands than he how to make words alive and hypnotic. No living poet better understands the necessity for physical and sensuous communication—without which mere content loses much of its power of appeal. But he has disparaged his pre-War poetry in justification of his latest work (which to many readers seems inferior), while he has still more recently shown himself a very uncertain judge and selector of his English and Irish contemporaries.

Except in the cause of Irish literature, Yeats has burned

with no crusading vigour. Christian themes which have occurred in his poems are not due to religious conviction, but are there because they are of the stuff of poetry. More real to him is the mysticism of India, for during his early period he came under the sway of the Theosophists.

Very different is A.E. (George Russell), to whom religion was a thing more vital than the form which conveyed it. He has to be read for his content, for his depth of vision, rather than for delight which he communicates by mere arrangement of words—though in some of his poems form and content perfectly combine. I think that there are quite a number of people, who if condemned to live for a decade on a desert island, intellectually and spiritually unsupported save by a bare score of books, would put a volume of A.E.'s poems in the short list. And for this reason—of all the poets who have written since the death of Tennyson he is the most spiritual, the most completely in touch with things eternal; he alone voices continually the omnipresence of God, the companionship of the All-Father. In the preface to his book *Homeward* he wrote:

I know I am a spirit, and that I went forth in old time from the self-ancestral to labours yet unaccomplished; but filled ever and again with homesickness I made these songs by the way.

Comparing A.E. with Yeats, Ireland's most recent literary historian, Stephen Gwynn, has said:

These two men were to dominate the entire literary revival, and affect the whole intellectual life of Ireland in their time. . . . Both were mystics. But whereas in George Russell mysticism appeared inseparable from his being, with Yeats it had the aspect of an exotic cult. Russell was of service to Ireland through the philosophy which radiated through his nature. It was in part a love of beauty, but more truly a love of humanity, of the divine in human nature.

To which one should add that though the first impetus came from W. B. Yeats, the movement might finally have flagged if it had not been for A.E.'s inspiring aid and personality.

The choice of the pseudonym A.E. at the beginning of his career came out of a strange accident.[1]   But though it is almost certain that Mr Russell did not immediately notice what the pseudonym might stand for, it can be used as denotative of the central theme of his work.   For pronouncing the first letter rather broadly as 'ah' (the pure European *a*), the two letters form a pure diphthong, denoting the letter 'i.'   But the ego of his poetry is not the ego of self-individuality, but the ego of space-individuality or spiritual identity—that is God:

> Out of the vast the voice of One replies
>   Whose words are clouds and stars and night and day,
> When for the light the anguished spirit cries
>   Deep in its house of clay.

Sometimes, as is natural, his intense mystical sense has interfered with his poetry, at any rate with that newness and strangeness of words which poetry demands.   It was nearly always A.E.'s idiosyncrasy to choose the simplest word to express his meaning, however threadbare and commonplace such a word had become, whilst most of his rhythms (though sometimes tending to that wavering quality so characteristic of Irish verse) are quite simple and conventional and lacking in pomp and glitter.   He never cultivated hypnotic obscurity, or strangeness of beauty, or electricity of phrasing after the manner of W. B. Yeats; and though he has been called 'the Irish Swinburne,' only at remote intervals do we detect the influence of Swinburne.   But though his output in verse has been comparatively small he was a very fluent poet, as fluent as Shelley, whom he more nearly approaches than Swinburne. According to his own confession, some of his verse was written as if with an automatic pencil, so that when he had finished the poem he read it with wonder and surprise.   He was controlled by an unseen world; he saw ghosts and celestial beings

[1] For the full account of the birth of the pseudonym see John Eglinton's biography, *A Memoir of A.E.*, recently published by Macmillan.

and strange spirits of the earth—fairies, though with the stature of men and women.

He was a painter as well as a poet. He painted the sea and the sky and the spirits that he saw and felt—with vivid passionate colouring reminiscent of a Van Gogh, though, I think, with even more luminous radiance and brilliance of celestial light. Perhaps he is greater as a painter than a poet, though difficult to assess as he was largely self-taught and not strong in technique, and his six hundred and more canvases are scattered all over England, Ireland, and America. He gave them away, or sold them at a quarter their value. He had no materialistic sense, and little feeling for property. He was a prophet and a saint to whom the trammelling of earthly possessions was a hindrance in his journey skywards. His poems are the only certain things of his that are completely and easily accessible, for though an exceptionally fine prose-writer,[1] much of his prose lies buried in the files of the *Irish Homestead* and *Irish Statesman*, signed not only A.E., but Y.O., and by other pseudonyms—though the poet Monk Gibbon has recently collected a large volume of it under the title *The Living Torch* (Macmillan).

His intensely human outlook drew him into the arena of philanthropy and strife for human betterment. The intellectual and imaginative dreamer developed into a man of action. He became—O most practical of mystics!—a leading authority on agriculture and a mainstay of wisdom to Irish farmers, while he also thrust himself into politics and journalism. And he adorned everything which he touched. The *Irish Statesman*, which he edited for so many years, achieved prominence for its remarkable qualities of vigour, freshness, and fairness, scintillating as it did with honest politics, honest criticism, and fine poetry. I think the *Irish Statesman* was honest as no English weekly has ever been honest. It was a

[1] Read, for instance, that masterpiece of open letters, *Ulster*, in which he scourges Rudyard Kipling for his political cheapness and wrongheadedness, and yet without ever losing sight of the man's exceptional qualities as a poet.

* E

platform for every Irishman (and for some disinherited Englishmen, too) who had anything real to say, so that few of the adverse elements which characterize 'highbrowism' disturbed its expressive pages. And yet A.E. never blew his own trumpet or ground his own axe. Though he liked to be treated with great respect, his modesty was really remarkable, and he was one of those exceptional poets who won recognition without a vestige of flamboyant effort or noisy self-advertisement. And he was always unusually ready to acknowledge merit in others, even at the cost of self-disparagement. In his foreword to Katharine Tynan's *Collected Poems* he wrote: 'When young, I was in despair, believing that I was not naturally fitted to use this precious art. I found it so difficult to make a shapely verse that I sometimes wondered at Katharine Tynan, to whom the craft seemed to come so easily, who had such a gift for melody.' However that may be, A.E. soon surpassed Katharine Tynan in expressed spirituality and strength of rhythm. No other British poet is so closely related to William Blake; and though the mystic in him may, at times, have striven to defeat the poet (in a Western sense), his feet were too deep-rooted in the earth for any such frequent reversal. But though so closely related to William Blake, the texture of his verse falls more frequently between that of the early Yeats and Walter de la Mare, while something of his content occasionally touches fingers with the fairy world of De la Mare—whom, of course, he preceded, and probably slightly influenced.

Fairies, gods, and goddesses move across his tapestry; but though all so real to him, his vision was of one god rather than many. Though not a Christian in any orthodox sense he was a profound deist. During the early part of his career he was in close contact with some of the leading theosophists and Hindu mystics, but he was too Irish and human-minded to lose himself in the coils of Hindu mysticism. Evidently he did not entirely achieve that Eastern tranquillity and self-renunciation which he aimed at—expressed so finely in *Hope in Failure*:

Though now thou hast failed and art fallen, despair not because of
 defeat,
Though lost for a while be thy heaven and weary of earth be thy feet,
For all will be beauty about thee hereafter through sorrowful years,
And lovely the dews of thy chilling and ruby thy heart-drip of tears.

The eyes that had gazed from afar on a beauty that blinded the eyes
Shall call forth its image for ever, its shadow in alien skies.
The heart that had striven to beat in the heart of the Mighty too
 soon
Shall still of that beating remember some errant and faltering tune.

Very rarely is his clear vision crossed by a sense of frustra-
tion, of doubt or bewilderment and grief at the world's
sordidness, for he wrote poetry during his more aloof moments,
when he was full of high disdain for things cheap and drossy.
A great journalist, he was never a journalist in his verse:

By many a dream of God and man my thoughts in shining flocks
 were led:
But as I went through Patrick Street the hopes and prophecies were
 dead.
The hopes and prophecies were dead: they could not blossom where
 the feet
Walked amid rottenness, or where the brawling shouters stamped
 the street.
Where was the beauty that the Lord gave men when first they
 towered in pride?
But one came by me at whose word the bitter condemnation died.
His brows were crowned with thorns of light: his eyes were bright
 as one who sees
The starry palaces shine o'er the sparkle of the heavenly seas.
'Is it not beautiful?' he cried. 'Our Faery Land of Heart's Desire
Is mingled with the mire and mist, yet stainless keeps its lovely
 fire.' . . .

Perhaps his best-known poem is *The Man to the Angel*, which
almost sounds like a contradiction of his heavenly vision and
a kind of blasphemy, unless we read it as symbolical and in
praise of humankind against the notion of the heavenly host

as attenuated beings of absolute purity without earthly experience. In this he approaches Swedenborg, who believed
that all angels began as men and women, moving through
successive stages of development:

> I have wept a million tears;
>   Pure and proud one, where are thine,
> What the gain though all thy years
>   In unbroken beauty shine?
>
> All your beauty cannot win
>   Truth we learn in pain and sighs:
> You can never enter in
>   To the circle of the wise.

Its six very fine stanzas must be read, not under the shadow of
theology or logic, but in the light of that imaginative unreason
which makes dark things clear by virtue of its passionate
spirituality.

The theme of Reincarnation—of which in various aspects
he was firmly convinced (indeed more than convinced)—dominated much of his spiritual outlook, lucidly told in *Babylon*,
and darkly unfolded in the more magnificent *Resurrection*:

> Let the dragons of the past
>   In their caverns sleeping lie
> I am dream-betrayed, and cast
>   Into that old agony.
>
> And an anguish of desire
>   Burns as in the sunken years,
> And the soul sheds drops of fire
>   All unquenchable by tears.

But to A.E. the whole mystery of present individual life was
bound up with a far-stretching past.

Towards the end of his life A.E. complained that the fire
which had gone to make his poetry was dulling, and that his
inspiration was not as it was. This, of course, was partly
due to the condition of his body, for poetry being partly a

physical thing is frequently affected by a man's age. But it was also due to the atmosphere of poetic disintegration by which he found himself surrounded on all sides, the growth of Modernism. In regard to this he wrote in a letter to a fellow Celtic poet, the Welshman Ernest Rhys, a short time before his death:

Certainly I would like to hear your Sun God.[1] Poetry is one of the things which I still can enjoy. Though there is still a great deal of very modern poetry which seems to me ashes and dust when one tries to absorb it. I read a volume of ultra modern verse a day or two ago and thought I was in a madhouse, but that may be because I had a bad cold and my head was stuffed, and I felt anyhow neglected and lost in the mire at the bottom of the universe.

The letter is characteristic: always wishing to see good rather than bad, he will suggest that perhaps he has been too hard on the misguided poet.

But where A.E. at the end of his life lost in spiritual joy he gained in technique, so that some readers may prefer his later to his early and middle periods. His later poems show a more fastidious use of words, and every now and again a new and original use of metre, nowhere more evidenced than in *Dark Rapture*, which is surely one of the most original technical feats of this century, and sustained in an equal key from its opening lines:

Ah, did he climb, that man, nigher to heaven than I,
   Babbling inarticulately along the road
His drunken chaotic rapture, lifting to the sky,
   His wild darkness, his hands, his voice, his heart that glowed. . . .

---

[1] The MS. of Ernest Rhys's most recent and probably finest volume of poems, *Song of the Sun* (Dent), published shortly after A.E.'s death. In this book Ernest Rhys has not only shown himself as young in spirit as in his twenties, but has added to his earlier achievements much metrical originality and subtlety. His post-War poem, *Pantoum of the Fellow-traveller*, showed his skilful command over an unusual form, but though he has always been notable for such skill, in *Song of the Sun* his technical prowess seems to have increased.

And in his blank-verse experiments (if you may call such finished poems experimental) he showed an increased verbal power, especially in *The Dark Lady*, where he censures Shakespeare with pitying dignity and deep imaginative passion for an unnatural affection—to which Shakespeare seems to have confessed in the *Sonnets*.

Of recent years A.E. has been neglected and set aside for W. B. Yeats; but the future will probably revive him as it has recently revived John Donne. He was a really great man, a towering personality, an artist who was curiously independent of art and poetry, realizing that there is something better and bigger than either—and that is Vision and Courage and Charity and Behaviour. He was entirely fearless, and the sort of man who would have cheerfully died for his loyalties and beliefs if he had been called upon to do so; for he was of the stuff of which saints are made.

The third most important poet of Ireland, James Stephens (though probably he should be bracketed as second, with A.E.), turned in the verse of his early and middle period to the human and grotesque rather than the mystical, and to the Ireland of to-day rather more than to the Ireland of the past. Most of his myth and folk-lore interest he left to his prose romances *Deirdre* and the *Crock of Gold*; but he is a very difficult poet to pin, for he is the most variable of the Irish school, more variable than Yeats, and as soon as you discover he is one particular thing you find out, turning over the pages, that he is equally something other and quite different —but always speaking through an instrument that can be identified with no one else's. He was included at the beginning of his career among the Georgian poets, though actually if he had been represented by his most characteristic verse he might have been judged something of a misfit among them. 'The quintessence of James Stephens is in the combination of the grotesque and the profound, all part of that naïve irreverence with which the poet contemplates terrestrial and cosmic phenomena,' says Ireland's literary historian, Ernest Boyd, and that judgment seems to sum him up rather accurately. He is mystical, fantastical, naïve, human, comical, almost brutal (though amusingly brutal), full of the Gaelic spirit, though generally avoiding the dreamy manner of A.E. and the early Yeats and the early Seumas O'Sullivan.

> If I asked her master he'd give me a cask a day;
>   But she, with the beer at hand, not a gill would arrange!
> May she marry a ghost and bear him a kitten, and may
>   The High King of Glory permit her to get the mange.

That stanza, though a partial translation (or reincarnation) from a Gaelic poet of the seventeenth century, furnishes an illustration of one of his frequent notes at its strongest. This, however, is often softened into the mouth of a child, resulting in some of the best poems of child psychology in English literature. In an indirect way, too, as in *Time's Revenge*, he can be penetratingly satirical, and while writing in the first person seem to write of another behind his back:

> And now a night-hag hath me down!
>   And I am staring, suddenly
> As one who wakens from renown
>   To staring notoriety—
>
> The king his diadem shall wear!
>   The half-king wear what gaud he can
> Until Time swings him by the hair,
>   No king at all, and scarce a man!

The influence of Blake in much of his verse, both in content and technique, is very plain to the senses. In his simplicity, too, he approaches Blake, and no English poet, even at his most fluent, can turn out a more trilling or spontaneous bird carol:

> I was singing all the time
>   Just as prettily as he
> About the dew upon the lawn,
>   And the wind upon the lea!
> So I didn't listen to him
>   As he sang upon a tree.

During his latest period the mysticism of the Bengali poets seems also to have deeply entered into his bones:

> Awake!
> Arise!
> Put glory on,
> Of which all Soul and Sense is wrought!
> Thou shalt be naught Thou dreamed upon
> Of good or evil thing! Nor aught
> That thought doth bicker at!
> Thou shalt be Naught!
> And Thou shalt be
> Thy Self, and Thine own mystery!
> Knowledge! Bliss! Eternity!
> For Thou art that!

What is perhaps his best book of verse is his most recent, *Strict Joy* (published 1931). A certain bony starkness and fibrous virility has always emerged from him, and in *Strict Joy* the thing is still more frequent. But in *Strict Joy* we are confronted by a poet of superb technique and, at times, of almost unfathomable profundity. He has become a poet of pure vision, contemplating beauty and eternity from an emotional angle that is held firmly in check by an intense intellectualism. The twenty-three short cantos of his *Theme and Variations* will not, I should imagine, be understood in entirety by many outside India—the difficulty of adequately dealing with such an immensity expressed by Stephens himself in the concluding lines of his 'Coda':

> But, well you know it, reeds are such,
> They pipe too little, or too much,
> Transposing music to a key
> Was not, is not, and should not be
> . . . And here I end my melody!

It is possible that this latest verse of James Stephens has been influenced by Neo-Platonism, and it is interesting to note that *Theme and Variations* was dedicated to his friend, the late Stephen MacKenna, known as the translator of Plotinus.

During the War years MacKenna was engaged in Dublin on his great task of translating the *Enneads*. The later Yeats, too, appears to owe something to the same source.

As regards Seumas O'Sullivan, his reputation as a bookman and critic, and intellectual stimulus behind much of the latter half of the Irish Literary Renaissance, has probably stood rather higher than that of a poet—for which the future will surely most esteem him. His output has not been extensive, but some beautiful and shapely lyrics stand to his jewelling, among them the finely finished *The Earth Lover* (which gave the title to one of his best books) and which very deftly expresses a supersensitive man's dissatisfaction with mere nature as he lives through the four seasons of the year, terminating with a stanza that specially invites quotation:

> And when white Winter's icy sway
> Held lake and hill and river-tide,
> He went with sorrow dumb, and sighed
> Because he heard how far away
> By frozen waters night and day
> The herons wild with hunger cried.

In his earlier work (which, however, in texture, is rather more Elizabethan than Irish) he is primarily like Yeats and A.E., a poet of the Celtic Twilight, delighting in semitones, pearly greys, and the dreamy, dignified utterance of sorrow and melancholy—so that A.E. wrote of him: 'He is the literary successor of those old Gaelic Poets who were fastidious in their verse, who loved little in this world but some chance light in it which reminded them of fairyland.' But in later years W. L. Phelps, a professor of English literature at Yale University, spoke of his realism, and said in his book *The Advance of English Poetry in the Twentieth Century*: 'the most original part of this poet's production is founded on reality.' For such lyrics as *Nelson Street, Merrion Square, Birds,* and *Saint Anthony* stand somewhat closer to the art of James Stephens (whom he is recognized as having preceded in the creation of that kind of human poetry), as also do such recent dewdrops of song as *Geese* and *The Convent*. His best-known lyric (and one of the most musical of this century):

> A Piper in the streets to-day
> Set up, and tuned, and started to play . . .

must, by now, have decorated over two score of English and American anthologies; but what is one of the profoundest stanzas he ever wrote—and for that matter one of the most deeply revealing in all religious poetry—has never been specially seized on:

> Sweetheart, be brave and face with me
>   The thing that we have done;
> Lo, in the quiet garden now
>   He prayeth all alone—
> The Lord we have betrayed; yet we
> May go with Him to Calvary.

Nevertheless, he is not a religious poet, and pagan elements thread through many of his lyrics and later satirical poems.

The poetry of Austin Clarke, on the other hand, is rather farther away from the Christian spirit. He is the visionary pagan, to whom an early Ireland, the Ireland before the coming of Saint Patrick, means everything, and the later Ireland a country of doubt and bewilderment. He is one with the elves, or 'little people,' knowing, in a present-day sense, neither good nor evil and revelling in a world of myth and pagan symbolism. His first book, *The Vengeance of Fionn*, published at the age of twenty-one, during the final year of the Great War, has never been surpassed, and in the opinion of many people is still his best. In this short, tangled epic he has struck something of an Homeric note and thrown upon the many-coloured canvas a rich profusion of wild mountain landscape. Action and heroic speech are interwoven with lavish descriptions of natural phenomena, the start of the poem typical of the key throughout:

> Upon a stormful nightfall when the plain
>   And mountains darkened and the fiery forge
> Of sundown under soot-black clouds of rain
>   Burned fiercest, like some angered demiurge

Brooding in iron through red-glowering smoke
  Smelted; up from the smouldering glooms one came
To Almhuin while the great slow raindrops broke,
  Hot ridden from the westward fogs and flame
To Fionn, telling of friendship and of feast. . . .

Immediately on its appearance the poem was greeted with
enthusiasm, and the *Irish Times* said of it: 'Not since Mr
Yeats first put on his singing robes has any Irish poet appeared
with such decisive claims to be in the bardic succession.'
The influence behind the poem was, however, not so much
Yeats as Tennyson and Keats, with something out of the
sleeve of Herbert Trench—though the tidal movement of the
iambic verse, interwoven rhyme so little obvious that it almost
sounds like blank verse, is stamped with so much originality
and individuality that one can regard it as something quite
new in the harvest of literary production. The story of Diar-
muid and Grainne is difficult to follow, for Austin Clarke
avoids telling a plain tale, but as a massive chunk of pure
poetry (it is fifty pages long) nothing has come out of the
century to surpass it. He has written other long poems of
epic quality, one of them, *The Fires of Baal*, developed from
an Old Testament legend. But he is always too occupied
with technique apart from lucidity of theme—glitter of words
and lavishness of imagery—so that in *The Fires of Baal*, where
we expect religious revelation and passion, we find ourselves
in a further world of pagan corridors and unrealizable Titan
shapes. He is too much like his frustrated eagle in *The Fires
of Baal*:

          In middle sky, the eagle soared
      A speck of ravenous rage, but its loud screams
      Taloned the remote unclutchable air
      And sank into a wail.

By such frequent magnificent passages he continually arrests
our attention, but the eagle of the human spirit escapes us,
clutching at unclutchable skies far beyond our ken. In *The
Vengeance of Fionn* he has managed to make us feel that when

we cannot follow him the fault is partly due to ourselves, but
in his later longer poems there is a more deliberate withdrawal,
a too self-conscious burrowing into the technique of his
brocaded art, to say nothing of lavishness of remote Gaelic
allusion—which estranges him from the average English reader.
He became, without quite knowing it, a baffling Modernist;
and it is exceedingly strange that all modernist anthologies
have overlooked him—especially as it is quite obvious that
two or three of the queerest of the younger men are in
his debt.

> I looked into the west
> And the claw had gone. But I saw blue-men heave
> Their backs in struggle, for they bore a seawoman
> Who prized the very shore. Bled, bled by scale
> Or fin they fought for that unreal breast.

The passage is characteristic Austin Clarke, but in his case
such lines do not in any way point to 'Dadaism' but are due
to his Gaelic background (the early language as much as
imaginative knowledge), and they are nearly always resolved
into meaning through intellectual effort. He is a very considerable scholar, and in a number of recent lyrics he has
experimented, as did certain Gaelic poets, with assonance or
half-rhyme in the place of complete rhyme:

> When the far South glittered
>   Behind the grey beaded plains
> And cloudier ships were bitted
>   Along the pale waves . . .

but from the standpoint of communicable poetry with frequent insufficient success to a normal English reader, for he
is a bard who has developed a strange manner too apart from
his earlier basic self, which functions best in the world of
Standish O'Grady. Speaking of a book published in 1929,
Padraic Colum says:

In the poems in *Pilgrimage*, Austin Clarke, through some strange
process, has been able to identify himself with the Gaelic poets of
the seventeenth and early eighteenth centuries, times which in

Ireland were an extension of the medieval period. He writes in the temper of these dispossessed men, as if he were actually trudging the roads they trudged, crossing the waters they crossed, and, like them, separating themselves from the people they sing to by dealing only with the most tragic figures in their tradition.

That may be so—but only to a very Gaelic Irishman. And the same applies to his strange, Gaelic-toned novels, *The Bright Temptation* and *The Singing Men at Cashel*, enthusiastically admired by some of the Irish intellectuals, but too remote from the consciousness of the normally imaginative English reader. It is only in the more fiery, energetic, or exquisite passages of his poems, particularly his long bardic poems, that he speaks to English readers. Only, and yet . . . there is at least one lyric, *The Lost Heifer*, which sings itself into daylight, and which like the best of the French Symbolist poems produces through its elusive imagery and the mere arrangement of the words a completely satisfactory sensation of enchantment:

> When the black herds of the rain were grazing
>   In the gap of the pure cold wind
> And the watery hazes of the hazel
>   Brought her into my mind,
> I thought of the last honey by the water
>   That no hive can find.
>
> Brightness was drenching through the grasses
>   When she wandered again,
> Turning the silver out of dark grasses
>   Where the skylark had lain,
> And her voice coming softly over the meadow
>   Was the mist becoming rain.

Imagination seizes upon every couplet of the poem, and it is bound together (unlike most of his other lyrics, with their deliberate halts and broken chords) into a co-ordinate whole. It is this co-ordination which seems to be so wanting in Austin Clarke. His *Music Healers*, a poem of twenty-one pages, full of opulent feeling for wild nature is thickly gemmed with dewdrops of this quality:

> in the hazels
> The sunlight dances with green heels. . . .

And yet it is nearly as effective read backwards, crossways, zigzag, in alternate pages—as you like—so lacking it seems in co-ordination or lucid development. Austin Clarke must be put into that company of poets who delight in talking to themselves—or to a strictly Gaelic-minded audience. What will be his next move we do not know, for he seems to be already changing and passing into closer contact with his English reader, and probably back towards a development from the amazing promise of his first book. His difficulty has been that he came right at the end of the Irish Movement, when the feeling for epic and heroic poetry was dying; and Yeats, recognizing this, had already changed his note.

Shortly after the appearance of Austin Clarke another distinctive Irish poet, F. R. Higgins—who seems to fall midway between Clarke and Yeats in manner—came upon the Celtic scene. He seems to have been influenced by both Clarke and Yeats, but has developed into a distinguished lyrical poet with an original and captivating manner. His background is never very remote, and though he frequently mourns an Ireland that is dead and gone, it is not the Ireland of the pagan years. The titles of two of his books, *Dark Breed* and *Island Blood*, give a sort of dark clue to his subject-matter. As with Austin Clarke his lines are charged with fine observation of natural phenomena, with an equally original manner of statement. Most of his virtues (as well as a few of his vices) are enshrined in his best-known and loveliest lyric, *Father and Son*.

But a more popular Irish poet (if more so in Ireland than in England) is Padraic Colum. His genius is transparently clear, and can be surveyed in a nutshell. He is a poet of the Irish people, a poet of the soil, a sort of Irish Burns, though he concentrates on description and simple observation rather than on the song. Subject-matter is to him of primary importance, but the form is neatly expressive of it. He is a very considerable artist, choosing his words with great care, but never allowing the mere form to intrude. As Ernest Boyd says of him: 'The poet is measured by the skill and congruity of his selection and elaboration. . . . With a minimum of artistic liberty he produced the maximum effect, giving us the stark poetry of life as it is felt by those living close to the soil.' He is a very interesting poet. His lyrics hold the attention in the way that good short stories and graphic prose sketches hold the attention. In this they are very different from the lyrics of F. R. Higgins, who tends to over-concentrate on his mere form, the clash between form and content occasionally alienating the whole poem. Nothing can be more apart than the manner of these two poets. Take, for instance, a typical stanza by Padraic Colum at his simplest and barest:

> I am sitting here
> Since the moon rose in the night,
> Kindling a fire,
> And striving to keep it alight;
> The folk of the house are lying
> In slumber deep;
> The geese will be gabbling soon;
> The whole of the land is asleep,

and then compare with it a typical stanza of F. R. Higgins at his most self-conscious and odd:

> Over their edge of earth
> They wearily tread,
> Leaving the stone-grey dew
> The hungry grass;
> Most proud in their own defeat
> These last men pass
> This labouring grass that bears them
> Little bread.

Here, though the words suggest in general terms a sufficiently clear twilight picture and vision of proud defeat, the lines tend to crumble in the fingers upon the first efforts of analysis, especially as some of the epithets are rather unusual. Such aloof word-spinning, which is entirely absent from the verse of Padraic Colum, occurs a little too often in F. R. Higgins, where artistry and verbal poise tend to stifle a rustic content that can sometimes be identified with the subject-matter made use of by the older poet.

But a poet with closer relationship to Padraic Colum is Joseph Campbell (who wrote also under the Gaelic name Seosamh Mac Cathmhaoil). He was one of the early comers, publishing his first books before the War. Though declared to be somewhat uneven, he has, at his best moments, a strong, simple quality of verbal magic, as in

> And who 's the wiser? I or he
> Who props a wall at Eden Quay,
> And spits innumerably between
> His drinks? While April like a queen
> Rides over noisome lane and street,
> Bringing the breath of meadow-sweet . . .

or in:

> The tall dancer dances
>   With slowly taken breath:
> In his feet music
> And on his face death.

One of his books, *Irishry*, contains a 'pageant of the types that stand for the nation of to-day,' drawn from almost every part of Ireland. He is much better known in America than in England.

Another genuine Irish poet who fitted himself very spontaneously into the movement, but disappointingly cheated expectations by suddenly disappearing, was Thomas Boyd. He seems to have been last heard of in London, where he was living with vagabonds and down-and-outs. His best lyrics have much beauty of form and romantic atmosphere.

A poet with rather less right of inclusion, but who is sometimes connected with the Irish School, is the post-War writer L. A. G. Strong, who has recently reached his richest fulfilment in the novel. He has one foot in Ireland and one in England, but in his poems he has more often resorted to West of England dialect and atmosphere than Irishry, though his lyrical wit is Irish in tone, and his affinity with, and descent from James Stephens is obvious—especially detectable in his best-known lyric, *The Mad Woman*.

But a traditional English poet who can be definitely connected with the Irish literary renaissance in that he has turned many Gaelic lyrics into English, is Robin Flower; and yet other lyrical translators are Frank O'Connor and Eleanor Hull —who have thus united themselves to the company of Douglas Hyde, Standish O'Grady, and Lady Gregory. Douglas Hyde, and a later poet Padraig Pearse (who lost his life in the Irish War), wrote their lyrics in Gaelic, and Lady Gregory has made English paraphrases from both of them.

One of the last of the Irish poets who have floated into the English eye is Oliver Gogarty, though he has long been known in Dublin as a wit and parodist, many of his poems being passed about in manuscript. His verse has a traditional English rather than Irish basis, and sometimes he strikes the old heroic note of pagan stoicism, reminiscent, too, of both A. E. Housman and the later Yeats.

An arresting young poet who has not up to the time of writing these pages collected his verse is Padraic Fallon; and in the same quarterly review, *The Dublin Magazine*, which has drawn attention to Padraic Fallon's poems, have appeared a large number of remarkable translations, by Michael Scot, of Villon's ballades, which have yet to be collected in book form. Also known through the *Dublin Magazine* (though he has published a very slim volume of verse, *Ploughman*, in Macmillan's shilling series) is Patrick Kavanagh, who has been a ploughman on his mother's tiny farm. His verse, though traditional, or not entirely unlike Humbert Wolfe's in technique, is sufficiently fresh and original, and full of odd original twists of thought and phrase.

But the Irish literary renaissance has produced many more —prose writers who have written poems, poets who like John

Eglinton have written little save prose, lyrists who were cut off in the flower of their youth by the Irish or European War, some complete in a small way, others made incomplete by death or an arrested development from the promise of their youth, others not yet confidently judged, some of them still writing, among whom should be mentioned Alfred Perceval Graves (the father of Robert Graves), Nora Hopper, Emily Lawless, Eva Gore-Booth, Thomas MacDonagh, John Todhunter, John Eglinton (W. K. Magee), Francis Ledwidge, Dora Sigerson Shorter, Susan Mitchell, Ella Young, R. N. D. Wilson, Stephen Gwynn, Monk Gibbon, Shane Leslie, Joseph Plunkett, James Joyce, Moira O'Neill. But these names by no means complete the list, for into a short space of less than fifty years has been packed one of the greatest European movements in pure and impassioned poetry since the time of the Elizabethans.

CHAPTER VIII

JOHN MASEFIELD prefaced his *Collected Poems* of 1932 with a poem called *Consecration*, from which the following lines are here taken.

Not of the princes and prelates with periwigged charioteers
Riding triumphantly laurelled to lap the fat of the years,—
Rather the scorned—the rejected—the men hemmed in with the
 spears;

The men of the tattered battalion which fights till it dies,
Dazed with the dust of the battle, the din and the cries,
The men with the broken heads and the blood running into their
 eyes,

 . . . .

Others may sing of the wine and the wealth and the mirth,
The portly presence of potentates goodly in girth;—
Mine be the dirt and the dross, the dust and scum of the earth!

Theirs be the music, the colour, the glory, the gold;
Mine be a handful of ashes, a mouthful of mould
Of the maimed, of the halt and the blind in the rain and the cold—
Of these shall my songs be fashioned, my tales be told.

 Those lyrical statements and implications, though they do not quite scoop the whole cream of Masefield's poetry, make away with a great deal of it. Masefield is many good things, but he is primarily the poet of the down-and-out who refuses to accept his defeat. He is the poet of the hunted, the derelict, the disreputable, the tortured, the beset, the beaten, the publican, and the sinner. All that, and yet more than that. For he is the poet of the man who wins, but who in his final or early striving sets out against fearful odds. In *Reynard the Fox*, a poem of many facets, the hunted and harassed human being is symbolized—as a fox. And the fox gets off. A shorter narrative poem, *The Wanderer*, takes the definite form of an allegory, and the *Wanderer* (a ship), after many bad beginnings, defeats what appears to be the determined hostility of Fate. In *The Everlasting Mercy*, in *The River*, in *Enslaved*, in *Right Royal*, in *King Cole*, in *Dauber*, there is again triumph and conquest. In *Dauber*, it is true, there is a strong element of tragedy, but the ship's butt and failure becomes a good sailor and finally earns the respect of the crew, though he loses his life as a result of it. Sometimes an element of luck, of heavenly fortune, but supported by brave optimism, brings about the final triumph—though character is the main element in determining it. The pull is generally on the side of hope, in the direction of a man winning if he makes up his mind to it, if he lets the light of heaven into his heart. But as Masefield is true to life—probably truer to actual life than most of our living novelists of realism—the other side is shown as well. So two or three of his greatest metrical tales end very unpleasantly. In *The Widow in the Bye Street* and *Daffodil Fields*, passion and weakness of character get the upper hand, and there is tragedy and complete disaster.

Masefield is the poet of the thrashed thews and the burning heart, the complete romantic who has managed to bring poetry down to the plain reader in the street. Moreover, he is the poet of sympathy, forgiveness, and excuse. There is nothing about him of the Hebrew prophet or the stern moralizer. Moralist he is often, but moralizer never. He does not set out to judge, but to delineate and show. So he delights in his riff-raff as much as in his regal people; and he writes of the motley assembly which sets out in the hunt against Reynard, as Chaucer wrote of his Canterbury pilgrims. To Masefield they are just human beings, and the most objectionable of them not really bad.

For a time Masefield helped to popularize modern poetry, especially among the people who read nothing later than Tennyson. By 1910 Kipling had had his day, his great vogue, and suddenly Masefield stepped triumphantly into his shoes.

But he went a great deal further in his verse than Kipling, besides being nearly as prolific in other directions. He has written plays and novels as well as poems, and the 'motives' in all of them are pretty much the same as in the poems. His colour, passion, and humanity set him beside Shakespeare as well as Chaucer.

Resemblances to Chaucer are, of course, rather obvious, though it was some time before they were noticed. Indeed, he is the greatest and most prolific story-writer in verse since Chaucer, greater than Byron or Crabbe (two opposite poets whom he has probably read with pleasure) or than Long-fellow, Tennyson, Scott, or William Morris. Probably it is not too extravagant to say that he is the greatest story-writer in verse in the English language, for being a modern he has better command of the machinery and technique of the story than had Chaucer, and he certainly does not digress from the main theme so frequently. In regard to Shakespeare his affinity is nothing like so plain, for he is not lavish with compelling phrases and memorable lines, and he has generally chosen to write in rhyme instead of blank verse, while there is not much of a deeply philosophic or contemplative character in his work. But his treatment of theme, his bite and snap, his florid romanticism, his realism interwoven with roman-ticism, his passion, his gift for strong, clear characterization, his command of plentiful vocabulary (archaic as well as ver-nacular and modern), and his way of giving the root, stalk, and leaves of poetry as well as the flower, fix him closer to Shake-speare than many other considerable English poets. And not the least of these evidences is his characterization. In the work (I speak chiefly of the verse) of no other English poet are there so many living, breathing, convincing people. He has given us a gallery of broad portraits and thumb-nail sketches, and though Sir Walter Scott has done rather more of it if you fling the novels upon the top of the verse, he was not par-ticularly strong in characterization, and Masefield as a poet is to be judged chiefly by his metrical work.

Moreover, his short critical study of Shakespeare reveals fundamental understanding as well as admiration; and in a small way of comparison it is interesting to note that the rhyme-arrangement of his sonnet-series is cast in the Shakespearian mould. Beyond that, all his verse is stage verse, in that it has been written to be spoken. This was evident from the very first, but in a post-War volume (by no means his best) he made it clearer, for on a frontal leaf to *Minnie Maylow's Story, and Other Tales* (a volume of 250 pages) he printed: 'I thank the beautiful speakers . . . who, in the speaking of these tales and scenes have deeply delighted me. . . .' His creative output has been enormous; and adding to the verse his novels and plays, it is possibly greater than that of any other English poet except Sir Walter Scott. Exuberance, too, was one of the features of Shakespeare.

None of which proves, or attempts to prove, that Masefield is a second Shakespeare or even stands very close to him; but it does show that he is directly of Shakespeare's company, and that he stands at his right side, even though there may be a very considerable space between the two, showing, too, that he is a hundred times more of an Elizabethan than such an overrated poet as T. S. Eliot.

It is not at all just to say that Masefield's romanticism is too dingy and everyday, too much of the nature of realism in tinsel robes. For what of his post-War volumes, particularly *Midsummer Night* (a book of poems which has never received its appreciative due), in which he revitalizes so many of the Arthurian legends and brings us back into the atmosphere of Malory and Edmund Spenser and the *Mabinogion*.

As a poet Masefield has always stood rather alone. During his early years of fame he had many followers; but soon adverse criticism got strongly to work and prevented anything in the nature of vigorous discipleship. Still, in the modern verse tale it is sometimes easy to trace his influence. J. Redwood Anderson started off as a Masefield follower before he struck into a completely different groove of his own, his *Flemish Tales* obviously influenced by Masefield. And Edward Thompson's recent prose play on Raleigh's last voyage [1] (a

---

[1] Recently put on the stage as *The King's Pirate.*

very fine piece of work) is closer to Masefield than is most other contemporary drama. Also worth mentioning in this connection is E. H. Visiak, who, though more important for his prose than his verse, is a poet of some quality who has been under the spell of Masefield's first lyrics.

Masefield's earliest volumes were composed of short lyrics, in which he shows admirations and influences coming from the old ballad, and from Stevenson, Kipling, Newbolt, Yeats, and even Arthur Symons (who was one of the most considerable influences on pre-Georgian verse). They were bright-blooded impulsive singing things—poems of passion and ecstasy, of nostalgia and dissatisfaction with bourgeois life, poems of the open road and the stormy sea. In the first volume there was much that was reminiscent of Kipling, and in each of them a strong human element and many thumb-nail sketches. One would have expected the immediate rapid success that attended Newbolt's *Admirals All* and Kipling's *Barrack-Room Ballads*; but this was not to be, and for a long time the appealing little books were in small demand—until the publication of *The Everlasting Mercy* brought Masefield before the eyes of a very wide public. Most of the contents to-day are well known, and a dozen of them are almost hackneyed; but what appears to me to be the pearl of them from the standpoint of pure poetry (*The Dead Knight*) has been left alone by most of the anthologists—a poem, too, which may have had influence upon T. S. Eliot in both *The Waste Land* and *The Hollow Men*, and which communicates most strangely and awfully in spite of some slight imperfections, and which is really cunningly original, in spite of its relationship to the Scotch ballad-song, *The Twa Corbies*:

> The cleanly rush of the mountain air,
>   And the mumbling, grumbling humble-bees,
> Are the only things that wander there,
>   The pitiful bones are laid at ease,
> The grass has grown in his tangled hair,
>   And a rambling bramble binds his knees.

To shrive his soul from the pangs of hell,
   The only requiem-bells that rang
Were the hare-bell and the heather-bell.
Hushed he is with the holy spell
   In the gentle hymn the wind sang,
And he lies quiet, and sleeps well.

He is bleached and blanched with the summer sun;
   The misty rain and cold dew
Have altered him from the kingly one
   (That his lady loved, and his men knew)
And dwindled him to a skeleton.

The vetches have twined about his bones,
   The straggling ivy twists and creeps
   In his eye-sockets; the nettle keeps
   Vigil about him while he sleeps.
Over his body the wind moans
   With a dreary tune throughout the day,
   In a chorus wistful, eerie, thin
As the gull's cry—as the cry in the bay,
The mournful word the seas say
   When tides are wandering out or in.

Then to that add *The West Wind*, with its lovely opening stanza:

It 's a warm wind, the west wind, full of birds' cries;
I never hear the west wind but tears are in my eyes.
For it comes from the west lands, the old brown hills,
And April 's in the west wind, and daffodils.

and then the lurid beauty and energy of *Third Mate* in such
stanzas as:

Grey were her eyes, and her hair was long and bonny,
Golden was her hair, like the wild bees' honey.
And I was but a dog, and a mad one to despise
The gold of her hair and the grey of her eyes.

And then the fierce realism of:

The town begins on the sea-beaches,
   And the town 's mad with the stinging flies;
The drinking water 's mostly leeches,

It 's a far remove from Paradise
Is Spanish port
Fever port,
Port of Holy Peter.

There 's sand-bagging and throat-slitting,
And quiet graves in the sea slime,
Stabbing, of course, and rum-hitting,
Dirt, and drink, and stink, and crime,
In Spanish port,
Fever port,
Port of Holy Peter.

Consider such poems and snatches, and one does get a sort of presage and epitome of the Masefield to come, though very few of his reviewers could see it at the time.

In 1911 he was a comparatively unknown writer, and when in that year he sent a poem (*The Everlasting Mercy*) of enormous dimensions to the *English Review* there was consternation in the offices. The editors, Austin Harrison and Norman Douglas, liked it mightily, but it was too long, a third the length of any issue of the *English Review*. Moreover it was full of oaths and curses, language to shock every drawing-room and literary *salon*. They were terrified of it. But how stirring it seemed! What was to be done? Should they attempt it? They did; and the *English Review* went straightway out of print. Masefield was made for life, and the *English Review* increased its circulation. Then the publishers Sidgwick & Jackson reprinted the poem in book form, and it went into edition after edition. The reviewers cursed and blessed it, and the Nonconformist clergy quoted from it in their Sunday sermons. It was even a bigger literary sensation than Kipling's *Barrack-Room Ballads*.

It had taken Masefield nine years to win his spurs, though actually he had deserved them earlier.

His poems had been born out of much experience and many vicissitudes. He had been a sailor, a pot-boy in an American public-house, an occasional scribbler. Continually a wanderer, a changer, a rover. His life has never been disentangled,

F

and probably never will be, for he has forbidden it and put difficulties in the way. At any rate he seems to have lived many years in London, enduring many grinding hardships there as elsewhere, just before his spring to fame. Many of his poems are manifestly autobiographical, or strongly touched with personal experience, even where such experience is transmuted and changed. Though one must take the opening lines of *The Everlasting Mercy* with a strong pinch of salt when wildbrained critics tell us that they have direct application to Masefield himself, for the only sense we can make of that is that the man died before he was born and is recording his pre-existence.

> From '41 to '51
> I was my folk's contrary son;
> I bit my father's hand right through
> And broke my mother's heart in two.
> I sometimes go without my dinner
> Now that I know the times I've gi'n her.
>
> From '51 to '61
> I cut my teeth and took to fun.
> I learned what not to be afraid of
> And what stuff women's lips are made of;
> I learned with what a rosy feeling
> Good ale makes floors seem like the ceiling
> And how the moon gives shiny light
> To lads as roll home singing by 't.
> My blood did leap, my flesh did revel,
> Saul Kane was tokened to the devil.
>
> From '61 to '67
> I lived in disbelief of heaven.
> I drunk, I fought, I poached, I whored,
> I did despite unto the Lord,
> I cursed, 'twould make a man look pale,
> And nineteen times I went to jail.
>   Now, friends, observe and look upon me,
>   Mark how the Lord took pity on me!

The Everlasting Mercy was followed by equally long verse tales. *The Widow in the Bye Street*, which came immediately

after, was greeted with a good deal of resentment, and abused
for what it was not, as much as for what it was. It was a short
novel that ought to have been written in prose rather than
verse. And it contained hardly any poetry, and was just hard,
bare, rhymed narrative, and was full of violence and unpleasant-
ness. Something similar had been said by the critics who were
adverse to *The Everlasting Mercy*; but now the chorus of disapproval was doubled. *The Everlasting Mercy* was passable,
particularly as it was about salvation, about the reform of a
sinner, ending up as it did with a strong Christian message;
but this new poem was just downright stark raving realism,
without a glint of sunshine in it. As a matter of fact, you
might nearly as aptly condemn a greater work, Shakespeare's
King Lear, for similar reasons. *The Widow in the Bye Street* is
probably the best of the verse-tales, judged solely from the
standpoint of its grip, its delineation of character, its unity,
and the way it mounts into the final tragedy. Such occur-
rences happen every day, exactly like that, save that a murder
and hanging do not always smash up the works. And the
atmosphere of the countryside and navvy life is very correctly
thrown upon the screen. The poetry lies in the pity. It lies
in 'the purification of the passions by pity and terror.' This
particular poem must be judged from its whole, not its parts.
And it is to be praised for its strong, forward-marching,
sustained rhythm. Nor is it entirely devoid of striking
passages—as for instance:

> Man cannot call the brimming instant back;
>   Time's an affair of instants spun to days;
> If man must make an instant gold, or black,
>   Let him, he may, but Time must go his ways.
>   Life may be duller for an instant's blaze.
> Life's an affair of instants spun to years,
> Instants are only cause of all these tears.

Or this reference to the wiles of a harlot:

> Love in her face hung out his bloody banner,
> And all love's clanging trumpets shocked and blew.

His blackest work, a play, *The Tragedy of Nan*, is written in prose, and is a sort of version of *Cinderella* with a dreadful ending. It is less even than *The Widow in the Bye Street*, for Masefield, to remind the reader that he is writing poetical drama, introduces a blind and very crazy old fiddler, who speaks out of the current mode. The old gaffer's speeches never get across to the reader, and they encroach on the very effective dialogue of the other *dramatis personae*. Indeed, in comparison with the wild poet's speeches in Yeats's *The Countess Cathleen*, they are strained and unreal. The influence of Synge as well as Yeats seems to be in it, and there are resemblances linking up with the German dramatists Sudermann and Gerhart Hauptmann—and with that grim Elizabethan, Webster. West Country dialect seeks to do the work of verse, and very effectively where the crazy fiddler doesn't butt in. The play is overwhelmingly sombre, and different from most of Masefield's other work in that poor Nan seems to be entirely the victim of Fate. Her final action does not seem to come from her own initiative. She is a gentle, fine-natured creature, but foully ill-used, and the madness of passion which transports her at the end seems to come from a horseplay of revengeful ghosts, who have taken possession of her. In spite of Masefield's inconsistent emphasis upon Fate, one is conscious of some element of free-will guiding the actions of the characters in *The Widow in the Bye Street*, so that its dreadful ending is compatible with the romantic idea of tragedy. But poor Nan seems to be a mere tool in the hands of Destiny; and that is definitely no part of Masefield's real 'message.'

A ballad lyric which occurs in a later book, *Lollingdon Downs*, and obviously thrown off from *The Tragedy of Nan* and *The Widow in the Bye Street*, has been much depreciated and attacked by the Georgian critics, although in its compelling music and original form it is a masterpiece of a kind, and nearer to the ancient Border-ballad in content and atmosphere and the intense pity and horror it evokes, than any other short poem in modern literature. . . . A drunken farmer beats his daughter. The son kills the father in a sudden passion of indignation. The son is hanged, and the daughter growing suddenly old from the shock walks the countryside demented, and soon after dies:

> Jane walked the wold
>   Like a grey gander;
> All grown old
>   She would wander.

> She died soon:
>   At high-tide,
> At full moon,
>   Jane died.

> The brook chatters
>   As at first;
> The farm it waters
>   Is accurst.

> No man takes it,
>   Nothing grows there;
> Blood straiks it,
>   A ghost goes there.

In the earlier part of the poem the odd rhymes 'daughter,' 'oughter,' and 'clubbed,' 'upped' have been adversely criticized, though they are consistent with the uncertain rhyming of old folk-lore poetry, sounding quite natural in their context.

Masefield has been attacked as a slipshod poet, for being careless and slapdash in his diction. But the Aunt Sally stone-flingers have rather overstated their grievance. It is true that he is sometimes disconcertingly uneven, and sometimes inserts nonsensical or inept words for the mere sake of effecting a correct rhyme. But this does not occur on every page, and it is better to be like that than to be merely bloodlessly competent. He is certainly no true-blue 'Georgian,' and even less of a 'Parnassian,' and there is a big gap between him and

Flecker. But in the frequent richness of his rhythms Flecker
and he do sometimes clasp hands across the severing chasm.

One of Masefield's most alienating rhymes occurs in that
really good and exciting narrative poem, *The Fight on the Wall*,
where Modred and his followers storm into the privacy of
Lancelot and Guinivere:

> 'Come out,' the dozen cried: 'No quarter
>   If we are forced to storm.'
> 'Go, Joure,' said Modred, 'to the dorter . . .
>   Bring up a form . . .'
>
> 'We 're bringing up a form to batter
>   The door about your ears . . .
> We 'll have your head upon a platter,
>   My prince, sans peers.'

Here may well be asked: Why bring in the atmosphere of the
schoolroom and office by introducing such an ambiguous substantive as 'form'? 'Bench' is manifestly the word needed,
only it does not rhyme. No, Masefield does not bother himself sufficiently, and gets on with the next job. Still, surely
Shakespeare sometimes did the same, for not quite all his
oddities are due to misprints or words that have changed in
meaning, or to good grammar that has become obsolete. Much
can be forgiven to any poet who gives so plentifully and
exuberantly. It is only where the output is small that we
must be exacting and demand continuous perfection. So we
may forgive Shakespeare and poets like Browning and Masefield where we ought to be harder upon John Donne and
Gerard Manley Hopkins.

Masefield is a poet of the emotions; and probably the
greatest poet of the primitive passions since Shakespeare. But
he is also the poet of the Quest—of the knight who sets out
to find the Holy Grail. He is a great seeker, if he is not
always a very certain finder. Despair has no place in his work,
for he is always looking forward. He hopes and desires,
setting no narrow limits upon belief, and has a childlike

fundamental faith in the goodness of humanity. Speaking for himself and his brother poets, he has said in one of his early lyrics:

Friends and loves we have none, nor wealth nor blessed abode,
But the hope of the City of God at the other end of the road.

And in another poem, written about the same time, he seems to see himself and all such seekers in *The Ballad of Sir Bors*:

Would I could see it, the rose, when the light begins to fail,
And a lone white star in the West is glimmering on the mail;
The red, red passionate rose of the sacred blood of the Christ,
In the shining chalice of God, the cup of the Holy Grail.

. . . .

It will happen at last, at dusk, as my horse limps down the fell,
A star will glow like a note God strikes on a silver bell,
And the bright white birds of God will carry my soul to Christ,
And the sight of the Rose, the Rose, will pay for the years of hell.

Such notes sound odd to-day, for though they are sane and necessary notes, they express hope and spiritual desire, and modern poetry is now 'modernist' and defeatist—in which circle Masefield has no place.

CHAPTER IX

GIBSON AND DAVIES

NATURAL REALISM has quite dropped out of English poetry. The newest natural poetic Realism, that of this century, started with Wilfrid Gibson, W. H. Davies, and John Masefield; and after being heavily propped by the soldier poets of the Great War, groaned itself to death under the smothering pillows of Surrealism and kaleidoscopic Symbolism.

Of all living poets of note, Wilfrid Gibson has been the most precocious, even more so than Roy Campbell or Robert Graves. Next to Masefield's, too, his output has been the largest. It might even be argued that his output has been as large as Masefield's, but that would mean ignoring the Poet Laureate's prose dramas, which are essentially poetical in atmosphere though written in quite simple prose.

He commenced to publish verse when a boy at school. He even appeared in highly reputable journals when in his teens —previous to this century.

His first book, *Urlyn the Harper* (1902), though it went into a second edition, was suppressed with two others when he published his *Collected Poems* in 1925—probably because he thought it too derivative and away from his natural manner. The book which brought him fame was his eighth, *Daily Bread*, published in 1910, after he had been writing and publishing for over a dozen years. Pre-War poets of this century had to win their spurs. Unless a first book combined high literary quality with popular features its author was not immediately acclaimed or much written about. Those few first books which put their authors among the recognized living poets were always the fruit of great care and assiduous toil, and were not written by very young men. Gibson, like many another, commenced to publish before he was quite ready—

before he had quite mastered his medium and knew exactly what he wanted to say.

Daily Bread made clear to himself and everybody else what it was his chief business to say. The theme which from henceforth was largely to occupy his attention was the struggle of human life in conditions of indigence and misfortune—suffering Poverty. His Muse was continually to concern herself with the struggles, passions, despairs, recreations, and simple doings of the working classes—of the cottage labourer, the miner, the industrial worker. Gibson had taken over the mantle of Crabbe. But he put rather more colour and glow into it, and there is much more of pure lyricism in his voice. Moreover, Gibson is more completely a poet of the poor than was Crabbe, who wrote frequently of the middle classes.

But Gibson was not to limit himself too narrowly to the working-class life of the towns. He has always been something of a pastoral poet, much more than Crabbe, and influences and admirations due to Wordsworth and his own life among the north country hills are continually thrust upon the pages. Through so many of his poems blows the scented wind that comes over wide expanses of gorse and heath, and the salt wind that comes over the sea. So every manner of human toiler gets into his verse; and behind them there is the romantic countryside. But perhaps it would be truer to say that the broad background is humanity, and that the foreground, Nature, is really secondary. In this he is quite different from Edmund Blunden, whose human background is less evident, the concentration upon mere Nature thrown heavily upon the screen.

The poems in *Daily Bread* were written in dialogue, bleak and drab and unbrocaded, rather too devoid of lyricism, and are probably not as good as they were judged to be at the time. But in 1912 he followed it up with a much better book on the same lines, *Fires,* straightforward narrative poems from which many of the weaknesses of *Daily Bread* had been eliminated. But in the meantime (in 1911) Masefield had published *The Everlasting Mercy,* which rather took the wind

*F

out of Gibson's sails. Gibson's book was independent of it, especially as the creation of most of the poems in *Fires* preceded or was simultaneous with *The Everlasting Mercy*. But from that moment Gibson's name was coupled with Masefield's, which would not have injured him if he had been considered equal; but his position as a mere disciple without romantic trappings did not add to his prestige. The same 'Time Spirit' had breathed upon both of them, but the texture of their work and the treatment of similar themes is so different that, though they stand in the same circle, they are at completely opposite sides of it. Only very casually can one compare Masefield with Crabbe, but Gibson has many affinities with him, and without in any way copying or repeating Crabbe he strongly suggests resemblances, more especially so if we ignore Crabbe's satire. Masefield uses his material like Chaucer or an Elizabethan dramatist, but Gibson's social verse is so social, so preoccupied with the 'workers,' that it almost smells like Socialist propaganda. Gibson at his weakest is just grey and drab and prosy, and even Sunday-schoolish in his inoffensive simplicity, but the comparable faults of Masefield (if they are faults) are the faults of violence and jet-black tragedy splashed with lurid crimson. Even their Nature passages are different, for Masefield stands much further away from Wordsworth than does Gibson; and, where the Old Ballad creeps into both of them, you are conscious in Gibson of strong superficial resemblances, whereas in Masefield there is generally complete change and transformation. Moreover, though Gibson is rather too prone to commonplace language and threadbare *clichés* he is generally a careful, non-committal craftsman, and even a little self-conscious, whereas Masefield lets drive with complete passionate abandon. Supposing a complete social change in the years ahead, much of Gibson's verse will then be read for its documentary value (as Crabbe's is to-day), rather than for its poetical or romantic value, as is likely to be the destiny of the equally realistic Masefield.

A very grim book published in 1922, *Krindlesyke*, is crowded

with strange North Country colloquialisms and dialect words.
So much so that Gibson jostles Edmund Blunden in that
particular sphere (though Blunden has not specialized to the
same extent in the colloquial phrase), and further adds to the
documentary value (in this instance philological) of much of
his work.   This book, too, is austerely free from those elements
of sentimentality which sometimes mar Gibson's best pages.
The characters are as harsh and unalluring as those in Masefield's *Tragedy of Nan*, so that Gibson seems to be caricaturing
certain peasant types of the North Country rather than seeking
to write about them sympathetically and faithfully.

Gibson's best book is probably *Fires* (1912), probably better
than any which followed, two or three of the stories written
with consummate mastery.   The most striking and moving
of them, *The Ovens*, certainly shows Masefield resemblances,
though the voice and technique of the verse and arrangement
of the material are peculiarly Gibson's own:

> He trailed along the cinder-track
> Beside the sleek canal, whose black
> Cold slinking waters shivered back
> Each frosty spark of starry light;
> And each star pricked, an icy pin,
> Through his old jacket worn and thin;
> The raw wind rasped his shrinking skin
> As if stark-naked to its bite:
> Yet, cutting through him like a knife,
> It would not cut the thread of life,
> But only turned his feet to stones
> With red-hot soles that weighed like lead
> In his old broken boots. His head,
> Sunk low upon his sunken chest,
> Was but a burning icy ache
> That strained a skull that would not break
> To let him tumble down to rest.
> He felt the cold stars in his bones,
> And only wished that he were dead
> With no curst searching wind to shred
> The very flesh from off his bones—

No wind to whistle through his bones,
His naked, icy, burning bones:
When, looking up, he saw ahead
The far coke-ovens' glowing light
That burned a red hole in the night—
And but to snooze beside that fire
Was all the heaven of his desire . . .
To tread no more this cursed track
Of crunching cinders through a black
And blasted world of cinder-heaps,
Beside a sleek canal that creeps
Like crawling ice through every bone,
Beneath the cruel stars, alone
With this hell-raking wind that sets
The cold teeth rattling castanets. . . .
Ay, heaven indeed that core of red
In night's black heart that seemed quite dead.

The poem is full of juxtapositions and contrasts: heat, cold; light, darkness; wet, dryness; sleep, wakefulness; virtue, vice; starvation, sufficiency; the industrial city, the unsoiled country —a panorama unfolded from material contrasts and memories evoked. Nearly all the powers of Gibson are here rather wonderfully condensed into less than a dozen pregnant pages.

This faculty for recording contrasts is perhaps the most striking feature of Gibson's genius. It recurs over and over again in ever varied and repeated forms, sometimes taking the shape of a dream, a sort of reaction of delight to compensate for the terrors of death or the drabness of material surroundings. In the special poem under discussion, *The Ovens*, the daydream turns both heads and tails to the striving soul:

Then in a reek of hot gas-light
He stood where, through the summer night,
Half-dozing in the stifling air,
The greasy landlord, fat with sin,
Sat lolling in his easy chair
Just half-way up the brothel stair
To tax the earnings they brought in,
With ear cocked for the copper's tread. . .

Then, shuddering back from that foul place,
And turning from the ovens' glare,
He looked into her dreaming face
And saw green sunlit woodlands there,
And waters flashing in between
Low-drooping boughs of summer green.

In the same volume (*Fires*) the poem entitled *The Snow* is a
very remarkable exercise in the technique of Suspense. Two
children set out joyfully from school in the snow, but get
into a thick storm on the moor-top, and struggle forward in
bewilderment. Then the girl lags and weeps, and the boy
heroically takes her on his back. Presently he loses the track,
falls down in exhaustion, and they go to sleep in the snow.
Dreaming, he sleeps the sleep of death (how good is Gibson
at that sort of thing!), and the two are given up by the reader.
But suddenly the boy wakes up, and the astonished reader
with him, to find that he and his little sister are in the cottage
bed, discovered at the last moment by their shepherd father.
It is a simple but delightfully told tale, and along with the
best of the others, marks Wilfrid Gibson as a master of the
simple narrative in verse. The fact that in quantity, length,
and variety of narrative-verse he has been ousted by Masefield, must not blind us to the obvious, that in the limits of
his own peculiar art Gibson is occasionally very good indeed
—even though one does feel that some of the tales might have
been better if they had been expanded and written in prose.

His iambic verse has a peculiar and individual movement,
the beat of the rhymes awaking few memories of other poets.
I would say no memories, if it were not that in Browning's
short narrative poem, *Porphyria's Lover*, there is the possible
origin of it.

He needs weeding. He has written too much for this un-
metrical age. His real quality could probably be more effectively masticated in a selection of between one and two
hundred pages.

That other realist, W. H. Davies, superior to Wilfrid
Gibson as a lyrical poet, but in no way a narrative poet, save

that some of his lyrics are anecdotes, originally belonged to part of that world which was on Gibson's canvas. His first book, *The Soul's Destroyer*, was written in, and published from, a doss-house. It was a book of genuine lyrical realism intermingled with meditations upon Nature. Bernard Shaw, when prefacing his autobiography (*The Autobiography of a Super-Tramp*) at a later date, suggested that one of his literary inspirations might have been Crabbe: 'His work was not in the least strenuous or modern: there was in it no sign that he had ever read anything later than Cowper or Crabbe.'

If, however, Davies had read Crabbe at all he was in no way dominated by him. More often—strange clash with his realistic vein!—does he remind one of Herrick, though his work is so naïve and free from literary taint that the early Davies may never have opened a volume of Herrick; and the only modern who seems to have touched him at all is A. E. Housman. It is easy to prove that he is a good 'Georgian' and just the sort of person who went naturally into Edward Marsh's anthologies, but it is equally easy to prove that he ought not to be there at all and belongs entirely to an earlier world. But I suppose that his distinguishing feature is a happy fusion of contradictions, for he combines a complete traditionalism with a very fresh individual unliterary way of his own.

Davies is a poet born, owing more to his natural gifts of feeling and observation than to his powers of imbibing and rejecting through reading. Added to this, he has a very sensitive ear for sounds. This, however, does not fully extend itself to rhythms. He has been blamed as a poet with a stammer; but the accusation was ill-aimed and unjust, and it was a long time ago, before the triumph of the Modernists. But few of his rhythms have much technical driving force or compulsion behind them. They are neither infectious nor dancingly musical. Newbolt, Dowson, Chesterton, Flecker, Swinburne, though not stronger in genuine emotion, are generally stronger in melody. And both Burns and Heine— poets with whom he has been compared—are quite different

in technique, especially as their best poems 'sing themselves.' Davies has, however, this affinity with both Heine
and Burns: he uses simple, homely language, and uses it
so effectively that there is never in his verse the slightest
suggestion of commonplaceness or cheapness. If few of his
lyrics have that perfection of music and form which we
associate with ecstatic singing—where perfection of art justifies
almost any kind of content—they are rich with erratic melody
of line and couplet and single stanza. His ear is for brief
combinations of words rather than for long musical passages.
If a rather inept comparison with birds be permissible, he is a
thrush, linnet, blackbird rather than a skylark or nightingale.
He is a poet of the earth rather than a poet of the high blue
spaces or the illimitable starry vastness of night. Compare,
for instance, his poem on the moon with Keats's *Ode to a
Nightingale*. Though one of the loveliest of modern lyrics it
is not exactly a poem of the ecstasy and pain of moon-drenched
starry night:

> Thy beauty haunts me, heart and soul,
>   Oh thou fair Moon, so close and bright;
> Thy beauty makes me like the child
>   That cries aloud to own thy light:
> The little child that lifts each arm
> To press thee to her bosom warm.
>
> Though there are birds that sing this night
>   With thy white beams across their throats,
> Let my deep silence speak for me
>   More than for them their sweetest notes:
> Who worships thee till music fails
> Is greater than thy nightingales.

And though in the last two lines we have an entire perfection
of musical form, there is less of it in the other couplets.

But everywhere in his verse beautiful short passages abound.
Everywhere occur such couplets as:

> Oh, happy wind, I say,
> To be alive this day!

even though they are rarely successive and sustained throughout a whole lyric.

Moreover, no other poet has quite so effectively combined talkiness with pure poetry. Call him a prosy talky poet if if you like, and one can immediately furnish examples to show that he talks much too effectively to be called prosy:

> The dog was there, outside her door,
> She gave it food and drink,
> She gave it shelter from the cold:
> It was the night young Molly robbed
> An old fool of his gold.

> 'Molly,' I said, 'you'll go to Hell'—
> And yet I half believed
> That ugly, famished, tottering cur
> Would bark outside the gates of Heaven
> To open them for her.

That poem makes a useful quotation for various reasons. It is one of his many anecdotes in rhyme, is typically expressive of his love of animals, and is also a memorable example from those clusters of verse occupied with the outcast and the darker sides of human life, showing his affinity with both Gibson and Masefield. There is wit in it too, though as a wit (and William Davies is a considerable wit) it does not show him at his truly wittiest.

He is sometimes called the 'Tramp Poet,' for a large part of his early life was spent on the roads, in complete vagabondage, both in this country and America. It speaks much for his character, and emphasizes the remarkable quality of his genius, that he was finally able to break free and fit himself for a life of concentration and literary application. Begging bread and selling laces along the high road is not conducive to industry; years of it entirely unfit a man for civilized life. William Davies is a sort of miracle.

Though not a very spacious poet he is a very fluid one. Not only does he sit in the same circle with Gibson and Masefield, but he also belongs to the pastoral company of

Edmund Blunden, Edward Thomas, Andrew Young, and Victoria Sackville-West. Indeed, many of his admirers seem to think that he fits more naturally with these poets of the English countryside, that though he is a modern realist (and after that a good Post-Elizabethan in that he sounds like Herrick's best brother) he is best assessed as a very sparkling poet of country life:

> It was the Rainbow gave thee birth,
> And left thee all her lovely hues;
> And, as her mother's name was Tears,
> So runs it in thy blood to choose
> For haunts the lonely pools, and keep
> In company with trees that weep.

So, at his wittiest and most imaginative range, he sings to the kingfisher; and whether his subject be birds, butterflies or flowers, winds or clouds, he writes always as a man to whom Nature is something real and intimate, more important than literature or the pleasures of the town. Indeed, in two or three places his personifications of Nature are sometimes almost too strong, as, for instance, where he seems to think of the wind as a person rather than as a god. At any rate he is a very considerable hedgerow realist, a knight of the woods and lanes, the friend of birds and all wild things—beautiful, human, impressive, and very interesting.

CHAPTER X

JAMES ELROY FLECKER

THE reputation of James Elroy Flecker has somewhat dwindled, if it is still unscathed. But for at least a decade it was in the ascendancy. He was one of the central figures of the first 'Georgian' Revolt (against William Watson, Rudyard Kipling, and others). He was one of the most powerful influences in the second 'Georgian' Revolt (against Masefield and others). And he might still become one of the most powerful influences against Modernist disintegration.

He was born on 5th November 1884. He died in Switzerland, of consumption, in the first week of January 1915, the sixth month of the War. Rupert Brooke, his friend, followed him a few months after. One of his earlier poems (although he could not have been thinking straightforwardly of himself) seems to prophesy his end:

> Not because I was weary of life
> As pallid poets are:
> My star was a conquering star,
> My element strife.
> I am young, I am strong, I am brave;
> It is therefore I go to my grave.

Strife—or rather, striving! It was his element. And his star was the sun! It is true that he was also the poet of twilight, of hours and moments shadowy and ghostly. Such is the other aspect. But all contrasting phases of diurnal phenomena exist in his work—of the sun of dawn; the blazing sun of noonday; the falling and sanguine sun of sunset; and of the spectre moments after, when the sun has ceased to reign:

When the words rustle no more,
  And the last work 's done,
When the bolt lies deep in the door,
  And Fire, our Sun,
Falls on the dark-laned meadows of the floor;

When from the clock's last chime to the next chime
  Silence beats his drum,
And Space with gaunt grey eyes and her brother Time
  Wheeling and whispering come,
She with the mould of form and he with the loom of rhyme . . .

He is less frequently the poet of Midnight and the Moon;
though terror of Death and its Afterwards is breathed into
some of his work; particularly into the weird, yet Virgilian
Town without a Market—Flecker's pronouncement of the
existence of Hell after the body's dissolution, for the self-
centred and unspiritual, a hell of dreadful loneliness, bore-
dom, and chill sensation. But the Sun was his dominant and
guiding symbol; and it was the Sun which consumed him.
He seems to have burnt himself up with the fire of his own
energy and fidelity to life and action. In his poetry, too, the
Sun is a consuming and testing force as well as a life-bestowing
force.

Wilt thou bloom red where she buds pale, thy sister rose? Wilt
    thou not fail
When noonday flashes like a flail? Leave, nightingale, the caravan!

That, from *Gates of Damascus*, admits of many inter-
pretations; but, at any rate, it asserts the very real difficulty
of living truthfully and individually; intimating also, perhaps,
the unlikelihood of Hypocrisy being able to continue long
with her ancient procession of shams and unrealities in the
face of any mind-shaking catastrophe, or beneath any shrivel-
ling and revealing system of human government. For the
insincere and untrue he prophesies consumption plain enough,
but an outward and visible corruption that shall leave behind
not even the dry bones:

The Sun who flashes through the head and paints the shadows
    green and red,
The Sun shall eat thy fleshless dead, O Caravan, O Caravan!

But Flecker was not of that company. He was one of those
vitally effective people whose fame Death heightens and en-
hances rather than lessens or holds stationary.

He was unusually gifted, and had packed much into his
short life. He was a good scholar, skilled in several
languages, and rated as an exceptional wit and conversation-
alist. He had travelled in many lands and earned respect as
a hard-grinding and capable official in an Eastern consular
office. And he had published a number of books (prose as
well as verse), and had shaped an instrument of exceptional
poetry, one that is little inferior to that of Keats. Though he
sometimes sacrificed sense to sound, his best lyrics and stanzas
seem to have the quality of something quite imperishable.
Their sensuous music and colour united to richness of phrase
and suggestion are sufficient support for such a prophecy of
high fame. His world is crowded with those hues and
shapes which spring from the energy of radiant day; though
the plangency of the style is apt, at times, to induce an
impression of glassiness and glitter. And yet how it delights!

> Had I that haze of streaming blue,
>   That sea below, the summer faced,
> I'd work and weave a dress for you
>   And kneel to clasp it round your waist,
> And broider with those burning bright
>   Threads of the Sun across the sea,
> And bind it with the silver light
>   That wavers in the olive tree.

Or these gloomier lines, where a young Greek is contemplating the beauty of his native city, and imagining it as already
overthrown before the assaults of the victorious barbarians:

No more on the long summer days shall we walk in the meadow-
    sweet ways
With the teachers of music and phrase, and the masters of dance
    and design.

No more when the trumpeter calls shall we feast in the white-light
    halls;
For stayed are the soft footfalls of the moon-browed bearers of wine,
And lost are the statues of Kings and of Gods with great glorious
    wings
And an empire of beautiful things, and the lips of the love who
    was mine.

But his best poem, of some length, *Gates of Damascus*,
seems to have crept out of the bed of French Symbolism.
What is it all about? And about what and whom are all its
apocalyptic prophecies? Nobody quite knows. Yet it is the
best English poem of its kind, better than Eliot's *Waste Land*.
It never irritates or estranges. It always speaks and passionately
communicates, casting a net of glamour round the brain—so
haunting that some of its stanzas almost hurt:

Pass not beneath, O Caravan, or pass not singing. Have you heard
That silence where the birds are dead, yet something pipeth like
    a bird?

Pass not beneath! Men say there blows in stony deserts still a rose,
But with no scarlet to her leaf—and from whose heart no perfume
    flows.

Flecker hovered between lyrical beacons. He proclaimed
himself a Parnassian, and then produced some effective Symbolism. Like Masefield, he was by preference a Sun poet,
and yet after his death became one of the central figures in
the revolt against Masefield's influence. We can write about
him from several points of view, and he himself seems to have
been aware of the tangle:

> I have done foolishly to tread
>   The footway of the false moonbeams,
> To light my lamp and call the dead
>   And read their long black printed dreams.

> I have done foolishly to dwell
>   With Fear upon her desert isle,
> To take my shadowgraph to Hell,
>   And then to hope the shades would smile.

He commenced with much admiration for Baudelaire, but at his death was moving into an atmosphere of religious mysticism.

And God shall make thy soul a Glass where eighteen thousand
    Aeons pass,
And thou shalt see the gleaming Worlds as men see dew upon the
    grass.

How are we to judge him? As a poet of perfect clarity, of finicking workmanship and restraint? Yes. And in that he was a Parnassian. As a poet who paid more attention to suggestive music and symbolism and the arrangement of his words than to clarity and logical content? Yes, but only sometimes—and in this he was a Symbolist. As a poet in the best Greek tradition? Yes, but though he was lightly tied to Swinburne and Keats he had no affinity whatever with Matthew Arnold. He appears to have been as much influenced by his Greek studies as by his Oriental and French pursuits, and when we compare him with Baudelaire we must remember that Baudelaire was a Parnassian rather than a Symbolist. Actually Flecker was too individualistic and original to permit of any labelling. In spite of his own declaration and labelling, and J. C. Squire's confirmation of them he was never strictly a Parnassian, the natural spiritual flame and romantic vigour in the man proving too strong for any narrow subjection to them. Indeed, like so many artists, he was never quite to be trusted when he spoke of himself. He knew it, and even confessed it. Writing to a critic about his preface to *The Golden Journey to Samarkand*, in which he had proclaimed himself a Parnassian, he said:

You know that Preface of mine, though it 's absolutely sincere, is a wicked piece of work! It is no good just writing poetry and flinging it at the public's head—especially if your poetry isn't all of one piece, but rather apt to vary with moods. If one wrote *only* Oriental poems, for instance, the critics would say, 'This follower of FitzGerald, etc. etc.' So I had to give myself a label. I had to proclaim a message. Of course, it succeeded. I have irritated some and pleased others—but now I am labelled.'

But besides the influences already mentioned, there were many more. One was John Davidson. And another was the Pre-Raphaelite, William Morris; chiefly reflected through his ballad poetry, while in one instance Flecker cunningly borrowed from him. For let us compare eight of the long lines in *Gates of Damascus* with a passage from the end of Morris's prose tale *Svend and his Brethren*.

Flecker's passage [1] runs thus:

Beyond the sea are towns with towers, carved with lions and lily
    flowers,
And not a soul in all those lonely streets to while away the hours.

Beyond the towns, an isle where, bound, a naked giant bites the
    ground:
The shadow of a monstrous wing looms on his back: and still no
    sound.

Beyond the isle a rock that screams like madmen shouting in their
    dreams,
From whose dark issues night and day blood crashes in a thousand
    streams.

Beyond the rock is Restful Bay, where no wind breathes or ripple
    stirs,
And there on Roman ships, they say, stand rows of metal mariners.

And the passage from William Morris runs thus:

Here ends what William the Englishman wrote; but afterwards (in the night-time) he found the book of a certain chronicler which said:

'In the springtime, in May, the 550th year after the death of Svend the wonderful king, the good knights, sailing due eastward, came to a harbour of a land they knew not; wherein they saw many goodly ships, but of a strange fashion like the ships of the ancients, and destitute of any mariners; besides they saw no beacons for the

---

[1] Sir John Squire has, however, written of this passage: 'A reading of Hérédia is surely evident.' Probably it is a case of both William Morris and Hérédia —the latter a Parnassian whom Flecker had absorbed.

guidance of seamen, nor was there any sound of bells or singing, though the city was vast, with many goodly towers and palaces. So when they landed they found that which is hardly to be believed, but which is nevertheless true: for about the quays and about the streets lay many people dead, or stood, but quite without motion, and they were all white or about the colour of new-hewn freestone, yet were they not statues but real men, for they had, some of them, ghastly wounds which showed their entrails, and the structure of their flesh, and veins, and bones.

'Moreover the streets were red and wet with blood, and the harbour waves were red with it, because it dripped in great drops slowly from the quays.'

But what are such far-away echoes?   And what are influences? Reading *Gates of Damascus*, one even has the faint suspicion that St John's Apocalypse may be one of them.   But everything in Flecker is so transmuted, and influences never detract from his originality and individual fervour and emotion.

Flecker has been reproached for being too aloof and too French and Oriental, that is because he did not write enough poetry for the People, for the Man in the Street, for folk of various shades of culture and activity—which is obviously the 'mission' of a Sun Poet.   But we must not blame Flecker for the insufficiency, we must blame Death for cutting him off; for it was plainly Flecker's gradual approach and trend. He believed that the most estimable poet is always a People's poet, which shows that in essentials he was no true Parnassian. Does not Ishak in the play of *Hassan* say: 'You loved music, too, and you could sing the songs of the people, which are better than mine'?   And does not the Caliph say questioningly to Hassan: 'Ah, if there should ever arise a nation whose people have forgotten poetry or whose poets have forgotten the people, though they send their ships round Taprobane and their armies across the hills of Hindustan, though their city be greater than Babylon of old, though they mine a league into earth or mount to the stars on wings—what of them?' While Hassan sententiously answers: '*They will be a dark patch upon the world.*'   And has not Flecker also made this theme the subject-matter of one of his most vital lyrics, one, too, that is undecorated, a definite gesture against his own Gallic gospel, and as un-Parnassian as Burns or Blake?

> A lad went piping through the Earth,
>   Gladly, madly, merrily,
> With a tune for death and a tune for birth
>   And a tune for lovers' revelry.
>
> He kissed the girls that sat alone
>   With none to whisper, none to woo;
> Fired at his touch their faces shone,
>   And beauty drenched them as the dew.
>
> Old men who heard him danced again,
>   And shuffled round with catching breath,
> And those who lay on beds of pain
>   Went dancing through the gates of death.
>
> If only he could make us thrill
>   Once more with mirth and melody!
> I listened, but the street was still,
>   And no one played for you and me.

Some time towards the end of his busy life he wrote *Hassan,* which, if not actually a poem, is at any rate a strong poetical drama, and one, in its various aspects, appealing to many kinds of people. Moreover, it seems to be one of the very few satisfying dramas in the department of tragedy since Shakespeare wrote *Hamlet, Lear,* and others of his master-pieces. It is true that it teases us with tiresome contradictory elements, and is sometimes marred by blotches of sensuality, violence, and cruelty, the expression of some morbid feature of Flecker's mind, or sprung from influences which, perhaps, may be traced to the later Elizabethan drama of extreme violence, lust, and bloodshed. But that does not alter the essential fact that it is a creation for the People, displaying characteristics which appeal to all sorts and conditions of men. Part of it bears definite resemblance to Justin McCarthy's one-time

popular and rather flashy play and novel, *If I were King*, about
the life and times of Louis XI and François Villon (where
Villon, with less than half an eye on veracity, is raised from
the position of a beggar to be the minister of a king and the
lover of a princess), and also to Maeterlinck's *Monna Vanna*.
In the latter drama, as in *Hassan*, an adventurer seeks to over-
throw the government of a city for the love of a lady. Such
subjects have always had an immense popular appeal. Moreover, much of *Hassan* is symbolical and religious, and the
man in the street likes 'religion' in his poems and plays,
especially when this is spiced and seasoned with wit and
laughter. *Hassan* even regales us with humour, a more important spiritual activity than that which goes to make mere
jests, of which there are a superabundance in the first acts.
The earlier part of the play is amusing enough to admit of
its being selected as a touchstone for the writers of comic
opera; while from the point of view of Aristotelian law
(framed for the requirements of a majority, those thousands
of serious and middle-minded Greeks who were always present
at the acting of any good tragedy) it does make a bold and rather
successful attempt at the 'purification of the passions' by
means of 'pity and terror.' Moreover, much of the play seems
to hit the times and to contain topical allusions. This can
hardly be due to calculating revision and insertion during the
first five months of war (when Flecker was chained to his
'mattress grave'), but it may be due to sheer vision and
prophecy, for the Procession of Protracted Death seems very
like the War in a nutshell; the sacrifice of Pervaneh very like a
noble feminine symbol for the sacrifice of England's youth in
the trenches of France; and the fantastic and outrageous
Beggars' conspiracy very like a Bolshevik upheaval. It is true
that in the play the Bolshevik or Beggars' conspiracy comes
before, and not after the human sacrifice, but following, all
the same, a period of cruel subjection and misrule, and its
failure is only typical of so many revolutions of hate and
violence. It is a play which scourges the tyranny of riches
and selfish power, which unveils the pride, lust, and cruelty

of Earth. There is no trifling with the main issues, and no palliation. If it is over-lustful in some scenes, it is also puritanical enough in essentials for a Salvation Army meeting-house. The Caliph is no less a tyrant and monster because he can discourse wisely and beautifully about poetry and art; and the soul of the unrepentant Rafi is no less damned because its owner's last decision on earth had been a noble one, and his courage all through of a most unmistakable calibre. It is a play to prick the sensibilities of a rhinoceros and frighten the most callous of scene-gazers; but the figure of Rafi, 'King of the Beggars,' as a sort of regal and glorified Barabbas, who adores and at the same time entirely misunderstands the female saviour Pervaneh, seems (from the point of view of mere dramatic criticism) to fit somewhat unsatisfyingly into the scheme of things, unless we care to drive the comparison further, and liken him to some harsh medieval Christian fanatic. His love for Pervaneh and his outcast fellow-sufferers only mildly atones for his ferocity towards their oppressors; while his chill damnation after death (considering that he consented to become a martyr) seems to savour as much of divine unfairness as it does of justice without mercy. Pervaneh dies by hideous torture (her own choice) because, in her own words:

Sweet life—we die for thy sweetness, O Lord of the Garden of Peace! Come, love, for the fire that beats within us, for the air that blows around us, for the mountains of our country and the wind among the pines you and I accept torture and confront our end. We are in the service of the World. The voice of the rolling deep is shouting: 'Suffer that my waves may moan.' The company of the stars sing out: 'Be brave that we may shine.' The spirits of children not yet born whisper as they crowd around us: 'Endure that we may conquer.'

So speaks Love, the Spirit of Love, as symbolized in a strong and radiant woman; and this and other passages of the play transmit to the reader or spectator something of the true sacrificial thrill. But why does this saviour so passionately love the bloody-minded Barabbas, signified in the person of

Rafi? Why after death must she also partially suffer, and be so aware of the poignant loneliness of *his* damnation? And why did she never reproach him for the revengefulness and horror of his revolutionary plans? Perhaps Flecker's meaning was more subtle and his thought more profound than we can readily probe. Perhaps it is just that, and not weakness of development or construction in the play. Perhaps, indeed, he was thinking dimly of Joan of Arc and a thwarted, brutalized French soldiery, and thus forestalling Bernard Shaw —whose enthusiasm for the play immediately upon its appearance was expressed in such warm terms that its influence upon *Saint Joan* may be taken for granted. At any rate Pervaneh, who is the incarnate spirit of Liberty, is a creature of pure nobility and chaste passion; Rafi, the elect warrior of the oppressed and wolfish rabble, is both her complement and her contrary—to be forgiven, at least, by *her*. Yet the drama as a whole, simple and easy as it is in expression, is a little bewildering. It is as if some violent Elizabethan, Hafiz, Saint John, and Heinrich Heine had collaborated to write it, and Gilbert-and-Sullivan had driven in a wedge.

After the fearful sentence of execution has been passed, Hassan is thrown from eminence and told to go back to his confectioner's shop because he dares to speak his mind to the Caliph—Civilization's Titan among cultured and callous plutocrats. He begins his expostulation with courteous and honeyed words: 'O Master of the World—the hour of the nightingale has not yet come'; but enraged by the Caliph's academic and exasperating sang-froid flares up into 'Hideous tyrant, torturer from Hell,' finally justifying his humane boldness with the simple but penetrating words: 'I am not ashamed to be a confectioner, but I am ashamed to be a coward.' And Ishak coolly turns his back on the magnificence of his office as poet laureate with: 'I am leaving this city of slaves, this Bagdad of fornication. I have broken my lute and will write no more qasidahs in praise of the generosity of kings. I will try the barren road, and listen for the voice of the emptiness of earth.' Then he and Hassan join the pilgrims who are preparing to make the Golden Journey to Samarkand. The city of Samarkand is, of course, symbolical of Paradise, and the Golden Journey over the stony desert and barren sand of that peace of mind which comes from self-denial and renouncement. The Dawn breaks over the desert hills, the dawn of Hope and a New Age, the first beams of whose light will shine upon the difficult path to the pilgrims' Holy City.

It sounds rather like a 'message' to a disillusioned Europe, for it was almost Flecker's final word.

CHAPTER XI

G. K. CHESTERTON AND HIS SCHOOL

SCHOOLS of verse, though they may sometimes help to keep poetry alive, are, nevertheless, equally often very troublesome and unfertile assemblies, especially when they become life-boats for floating and saving literary journalists. The least scrupulous manage to triumph by mere weight of numbers, by quantity rather than by quality. Making friends with considerable sections of the press and the pundits of minor criticism, they arrange for the prominence of their own particular wares, boycotting or squeezing into a corner every volume that sounds like a challenge or opposition. The apparent result is the domination of one kind of lyre—which in the end may emerge as a very indifferent instrument, perhaps a tin-can lyre, perhaps a super-sleepy violin, perhaps a thing of harsh metallic wires. The bad poets triumph with the good, and the good are in the end smothered by the worst efforts of their own fellows. The development, too, is always in the direction of war, a guerrilla strife between parties, outstanding individualists who refuse to submit being put to bed and told to cuddle the pillow of their unimportance.

But there also exist schools of poetry whose members hang together so loosely that their influence does no hurt to other fraternities or to outstanding individualists. They form nothing in the nature of an aloof coterie or hostile clique.

G. K. Chesterton at one time seemed to be the centre of such a school or division. Its journals of outlet were *The New Witness* and *G. K.'s Weekly*, and its characteristics were such that one might almost call it the Modern School of the Medieval Elizabethans, which though an unwieldy contradiction in three terms will perhaps partially describe its comely features of quarrelling Romanticism.

The chief members of this division, which began to show

itself dimly between the beginning and end of the War were
G. K. Chesterton, Hilaire Belloc, Wilfred Rowland Childe,
W. R. Titterton, and William Kean Seymour. Its most obvious characteristics were robustiousness, rapture, medievalism,
Roman Catholic Christianity, the exaltation of the humble and
homely, traditional music, the cult of the tavern, songs of
liberty. It was also characterized by Puritanism. Indeed,
Chesterton, who pretended to be the great opponent of Puritanism, rode his hobby-horse with a rather grinning mouth and a
long tongue in a very bulging cheek. For the essence of
Puritanism is the putting of the Christian religion into all the
deeds of daily life, speaking about religion in daily speech and
writings, the cultivation of justice, of fair play and sincerity of
speech, and the exaltation of sex purity in celibate and family
life. It is this last which is the plainest badge of the Puritans.
It is true that the chief leaders of Puritanism in this country
have sprung from the Nonconformist churches, but Non-
conformity is not necessarily Puritanism, though the Elizabethan dissenters were called Puritans, and the Puritan movement owes most of its tenets of faith to them. For, to-day
it is probably among the Catholics of Ireland that you will
find the greatest power of Puritanism, manifest peculiarly in
the rigorous workings of the literary censor (moralist rather
than political) in that green and rain-lashed country. So when
wilful enthusiasts about the work of D. H. Lawrence (enthusiasts who want to give him special moral backing) claim
that he was a great Puritan they do not speak at all correctly
about him, for D. H. Lawrence, although the child of
Congregationalists (and very lax Congregationalists), was in
continual rebellion against the church of his fathers. But
when Chesterton wrote:

> But the song of Beauty and Art and Love
> Is simply an utterly stinking song,
> To double you up and drag you down
> And damn your soul alive . . .

he expressed the Puritan attitude in entire completeness

towards sensuous and sensual art, the reverse of which
D. H. Lawrence may not have quite crystallized in his verse,
but which is often flamboyantly and disturbingly manifest in
his lurid, though magnificent prose.   Where Chesterton showed
his severance from Puritanism was in his very non-moral
drinking songs, for Puritanism in part means rigid temper-
ance, if not teetotalism, and alcohol as a theme for poetry is
taboo.   Even his attempt in the ultimate stanza of *Wine and
Water* to effect a sort of compromise (a very droll compromise)
does not clear him of a very strong bias:

But Noah he sinned, and we have sinned; on tipsy feet we trod,
Till a great big black teetotaller was sent to us for a rod,
And you can't get wine at a P.S.A., or chapel, or Eisteddfod,
For the Curse of Water has come again because of the wrath of
    God,
And water is on the Bishop's board and the Higher Thinker's
    shrine,
But I don't care where the water goes if it doesn't get into the wine.

All through his poems he sings in praise of the tavern, of
jolly roistering, but roistering in which (here is the real
Puritan) women and sensual debauch have no place.   His
drinkers are unattached medievalists, men-at-arms with no
mistress, plump-cheeked fighters in the chaste cause of right
and liberty, Sir Galahads taking a day off and shouting their
exploits over the wine-barrel.   He is the apostle of a sort of
drunken Puritanism, the poet of Falstaffian Christianity.   He
almost unites priest and publican, and ignores every movement of the Modern Age save as something to criticize and
condemn.   Of all English poets of this century he belongs
foremost to an earlier age.   Paradoxically though, he is a social
propagandist—probably more propagandist than any poet of
importance ever born.   In the years which immediately preceded his death, his poetry became hidden and embedded in a
crush of social rhymes, the artist receding more and more into the
background.   But this is not the characteristic Chesterton, for in
him the artist and propagandist often marvellously combine:

It has not been as the great wind spoke
  On the great green down that day;
We have seen, wherever the wide wind spoke,
Slavery slaying the English folk:
The robbers of land we have seen command,
  The rulers of land obey.

We have seen the gigantic golden worms
  In the garden of paradise:
We have seen the great and the wise make terms
With the peace of snakes and the pride of worms,
And them that plant make covenant
  With the locust and the lice.

He is writing of the present England, the people of to-day,
for according to Chesterton, personal liberty has been almost
entirely lost under the tyranny of capitalism. And in his
strangely communicating, if rather wild and nonsensical poem,
The Old Song, the revolutionary note is even more passionately
intensified:

I saw the kings of London town,
  The kings that buy and sell,
That built it up with penny loaves
  And penny lies as well:

And where the streets were paved with gold, the shrivelled paper
    shone for gold,
The scorching light of promises that pave the streets of hell.
For penny loaves will melt away, melt away, melt away,
Mock the mean that haggled in the grain they did not grow;
With hungry faces in the gate, a hundred thousand in the gate,
A thunder-flash on London and the finding of the foe.

And yet he never advocated Communism, nor even Socialism
of any very levelling nature. Distribute wealth and goods a
little more evenly, and let us be ruled by Englishmen with
national and social interests at heart, people who have sprung
from the agricultural land of Anglo-Saxondom, and we shall
be glorious and happy once again:

G

They have given us into the hand of new unhappy lords,
Lords without anger and honour, who dare not carry their swords.
They fight by shuffling papers; they have bright dead alien eyes;
They look at our labour and laughter as a tired man looks at flies.
And the load of their loveless pity is worse than the ancient wrongs,
Their doors are shut in the evening; and they know no songs.

A critic who tries to yoke him to any of his English predecessors has a difficult task. Maybe at moments he sounds
a little like Lord Macaulay, and at another time like a sort
of ghostly fusion of Marlowe and Blake, or of Swinburne
and Blake; but the resemblance at closest is not very pronounced. He manifestly read all the old ballads written
in the English tongue, and he may have read all the few
existing epics and fragmentary poems of the Saxon scops.
Add to that, if you like, everything else Teutonic, be it
Danish, Icelandic, or German, introducing into their midst
some very odd or strange foreign matter, such as the employment of paradoxes, and even such a destructive element as
French Symbolism (his poem on old age, *A Second Childhood*,
sounds uncommonly like a piece of glorified Surrealism), and
the Chestertonian framework knottily emerges. I doubt if
he ever bothered himself with German poetry (he was no
great friend of the Germans), but, turning over the pages of
representative German anthologies (one of them a students'
drinking-song book), one is continually confronted by re-
minders, particularly noticeable in the strong racial outlook,
and something straightforwardly musical, resonant, and rhetorical in the language—to say nothing of the wine- and beer-
imbibing enthusiasm. One is moderately certain that poets
like Bürger, Schiller, and Liliencron, and probably also the
divine and demoniacal Heine, would have derived pleasure
from Chesterton once they had sifted away the paradoxes
and the lyrics containing the most extravagant figures of
speech. Affinities, too, exist between him and a more recent
German poet, Börries von Münchhausen, so eminently Teutonic is the man. There is a royalist strain in him, certainly,
for you may sing of liberty and shout 'Down with Tyrants!'

as hard as you like, but you cannot be quite so enthusiastic about medievalism without suggesting that you believe in kings more than presidents, soviets, or republics. One can almost believe that in remote times he thrilled the hearts of the thanes guarding King Alfred, and that his hand tintinnabulated on the harp whilst that great monarch at repose was watching his clock-candles and planning another onslaught on the Danes. Yet there is rather more of the modern brass band in his verse than the harp, and considering his verse from the viewpoint of the orchestra, the harp comes midway between the brass instruments and the violins and 'cellos. His orchestra, if sufficiently complete, is rather too one-sided, and though violins and 'cellos break through the general blare they are not at all frequent. And yet it seems rather odd to hear a brass band playing this kind of thing:

> You may be tired and tolerant of fancies as they fade,
> But if men doubt the Charter, ye shall call on the Crusade—
> Trumpet and torch and catapult, cannon and bow and blade,
> Because it was My challenge to all the things I made.

Because what have we got to do to-day with bows and catapults? and though such songs of liberty are given a backward atmosphere, their application is always quite obviously contemporary.

His longest poem, a complete book, and a very long poem, *The Ballad of the White Horse*, takes us right into Saxon times and the press of nobles around King Alfred; and from that and the general tone of his whole output one gets the view that though a medievalist, he is an early medievalist, believing that since the battle of Hastings the English have always been an oppressed and downtrodden people who have yet to come into their own. His best poem, *The Secret People*, in which he briefly surveys the whole of English history since the Norman Conquest, and agreeably fuses propaganda with poetry and historical substance, quite plainly advocates that idea, its concluding lines being among the most memorable things he has written:

It may be we shall rise the last as Frenchmen rose the first,
Our wrath come after Russia's wrath and our wrath be the worst.
It may be we are meant to mark with our riot and our rest
God's scorn for all men governing. It may be beer is best.
But we are the people of England; and we have not spoken yet.
Smile at us, pay us, pass us. But do not quite forget.

His verse is full of preachings, politics, and arresting hymns of hate. Anger, witty expostulation, impish satire, and hilarious mockery are the currants and raisins in his holly-decked plum-pudding. Green and prickly is the holly, and red are the berries—red for the wounds of Christ and the scarlet robes of an idealized papacy. He is a Christian poet, and therefore being a poet of festivities a prominent Christmas poet:

> There fared a mother driven forth
>   Out of an inn to roam;
> In the place where she was homeless
>   All men are at home.
> The crazy stable close at hand,
> With shaking timber and shifting sand,
> Grew a stronger thing to abide and stand
>   Than the square stones of Rome.

But Chesterton has always been much more popular as a prose writer than as a poet. Probably it is owing to his propagandist vein, for the educated man in the street seems to like his poetry unadulterated, at any rate not infused with any strong sense of social indignation. You may quarrel with capitalism and the Government as much as you like, and be popular, if you do it only in prose; but as soon as you ignore the general aloofness of art to the turmoil of everyday change you are not only apt to spoil your poetry but to lead people into the belief that you are doing so when your hands are exceptionally untarnished. G. K. Chesterton, in spite of his frequent blare and bombast, has been extraordinarily successful in infusing true poetry into his thundering orchestra. God speaking through him, he knows no restraint, but comes at you, marches up the street and round the corner, a rage of music and colour that seeks to hold up the traffic, so that your spirit stands still, and for a moment you stop work and 'down tools'—bemused, feet going, and head awhirl, intoxicated by a rushing rhythm of bacchanal or religious emotion. But poetry that is merely like that does not necessarily contain the enduring line, the wonderful stanza, and it is astonishing that in the verse of Chesterton there is so much of what is really fine, as for instance:

> Ruin is a builder of windows; her legend witnesseth
> Barbara, the saint of gunners, and a stay in sudden death.

Or:

> But all beyond was the wolfish wind
> And the crafty feet of the snow.

Or:

> Tip-toe on all her thousand years and trumpeting to the sun.

Or:

> We have seen the gigantic golden worms
> In the garden of Paradise.

Or:

> There is a game of April Fool that is played behind its door
> Where the fool remains for ever and the April comes no more.

Or:

> There is always a thing forgotten
> When all the world goes well;
> A thing forgotten, as long ago
> When the gods forgot the mistletoe,
> And soundless as an arrow of snow
> The arrow of anguish fell.

Or in a rather more everyday vein:

> The rolling English drunkard made the rolling English road.

Or:

> When you and I went down the lane with ale-mugs in our hands
> The night we went to Glastonbury by way of Goodwin Sands.

Or, triter in speech, but little less memorable:

> The happy men that lose their heads
> They find their heads in heaven.

There is plenty of magic in Chesterton's verse, not exactly
the delicate elfish magic of Yeats or Walter de la Mare, a rather
flick-in-the-eye magic if you like, but none the less evident.
Sometimes, indeed, he achieves it when flying right into the
jaws of bombast he steers miraculously clear, or when formulating a paradox he gets beyond the truth of paradox to the
creation of the rose that shines upon the lips of truth.

Then there is the Chesterton who is memorable because
he says something very droll, even though it be penetratingly
satirical:

> Half of two is one,
> Half of four is two,
> But half of four is forty per cent if your name is Montagu:
> For everything else is on the square
> If done by the best quadratics;
> And nothing is low in High Finance
> Or the Higher Mathematics,

winding up with the very brilliant and veracious:

> Where you hide in the cellar and then look down
> On the poets that live in the attics;
> For the whole of the house is upside down
> In the Higher Mathematics.

At moments he had a scathing tongue, and did not always
avoid the libellous (at any rate not in his prose), though who-
ever he may mean by Montagu steers clear of that. A more
venomous stanza from another poem is fired at the head of an
inanimate substance:

> Tea, although an Oriental,
> Is a gentleman at least;
> Cocoa is a cad and coward,
> Cocoa is a vulgar beast,

> Cocoa is a dull, disloyal,
> Lying, crawling cad and clown,
> And may very well be grateful
> To the fool that takes him down.

But Chesterton was a sort of God's fool, the Almighty's chosen jester, who fearlessly took liberties, secure in most instances beneath his cap and bells.

When his first book of poems came out he was linked up with John Davidson, and though his verse is more like that unfortunate poet's than anybody else's, the coupling seems to have been a little displeasing to both of them. A strong Davidson influence was probably present, but it was no more than an influence and for the most part entirely transmuted and transformed. But hear what he himself has said about it in his autobiography:

My little volume of verse was reviewed with warm and almost overwhelming generosity by Mr James Douglas, then almost entirely known as a leading literary critic. Impetuosity as well as generosity was always one of Mr Douglas's most attractive qualities. And he insisted, for some reason, on affirming positively that there was no such person as G. K. Chesterton; that the name was obviously a *nom de plume*; that the work was obviously not that of a novice, but a successful writer; and finally that it could be none other than Mr John Davidson. This naturally brought an indignant denial from Mr John Davidson. That spirited poet very legitimately thanked the Lord that he had never written such nonsense; and I for one very heartily sympathized with him.

As time went on the severance between Chesterton and John Davidson became only too plain, because where Davidson was bitter, Chesterton was passionately indignant or amusingly malicious; where Davidson was religiously destructive, Chesterton was eminently Christian. Moreover, much in Davidson seems to reveal the influence of Nietzsche—who was Chesterton's stock abhorrence. Chesterton was always on the side of the humble and the downtrodden; but though John Davidson's sympathies also went to the underdog, and though he was in more ways than one the poet of social unrest, admiration for heroic passivity and humility was hardly part of his stock-in-trade. So Chesterton's best-known lyric, *The Donkey*, could not possibly have been written by John Davidson. Moreover, while John Davidson's verse is somewhat formal and syllabic, Chesterton's is infinitely flexible, built upon the ballad, which Davidson did not fully appreciate, in spite of the fact that he called some of his poems 'ballads.' What had John Davidson in his short-lined poems to do with rolling and shifting stress, or sprung rhythm, or anything relative to sprung rhythm? At any rate, not very much.

Hilaire Belloc has always been yoked with Chesterton, and his verse shows strong resemblances. Indeed, in some instances it would be difficult without appended authorship to tell which poem is by which; but though there was manifestly a good deal of interchange, Chesterton seems to be the greater poet, with a larger and more memorable output. Belloc, too, has always been more formal and restrained. He is a sonnet writer of originality, and some of his lyrics are very finely shaped. The pure artist has often triumphed where the passionate lyrist of spontaneity would have failed. Rage and indignation are rarely present in his verse, though in *Lines to a Don*:

> Remote and ineffectual Don
> That dared attack my Chesterton . . .

he seems to let himself go, and in lines which are nearly as rich with anathema and curses as William Dunbar's *Flyting of Kennedie* soundly scourges some real or imaginary foe. Christianity does not enter here, though Belloc as an occasional religious poet is one of the stars in the Catholic diadem.

> Of Courtesy, it is much less
> Than Courage of Heart or Holiness,
> Yet in my Walks it seems to me
> That the Grace of God is in Courtesy.

The rest of this well-known lyric, which charms the ear with its variable rhyme arrangement, most appropriately develops

Catholic *motifs*, and together with a bright sprinkling of similar lyrics sets Belloc among the religious poets of this century.

Yet if one cared to make a distant comparison it would be with the medieval French poet, François Villon, for Belloc's verse has much of Villon's conciseness and hardness of outline, much, too, of Villon's wit, satirical attack, and human irreverence. But it is the genuine expression of Belloc's rather complex, earthly mind, so it is not surprising that in *The Prophet lost in the Hills at Evening* (which probably should be read as semi-personal) he should write:

> It darkens. I have lost the ford.
>   There is a change on all things made.
> The rocks have evil faces, Lord,
>   And I am awfully afraid.

As regards Wilfred Rowland Childe, he is possibly the equal of Belloc as a poet, and certainly beyond him in the amount of his output; but for some reason or other, probably because while a contemporary with the later Georgians he was excluded from Edward Marsh's anthologies, he is a great deal less known than he ought to be. But he is not a characteristic Georgian, being very colourful and ornate, and rubbing shoulders with many of the despised Victorians, particularly William Morris and Francis Thompson, and occasionally echoing poets like Ernest Dowson, as in the gilded tag, 'between the viols and the wine.' Of the poets of this century his position of form and content lies somewhere between G. K. Chesterton and Elroy Flecker.

He also is a religious poet (indeed a Catholic poet of distinction), and, like Chesterton and Belloc, is chiefly inspired by the symbols and beliefs of Christianity and medieval chivalry; and even more than they delights in ritual and embroidery, though as an occasional nature poet he has another side to him. Unfortunately his lyrical tapestry is occasionally dulled by cheap prettiness and the sentimental, commonplace *cliché*. Not all his admirers can approve of every single poem he has published, but when the tinsel and

* G

the chaff have been taken away there remains a firm body
of work which may be remembered in a future age, especially
as he is the last poet to-day writing in that particular vein,
and is likely to be the last for a long time to come. His
Song of the Folk in the Industrial Cities is a miracle of musical
form, a metrical feat of great skill and beauty. It is, too,
sufficiently moving to be convincing, though it totally ignores
the tyranny of the medieval Catholic Church and the ecstatic
vision of the reformers:

We had a loving Mother once, she pleased us with her shows,
A silver Lily in each hand and on her head a Rose,
And on her head a Rose, Jhesu, and on her head a Rose,
And in her hand a Crook, Mary, against the poor flock's foes.

But then rose up the cotton-lords, the iron-lords, the printing-lords,
But then rose up the merchant-lords and they became our kings;
They cut our Mother's cornfields down, they drove her dumb
    beasts out of town,
They trampled on her crystal crown and tore away her rings.

Oswald's green banner down the dales at rush-bearing still sweetly
    sails,
And there are white monks singing sweet in white isles of the sea
    of Wales;
But no more now she singeth sweet, our Mother, in the shouting
    street,
We only hear the noise of wheels, our sick ear feels the stamping feet.

She showed us deaths of Martyrs painted, and when at times our
    spirits fainted,
The precious blood of Brothers sainted burned like a flame through
    drudging days;
But we are become the Martyrs now, the thorns are pressed upon
    our brow,
The wool-lords worship Dividends, they have forgotten Blaise.

Why have you taken away the dolls that the King's Lady gave to us?
They smiled on us when we were sad, they blessed when we were
    dolorous,

Those little dolls that were so fair, with painted wings and gilded
    hair—
You have taken away the toys of a child, you are so tyrannous.

Almost we welcome death and pain, to have our Mother back again;
She bore a Lily in each hand, a silver Lily clean and plain:
We cannot read their books, Jhesu, that are so proud and high,
But we would bring our souls to You, to see the red rose bloom anew,
To have it washed in holy dew, the colours of the sky. . . .

The chief weakness in the poem lies in the two lines beginning
'Oswald's green banner,' for they are obscure and fantastical,
and, moreover, seem to echo Flecker's much more enchanting
Parnassian-*cum*-Symbolist nonsense:

> Evening on the olden, the golden sea of Wales,
> When the first star shivers and the last wave pales:
> O evening dreams!
>   There's a house that Britons walked in, long ago,
>   Where now the springs of ocean fall and flow,
> And the dead robed in red and sea-lilies overhead
>   Sway when the long winds blow.

Mr Childe is also at his best in the satirical *Repentance
of Doctor Faustus* (perhaps the best short poem ever written in
defensive explanation of the stability of organized Christianity):

> The Devil found that curiosity
> Was a most potent goad for human pride.
> What is the colour of a worm's inside?
> How many eyelids has the female flea?
> What is the shape and weight of a man's soul?
> Faustus was much intrigued, and he pursued
> His studies lost in stately solitude,
> Delving far deeper than the patient mole.
> But by long process of analysis
> He came at last on a destructive power,
> That smote him with the claws that stain and stun;
> Then, reeling back from the amused abyss,
> He rushed outside and saw like a white tower
> The Church stand upright, shining in the sun. . . .

Mr Childe has given out that his chief recreation consists in 'regretting the Reformation,' which may suggest moping in his spare time, but more likely implies an enthusiastic, active admiration of medievalism. The titles of some of his books of verse include such defining symbols as *The Gothic Rose* and *Ivory Palaces*; and many of his best lyrics, though somewhat lacking in searching vision or ethical content, are at least vivid tapestry pictures which would have delighted the Pre-Raphaelites. Such a one is *Âge Gothique Doré*, which was originally issued from Magdalen College, and decorates the *Oxford Poetry* volume of 1918.

A poet less known, and one who has insufficiently developed his gift, owing to his devotion to socialistic and iconoclastic journalism, is W. R. Titterton, Chesterton's chief editor. Some of his articles in *The New Witness* and *G. K.'s Weekly* were so admirably written as to be mistaken for Chesterton's own, and in some of his verse also, at any rate in his drinking and convivial songs, he has proved himself an admiring disciple. A book of verse which he published during the War with the flamboyant title *Guns and Guitars*, prompted a facetious reviewer to say that as the title suggested cater-wauling, Mr Titterton must not mind being taken at his word. But though inclined to be very robustious he does not caterwaul, for he has always shown himself a sufficiently tradi-tional craftsman and student of form and order. Conviviality, the girls of London, John Davidson, Richard Middleton, and the madness of modern art and poetry, are among his themes.

His poem on Richard Middleton rates that unfortunate poet rather too highly, though it convinces as a very apt character-sketch:

> Calmly he rests whose soul was like a sea
>   Whippèd by desires unsatisfied, unnamed,
> Was like a trapped god struggling to be free,
>   A fire that never flamed.
>
> .   .   .   .   .
>
> Part woman, part swashbuckler. and part child,
> He was a lord of song.

But Titterton is often at his best in hyperbole, as in:

> King Solomon had ten thousand wives
>   In his house of cedar wood.
> There was Sheba's queen, and Helen of Troy,
>   And little Red Riding Hood.
> But whether their skins were white as milk,
>   Or black as a chimney-sweep,
> There were no flies on the shy gazelles
>   King Solomon used to keep.

That other poet who can be associated with the Chesterton School, though perhaps not directly of it, is William Kean Seymour. His zest and joy of life, and something old-fashioned and right-wing in his speech set him rather apart from the Georgians—among whom one might have expected to find him. He has been a frequent contributor to Chesterton's *New Witness* and *G. K.'s Weekly*, though he has not been very securely caught in the net of their intense loyalties. His *Caesar Remembers*, one of the best, as well as best known, of modern lyrics, is not in any sense political, medieval, or religious, but in its turning away from glory to simplicity, from the contemplation of the achieved summits of ambition to the enduring joys of home and family life, it is distinctly Chestertonian:

> But Caesar cared not
>   For dyke and wall,
> Faint and remote
>   Came the bugles' call;
>
> Soft in the shadows
>   He saw, and heard
> A Roman garden,
>   A Roman bird.

But though Mr Seymour writes more frequently of the wild woodland than the well-ordered garden there is something rather trimmed and tidied (to say nothing of imagist and pictorial) about his zest, as if in putting together his books his thoughts ran on flower-beds. Even in his free-verse experiments there is a sort of familiar compactness, a standing still of Time (*Time stands* and *Caesar remembers* have been the title of two of his books) and once when he wrote of the moorland he was so backward as to set the time-honoured swan among the curlews. His lyric, *Ghost in Garden,* beginning:

> This way, blanched phlox, this way, dim mignonette,
> She trod this path,—do you so soon forget
> How in a charmed obeisance your frail heads
> Bent in the air where still her phantom treads?

is probably one of his half-dozen best poems, and with rather more strangeness and wildness of beauty in it than we have come to expect from him, though his debt to the Elizabethans has always been pretty plain—to say nothing of Chesterton himself in his earlier verse. He is good, too, in a satirical vein, and it is a pity that satire has not more frequently occupied his attention. Also he has played a considerable role as a critic and shepherd. His two volumes of parodies are among the best works of that kind, and his anthologies have helped to draw the public attention to some good poets whom Edward Marsh omitted. Very few contemporary poets have clearer understanding of the technique of verse and the scope and limitations of their fellow-artists than has Mr Kean Seymour.

Not necessarily connected with Chesterton and his followers, but prompting special mention in this chapter are all the poets who may in any way be termed Christian or religious. There are not many of them in this century, and very few who have flowered abundantly since the War. So unprominent are they that W. B. Yeats seems to think that there is only a fraction of one, for in the preface to his extremely odd recent anthology, *The Oxford Book of Modern Verse,* he says:

> When I was young there were almost as many religious poets as live poets and no philosophers. After a search for religious poetry, among the new poets I have found a poem by Force Stead, until lately chaplain of Worcester.

But W. Force Stead is not a new poet, being one of those who were continually passed over by Edward Marsh, and then suddenly rescued by W. Kean Seymour in his *Miscellany of Poetry*, 1920–2. Mr Yeats, in this connection, might nearly as aptly have mentioned Lord Gorell and Edward Thompson, though they are both, particularly Lord Gorell, rather more conventional in their vocabulary and rhythms than is W. Force Stead—a very real poet whom there is no intention to disparage.

But what really do we mean by a religious poet? I suppose it is one who concentrates on Love in its spiritual aspects, on the love of God, on eroticism in relation to God, on love viewed from the angle of Eternity, on reverence and devotion to God, on the continuance of existence beyond this planet, the relationship of Good to Evil in matters Absolute, the rewards and punishments of Good and Evil.

So it is quite clear that others besides W. Force Stead have claim to the title 'religious poet'; among them Gilbert Thomas—the author of the best life of Cowper and his period [1] yet published. In the light of the two fine studies by Lord David Cecil and Hugh I'A. Fausset such praise may sound too superlative, but setting aside the fact that their books must have helped him to write it, there is this special thing to be said about Gilbert Thomas's *Cowper*: it not only shows a very intimate understanding of Cowper's mind and malady, but also a very scholarly knowledge of the religious and social atmosphere which enveloped him, so that one may say with confidence that few better books on English evangelicalism have ever been written—few more human, more contemplatively spiritual, or more creative in their own peculiar Puritan sphere. Mr Gilbert Thomas has been reared in that peculiar Puritan atmosphere (Methodist rather than Congregational or Presbyterian, Arminian rather than Calvinist) which makes him the completely right person to deal with Cowper; and his own verse, sincere, though conventional, is not entirely unlike Cowper's, for we are confronted by similar religious motives, an equal variety of theme, and stress

[1] *William Cowper and the Eighteenth Century.*

upon lucid content rather than verbal magic and dynamic strangeness of form. It is both difficult and unsatisfactory to prove his quality in a single selection, but this lyric from *Mary of Huntington* should give some idea of his religious fervour, and his outmoded language and rhythms at their best:

> I drew the blind on Christmas Morn,
>   The sky was one wild riot of red.
> Its glory told me Christ was born,
>   Yet filled my soul with dread.
>
> Against the dawn's too radiant light,
>   There stood a solitary Tree,
> Its naked arms were black as night
>   And grim with prophecy.

It is probably the consciousness of all that Christianity means (embodied in that strong outburst of spiritual passion) which has shackled modern poets and prevented them from giving expression to Christianity—which makes ardent demands upon Life, but leaves Art (and, I suppose, necessarily so) rather as a decorated aside. Life has so changed and is so much in the melting-pot, that Art seems to be of no consequence. You must either devote your service to science and the machine, or throw in your lot with the self-sacrificing individualists, the Christian workers for the uplift of the working classes. Declarations of Christian fervour too often sound like insincere verbiage, a luxury of emotionalism which is to take the place of social action. The same applies to pulpit preachings, and probably explains the unpopularity of the clergy. The artist feels himself entirely useless, and such being the case, he prefers any kind of uselessness to the uselessness of mere verbal Christianity. The heroic accept the situation and say: 'I say this because I must say it, because the Deity wills me to say it, and I must take no notice of aims and results.' But how next to impossible is it in these latter days to be heroic, to do a thing well for the mere sake of doing it, to say a thing finely for the mere sake of saying it.

Among religious poets, or religiously inclined poets of great early promise, who made an uncertain contemporary reputation, but who finally gave up poetry for criticism, are Hugh I'A. Fausset, J. Middleton Murry, Max Plowman, and R. Ellis Roberts. They have probably got more lasting satisfaction out of praising and saving others, though anthologies occasionally disclose a short poem from one of them which makes us glad that they did not quite bury the blooms of their early flowering. None of these poets were as the Georgian fairies, knowing neither good nor evil, and probably the deeply philosophic and contemplative nature of their outlook was an aesthetic hindrance. Middleton Murry, who is, I believe, our greatest living authority on Keats and Shakespeare, has published several little books of verse that promised splendid things to come, and in which an aspiring, if somewhat too tortured and groping imagination does sometimes successfully free itself. But he chose not to go on. Some of Ellis Roberts's lyrics are still uncollected (he is clearly religious minded, and has high-church sympathies); but Max Plowman (the least prolific of the four as a critic) and Hugh I'A. Fausset (who has probably published more good volumes of literary criticism than any man living) have many little books of verse to their names, the value of which has perhaps not yet been truly assessed. For I wonder how many know that little pearl of modern lyrics by Max Plowman:

> I heard them say, 'Her hands are hard as stone,'
> And I remembered how she laid for me
> The road to heaven. They said, 'Her hair is grey.'
> Then I remembered how she once had thrown
> Long plaited strands, like cables, into the sea
> I battled in—the salt sea of dismay.
> They said, 'Her beauty's past.' And then I wept,
> That these, who should have been in love adept,
> Against my fount of beauty should blaspheme,
> And hearing a new music, miss the theme.

They have concentrated on theme (chiefly the theme of Love) rather than form, and yet there occur occasional moments in the work of all of them when theme and form triumphantly interlock and produce the striking or memorable passage.

CHAPTER XII

THE GEORGIAN MOONLIGHT SCENE; AND THE SECOND GEORGIAN REVOLT

A SUCCESSOR to the first volume of *Georgian Poetry* was published during the second year of the War. Its longest feature was a short play by Gordon Bottomley, *King Lear's Wife*, one of his several one-act plays. Here was something of the language and mind of Shakespeare, but with less of his gift of sentence and phrase, less than half his bite and snap, and insufficient of his dramatic stir and movement—the main influence seeming to come from W. B. Yeats (the dialogue is very dreamy), particularly his play *The Countess Cathleen*. But Gordon Bottomley stands closer to the Elizabethans than do most of the other Georgians, and it has been to his disadvantage that he has not concentrated more on dramatic machinery and less on pure poetry (the poetry of lyrical drama and its involved restraints), otherwise he might as a popular dramatist have taken the place of Stephen Phillips—who, however, never had his fine gifts of song. Mix together Masefield and Gordon Bottomley with an infusion from Lascelles Abercrombie and one might be rather sure of producing the best European dramatist in the romantic current since Shakespeare. Perhaps such epithets and substantives as 'gorgeous' and 'gorgeousness' as applied to him by one of his greatest admirers, R. L. Mégroz,[1] are too superlative to describe his best true qualities, though there is no doubt that he has never been given the high place which is his due. His shorter poems, too, have much imaginative depth, and his semi-satirical *To Iron-founders and Others* (of which I quote two powerful stanzas) is still the one supreme lyric against our erring civilization, though it is a pity that it was written too

[1] See Mégroz's critical study, *Modern English Poetry : 1882–1932*.

early in the century to include tarred roads and recent vulgar architecture:

> You have brought down the firmament
> And yet no heaven is more near;
> You shape huge deeds without event,
> And half made men believe and fear.
>
> Your worship is your furnaces,
> Which, like old idols, lost obscenes,
> Have molten bowels; your vision is
> Machines for making more machines.

A formidable newcomer turned up in the person of Ralph Hodgson. His small early book, *The Last Blackbird*, published in 1907, had not been successful; but in 1913 he issued two short lyrics, *Time, you Old Gipsy Man* and *Eve*, and some tiny scraps, in a thin paper-backed volume, the two lyrics reprinted from the *Saturday Review*. Their technique and music were such that they brought him immediate fame. Probably no poet on so small an output has ever been so whole-heartedly acclaimed; but his verse had worked a miracle, for it united a popular note with the highest literary and artistic achievement. The note, too, seemed new, though actually it was a resurrection of something whispering through James Hogg, the Ettrick Shepherd, particularly his lovely lyric to a skylark:

> Bird of the wilderness
> Blithesome and cumberless,
> Sweet be thy matin o'er moorland and lea! . . .

From Hogg, Ralph Hodgson turned to William Blake and Christopher Smart, the technique of Blake obvious enough in *The Bull*, and that of Smart in *The Song of Honour*. Both these rather long poems were reprinted by Edward Marsh. But Ralph Hodgson wrote little more. A very thrifty rhymer, he had little to say, and what he did say was shaped with consummate mastery. Whether or not, like Crabbe, he will write again and break silence in his old age, is a question for hope rather than probability, for there is a radiant bubble of extreme youth in his verse—and that can rarely be repeated.

Another newcomer was the Irish peasant poet, Francis Ledwidge. Here was a poet more apparent in promise than actual performance. If he had lived he would certainly have gone a long way, possibly as far as James Stephens. Unfortunately he was killed in the War.

On the whole, this second Georgian anthology is better than the first. It contains more poems of distinction, more memorable lyrics. Harold Monro is shown at his very best, and his swing towards the Left-wing is only dimly discernible. He was ultimately to move away from Georgian poetry, to land himself in the awful impasse of *Bitter Sanctuary*, a poem that may be good once you hold the key, but bewildering and unsatisfactory to most readers, as it does not explain itself, and is expressive of pain without that magic of phrase and line which makes the contemplation of pain tolerable or even alluring. Harold Monro was often at his best in verse of not very profound significance, such as *Milk for the Cat*, and his tendency to overreach himself, to express some dark turmoil of his under-mind, was sometimes defeating, for he could not quite communicate what he insufficiently held in the palms of his hands. As an objective poet contemplating the house furniture or animals or trees, he was good so long as he did not mix his own being too morbidly in the coil. He turned aside from God and all higher romance, at any rate he was against traditional loyalties, and *Children of Love* (included by Edward Marsh) not only seems expressive of the rather non-Christian, non-religious character of Georgian poetry (though Georgian poetry was nearly all quite innocent in its non-morality), but is intensely expressive of Monro's own anti-Puritan attitude. In the volume named *Children of Love* (after the best lyric in it) he wrote:

> God, I've stayed thy hated guest
> In thy tavern far too long,

and

> God, thou melancholy host,
> Greybeard without any jest.

But God is spoken of rather more reverently in *The Rebellious Vine*, which is possibly the best short lyric expressive of the purely *fatalist* attitude to life ever written.

On the cover of *Children of Love* there is a black-and-white picture of Cupid shooting from a bow, and it is interesting to note that not only is the bow a little fantastical in shape, but it is reversed, and doing something that is against the nature of a bow. Here, at any rate (1914), was one of the beginnings of Modernism. Monro's imagination moved more and more in the direction of the sombre and nightmarish; but his handling of words was fresh and simple (sometimes, indeed, powerful) and his literary derivations not too obvious—though Cowper, strange to say, seemed to be one of them, and A. E. Housman, whom he professed to despise, unconsciously seemed to be another. After them, at a later date, among his admirations came T. S. Eliot and the three Sitwells. But because snatches of his book, *Children of Love*, particularly a part of the realistic poem *Suburb*, really do emphatically remind one of something in Eliot in his more lucid moments, and the book preceded nearly everything written by Eliot, the boot may be chiefly on the other leg.

Monro had three distinctly different notes, but though as a Nature poet he was a mere week-ender, the future will probably esteem him for his sincere attempts to show the affinity of man with the natural life of the soil, and for his frequent domestic poems, and for such odd genial stanzas and couplets as:

> Life is no good unless the morning brings
> White happiness and quick delight of day.

The Georgian anthologies were published from Harold Monro's Poetry Bookshop in Devonshire Street; so, of course, he had to try to serve two masters. After the appearance of the third of them (1917), Monro's influence seems to have started giving way to that of J. C. Squire (now Sir John Squire), a formidable poet who chose too often to be merely experimentally bad, and the 'Solomon Eagle' of many learned *Observer* and early *New Statesman* essays in contemporary criticism. And here we come to an important cross-roads in literary history—the Second Georgian Revolt, which was followed shortly after the War by the foundation by J. C. Squire of the *London Mercury*.

The first Georgian anthology wobbled a little, it seemed not to know completely where it was; the second crystallized its purpose and aims, though the inclusion of Elroy Flecker's Pre - Raphaelite - *cum* - Parnassian - Symbolist poem, *Gates of Damascus*, constituted a curious anachronism. But in the third (1917) there is not only a further emphasis of crystallization, but a forward movement towards completer exclusiveness. Impressionist Nature poetry was from henceforth to be the central pivot round which all was to circulate, and the boisterous influence of Masefield (a Jonah in the Georgian boat) and other ruddy poets was to be thoroughly checked. But the sky was to be one of night rather than day, the light which bathed the landscape the light of the moon rather than the light of the sun, and the Celtic Twilight (which exercised a good deal of influence upon Georgian poetry, particularly in its later developments) was to be translated into Anglo-Saxon moonlight. But there was also present something foreign, 'Parnassian,' in fact—for French influences, Parnassian as well as Symbolist, had got into a little of both Flecker's work and J. C. Squire's, and these two poets wrought upon the general atmosphere of the later Georgian period.

The most notable and original poem (the very key and centre of it) in this third Georgian anthology is J. C. Squire's *Lily of Malud*. It covers several pages, of which the early part is very good, and most of the rest uncertain or uneven, though the long stanza of the end is effective enough.

But the first thirty lines are rich with strange beauty, mysterious nonsense, alluring magic:

The lily of Malud is born in secret mud.
It is breathed like a word in a little dark ravine
Where no bird was ever heard and no beast was ever seen,
And the leaves are never stirred by the panther's velvet sheen.

.   .   .   .   .   .

When the world is full of night, and the moon reigns alone
And drowns in silver light the known and the unknown,
When each hut is a mound, half blue-silver and half black,
And casts upon the ground the hard shadow of its back,
When the winds are out of hearing and the tree-tops never shake,
When the grass in the clearing is silent but awake
'Neath a moon-paven sky:

Then suddenly occurs not only the very best passage in
Squire, but also one of the most enchantingly beautiful in
modern poetry:

From the doors the maidens creep,
Tiptoe over dreaming curs, soft, so soft, that not one stirs,
And stand curved and a-quiver, like bathers by a river,
Looking at the forest wall, groups of slender naked girls,
Whose black bodies shine like pearls where the moonbeams fall.

Such passages appear to constitute the central orbs round
which so many of the poems in the third, fourth, and fifth
Georgian anthologies seem to circulate. It has, I think, by
now been forgotten that there was a time when Squire was
as much a force as Eliot, and though his power and influence
were not entirely due to literary hypnotism, his personality
in one way and another exercised a dominating influence,
considerably more dominating than that of Harold Monro—
who for many years jostled him for the position of poetry
dictator.

Squire's next most important poem is probably his long
ode *The Moon*, published separately in a slender volume in
1920, and overlooked by the anthologists. It is considerably
more even than *The Lily of Malud*, infinitely better than *Rivers*
(a flat, machine-made piece of work), and rather better than
Birds—the three longest poems by which up to the present he
is best known. It asserts his aesthetic vision more clearly
than does *The Lily of Malud*, and with the exception of *To a
Musician* and *To a Roman* (a very interesting and gripping poem
about Catullus) is less thickly streaked with prosy and commonplace lines and passages than is so much of his longer
work. For there is this to be specially noted about Squire:

his Parnassian craft, though sufficiently obvious, and well sustained in many of his short poems—clear, pictorial, cool, thrifty, musical—is also continually breaking down, and even dissolving into wobbling verbiage. And he even deliberately runs away from his best self, searching, it seems, for newer and more flexible forms. But that is not the real Squire, the poet of silvery quietness and sombre meditation, the poet of Diana:

> High over all this England will she ride;
>   She silvers all the roofs of folded towns,
> Her brilliance tips the edge of every tide,
>   Her shadows make soft caverns in the downs;
> Even now, beyond my tree serenely sailing,
> She clothes far forests with a gauzy veiling.
>   And even as here, where now I stare and dream,
> Standing my own transfigured banks beside,
>   On many a quiet wandering English stream
>   There lies the unshifting image of her beam.
>
>   .   .   .   .   .   .
>
> A night there was, a crowd, a narrow street,
>   Torches that reddened faces drunk with dreams,
> An orator exultant in defeat,
>   Banners, fierce songs, rough cheering, women's screams;
> My heart was one with those rebellious people,
> Until along a chapel's pointing steeple
>   My eyes unwitting wandered to a thin
> Crescent, and clouds a swift and ragged sheet;
>   And in my spirit's life all human din
>   Died, and eternal Silence stood within.

Very few of its other twenty-nine stanzas fall behind that luminous unveiling—but the poem is much more effective as a whole than in any of its parts.

J. C. Squire's Moon! His own verse is hag-ridden by it; and it was on the banner of all the New Poetry. On the banner of the new-comers—Shanks, Freeman, and W. J. Turner—casting its silvery beams across the whole landscape of Georgian verse. Even a hurried glance at the third, fourth, and fifth volumes is sufficient to thrust away any doubts.

And even in the second volume we see it coming. One of
the best of Davies's lyrics begins:

> Thy beauty haunts me heart and soul,
> Oh thou fair Moon, so close and bright!

And the white saucer prepared for Harold Monto's cat descends
from the table like 'some full moon,' and the nymph of his
Overheard on a Saltmarsh tells the goblin that she stole her beads
'out of the moon.'

Even though the moon be not mentioned by name it is
frequently felt. The landscape is hushed. The winds are
still, with just faint clouds trailing their gauzy edges across
its disk. The music of the verse is slow and mournful. The
colours are uncertain, tending to dissolve into greys and dark
greens and silvery blues. The Celtic Twilight has moved
forward into the Georgian Moonlight. But the glamour is
less, the suggestion of hope is less, and the romantic attri-
butes are fewer. Still, how beautiful are some of these moon
poems, and among the very choicest of the Georgian exhibits,
including John Freeman's *Moon-bathers* and his still lovelier
It was the Lovely Moon, John Drinkwater's *Moonlit Apples*, and
V. Sackville-West's *Full Moon*.

But Victoria Sackville-West's *Full Moon* (which appeared
in the fifth Georgian anthology) is rather apart from her other
work, and looks like a gesture of homage to the new school.

> She was wearing the coral taffeta trousers
> Someone had brought her from Ispahan,
> And the little gold coat with pomegranate blossoms,
> And the coral-hafted feather fan;
> And she ran down a Kentish lane in the moonlight
> And skipped in the pool of the moon as she ran.
>
> She cared not a rap for all the big planets,
> For Betelgeuse or Aldebaran,
> And all the big planets cared nothing for her,
> The small impertinent charlatan;
> But she climbed on a Kentish stile in the moonlight,
> And laughed at the sky through the sticks of her fan.

A gesture of homage?   But equally likely a gesture of derision:
'The small impertinent charlatan.'   And it was the planets
which were big and important rather than the moon.   An
odd, delightful, jaunty little lyric, which, in spite of its title
Full Moon, does *not* really get the moonlight atmosphere of the
new domination, and makes no particular bow to the Man
in the Moon, whether that be J. C. Squire or a mere allegorical
presence.

John Drinkwater's *Moonlit Apples*, in the fourth Georgian
anthology, is more obviously a piece of hat-lifting, but gets
the atmosphere with great beauty, and with rather more energy
of movement than characterizes most of such work:

> They are lying in rows there, under the gloomy beams
> On the sagging floor; they gather the silver streams
> Out of the moon, those moonlit apples of dreams,
>   And quiet is the steep stair under.

The high priests of the Georgian moonlight tabernacle were,
of course, not John Drinkwater, or V. Sackville-West, or
W. H. Davies.   The school is really made up of J. C. Squire,
John Freeman, W. J. Turner, and Edward Shanks, with
Walter de la Mare (a technical and atmospheric influence)
running round them and perfuming the skirts of their flowing
robes.   Edward Shanks, however, is rather less obviously in
the group, though much of his verse conveys the unmistakable
atmosphere.

Turner, as time went on, began to show his feet in two
camps, changing from Georgian into neo-Georgian and then
into Modernist.   He is the most intellectual of the four, and
the most expanding and strange.   The exoticism of Squire's
Lily of Malud (a tropical night under moonlight) threads through
all his early and middle work, occurring again and again in his
later pages.   Poe, Keats, and Baudelaire seem to have been
among his literary admirations, and like Poe he has sought
to capture the speech of Music (an impossible feat) and set
it into the net of words.   His position as musical critic on
the *New Statesman* has brought him before a rather wide public,

but not all of his admirers know that he is a poet, and his
enthusiasm for orchestral music has probably been at variance
with his literary instrument.   His world is a dream world—
a deeper dream world than that of the more fantastical and
nonsensical Edith Sitwell—and his verse is more symbolical
(and therefore potentially more truly poetry) than that of his
contemporary spiritual comrades.

> In Time like glass the stars are set,
> And seeming-fluttering butterflies
> Are fixèd fast in Time's glass net
> With mountains and with maids' bright eyes.
>
> Above the cold Cordilleras hung
> The wingèd eagle and the Moon.   .   .

A little of his verse is incomprehensible on a first and second
reading, one has to enjoy it for its felicity of line and music
and strange imagery.   It is as if violin and 'cello had set up
some untranslatable emotion, to crystallize itself more perfectly in sleep, from which state, half rousing himself, he has
essayed to write.   He is a mystic, but not a religious mystic,
and every now and again he drifts into uncompromising
bitterness:

> I no longer seek to hold
>   Beauty with enchanted eyes;
> 'Tis vain, for beauty dies, I know,
>   I know beauty dies.
>
> Ring the merry marriage bells,
>   That most melancholy sound!
> When the bridegroom and the bride
>   Go to find what none has found.

The fire in him is a dark cold fire, the light sombre, the
emotion very restrained, and when he writes of Nature (and
Edward Marsh, of course, strove to show that infrequent side
of him), it is in a strange windless silence of grey-white light,

his eyes frequently cast upon an aspect of life that is dead and gone:

> He carved the red deer and the bull
>   Upon the smooth cave rock,
> Returned from war with belly full,
>   And scarred with many a knock,
> He carved the red deer and the bull
>   Upon the smooth cave rock.
>
> The stars flew by the cave's wide door,
>   The clouds wild trumpets blew,
> Trees rose in wild dreams from the floor,
>   Flowers with dream faces grew. . . .

And in his *Search for the Nightingale* which he sub-titles 'Recollection of reading Keats's Ode when a boy near Mount Olinda, Australia,' he chants gloomily:

> And then I came unto an older world:
> The woods were damp, the sun
> Shone in a watery mist, and soon was gone;
> The trees were thick with leaves, heavy and old,
> The sky was grey, and blue, and like the sea
> Rolling with mists and shadowy veils of foam.
> I heard the roaring of an ancient wind
> Among the elms and in the tattered pines;
> And riding out into a pale lagoon
> I saw with gauzy sails a scudding Moon.

But in one of his least effective poems he brandishes a glaring inaccuracy, one of these faults against naturalism which have helped to get the Georgian pastorals nicknamed 'the week-enders.' He tells us that the music of streams among chalk hills has a tin-canny sound, and that the tin is polished. (What exactly is meant by 'polished tin'?) Worse still, the streams fall down from the chalk-hills—which of course does not happen, the behaviour of running water being very different from what it is in the rocky mountainous country of the north and west. Chalk being porous, the rain sinks into underground reservoirs under the hills, and so the streams have no fall, but issue from the bases of the hills, and nothing like this:

> In low chalk hills the great King's body lay,
> And bright streams fell, tinkling like polished tin,
> As though they carried off his armoury
> And spread it glinting through his wide domain.

But Sir John Squire set a similar bad example of inaccuracy when he wrote in the initial stanza of his worst long poem, *Rivers*:

> And streams down-tumbling from the chalk hills
> To valleys of meadows and watercress-beds.

There has manifestly been some interchange between the two poets; for there is also a tinge of similarity between Squire's *Lily of Malud* and Turner's *Talking with Soldiers*. At any rate there is a faint suggestion of similarity in such a stanza as:

> The mind of the people is like mud,
> From which arise strange and beautiful things,
> But mud is none the less mud,
> Though it bear orchids and prophesying Kings,
> Dreams, trees, and water's bright babblings.

Mr Turner is a typical Georgian in that he is somewhat deficient in ecstasy, and when he labels one of his most beautiful lyrics *Ecstasy* (a blank-verse poem which is so mellifluous in its language that it cajoles you into thinking it is written in rhyme) one feels that he is using the term a little exclusively:

> I saw a frieze on whitest marble drawn
> Of boys who sought for shells along the shore,
> Their white feet shedding pallor in the sea,
> The shallow sea, the spring-time sea of green
> That faintly creamed against the cold, smooth pebbles.

Both Freeman and Shanks are better and broader nature poets than either Squire or Turner, more correct, and much more in the current of the Wordsworthian tradition. Actually, of course, Turner isn't a nature poet at all, for his lyrical mind is semi-tropical and shut off from the contemplation of the phenomena of the English countryside, while Squire has been little more than a 'week-ender,' glad of a brief escape from the pavement, but never quite at one with any natural landscape. It is necessary to diverge like this, because the poets who clustered around Squire have been called 'Jack Squire's Country Boys' and the inner centre of that clustering 'The Squirearchy.' Strictly speaking the Squirearchy was composed of Squire, Shanks, and Freeman—though W. J. Turner has been included in the minds of many, and the second Georgian Revolt is almost identical with the triumph of the Squirearchy.

When we turn to John Freeman and Edward Shanks, though we are still among the moon-bathers, we are for the most part freed from the tropical greenhouse and from Nature contemplated from the unsafe limits of the library.

John Freeman is a poet of country life and the sky. When he was not at business (he was the secretary of a highly successful insurance society) he was contemplating Nature and writing about her with charm and strong fancy. His voice sounds original, and his technique pleasantly striking. But much of his verse lacks colour, sinew, and incisiveness; and though some readers may dimly think of Wordsworth, they will be more conscious of trees than rolling hills, and of white moonlight than illuminating sunlight. His gentle, melancholy, rather intangible verse rustles and rustles without pause; but it is shot through with frequent meditation, developing occasionally (chiefly in his later poems) into really profound thought—though almost stifled by the hush, hush, hush of night and twilight winds. Here is beauty, some-times exquisite, though the colours of it are rather too monotonously silver or pearly grey, and very little of it, owing to his avoidance of striking phrases (a typical Georgian idiosyncrasy), remains permanently rooted in the mind. But though some of his lines are tinged with echoes from his favourite poets (for instance in the lyric beginning 'The joyous morning ran and kissed the grass' there are distinct echoes from FitzGerald's rendering of the *Rubáiyát* of Omar Khayyám), he generally speaks through his own particular instrument. He has a manner which, however much he has been influenced by his readings, is sufficiently his own, nowhere more clearly evidenced than in *Stone Trees*:

> Last night a sword-light in the sky
> Flashed a swift terror on the dark.
> In that sharp light the fields did lie
> Naked and stone-like; each tree stood
> Like a tranced woman, bound and stark.
>   Far off the wood
> With darkness ridged the riven dark.

But in some of his lyrics, such as *Moon Bathers* (where there is a very arresting movement in the blank verse), he is technically not unlike the early Laurence Binyon of the shorter poems:

> Falls from her heaven the Moon, and stars sink burning
> Into the sea where blackness rims the sea,
> Silently quenched. Faint light that the waves hold
> Is the only light remaining; yet still gleam
> The sands where those now-sleeping young moon-bathers
> Came dripping out of the sea. . . .

Yet rarely is he as sombrely powerful as in:

> the light hung still

> Like a painted thing, and deadly.
> Then from the cloud's side flickered
> Sharp lightning, thrusting madly
>   At the cowering fields.

His greatest admirer has always been Sir John Squire, who has pointed out that, besides pastoralism, one of the themes which most firmly and widely occupied the attentions of his Muse, was the theme of Love. It is to be expected, of course, in so meditative a moon-poet, especially as one of his few colourful lyrics is about Venus:

Rose-bosom'd and rose-limb'd
With eyes of dazzling bright
Shakes Venus mid the twined boughs of the night;
Rose-limb'd, soft-stepping
From bough to bough . . .

In the course of a very sympathetic preface to a large volume of posthumous poems, J. C. Squire says of him:

Were all his love poetry assembled Swinburne's words might far more aptly be applied to it than to Gautier's scented novel: 'This is the golden book of spirit and sense.' The deepest abysses of Love's hell he had plumbed, and, for such a man, the blackest of all where abides the agony of self-reproach. . . . Every doubt, craving, jealousy, sullenness, resentment known to lovers was familiar to him, all the unachieved communions of the brain and all the frustrated desires of the insatiable flesh: and every experience was to him, it may be, peculiarly intense, because of the imminent shadow of death which overhung him, lending a deeper gloom to discontent and a sharper edge to joy.

There is probably a tinge of exaggeration in some of that, for when one is writing about deceased personal friends the sympathetic heart is apt to give a man rather more than his lawful due; but the central evidence is manifest enough, and no anthology of love-poetry would be complete without some emphasis upon John Freeman.

That other associate with J. C. Squire, who was for many years his assistant-editor on the *London Mercury*, Edward Shanks, is another who has dwelt frequently upon the theme of frustrated love, but with perhaps more of philosophical resignation than John Freeman—especially recorded in his memorable:

I have known love, and thrice or more
Has beauty on my pleading smiled,
For one or two my heart was sore,
And one I loved was a fairy's child.

Fairies are neither good nor evil
But strange: they follow different laws.
Fool that I was in her to level
Human effect and fairy cause!

With that deception sick and spent
I wept alone, but now I see
She was, though wide her footsteps went,
Faithful to love if not to me.

But many of his poems speak also of satisfied and comforting love, as in *Song, The Triumph of Love,* and *Reality.* He has many affinities with John Freeman, but he is less profound in his contemplative pieces, and the movements of his verse are rather more Victorian and traditional. He is more of a pastoral poet than John Freeman, the hues on his pages are a brighter green, his contact with Nature rather more physical. He rides on horseback, rambles through the country, stares round him and looks aloofly at the people, goes down to the river or seashore, swims, and I dare say shoots rabbits. But one has continually the feeling that he likes the evening best, and that, though melancholy in the night, he is happy in the night, and that he is another Diana worshipper. Though he is not quite so haunted by the moon and the silvery silences of the night as is John Freeman, he nevertheless is haunted. His daytime landscapes never really burn with the sun, and he never gives himself up to any ecstasy of morning joy. He is at his best in such poems as *A Night Piece,* which starts with two stanzas which are among the most felicitous in modern verse:

Come out and walk. The last few drops of light
    Drain silently out of the cloudy blue;
The trees are full of the dark-stooping night,
    The fields are wet with dew.

All 's quiet in the wood but, far away—
    Look down the hillside and across the plain—
Moves, with long trail of white that marks its way,
    The softly panting train.

But he has written more than one night piece, and in *The King's Dancer* he tells the story of a moon-worshipper in delicately wrought blank verse:

H

> But he came one night
> Through the black shadows of the mighty trees,
> Black and immense beneath the risen moon,
> Unseen, unheard. The negroes crept behind
> Blotted in shade. He picked his way to the gate
> And through the filigree of coiled gold
> He saw her little garden full of light,
> Wherein she danced alone and not for him,
> But with her moon-white arms to the risen moon
> She offered her beauty and her sacred steps.

In the same poem occurs one of those glaring examples of stark fancy, where mere fancy takes the place of imagination —one of the most frequent Georgian pitfalls:

> The scattered and stricken clouds that fly in shreds
> Across the face of the moon and are lost in night
> And die in bitter space for love of the moon.

Perhaps there is more of fancy than imagination in the art of Edward Shanks. . . . In the same poem the king orders the dancer's ankles to be broken as a punishment—for what? For putting the moon in front of His Royal Highness? Is that faithful to any kind of central or imaginative truth? Or is it just a mere unreining of Edward Shanks's pleasure in the macabre? But he did not often thus let himself go. He was too well-ordered a Georgian for that. It did not suit the new vogue—which avoided the grim and unpleasant as much as the passionate.

One of his best short poems is *Searchlights*, which he says is 'in the manner of Paul Fort.' But surely the comparison is nonsensical. Surely it is much more in the manner of Elroy Flecker (see *Gates of Damascus*), a poet whom, I believe, Edward Shanks much admired—though he rarely has his plangency or symbolism:

O searchlights, pierce the nights with swords and drive the stars in ruin thence; the moon in cold indifference looks down upon your leaping hordes.

Storm the old ramparts of the sky and shake the planets all awry,
pull, if you can, the young moon down upon the house-tops of the
town.

He has written out the stanzas as prose lines. But let us
rearrange and then compare them with the stanzas in *Gates
of Damascus*:

O searchlights, pierce the nights with swords and drive the stars
    in ruin thence;
The moon in cold indifference looks down upon your leaping
    hordes.

Storm the old ramparts of the sky and shake the planets all awry,
Pull, if you can, the young moon down upon the house-tops of the
    town.

The texture of line and division of line is exactly the same,
and though in the first stanza you may point to Oscar Wilde's
Sphinx (Tennyson's *In Memoriam* stanza written out as two
lines instead of four), in the second the rhyme arrangement
is more conventional—and thus the same alternatives of two-
rhyme arrangements are used as by Flecker in *Gates of
Damascus*.

And now because of certain indelible happenings it seems
necessary to push myself into the arena. What, I would ask,
was my own personal attitude to the new poetry? . . . It
was becoming more and more adverse. This worship of the
moon, which suggested an approaching disease of literary
anaemia, and an acceptance of some of the worst post-War
conditions of passive materialism, began to pluck hard at my
nerves. Admiration and pleasure were, at moments, completely smothered by a very critical hostility. I felt that the
lordly sun was not getting his fair fee, that he was in a decline,
and that the English landscape was in danger of completely
sinking into the lullaby arms of Night. English poetry was
gradually getting dominated by the School of the Lunar
Pastorals, and the moon was becoming the symbol of too much
that was spiritually frightening. So after the War some hard

stones were flung by me into the Georgian camp, among them a *Denunciatory Ode to the Moon* which was printed in the *Saturday Westminster*, and of which here are the first two stanzas:

As I was moorwards faring
 I was aware of eyes,—
A wrinkled visage staring
 From out December skies,—
The Moon, an astral shilling,
Her silvern radiance spilling
Like mammon light in darkness
 Along the moorland rise.

I know thee, ghastly symbol,
 How once on sulphurous morn
When skies swung harp and timbrel
 Thou wast conceived and born,—
God's sign of slow damnation;
Drear whirling desolation!
I have discerned His meaning,
 And render Fate my scorn.

The ink was scarcely dry when it was answered by John Freeman in the *Spectator* with a poem he entitled *The Murdered Face* (of which here is the last stanza):

But as a murdered face in agitation
Of windy flaw,
The argent moon wrinkles in angry pain;
Eyes stare in dream of pain.
Wind on the willow's bosom falls and moans,
Hiding in floating cloud the moon's torn face.

But what did all this, in a beneficial as well as noxious sense, really mean? . . . It meant that passion was dying, that it was thought better that it should die, that emotions during the early part of the War had been keyed to too high a pitch, and that henceforth poets must seek strength in completer escape, in farther withdrawal from the turmoil of religion, of politics, of patriotism, of active life. The sun, the old life-giver, had gone corrupt; the moon, the new life-giver, was to be the symbol of the new serene order in the world of poetry, of art, of human life. Suppression! Resignation! Restraint! The key-notes of the first two Georgian anthologies were strengthened, and the aesthetic tendencies of the New Age more fully revealed. The third Georgian anthology is more completely Georgian than the first two, the fourth and fifth still more so.

But, of course, the change could not be too drastic, and some adverse elements continued to be admitted. For instance, in the third Georgian anthology the War poets first made their appearance, for they could not be kept out. And though in most of the poetry of Siegfried Sassoon there is a complete turning away from the old contemplation of the glamour of war and its exaltation, in Herbert Asquith's short lyric *The Volunteer*, there is a revival of the Victorian attitude, while in Robert Nichols's *Assault* and Robert Graves's *It's a Queer Time* the sensational excitement of war is again portrayed. The chief technical influence upon these War poets was John Masefield. But A. E. Housman was claimed by Sir Edmund Gosse as their chief written inspiration; and there is also little doubt that Wilfrid Gibson, William Davies, and even Thomas Hardy had been specially cultivated by them.

But all strong emotionalism, as well as war clamour, was in the way. It was a barrier against the new movements in poetry, and acted as a stifling influence upon the new poets —whose leader now was quite obviously J. C. Squire. So in 1917 (two and a half years after the start of the War) he issued a volume of parodies called *Tricks of the Trade*, and it was so successful that before the end of the War it had run into a fifth edition. The chief enemy appears to have been John Masefield, and of its eighty peppery pages, sixteen were devoted to ridiculing and parodying him. Some of it, though side-crackingly funny, is rather unfortunate, for it seems to ridicule the Salvation Army and emotional evangelicalism as much as John Masefield, the content of spiritual passion rather than the outer sun-fire expression of it—which, of

course, parody should not do. And it gives the victim no
marks at all; and parody should be rather fairer than that:

> The mother swooned; the children joined in prayer
>   That Flo should not decide in such a fast time;
> But the fierce heavens cried beer was a snare
>   And skittles was a most immoral pastime;
>   So that that evening for the very last time
> She washed the pots and locked the 'Fountain' door,
> As she had done so many nights before.

> Next day she went out early without warning
>   Down the wan street; and later in the day,
> That is to say well on into the morning,
>   She sent a District Messenger to say
>   That she had definitely gone away
> To join the Battersea Salvation Army.
> 'Swipe me,' her mother moaned, 'the gal's gone barmy.'

The stanza that precedes the first of these is almost too
irreverent to reprint—and it may well be asked, when did
Masefield ever write anything quite like this, especially as
the convert to religion has just committed a ghastly murder,
and, with insufficient bearing on any happening in the poems
of Masefield, could not morally dodge punishment and become a shining light of the Salvation Army—as takes place
in Squire's parody? There is not much in *The Everlasting
Mercy* which evangelical Methodism regards as impossible,
which indeed has not happened many thousands of times;
and what Masefield has perhaps failed to communicate con-
vincingly is the transition period between brutal abandon and
the moment of conviction of forgiveness of sin, the man's
conversion being, as regards point of time, perhaps a little
too sudden. But in the religious world the strangest and most
sudden things do happen. What is so immensely difficult
is to show that sudden change, and make the reader completely realize it.

As regards Squire's parody (where, of course, *The Widow
in the Bye Street* and *The Everlasting Mercy* have become fused),

form and content are rather more accurately hit on the nail
in such amusing stanzas as:

> Death laughed; Life winced; for in the neighbouring borough
> Old mother dwelt and bided her own hour,
> Whetting a carving-knife with motions thorough,
> Practising stabs of accuracy and power.
> The scythe must fall, and then must fall the flower,
> The day must die and then must sink the sun,
> And all things end that ever have begun.

And when Squire writes:

> Until at last came Fate in Fate's own time,
> And ravelled her in the dark nets of crime,

he does dwell on a possible fault in Masefield, who has been
known to drag in Fate to his assistance when Fate has slight
hand in the development of the tragedy—most events being
decided by character and behaviour.

Turning to another parody, *If Mr Masefield had written
'Casabianca,'* he is farther off the nail than ever, though at
his most amusing, and reminiscent enough of Masefield in
the rhythm and repetitive manner:

> The deck was getting hot and hotter,
> 'Father!' he screamed, 'you —— rotter!'
> The deck was getting red and redder,
> And now he thought he'd take a header,
> Now he advanced and now he funked it . . .
> It had been better had he bunked it,
> For as he wavered thus, and swore,
> There came a slow tremendous roar.
>
> Lord Nelson suddenly woke up.
> 'Where is Old Cassy and his pup?
> "Don't know," you say? Why, strike me blind,
> I s'pose I'd better ask the wind.'
> He asked the wind; the brooding sky
> At once gave back the wind's reply:
> 'Wotto, Nelson!'

In a short introduction to the first Masefield parody, Squire says:

> But enough at least has been printed to indicate that it is a production of the School of Real Human Emotion that is leading a return to Life and Religion and Natural Action and away from the refined aestheticisms of so many of our modern poets.

Which, of course, includes Wilfrid Gibson, though Wilfrid Gibson, for various reasons, has been left severely alone. W. H. Davies, however, gets his nose mildly thumped, chiefly on account of his naïveté:

> I saw some sheep upon some grass,
>   The sheep were fat, the grass was green,
> The sheep were white as clouds that pass,
>   And greener grass was never seen;
> I thought, 'Oh, how my bliss is deep,
> With such green grass and such fat sheep!'

Which, however, does give the victim a few marks, though it is doubtful if Squire gives him any in the hedgerow realism of the second parody:

> He has a cough,
>   Bad boots he has;
> He takes them off
>   Upon the grass.
>
> He does not eat
>   In cosy inns
> But keeps his meat
>   In salmon tins.

Another influential emotional nuisance who had to be disposed of was Sir Henry Newbolt—so he gets it like this:

> It was eight bells in the forenoon and hammocks running sleek
>   (*It's a fair sea flowing from the West*),
> When the little Commodore came a-sailing up the Creek
>   (*Heave Ho! I think you'll know the rest*).

Thunder in the halyards and horses leaping high,
Blake and Drake and Nelson are listenin' where they lie,
Four and twenty blackbirds a-bakin' in a pie,
    And the *Pegasus* came waltzing from the West.

But that treats its victim with a certain amount of respect,
as also do the two parodies of Hilaire Belloc, and to some
lesser extent the one on G. K. Chesterton—whose most
extravagant features are well caught in the lines:

> When I leapt over London Bridge
>   They quailed to see my tears,
> As terrible as a shaken sword
>   And many shining spears.

And to what extent did J. C. Squire approve of Swinburne?
At any rate it cannot have ever been very wholeheartedly,
for he was the complete antithesis of what the Georgian strove
to erect.   Still, in *If Swinburne had written 'The Lay of Horatius'*
the note is sometimes so well caught that one feels he admires
him beyond his own aims and theories:

May the sword burn bright, may the old sword smite, that a myriad
    years have worn and rusted?
  May an old wind blow where the young winds go immaculate
    over the eager land?

These lines actually speak, and rather forcibly, but in the
rest of the poem there is sufficient nonsense to justify the
poem as a parody.

Sir John Squire started his literary career as an admirer of
Baudelaire. One of his early volumes was Baudelairian
enough to be called *Poems and Baudelaire Flowers* (1909), though
his later *Lily of Malud* shows the influence clearly. Here, of
course, is the cup of wine which blurred his vision of the
sun, and helped to generate those literary antagonisms which
put Masefield in the foreground. Strange to say, at his
prosiest he is more prosy than ever was Masefield. His poem
The Rugger Match is an irritating instance of halting prosaic experimentalism, and *To a Bulldog* waddly enough to make one

* H

suggest that the dear animal had developed hydrophobia and bitten him. But when he tightens himself into a simple conventional rhythm with an exacting rhyme arrangement, particularly when he has art and the artist for his theme, he can hold his reader's attention to the end, and even move him. His poem on the moon has been discussed, but add to that his three-page descriptive poem on Catullus, and even better, a poem of similar length, *To a Musician*, in which, strangely enough, he makes a sweeping bow to the sun:

> Musician, with the bent and brooding face,
>   White brow and thunderous eyes; you are not playing
> Merely the music that dead hand did trace.
>
> Musician, with the lifted resolute face,
>   And scornful smile about your closed mouth straying,
> And hand that moves with swift or fluttering grace,
>   It is not that man's music you are playing.
>
> The grave and merry tunes he made you are playing,
>   Each march and dirge and dance he made endures,
> But changed and mastered, and these things you 're saying,
>   These joys and sorrows are not his but yours.

In simple flowing speech, which, though it sometimes falters, never fatigues or cloys, he bares the soul of a foreign fiddler, adroitly extending a hand of sympathy to any sensitive reader and making him at one with the fiddler:

> Through battering tempests you have blindly won,
>   And lived, and found a medicine for your scars
> In resolution taken from the sun
>   And consolation from the unsleeping stars.

But unfortunately for Sir John Squire, the bulk of his work reveals only a slender intellectual and spiritual content, which would not have really mattered if he had *always* written thriftily and given himself only as an artist. But the weakness of his position was such that the disgruntled people were able to join hands with the Philistines and bludgeon him out of recognition—though at his best he is a really fine poet.

That quarter of his verse which within its limitations was good or very good was, under the eyes of antagonism, so obscured by the three-quarters of bad and indifferent that it simply didn't exist at all. Moreover, Squire had rather too sharply attacked a poet who was more complete than himself, and his position of anthologist and critic and editor of the *London Mercury* and 'Solomon Eagle' of the *Observer* and other journals had put responsibilities upon his shoulders which were not always easy to fulfil. His position as literary dictator (and he was certainly that for quite a decade) gave him unique powers; and he was certainly too generous to some poets, and insufficiently appreciative of others. For many years it seemed as if no poet could get a public, or even, in some instances, secure a publisher for his books, unless J. C. Squire and the Squirearchy approved of him; so that several meritorious poets feel to-day (though, of course, not always quite rightly) that they have to thank a literary dictatorship for a neglect from which they may not hope to recover during their lifetime. But Squire stood for carefulness and clarity in verse, encouraging all that had affinity with the French Parnassian marmorealism as well as the Wordsworthian tradition of pastoralism, and in justice to him it must be said that he strove to erect a barrier against the growing tide of nonsense and wilful obscurity—much of it sheer wickedness. His parody in *Tricks of the Trade* of some of the worst efforts of the free-verse writers is one of the most praiseworthy things in that exciting and irritating armoury, and if only some of his defences had been stronger and he had widened his *London Mercury* horizon to let in the most traditional verse of the Left-wingers with rather more poems from the Right, it is quite possible that the seas of desolation would never have broken through.

I suppose that J. C. Squire's strongest opposers were the three Sitwells and myself; and though the most virulent attack came from Roy Campbell in *The Georgiad*, that long

satirical poem was not published till 1931, by which time
the power of the Squirearchy had dwindled into insignificance.

Of the three Sitwells, Osbert the satirist was the loudest
spokesman against the Squirearchy and his *The Jolly Old
Squire, or Way down in Georgia* (published by Harold Monro
from the Poetry Bookshop in 1922) his principal manifesto.
But the poem is not entirely effective, its faults being sufficiently obvious in the opening lines:

> Come, Tragic Muse, come near me, to inspire
> This awful tale of poets and hell-fire,
> Of fell cross-purpose, of how Destiny
> Tangles the tentacles of Squirearchy. . .

The poem, which occupies ten pages, is copiously annotated
and introduced by a prose statement of scene, and it is pointed
out that the chief members of the Squirearchy are Sqxxre,
Shxxks, Frxxmxn, and Txrnxr—the names, after the opening
stanza, for some unknown reason are half blindfolded in the
letter x—with special emphasis upon Sqxxre and Shxxks.
They are week-end rustic poets living at Chiswick in London
'where Hawthornden more sweet than hawthorn blows' because Shxxks and Frxxmxn had both been awarded the
Hawthornden prize. Here 'more rain of ink than rain of
heaven flows' and they spend half their time playing cricket,
taking in one another's washing, and entertaining one another
at tea and dinner parties. Naturally they haven't time to
do their own work thoroughly, and they don't seem to know
quite what they have written, so that when Satan puts a stanza
from Shelley into the desks of Sqxxre and Shxxks they both
think it is the fruit of their own brains (an obviously bad
shot from Mr Sitwell, and utterly pointless even as satiric
criticism). The Squirearchy leader is referred to as the new
Alexander Pope, and a multitude of smaller poets—'poetic
mannequins'—gather round to display the spring and autumn
fashions and write about all kinds of birds and their songs.
Mr Shxxks admires his own works tremendously because it
is 'a kind of hollow hallowed emptiness,' and struggling with

a verse that he doesn't remember writing, because it has as much content as form, he cries to his Pegasus, his 'Shanks' Mare,' to 'inspire this verse, create a vacuum.'

Truthful and amusing passages in Mr Sitwell's poem fail to quite save it from the prosy and commonplace, together with something much too juvenile or even schoolboyish in its general make-up. It hits below the belt, but doesn't hit firmly enough to incapacitate its victims, and the special weakness of Mr Sitwell's position as spokesman for himself and the other two (for the motive behind the poem is surely rather personal) is that the verse of the Sitwell triune up to date, is no better than and probably not two-thirds as good as that of the Squirearchy triune, and if we include the fourth knight of the London Mercury castle guard (W. J. Turner) the whole body of it is not half as good. At any rate Masefield had been mildly avenged (though I am sure that Mr Sitwell had no such intention) and the aggressive character of the Left-wing, which the Sitwells at that time seem to have been endeavouring to lead, made very evident.

The Georgian poets constituted a sort of Centre. On the Right-wing were Newbolt, Chesterton, Bridges, Watson, and their kin (the Sun Poets). Masefield, who sat awkwardly in the Centre and who belonged obviously to the Right with a slight infusion of Left, moved away from the Georgians more and more, partly pushed away—for this second Georgian revolt, as has been pointed out, was largely directed against Masefield, their fellow-member. At the hands of Georgian reviewers and critics he was slanged and depreciated at every bend of the road, and held up as an example of how one ought not to write. In rough general terms one might describe him as another poet of the Sun, indeed the most sunshiny of them all, a sort of English Victor Hugo, the Georgians corresponding to the French Parnassians who had shattered the Victor Hugo vogue and instituted a new literary vogue of carefulness and restraint—for Victor Hugo frequently tended towards the sentimental, the rhapsodic and rhetorical. The comparison is surely not too far from fidelity, though I am inclined to think that the only true Parnassian after Flecker (who was, however, all sorts of things) was Edward Davison, a poet who first made his appearance shortly after the War, and became associated with the Georgians and J. C. Squire.

> At last the cygnet, preening his plumed snow,
> Wins the mid-stream. Mark his new beauty well!
> Erect, uplit he sails; in the clear flow
> > Reflected, breast and wing,
> > And proud beak, winnowing
> The April air, all carved like a sea-shell.

Those lines, very typical of Davison at his best, may illustrate what I mean by English Parnassianism, Georgian Parnassianism, though you can go back to Ernest Dowson and Arthur Symons and their kin for something similar—who if they had rather more of the true Parnassian shape in their make-up, displayed also rather too much of that emotionalism which the French Parnassians strove to restrain, and which the true-green Georgians followed them in doing.

Thus it seems that the School of the Rhymers' Club had changed into the Georgian Squirearchy School, for the red rose of the London taverns had got blown into the country, from whence it had ascended into the lower skies and blanched into a pale round moon. It was presently to dwindle into a blunt edged sickle moon, and then tumble to earth and change into a hard terrestrial bone of unseizable oblongitude, the unwieldy fleshless bone of Eliot and his kin.

CHAPTER XIII

THE GEORGIAN PASTORAL SCENE

In the third Georgian anthology (1917), bound in a daytime green which is somewhat at variance with the night hues of J. C. Squire's *The Lily of Malud*, to say nothing of John Freeman's *Pigeons* and *Stone Trees* and much of the verse by the War poets, there is a slight but exquisite lyric by John Drinkwater which seems to express the main tenets of the Georgian faith, and the non-moral intentions of its art:

> I do not think that skies and meadows are
> Moral, or that the fixture of a star
> Comes of a quiet spirit, or that trees
> Have wisdom in their windless silences.
> Yet these are things invested in my mood
> With constancy, and peace, and fortitude,
> That in my troubled season I can cry
> Upon the wide composure of the sky,
> And envy fields, and wish that I might be
> As little daunted as a star or tree.

A contradiction in it is 'I do not think . . . that the fixture of a star comes of a quiet spirit,' but otherwise it very finely expresses the point of view of the mere artist, and defines the Georgian arena, about which nobody can have any doubts from the anthologies which followed the 1917 issue. But about John Drinkwater himself one may be permitted to have some doubts, especially as his plays *Abraham Lincoln* and *Oliver Cromwell* are very moralistic, and some of his poems acknowledge the existence of a great and beneficent God. It has been said of the Georgian poets that they were as the fairies, acknowledging neither good nor evil (which, of course, puts them rather apart from their pastoral grandfather

Wordsworth, as well as Tennyson and Browning) and though
John Drinkwater was, more often than not, a typical Georgian
pastoral poet and struck his finest note in such lines as those
already quoted, and in such surprising stanzas as:

> The scent of the ploughlands is calling me away,
>   The chatter of the rooks, the open skies,
> And she I know is waiting with the glory of the day
>   And the shadow of the night in her eyes,

he could be effective in a vein of religious reverence:

> So I forgot my God, and I forgot
> The holy sweet communion of men,
> And moved in desolate places . . .

and both religious and aphoristic in such lines as:

> My weapon was a little faith,
> And fear was my antagonist.

> Not a brief hour of cannonade,
> But many days of bitter strife,
> Till God of His great pity laid
> Across my brow the leaves of life.

But that kind of verse was generally avoided by Edward
Marsh, and the rural, non-committal atmosphere which he
helped to create was not such as John Drinkwater could
easily expand in.

Each of the post-War Georgian anthologies (1919 and 1922)
is excessively pastoral. Now we are definitely confronted by
the poetry of escape, not only from the ardours and horrors
of War, but also from the demands and decisions of the
Peace that followed it. Here are copious selections from more
than forty books by more than twenty poets, and they seem
to conspire together to suggest that nothing unusual has happened, or if it has happened that it had much better be forgotten. . . . I do not, of course, want to suggest that poetry
should always concern itself with moral theme and ethical

content, for I do firmly believe that art in general, if not in totality, should know (and actually does know) no morality, and that the moral artist will actually defeat his genius or his daemon, and even the Holy Spirit when it descends upon him, if he tries too assiduously to preach and teach and lets any strong consciousness of right and wrong (particularly when it is not absolute), residing in the upper strata of his mind, defeat his sub-conscious vision of truth; [1] but here in these two post-War Georgian anthologies the non-moral, non-religious, non-social side of poetry is definitely overdone. Whatever you may say of poetry, escapism should not dwindle into exclusivism, otherwise you end up by creating a sort of vacuum into which all sorts of unpleasant hostile forces may presently rush. (Which, of course, is exactly what did happen.)

It is therefore not surprising that the fourth Georgian anthology was badly received by the press, that its sameness and lack of passion made critics and reviewers sniff contemptuously; so that in prefacing the fifth and final volume Edward Marsh had to write:

When the fourth volume of this series was published three years ago, many of the critics who had up till then, as Horace Walpole said of God, been the dearest creatures in the world to me took another turn. Not only did they very properly disapprove my choice of poems: they went on to write as if the Editor of *Georgian Poetry* was a kind of public functionary.

Then he goes on to say that 'much admired modern work seems to me, in its lack of inspiration and its disregard of form, like gravy imitating lava.' Which, probably, points to the beginnings of the Modernist racket, though perhaps it would have been more closely descriptive of their worst work if he had written 'like wood-shavings imitating clouds,' or 'like putty imitating marble.' Then he suggests that the upholders of Modernism regard Georgian poetry as 'tapioca

[1] And has not Elroy Flecker written: 'It is not the poet's business to save man's soul, but to make it worth saving'?

imitating pearls,' and that though inspiration may be as non-existent in the one as the other, he nevertheless prefers his own peculiar brand.

Unfortunately, however, there are too many misses from the ranks of the formalists. At least half a dozen meritorious young poets who wrote with conscientious feeling for form and crystallization were completely omitted. It is true that two or three whose appearance was hoped for or anticipated, did turn up in these two final volumes; but others as good or nearly as good were still left outside in the cold. Arthur L. Salmon, a pastoral, mystical, and meditative poet of the West Country, a little of whose work was so much of the land that it was written in dialect, was almost certainly omitted because he was too old, for the first of his many books was published in 1895, and his third in 1906. In *The Crown deferred* Arthur Salmon chides depreciators and wilful neglecters, not necessarily of poets, though he is probably thinking of himself:

> There is a paramount and vital cause
>   Why we delay our praises and thanksgiving;
> We must defer our suffrage and applause—
>   The man is living.
>
>   .   .   .   .   .
>
> A little just appreciation now
>   Might pamper him and render him unsteady.
> We have a wreath preparing for his brow—
>   But 'tis not ready.

He was unlucky in his age (he was born in 1865), a passable Georgian poet (though with his deepest roots in Tennyson) who preceded the movement, and therefore had to be overlooked.

An actual miss, and a bad one, was the young poet Frederick W. Harvey, whose first volume of verse, *A Gloucestershire Lad*, was unusually successful and ran into six editions. His most appreciated poems are *Ducks* and *The Bugler*; but *François Villon* contains passages quite as good:

And in his favourite tavern worlds away
Sits poet Villon, vagabond and worse,
Whose head is aching sore: as well it may,
Within whose pocket is an empty purse.
And to forget how worldly pleasure roves,
For joy of lively words, and for the sake
Of one old simple woman whom he loves,
And to forget how much his head doth ache,
While that his fellows quarrel, game, and curse,
The poet Villon sits and scribbles verse.

But there is nothing of Villon in the mind and art of F. W. Harvey. He is too much of the countryside for that.

The worst miss of all from the viewpoint of pastoralism was Edward Thomas. He has probably of recent years been over-rated as poet, though certainly not overrated as a prose writer and naturalist. His verse never descends into monotony, but some of it seems a little formless in that, though always metrical, it lacks strong compulsion and has to be read almost as condensed, rhythmical prose. Great beauty and perfection of form jostle verse which lacks incision and conciseness, some of which may have called forth from Edward Marsh the censure, 'gravy imitating lava'—which, however, could not apply to such memorable stanzas as these:

I have come to the borders of sleep,
The unfathomable deep
Forest where all must lose
Their way, however straight,
Or winding, soon or late;
They cannot choose.

Here love ends,
Despair, ambition ends,
All pleasure and all trouble,
Although most sweet or bitter,
Here ends in sleep that is sweeter
Than tasks most noble.

But Edmund Blunden and Victoria Sackville-West entered the caravan; and these along with the omitted Edward Thomas constitute the most formidable trio of pastoral poets of this century—pushing both John Freeman and Edward Shanks into the shade. Their inclusion in the final Georgian anthology (1922) helps to make that issue even more pastoral than any of the preceding volumes, and puts the steeple on it if there had been any doubts up to that moment in what direction Georgian verse was tending. Now has the ultimate virtue really become a fault—because inclusive exclusivism was really acting as a check on poetry's development.

But if Edmund Blunden is shown at his most pastoral, Victoria Sackville-West is left a little more to surmise. One of her selected poems, *Bitterness*, is much more symbolical than is usual with Georgian poetry, and her frequent inclination to write of the passions and adventures of the human soul is somewhat at variance with her country-life aloofness. Her landscapes are sunnier and hillier to the visual sense than Edmund Blunden's, though many think her less effective, as her use of words is more conventional. Edmund Blunden for a long time was dominated and influenced by John Clare, though there is very little in his language which is directly reminiscent of John Clare. In his best passages there is a rough musical plangency more reminiscent of Browning than Clare, but this frequently breaks down, so that not all his poems are successful from the reciter's standpoint. He is, like Masefield, a very uncertain artist, though his weaknesses are quite other than those of Masefield, who is an excellent poet for the reciter. Blunden will be anything rather than cheap and easy, for though he is entirely unpretentious, he is too dominated by the literary sense, and almost seems to look for dissonance and harshness when he feels himself falling into a conventionally mellifluous stride. The plodding deliberateness with which he heavily loads every rift with ore really sets him away from Keats—whose exuberance was entirely spontaneous—but, nevertheless, helps to create a body of poetry rather different from anything preceding. There is no doubt

as to the originality and individuality of Edmund Blunden's
voice, though in its too strenuous flight from the reminiscent,
while it avoids the nonsensical, it falls frequently into dullness and a sort of staccato monotony. His landscapes, as may
be expected, are more expressive of autumn than summer or
spring—damp and yellow and brown with dying leaves; fog-
benighted, rain-sodden; sighing, wailing stretches of wet,
fading woodland and corn stubble, intersected by hedgerow
and blackberry tangle; the moon (as was characteristic of
'Georgian' verse), rather than the sun, shining over everything:

> Now ragged clouds in the west are heaping,
> All the hedges fall a-weeping,
> And in a thin green distance flowers
> The moon, the blossom of lonely hours.

His landscapes are low and rural rather than exulting and
mountainous, crossed by canals and sluggish streams, and
dotted with green pond and marsh. The fish he frequently
mentions by name are such humble creatures as inhabit waters
that are silent or do not move swiftly—perch, and roach, and
pike, never salmon or grayling or trout. Modesty, unpre-
tentiousness, melancholy, mossiness, dampness, decay, a lonely
turning of the head on something beautiful that has gone—
these are some of the most salient features of his unique
pastoral verse:

> How shall I return and how
> Look once more on those old places!
> For Time's cloud is on me now
> That each day, each hour effaces
> Visions once on every bough.
>
> . . . . . .
>
> Spider Dick, with cat's green eyes
> That could pierce stone walls, has flitted—
> By some hedge he shakes and cries,
> A lost man, half-starved, half-witted,
> Whom the very stoats despise.

Strange! And almost odd. And even stranger is the poem
April Byeway, in which he sings rather too huskily to an unseen
friend (a friend he has never met or seen), presumably an
attendant spirit—that of John Clare—and which ends with
a stanza that is atmospheric and symbolic (as so frequently)
of October rather than April:

> But the old forge and mill are shut and done,
> The tower crumbling down, stone by stone falls;
> An ague doubt comes creeping in the sun,
> The sun himself shudders, the day appals,
> The concourse of a thousand tempests sprawls
> Over the blue-lipped lakes and maddening groves,
> Like agonies of gods the clouds are whirled,
> The stormwind like the demon huntsman roves—
> Still stands my friend, though all 's to chaos hurled,
> The unseen friend, the one last friend in all the world.

He is the melancholy naturalist of rurality. He might
have been a gamekeeper in some eastern or midland
preserves. If you do not care for his poetry as poetry
you may read it for its atmosphere and interest. Hudson
and Richard Jefferies wrote only in prose, Edward Thomas
largely in prose, but nearly the whole of Edmund Blunden's
pastoral sympathy and intimate knowledge of the English
countryside has gone into his meditative and often rather weird
verse—slightly relative to Hardy's. And though he does
not write in dialect, and though his bucolic but rather too
shadowy human beings do not converse with one another, he
has, more than any other modern poet I know of (even more
than Wilfrid Gibson), introduced strange dialect words into
his verse—such odd titmice as 'goistering,' 'glinsy,' 'thaive,'
'hop-dog,' 'dor,' together with many other kinds of words,
which, if not strictly local, are as unusual as they are strange,
and rooted in the beginnings of language. His speech is
eminently Teutonic, Anglo-Saxon, far removed from urban
influences, and as far as possible from Latin culture. And
though in his pleasure in the bucolic and the recording of

natural phenomena he has sometimes forgotten poetry as poetry, and ignored some of the obvious demands of art and the craft that triumphs because it throbs and sings, he does most definitely command our attention, and will continue to do so for many years to come. More than any other pastoral poet of this century, more even than Victoria Sackville-West, he has given idiosyncratic hue and shape to the poetry of rural landscape, so that many have turned to him for instruction and inspiration. To what extent that more recent sensitive pastoral poet Andrew Young is indebted to him for inspiration I am not quite sure, but it is certain that Edmund Blunden has exercised a bestowing influence upon many of his contemporaries. Even since the decline (nay débâcle) of Georgian pastoralism, Edmund Blunden, almost equally with Edward Thomas, has continued to be respected, even by the poets who sail in the Modernist petrol-boat. It is true that his work has of recent years somewhat changed, being less pastoral and more intellectual than in earlier days, but in effecting the change it has probably lost something of its old allure. But he has never sunk into the mere versifying competence of John Drinkwater (a good and true poet who chose too often to be merely competently bad) or into the morass of the same poet's earnest silliness:

> Beyond my window in the night
> Is but a drab inglorious street,
> Yet there the frost and clear starlight
> As over Warwick woods are sweet.

No! Edmund Blunden was never capable of sticking so fast in lyrical mud as to write of 'starlight' as 'sweet,' and provoke an image of whiteness that makes you think of frost as sprinkled sugar. Nor was he ever capable of writing such a bad angling poem as Drinkwater's *Pike Pool*, with its weak similes and forced rapture and only half understood allusions, and associations of pike and mayflies (because I suppose John Drinkwater did not know that the trout stickle in the little river Dove called 'Pike Pool' was named after a rock and not after a voracious fish). Edmund Blunden was never like that, for he has always been clear in mind as to what he was writing about, and was never a countryside week-ender.

One of the best of all the Georgian outdoor poems is Martin Armstrong's *Buzzards*, included by Edward Marsh in the final Georgian anthology, a poem that entirely justifies itself and makes one cry for more. Martin Armstrong hovers between pictorial pastoralism and deep adventures into the cultured inquiring spirit. His ambiguously entitled poem *To Hate* is not the sort of thing that Edward Marsh chose for the later volumes, but it is probably his finest, and quite certainly one of the best lyrics of intellectual passion which the century has produced—never falling away from its fine opening lines:

> Come, holy Spirit, pentecostal Flame!
> Out of the deep we cry to thee. The shame
> Of feeble virtues, mild complacencies
> Clings to our bodies like a foul disease.
> Eat us as acid eats: burn us with fire. . . .

Other pastoral inclusions who should not be overlooked are Richard Hughes and Francis Brett Young. Richard Hughes was somewhat influenced by Robert Graves in his technique, though Graves himself was never much of a country poet, and his Georgian incursions into that kind of verse are only half realized. Probably the silliest lyric in all the Georgian anthologies is Richard Hughes's *Poets, Painters, Puddings*, beginning:

> Poets, painters and puddings; these three
> Make up the world as it ought to be. . .

One recognizes at once the early jolly schoolboy vein (via Skelton) of Robert Graves, but Graves never committed himself to quite such a crude absurdity of traditionalism. Otherwise the poems of Richard Hughes are sometimes very good, and have never been quite neglected.

Francis Brett Young (not to be confused with Andrew

Young) contributed many pages of country-life verse to the final Georgian anthologies, but for some reason or other he has been more heard of since as a novelist than as a poet. But his short lyric (a true lyric) entitled *Song* is quite unforgettable in its musical first stanza:

> Why have you stolen my delight
> In all the golden shows of Spring
> When every cherry tree is white
> And in the limes the thrushes sing?

Four other pastoral poets (at any rate their verse is mainly pastoral) who, between them, contributed twenty-four pages to the final anthology, were Peter Quennell, J. D. C. Pellow, W. Kerr, and Frank Prewett. Of none of these have we recently heard much as poets, though some later-written verse of Quennell's is of intellectual significance. In two of Prewett's poems the influence of Thomas Hardy is very evident, while in another, *The Somme Valley, June 1917*, he has contributed a first-rate lyric to the poetry of the War.

Another Georgian poet who deserves especial mention is Thomas Moult. He promised very highly and then seems to have more or less stopped writing verse. There is metrical originality in *For Bessie* and *Truly he hath a Sweet Bed* (see *Georgian Poetry*, 1918–19), and much delicacy of colour and tone. But he did not develop an art which in *Georgian Poetry* and his one important book, *Down here the Hawthorn*, seems to have been partly experimental.

> To the heart, to the heart the white petals
> Quietly fall.
> Memory is a little wind, and magical
> The dreaming hours.
> As a breath they fall, as a sigh;
> Green garden hours too languorous to waken,
> White leaves of blossomy tree wind-shaken:
> As a breath, a sigh,
> As the slow white drift
> Of a butterfly.

Before finishing with the Georgian pastoral scene (which, as I have shown, has not been completely represented by Sir Edward Marsh) it is necessary to mention Charles Dalmon, a country-life poet with a very fresh, individual voice, who possibly had some slight influence upon W. H. Davies. But he chiefly belongs to the end of the last century, though he published a book, *A Poor Man's Riches* (1922), just at the end of the Georgian anthology period. Writing of him in 1914, Edward Thomas said: 'It is rumoured that Mr Charles Dalmon is still alive. . . . Before Mr Belloc and Mr Kipling, Mr Dalmon was a Sussex poet. . . . He saw strange visions. For example, he saw Cupid and two or three gods down in Sussex; and even in Chiswick he knew a dryad. She haunted a mulberry tree in an old garden.' Whether or not Charles Dalmon really did see these things, or whether it is only a supposition culled from imaginative statements in his verse, or whether he had to some of his friends exaggerated the form of his mental visions under the influence of many draughts of cider—for of cider he sang frequently—I am not in a position to judge, though he certainly has a very naïve Blakian voice.

After the cessation of the Georgian anthologies, Thomas Moult carried on the tradition in his *Best Poems of the Year* series—yearly reprints from the literary journals. But he has been rather more catholic and variable in his choice than was Edward Marsh, and also extended his pages to include American poems. So the first issues were only in part 'Georgian.' To what extent he has included all the very best of the yearly output of America I cannot judge, but as regards this country he seems as a general rule to have scooped about seventy per cent of the best poems, so that in spite of a number of unfortunate omissions the anthologies are fairly representative of each year's best output, and, while giving prominence to the pastoral, have rarely over-emphasized it.

CHAPTER XIV

THE POETRY OF THE GREAT WAR

THE Great War gave birth to a tremendous sheaf of war poetry, written from every point of view, some of it very good, and only a little of it wholly bad. No war in historical memory has called forth a quarter of such quantity united to high quality, for the plain reason that national emotions never before, for any length of time, ran at such flaming heat. Most of the enduring poems were written by actual soldiers, as, of course, they should have been; and out of a notable score one calls quickly to mind Julian Grenfell's *Into Battle*, Rupert Brooke's *The Soldier*, Wilfred Owen's *Greater Love*, Major Maurice Baring's *In Memoriam*, A. H. John McCrae's *In Flanders Fields* (the poppy-poem of Armistice Day), this last strangely misapplied, because the symbol of the poem being really the blue forget-me-not, the red poppy of Oblivion should be surrounded by a fringe of these flowers.

I suppose that the first War poem of any consequence was a lyric by Harold Begbie published in a daily newspaper a few weeks after the commencement of hostilities. As a stirring piece of propaganda and call to arms it was effective enough, but could not in any way stand for more than a period. Another early war poem, much better, and rather unfortunately obscured by time (written also during the first months of the War), is Ford Madox Hueffer's *Antwerp*. It was published by Harold Monro's Poetry Bookshop, and occupied seven sheets. On the cover was a rhapsodical Futurist (or Vorticist) design of a Belgian soldier by Wyndham Lewis, and the poem, which combined Futurism with traditional measures and rhyming, was written in something of the same key. Though a reckless and occasionally nonsensical piece of work, it is a pity that it has been forgotten, for it is full of gorgeous things of this quality:

For the white-limbed heroes of Hellas ride by upon their horses
Forever through our brains.
The heroes of Cressy ride by upon their stallions;
And battalions and battalions and battalions—
The Old Guard, the Young Guard, the men of Minden and of
　　Waterloo,
Pass, for ever staunch,
Stand for ever true;
And the small man with the large paunch,
And the grey coat, and the large hat, and the hands behind the back,
Watches them pass
In our minds for ever . . .
But that clutter of sodden corses
On the sodden Belgian grass—
That is a strange new beauty.

Many of the other known poets, including Watson, Hardy, John Masefield, and Ernest Rhys, contributed in one way or another to the passionate outburst of resentment, patriotism, and sorrow. But the war verse which was to stir the imaginative and cultured public to attention, chiefly came from the soldiers themselves, and was written during their military preparations in England, or scribbled on bits of paper between their long hours of active service in the trenches. The note at first was patriotic enough, the key poems supplied by Rupert Brooke's sonnet *The Soldier* and Julian Grenfell's *Into Battle*, with its eternally memorable:

> And Life is Colour and Warmth and Light,
> 　And a striving evermore for these;
> And he is dead who will not fight;
> 　And who dies fighting has increase.

And that distinguished naturalist and pastoral poet, Edward Thomas (not to be confused with another soldier poet, Edward Thompson) joined in with:

> Up with the light,
> To the old wars;
> Arise, Arise!

Rarely, strange to say, was there any strong denunciation of
the enemy, though Lord Gorell voiced the more general
national feelings during the middle of the War with *Song before
Battle,* culminating in a very stirring battle stanza:

> We are rising now, a nation's tide,
> And you must dig and wire and quail,
> *Your* turn at last beneath our guns,
> *Your* turn to find defences frail.
> We are bursting in, we are breaking through;
> The great sea sweeps your barriers down.
> You urge anew your claim on God,
> But He is silent as you drown,
> Look to yourselves, O Huns!

That, of course, like Julian Grenfell's stanza, can be otherwise applied (as much real poetry can be reapplied) and invested
with a symbolical significance. As regards something better
known, it was the symbolical or universal side of John
McCrae's Armistice Day poem which set it on the shelf of
permanence, though actually it was a call to arms:

> Take up our quarrel with the foe:
> To you from failing hands we throw
>   The torch; be yours to hold it high.
>   If ye break faith with us who die
> We shall not sleep, though poppies grow
>   In Flanders fields.

Save Julian Grenfell's *Into Battle,* nothing better woven in
the old-fashioned knightly spirit came out of the War than
Maurice Baring's *In Memoriam, A. H.* Maurice Baring has
been connected with the Georgian revolt, and one of his
distinguishing features is a studied conversational simplicity,
so that in his numerous sonnets of a most transparent clarity
he seems to be almost aiming at poems in monosyllables—

though not always with complete success.   But in *In Memoriam,
A. H.*, a poem with a metrical texture rather similar to
Milton's *Lycidas*, Maurice Baring not only reached the culmination of his lyrical powers but achieved one of the greatest
elegies in the English tongue.   Nearly every part of this
colourful, beautiful poem is quotable, none more so than that
which tells of the dead soldier's ascent into Paradise:

> Surely you found companions meet for you
> In that high place;
> You met there face to face
> Those you had never known, but whom you knew;
> Knights of the Table Round,
> And all the very brave, the very true . . .

But it was not Milton and the Elizabethans to whom the
soldier-poets went to school, but rather A. E. Housman and
the realistic John Masefield.   Sir Edmund Gosse during the War
said that they had put A. E. Housman's *Shropshire Lad* into their
knapsacks.   This is not always quite plain, though the note of
Housman seems to thread through much of their work.   Well
transmuted, it is certainly present in Edward Thompson's:

> And Tigris, racing seaward,
>   Remembers here a space
> The storm of human anguish
>   That swept the desert's face.
> The flocks are grey hyenas
>   And here the jackal feeds—
> On the pastures of Sannaiyat,
>   Sannaiyat flanked with reeds.

At any rate much of the hard acidity in Housman's *Shropshire Lad* crept into the later War verse.   The notes of Brooke,
Grenfell and Maurice Baring die down into realism and disillusionment—sometimes softened into bravado, or crossed by
dreams of home, as in Robert Graves's *It's a Queer Time*:

> The trouble is, things happen much too quick;
> Up jump the Bosches, rifles thump and click,
> You stagger, and the whole scene fades away;

> Even good Christians don't like passing straight
> From Tipperary or their Hymn of Hate
> To Alleluia-chanting, and the chime
> Of golden harps . . . and . . . I 'm not well to-day . . .
> It 's a queer time.

The 'whole scene fades away' is a reference to the scene of home and childhood; and this nostalgia ever creeps through the bitter contemplation of battlefield horrors and the pictures of maimed and ruined youth, as in Sassoon's:

> Return to greet me, colours that were my joy,
> Not in the woeful crimson of men slain,
> But shining as a garden; come with the streaming
> Banners of dawn and sundown after rain.

But Sassoon, fine soldier (like Lord Gorell and Edward Thompson he was decorated with the M.C.), fine poet, penetrating satirist, and master of words, if not always going quite as deep as he might, and sparing of the suggestive use of symbols (though his weird *Haunted* has a very symbolical content), writes equally frequently in this manner:

> 'We 're none of us the same!' the boys reply.
> 'For George lost both his legs; and Bill 's stone blind;
> Poor Jim 's shot through the lungs and like to die;
> And Bert 's gone syphilitic; you 'll not find
> A chap who 's served that hasn't found *some* change.'
> And the Bishop said: 'The ways of God are strange!'

The manner of realistic speech had been made possible by Masefield's *Widow in the Bye Street*; and the influence of Masefield is still more obvious in the little anecdote of the suddenly uplifted soldier who was about to be killed, and didn't know what he was fighting for:

> So Davies wrote: 'This leaves me in the pink,'
> Then scrawled his name: 'Your loving sweetheart, Willie,'
> With crosses for a hug. He 'd had a drink
> Of rum and tea; and, though the barn was chilly
> For once his blood ran warm; he had pay to spend.
> Winter was passing; soon the year would mend.

The real Sassoon note, however—and there is a Sassoon who
stands entirely on his own platform—is struck more plainly in:

> The House is crammed: tier beyond tier they grin
> And cackle at the Show, while prancing ranks
> Of harlots shrill the chorus, drunk with din;
> 'We're sure the Kaiser loves the dear old Tanks!'
>
> I'd like to see a Tank come down the stalls
> Lurching to rag-time tunes, or 'Home, sweet Home,'—
> And there'd be no more jokes in Music-halls
> To mock the riddled corpses round Bapaume.

The poem reminds us of many strange things, not merely that
the English were first to use tanks, but that among many of
the soldiers any bitter feeling that they may have earlier enter-
tained against the enemy was completely dying away, and that
they were transferring their animosity to the civilians who had
comfortable jobs at home and shouted patriotism while only
too glad to keep out of trouble. Not only Sassoon, but also
Charles Hamilton Sorley, a soldier-poet of great promise who
was killed (but who wrote little verse directly applicable to
the War), voiced this feeling of forgiveness to the enemy.
In his sonnet *To Germany* he cries 'You are blind like us,'
and adds:

> When it is peace, then we may view again
> With new-won eyes each other's truer form,
> And wonder.

Pride in their military calling after the first ardours had
died down was rarely expressed in the verse of these soldier
poets; so that when it does occur it is to be wondered at and
almost admired. Perhaps it was struck more frequently after
the War was over, a notable example being Edward Thompson's *The Author writes his own Epitaph*:

> Stranger, if passing by you seek to learn
> What man was he whose ashes fill this urn—
> Know: there's a ghost remembers now by Styx

> He marched with Maude, was with the few who first
> The embattled sandhills of Samara burst,
> And once hit Faulkner over the ropes for six.

But the speech is very restrained. Of exultation there is little, for the great *in memoriam* and heroic note of Laurence Binyon's *For the Fallen* was hardly possible of expression by the soldiers themselves.

The soldier poets who came chiefly before the eyes of the public during the War were a trio—Robert Nichols, Robert Graves, and Siegfried Sassoon. Of these the only one who strove to give anything like a complete picture of individual outlook and development, from the opening of the conflict to the final contemplation of the horrors of the battlefield, was Robert Nichols. He divides the first part of his war-time book (the part dealing with the War), *Ardours and Endurances*, into six parts: (1) The Summons, (2) Farewell to Place of Comfort, (3) The Approach, (4) Battle, (5) The Dead, (6) The Aftermath. It must be read as a whole rather than in parts, for none of the poems save the well-known *Fulfilment*, beginning:

> Was there love once? I have forgotten her.
> Was there grief once? Grief yet is mine . . .

is especially good in itself, though very many stanzas pin the attention:

> Sometimes a sniper's bullet whirs
>   Or twangs the whining wire;
> Sometimes a soldier sighs and stirs
>   As in hell's frying fire.

Robert Nichols was not long in France (see Robert Graves's autobiography, *Good-bye to All That*) and probably some of the poems, particularly the well-known *Assault*, were not written as complete individual experiences, though, at the time, they were very effective. Robert Nichols (who was one of the poets specially selected for Edward Marsh's Georgian anthologies) is at his best in an Elizabethan vein, his *Sonnets to*

I

Aurelia among his most powerful and interesting work.   To-day his war poems are of little value, these having been superseded by the passionate and bitter rhymed documents of Sassoon, who with Robert Graves served through nearly the whole period of war.   Once or twice they addressed their poems to one another; and both suffered to the full the disintegrating horrors of trench and field.

The war poems of two others with complete periods of service to their honour, Edmund Blunden and Wilfred Owen, were published long after the cessation of hostilities.   As one would expect in Edmund Blunden's verse, the landscape is in the foreground, the soldiers chiefly present to give the earth articulation.   His memories are of

> A whole sweet countryside amuck with murder,

rather than of the actual individual human beings in the struggle.   These beautiful and mournful poems belong nearly as much to the kingdom of pastoral as war verse, and invite our attention to the experiences and rustic personality of the brave man who wrote them rather than to the struggle itself.

The war poems of Wilfred Owen are, on the other hand, of quite a different calibre.   First published in 1920, with an introduction by Siegfried Sassoon, they startled immediately by a vigour as great as Sassoon's, but with less of bitterness and an almost greater infusion of pity.   They were much less carefully worked over than Sassoon's, and abounded with difficulties, if not obscurities—which is probably one of the reasons why the Eliotites have recently cast such favourable eyes upon them.   But Wilfred Owen was killed in the War; so we are probably right in looking upon many of the supposed virtues of these poems as minor faults.   The MS. had received no final revision, many half-lines are entirely missing, and Owen's proof-readers had to be Sassoon and Blunden in place of the poet himself.   The most magnificent lyric of all, *Greater Love*, contains faults, and yet, for all of them, is probably the most passionate and intense song that came out of those awful years.   In this poem Owen addresses the woman of his love, telling her that as objects of affection he prefers the men who are dying at the front to any woman born of Adam's seed:

> Red lips are not so red
> As the stained stones kissed by the English dead.
> Kindness of wooed and wooer
> Seems shame to their love pure.
> O love, your eyes lose lure
> When I behold eyes blinded in my stead!
>
> .   .   .   .   .   .
>
> Heart, you were never hot,
> Nor large, nor full like hearts made great with shot;
> And though your hands be pale,
> Paler are all which trail
> Your cross through flame and hail:
> Weep, you may weep, for you may touch them not.

The poem is really a very patriotic outburst, and rather different in sentiment from most of Owen's later work—which, as in *Anthem for Doomed Youth*, is verse of warning:

> What passing-bells for these who die as cattle?
>   Only the monstrous anger of the guns.
>   Only the stuttering rifles' rapid rattle
> Can patter out their hasty orisons.

Says Owen in some notes which he left for a preface: 'Above all, I am not concerned with poetry. . . . My subject is War, and the pity of War. . . . The Poetry is in the Pity. . . . All a poet can do to-day is to warn.' Nevertheless, the poet triumphed over the propagandist, so that (though perhaps in a rather remote sense) some of the verse is almost too self-consciously poetical. At any rate Wilfred Owen sought to free himself from anything relative to doggerel or the easy prose line. Probably there is a more intense and memorable revelation of the seamy side of war in these poems by Wilfred Owen and Siegfried Sassoon than in all modern prose writings put together. So much they gloriously achieved—an almost impossible feat in these days of much-read and much-written prose.

Among others whose war verse was not published in accessible book-form till after everything was over—and also revealing the seamy side of the struggle—should be specially mentioned Edgell Rickword, Richard Aldington, Isaac Rosenberg, and that extremely odd poet Herbert Read. Edgell Rickword's contributions are few in number, though one or two are among the best things in his strange symbolistic cupboard. But Richard Aldington in *Images of War* (1919) has given us a completer picture, and were it not that these carefully executed cameos of beauty and terror are written in free verse, and are therefore lacking in carrying power, they might have been placed near those of Sassoon. As regards Herbert Read (a D.S.O. and M.C. soldier), he has always been too intellectualized to be effective as a war poet. Half stifled under his acute self-consciousness and literary affectations, his war agonies are less effectively recorded than those of Richard Aldington—with whom as Modernist he has some slight affinities.

As regards Isaac Rosenberg, his now well-known *Dead Man's Dump* shows to what imaginative ardours free verse can actually rise if there is a passionate impulse to inform it. Nevertheless, the poem is not entirely successful. Rosenberg's sense of rhythm was always a little shaky, and during his period of active service it certainly did not increase. Unfortunately he was killed, and one of the really promising geniuses of our time brought to an end. Nearly every scrap of his work has been recently collected,[1] and it reveals an apocalyptic, if somewhat hunchback imagination striving in the net of an insufficient education. Tortured, only half articulate, intellectually violent, but often beautiful and powerful, he might have fully discovered himself, and in spite of some apparent

---

[1] See *The Collected Works of Isaac Rosenberg* (Chatto & Windus, 1937), edited by Gordon Bottomley and Denys Harding. It speaks much for Rosenberg's imaginative quality that he has so interested Gordon Bottomley, though the bulk of the work was done by Denys Harding.

deformity in his imaginative physique have risen to be among the first three or four poets of our time. But his gods willed otherwise, and *Dead Man's Dump* is his revered monument and full stop.

But there is one special and unique poem, less esteemed, which in spite of its somewhat conventional language the future will, possibly, prize over all. I give it here in full:

> By all the glories of the day
> And the cool evening's benison,
> By that last sunset touch that lay
> Upon the hills when day was done,
> By beauty lavishly outpoured
> And blessings carelessly received,
> By all the days that I have lived
> Make me a soldier, Lord.
>
> By all of all man's hopes and fears
> And all the wonders poets sing,
> The laughter of unclouded years,
> And every sad and lovely thing;
> By the romantic ages stored
> With high endeavour that was his,
> By all his mad catastrophes
> Make me a man, O Lord.
>
> I, that on my familiar hill
> Saw with uncomprehending eyes
> A hundred of Thy sunsets spill
> Their fresh and sanguine sacrifice,
> Ere the sun swings his noonday sword
> Must say good-bye to all of this—
> By all delights that I shall miss,
> Help me to die, O Lord.

The author of the poem, which bears the date 29th June 1916, was William Noel Hodgson (not to be confused with Ralph Hodgson, a poet of greater fame). Two days after he wrote it, on 1st July, he was killed in the battle of the Somme.

To few soldiers was given such knowledge of the certainty of approaching death. Still fewer were able to achieve entire reconciliation with that fact and uncomplainingly renounce all the delights of their youth, and then write a really fine lyric out of the experience. The mind that can so pull itself together in strength and exaltation has something in it of the sublime as well as the heroic.

The poem was evidently written at white heat. It bears all the impression of having been composed in one short hour, not resembling any of those creations which have been slowly polished into perfection and then dated on the day of final completion. For instance, the 'By that last sunset touch that lay' would have been revised (to avoid the clash of the two 'thats') if the young poet had had sufficient time to think of the final effect of his words; while something throbs through the whole of it which reveals the swiftness of unalloyed inspiration.

Like every exceptional poem, it communicates from within as well as suggestively from without; and contains an image of remarkable revelation, strengthened by a brilliant ambiguity, pun, or homonym:

> I, that on my familiar hill
> Saw with uncomprehending eyes
> A hundred of Thy sunsets spill
> Their fresh and sanguine sacrifice.

For there can be no true mental and spiritual progress without pain, no continuous joy (at least not in the collective life of the human race) that has not been introduced by suffering, trial, or agony, no permanent satisfaction without sacrifice; all of which should, of necessity, be accompanied by a mental act of faith—the sanguine (bloody) sacrifice an offer of the sanguine (confident) will. Is not the image a perfect expression of reality? And further, the worn-out day that plunges down in blood-red fire gives promise of a new unclouded day, is 'the shepherd's promise' of a fine morrow, let the night intervene as it will.

And yet how vulgar and insufficient seems the language of prose when one seeks to paraphrase these naïve, red-hearted stanzas! And how trivial and commonplace seem all explanations beside the supreme comment: 'Saw with uncomprehending eyes.' Nature is florid with signs and symbols, the flares and fingers of unshakable truth, day by day passed by unheeded. During recent time pacificism has been so often spiteful and knock-kneed, and so much has been done to belittle the sacrifice of English soldiers during those unimaginable years, that the mind of the reasonable pacifist feels itself revolted, and finds the words of this unfulfilled poet glowing with a peculiar significance. For though war must be avoided at a thousand costs, it cannot be avoided at all costs, and until the heart of man is entirely cleansed and changed, a nation's defence and self-preservation by means of war has to be shudderingly contemplated.

CHAPTER XV

SOME PROMINENT INDEPENDENTS

IN all ages the tendency of poets has been to run in droves, to form cliques and schools (partly for the purpose or convenience of patting one another on the back), though, I think, never since the conclusion of the War has this phenomenon been so exasperatingly pronounced. But certain poets to-day stand out as being neither of the Georgians, the Irish School, nor the Eliotites—prominent among those who revealed their leading characteristics after the War being Humbert Wolfe, Richard Church, Roy Campbell, and J. Redwood Anderson. All four of them were contemporary with either the earlier or later Georgians, save perhaps Roy Campbell, who published his first book, *The Flaming Terrapin* (1924), soon after Edward Marsh issued the last of his anthologies.

Humbert Wolfe's first books, *London Sonnets* (1920) and *Shylock reasons with Mr Chesterton* (1921) received little attention; but shortly after that, with *Kensington Gardens, The Unknown Goddess, Lampoons,* and *Humoresque,* he began to make himself felt, succeeding in throwing his weight about very advertisingly. With *News of the Devil* and *Requiem* (very nearly his worst book) he became a best seller, if he was not already that before. In fact, no new poet of consequence since the War sold so extensively, and his success reminded people of Masefield's early years. His *Requiem* went into the teens of thousands, and the other volumes followed quick behind. Robert Bridges's *Testament of Beauty* (a more disciplined work) competed with it in popularity; but none of Bridges's other works were as sought after as those by Humbert Wolfe. He is a disconcerting mixture of very bad and very good, and his reviewers, wishing to emphasize his great merit, made remarkable fools of themselves in the criticism of overstatement. 'A poet of whom it is difficult to speak with moderation'

—such were the comments by young reviewers who were sick to death of the Georgian tyranny and anxious to crush it by weight of an antagonistic laudation—by means of a poet who combined mysticism, rapture, recklessness, spontaneity, variety of music, wit, and tripping satire, so many qualities that the Georgians (especially the later Georgians) in a body seemed to lack. After that they veered round, conferring their attentions upon T. S. Eliot and his followers. One extreme to the other! They are now as unfair in their under-estimation of him as they were formerly fulsome in their admiration. Perhaps they never read him very carefully, for very careful attention would have shown them that he was even more committal than Swinburne, blurring his glittering pages not only with a maximum of sound into which sense did not always sufficiently enter, but also giving too lucid expression to over-many comfortable heresies and odd per-versions of rationality. There was nothing absolute about Humbert Wolfe's vision save when he fixed his eyes upon pure beauty. 'His realm is that of pure beauty,' most truth-fully shouted one critic, and it is a pity that so much nonsense has got into him from . . . perhaps the pages of Edith Sitwell and the French Symbolists; for at his best he has thrilling fingers, a really magical touch. More than that, I think that no poet ever committed verse to paper who has better combined ordinary speech cadence with metrical cadence. His natural tendencies seem to be in the direction of lucidity, the quotable line, the quotable stanza—this in spite of the fact that so much of his verse is neither lucid nor quotable. He is a skylark of the serene blue, but too often lost in the obscurity of night. He is a nightingale of the moon-drenched wood, but too often twittering his life away in the suburban girdle of a smoky or garish day. But as a technical artist he scarcely ever errs. In this he is the equal of Yeats, Walter de la Mare and Robert Bridges. His pages are hypnotic, ear-snatching, very pleasure-giving. He holds the attention, and excites the imagination—this in spite of his frequent obscurity, vagueness, wrongness, inflation, and syntactical queerness.

* I

His anarchical tendencies exasperate the critical sense rather than dull the page. As regards suggested influences, too, he is almost anarchic—Heine, Ronsard, Swinburne, Browning. He reminds us a little of all of these—though his voice is really very individual and generally beats right through his admirations, including certain of the moderns—tags of whose verse occasionally stick to his tongue.

At the beginning of years of fame he was compared with Heine, and the comparison was frequently repeated. But it is a rather misleading coupling. Every now and again the real Heine does steal out, but more often than not he gets right away from Heine. One might nearly as accurately have compared Humbert Wolfe with Longfellow—who really did come under Heine's influence. It is necessary to realize that Heine was a song poet, a very simple poet, and, perhaps, with the exception of Robert Bridges, the most careful verse craftsman who ever adorned language. Humbert Wolfe, for all his metrical cleverness, adroitness, and technical efficiency is not a careful verse craftsman, since he is thinking of his words in advance of his meaning. He lets his spontaneity run away with him, and rarely seems to revise. The form continually crushes the content. Form and content are frequently insufficiently locked or fused. Heine was never nebulous, diffuse, or illogical. Heine was always right on the nail. Heine used simple colloquial speech—which is quite a different thing from colloquial cadence—and used it with consummate mastery. Moreover, Heine was considerably influenced by German and English folk-lore poetry, the English ballad coming to him via Percy's *Reliques*. There is little of folklore poetry or the ancient ballad in Humbert Wolfe—whose translations of Heine generally miss the metrical peculiarities, particularly the ballad lilts. Still, when he writes (not in one of his translated pieces):

> But now to veins bloodless and arid
> by their own volition drawn
> through the shoals of a faith miscarried
> flow the red tides of dawn,

he does most emphatically remind us of Heine, though Heine would have rewritten his second line—which, though clear in itself, holds up the rest of the meaning. But the general technique of that particular stanza is the Heine technique. For, of course, good verse technique is always vocal, a captivating thing of the tongue and ear rather than of the brain or nerves. Mr Humbert Wolfe, with his very individualistic sheaf of violin tones and captivating syllabic mannerisms, can fairly bamboozle the nightingales; though the contemptuous wise owl may keep swooping down into the midst of them with a 'What the hell is it all about?' or 'Why couldn't the wild man look more carefully at his proof-sheets?' What one is so strongly aware of in reading Humbert Wolfe is something southern, particularly French. But though he seems to have imbibed from the French Symbolists (by no means to his good), more often French poets of the traditional type are paramount. So when he set out to translate Ronsard he probably got into touch with his basic self. Indeed, I think, he has occasionally translated Ronsard as if he were the man himself come back to enchant our tar-filled ears with songs of love and the rose and the nightingale—and the blighting wickedness of the grave; though we are too often bewildered by passages whose English is more obscure and difficult to read (to an Englishman) than the original French. That is the paradox, another anarchic touch in Humbert Wolfe. And it is perhaps one of the reasons why the critics have given him up; he is too difficult to discuss in compressed sentences. He seems to write like a traditional French poet (particularly Ronsard), but overlooks their consistent clarity and logical movement. How good he is when he is lucid! And how odd it is that he should be so frequently triumphantly lucid and yet not consistent in his lucidity! And why does he so frequently perpetrate hyperbolic nonsense like this?

> The feathers in a fan
> are not so frail as man;
> the green embossed leaf
> than man is no more brief.

> His life is not so loud
> as the passing of a cloud,
> his death is quieter
> than harebells, when they stir,

when he can equally often write unquestionably lovely things like this:

> Thus it began. On a cool and whispering eve,
> when there was quiet in my heart, she came,
> and there was an end of quiet.

Or aphoristic, epigrammatic stanzas like this:

> As this blind rose, no more than a whim of the dust,
> achieved her excellence without intent,
> so man, the casual sport of time and lust,
> plans wealth and war, and loves by accident.

Or molten lumps of magnificent, imaginative bitterness of this quality:

> Knit your great brows of granite, Kofel. Tighten
>   the hammer at your wrist. The time is now.
> Vast shadows darken, forked destructions lighten
>   over your village of Oberammergau
>   and, as they burn,
> giant, look to the West and strike! Your gods return.

Or (in a verse-comedy, *Reverie of Policeman*, distinguished by unusual obscurity) many lines of such imaginative clarity as:

> When with gold brooms the reasonable sun
> sweeps up the litter of night, and dreams are done,

and:

> The walls of day, the ragged fences
> between the spirit and the senses.

The rhymes in the last are very adroit, and point to one of Humbert Wolfe's distinguishing qualities. He is an astonishing rhymer, as prolific as Robert Browning. He is never hard up, never at a loss, his head seemingly crowded with the dictionary:

> And then let 's travel back to father Noah
> and speculate upon the protozoa
> that in their fairy-like and Andrew Lang-way
> dreamily oozed in pairs across the gangway.

Any kind of rhyme will serve his purpose if it fits mellifluously into the general texture of the line; while he shows his debt to German poetry in his frequent use of disyllabic rhymes —rhymes with a feminine ending:

> I have held out my hand, but more than that was needed.
> I have held out my heart, and that was not enough.
> I have prayed in all your heavens. Did I pray unheeded?
> What must I give, what more do you ask of me, love?

Very skilfully, also, in the place of pure rhyme, he makes use of partially coinciding assonance, or even coinciding consonantal effects freed from assonance. It will be noticed in the above that he rhymes 'enough' with 'love,' while in the succeeding stanzas he rhymes 'possession' with 'compassion' and 'tamarisk' with 'dusk'—all pleasing and satisfying to the ear because of his metrical skill. This metrical skill, however, sometimes resolves itself into very odd arrangements:

> Kitty 'ad found
>   religion and
> joined the Salvation
>   Army Band,

but which sometimes point to Humbert Wolfe's exceptional sensitiveness to pause and caesura.

As a light mordant satirist he is, perhaps, the foremost poet of this century. Milne can be equally clever and amusing, though Milne is a humorist rather than a satirist. But when

Humbert Wolfe in one of his epitaph poems wrote of Chesterton:

> Here lies Mr Chesterton,
> who to heaven might have gone,
> but didn't, when he heard the news
> that the place was run by Jews,

he not only reproved Chesterton very adroitly for his anti-Semite activities (Chesterton really did try to be a consistent Catholic medievalist) but triumphantly pointed to the basic creative authorship of our conceptions of heaven and hell, so curiously ignored by the medieval Catholic Church, and which to-day is equally ignored by the Nazi Christians of Germany—again scourged by Humbert Wolfe:

> Gangster by choice, storm-trooper, and then putscher,
> his civic occupation as pork-butcher
> made it seem more than probable that he might
> have been designed as Nature's Anti-Semite
> by God and by His first Pan-German Bishop
> to visit Oberammergau, and dish up
> a Passion-Play, purged of the ugly libel
> that the Jews had some connection with the Bible.

But enough! Let me conclude on Humbert Wolfe with what is probably his supremest and most lovely poem—*The Immortal Hour*:

I. SEMI-CHORUS

> We have no tears, who are the source of weeping,
>   and what is laughter to us, whose laughter first
> of laughter woke in man the sweet unsleeping
>   hunger and thirst?
>
> We are the words the poets hear and fail of,
>   we are the note beyond the fiddle's cry,
> we for all lovers of beauty are a tale of
>   beauty that passes by.

II. SEMI-CHORUS

Cried a ghost-king by night, 'Divine Augustus!
 you tread the ends of the world only to find
that the long roads of dreams go sweeping past us
 into a world behind.

'A fleeting throne, a shadow godhead these are,
 whose symbol is the axes and the rod,'
saying, 'There is another kingdom, Caesar,
 a further heaven, God.'

I. SEMI-CHORUS

We walk with the wind's feet, and do not rest,
 we walk between the leaves in the high meadows,
our hair with their green wings of light, our breast
 stained with the soft green shadows.

Fleeter than the heart's desire, one by one
 we leave delights that are well spoken of,
and far behind us echo, as we run,
 the tired feet of love.

II. SEMI-CHORUS

We are impatient of truth, that is no more
 than finite stain upon the infinite,
a fading seamark on a distant shore,
 and we have gone from it,

whose lips, though grave, are not too grave to smile at
 the heart of man crying in his vext youth:
'What is the truth?' and to make answer, 'Pilate,
 we are the truth.'

A complete opposite to Humbert Wolfe is J. Redwood Anderson—in nearly everything. Moreover, his public has always been extremely small. As the *Manchester Guardian* said of him, his 'recognition as a poet comes altogether short of his powers of achievement.' In fact, of all our poets of real quality and extensive output he is the least sufficiently known, the least widely distributed. His books (twenty-five years of them) have never sold. Very few anthologists have included him in their volumes. A poem from his pen rarely appears in the press. There is an opaque wall between him and the public. But what of the future?

The future has a very odd way of reversing the judgments of the present—particularly in regard to poetry. One might say with something like certainty that most of the judgments of one decade are completely reversed in the next. After that there is more reversion, then careful rectification and revision —so that looking back on a past century we discover that although half the number of poets who were really famous in their own day continue to be famous in this, the other half are now entirely unknown or regarded as the merest pigmies. But into their shoes have stepped certain poets who in their lifetimes were little recognized, or not recognized at all.

The contemporary critic is necessary and useful. And yet, and yet!—it is only Time that really writes criticism. For the final judgment seems to lie with the educated Man in the Street and along the Lane—call him 'Everyman' if you will.

One reason for the neglect of Redwood Anderson is that he has no publicity talents. Moreover, he lives in Yorkshire, in Hull—far away from literary drawing-rooms and literary cliques. He concerns himself with no literary movements, and goes on steadily with his school-work (for he is a public school master of unusual scholarly attainments) and his creative work. He makes no gesture, curries no favour, writes no praise or blame of others. He ignores his contemporaries almost as much as his contemporaries ignore him. And yet some of his verse has the real contemporary ring, and is sometimes an unusual revelation of our age. But, although his wilderness and 'waste-land' poems are among his best, he does not believe, like so many of us, that civilization has run off the lines. Rather does he see in the present-day ugly phases of civilization a necessary and inevitable development:

I did not see the city spread
Square mile on mile upon the plain.

I saw instead
The cone
Of a gyrating, black, immense,
Tumultuous cyclone.
And there were cannon-bursts of pain
And spears of agony that pierced
Its multitudinous thunder; there were cries
Of formidable triumph, and the call
Of mighty laughter and shattered gales of song;
And under all
The long
Surge of titanic effort.

    .   .   .   .   .   .

And in the elemental, roaring strife
I could discern, through all unrest,
The motions of eternal law;
While at the fringe of its huge storm I saw,
Driven through the blinded scud like a sharp knife
One blood-red ray from the hid sun of love.

I did not see the city spread
Square mile on mile upon the plain.

He is one of our very best technicians, combining effective
originality with effective traditionalism, and is, I think, of
all living poets nearest to Milton as a verbal organist. He
chiefly uses the conventional iambic line (iambic pentameter),
but frequently splits it up and arranges it according to the
laws governed by pause and caesura—with, of course, trochaic
and spondaic insertions. Thus it may be nothing but a
flexible adaptation, with internal rhymes used as end rhymes,
of the verse we know so well. His seemingly erratic lines
are often fundamentally conservative, his short lines com-
ponent parts of longer ones—written for the ear and voice
rather than the eye. Indeed, he is something of a platform
poet, though a glorified platform poet. But his notes, unlike
those of Humbert Wolfe, are of a church organ rather than a

violin or harp, of stately solemnity rather than lyrical abandon, and his best poems are narratives rather than lyrics. To rightly appreciate him, to glow to him, one must needs read him aloud, sonorously, in great gushes, half a page, one page, two pages, without halt or hesitation, observing all the devices of the elocutionist. There is, I know, sometimes too much downright rhetoric in him, but it is rhetoric shot through with real thought and imagination, and all that sensitiveness of perception which distinguishes the actual poet from the merely competent versifier.

At his best, his note is a cathedral note of very radiant and remarkable elevation:

> And the wind blew
> through all the winter of the Boreal night:
> and the wind wailed
> above the arctic stark paralysis
> that roofed in death the living sea's abyss;
> and the wind failed,
> for all its terror, all its might,
> all its splendour and its love,
> for all its trumpet-majesties,
> to move
> one tittle of compacted ice
> or wake one ripple on that rigid sea.

Yet although Redwood Anderson is much more than a poet's poet, his work stamped with the mark of our age, he frequently asserts an aloofness that is remindful of O'Shaughnessy's description of the poet as one 'wandering by lone sea-breakers and sitting by desolate streams,' nowhere more wonderfully and powerfully expressed than in his symbolical poem, *The Goat*, which appeared in his *Haunted Islands* of 1924—of which here is a substantial part:

> One day
> Its rope of twisted straw
> Snapped, and it passed away
> Forever from the circle of man's law,
> Up to the tameless hills to be untamed as they.

Sheer
Buttress on buttress, scarp on scarp,
Sheer and sharp,
Covered with time's worn hieroglyphs,
The cliffs
From the white cloud to the white surf
Fell.

They were a temple where the sea
Sang eternally
The anthems of its fear;
They were a citadel
Where the old gods and blind
Still defied
The pride
And prowess of mankind.

   .   .   .   .   .

Here,
Nevertheless, he dwelt
Year after year
Upon the world's last barren edge.
The ledge
Gave him a lodging, and the splintered rock
A shelter from the shock
Of the gigantic
Winds that raved
Over the leagues of black Atlantic.
Hardly he clung to the thin strip of life,
Never knew comfort, and lay down at night
With hazard and awoke again
To hunger and to strife.

But he had saved
The little spark of the eternal light
That smouldered in the lantern of his brain
From utter death. . . .

Sometimes, indeed, his experiences may seem too aloof from
the experiences of the normally sensitive, for there is a side to
Redwood Anderson which is strangely lonely and withdrawn;

but this very aloofness helps to equip him at moments with unusual power and insight. No one has written with greater clarity of the would-be supermen (for how rare are the real supermen!), those personalities which strut and strum and make mesmeric, Mussolini-like gestures and noises. Often, indeed, they conquer—for a time. But that is only because they believe so inexorably in themselves, because they completely exert the might of the will, although their wills are out of touch with the Absolute, with the Divine. To will sufficiently is always to perform, and to be or to seem divine. But selfishness, which dwells too usually at the centre of egotism, unconsciously manufactures a full stop; and disregarded humanity writes the next sentence. So listen to Redwood Anderson's Marlowesque Nimrod (the chief character of his blank-verse play *Babel*, later reprinted under the title of *The Tower of Heaven*):

> O horrible stars! Millions of peering faces
> crowding the malign infinite of night!
> Why will you look at me? I am a man
> made miserable in his own conceiving!
> I am the man who scorned humanity
> and whom humanity has laughed to scorn!
>
> .   .   .   .   .
>
> O let your horrible visages have rest!
> Gibber not at me! Let your thin arms cease
> their wild menace above me! Here I stand,
> a man alone with his savage delusion,
> locked in the windy summit of this tower,
> alone with his intolerable thoughts!
> See, I reverse my cries! I will go down,
> crawl on my knees to the feet of mankind,
> beg of the nearest the contemptuous bread
> of charity, and become man once more:
> for solitude is the cold cloak of God,
> and only God may wear it.

Anderson seems to have begun as a disciple of Masefield and Wilfrid Gibson, an early volume, *Flemish Tales* (1913), being clearly in the Masefield arena of tale-telling. But he has deviated a long way from both of them since that early coupling, and now the only living poets he at all resembles are Lascelles Abercrombie and H. D. (bewildering opposites). He is as confident a master of blank verse as Lascelles Abercrombie, and sometimes produces in his short lines similar effects to H. D. His best works are *Haunted Islands* (1924) and *Transvaluations* (1932), though all his volumes yield good poems and fine passages. His knowledge of prosody is wide and scholarly, and his approaches to form and content always logical. Indeed, he is almost too logical, the argument often overpowering the poetry. His greatest fault is *that*— together with a tendency to monotony and long-windedness. In spite of his exactness of epithet and figure of speech he insufficiently bestows on us the striking phrase, the detachable single line. He has not loaded every rift with ore, and his exceeding nakedness reveals too many hard distending ribs. He has, too, a tendency towards inflation and bombast, though generally, like Chesterton, steering right into the jaws of bombast he miraculously saves himself at the edge of disaster. His sins of inflation are different from those of Humbert Wolfe in that they are never devoid of meaning. Very different he is from Humbert Wolfe, who tends to sacrifice logic and sense to the mere physical communication of sound, and carelessly use suggestion freed from content.

Humbert Wolfe even more than Roy Campbell was hailed as a gold broom for sweeping away the superfluous silver dust of the Georgian smithy. On much of the minor poetry of the day his influence was for a time very plainly discernible, but Fate finally willed that he should give way to T. S. Eliot, and that such an invigorating life-giver as Redwood Anderson should also continue to be unread.

Fate also ignored Richard Church, who is half-Georgian and half-Modernist, a quaint combination of seeming opposites, and I believe derisively and unfairly called 'a pseudo-Georgian.' He is uncertain under the critical microscope, elusive and difficult to pin. He bothers himself tremendously

with his words and at times seems wilfully to obscure his
content:

> Ah! It was good to rise
> And watch, above the wold,
> The king with fiery eyes
> Stride as of old.
>
> Gone was the lonely doubt
> Which the night wrapped me in:
> Here was a foeman stout,
> Here was a crown to win!

The above short lyric prefaced one of his books (*The Glance
Backward*), and the lines are specially quoted here because they
are, I think, both illustrative not only of his virtues but also
of certain obscurities and faults. In an oblique way he
appears to laud the sun (perhaps as the symbol of right-wing
poetry struggling to reassert itself), and yet, it seems, as a
desired enemy rather than as an immediate friend. Richard
Church scarcely belongs to the school of the later Georgian
poets, the school of the Lunar Pastorals; but such stanzas,
when put in positions of prominence, are rather puzzling, and
prepare us for many half-spoken passages and their atmosphere
of half-dawn. He would embrace brilliant lights and at the
same time strive against them. He would bow down, and
at the same time withhold his service. He would revere that
he might conquer and deprive.

Had Richard Church not been such a late-comer he would
assuredly have been included in Marsh's Georgian anthologies
and achieved some reputation as a nature-poet. Though his
strongest affinities seem to be with John Donne, there is a
touch of something Wordsworthian in him, while now and
then the incisive jingling qualities of lighter Victorian verse
are flicked skilfully and enchantingly across his uncertain
sky-line:

> Walking along the pavements in the rain,
> I thought of summer, and the ripened grain
> Rolling its golden billows in the lowland valley.

> I heard above the dun rain and the din,
> Lazy yellowhammers in the whin.
> And I snuffed the scent of apples in the wet brick alley.

But perhaps he shines more brightly in the orthodox un-rhymed medium; for his blank verse at its best is intriguing, and is somewhat reminiscent of the Caroline poet, James Shirley, the last of the great Elizabethan dramatists:

> It was enough, to see her walk away
> Out of the room, out of his world of life.
> He bowed, submissive to the deathly stroke;
> But courtesy was cruel at the edge,
> A knife secreted in a rebel's hand.
> Farewell! Farewell! rang wildly in his heart.
> But hatred was the echo that returned!
> And then he knew her absence utterly,
> Knew that all sympathy and gentleness
> Were gone with her, leaving him hard of heart,
> A prince without a kingdom of content,
> With none to serve him, and with none to serve.

No poet of any consequence is quite independent, all are tied to tradition and the past. John Donne and James Shirley—these seem to be the important poets with whom Richard Church has the closest affinities. The former he has certainly cultivated, the relationship to the latter may be chiefly accidental. He is an Elizabethan gone lost—in the alleyways between the Georgians and the poets of the Celtic Twilight, in the lonely corridors between the Modernists and the Victorians.

Much of Richard Church's work is shot through with a depressing melancholy. He is nearly as despairing as Thomas Hardy. The struggling optimism of former days has given place more and more to a resigned pessimism. But he is not at one with the modern Poets of Despair, for he has always realized the necessity for form (even in his free verse), and at least some of his obscurities suggest that it is ourselves, his readers, who are at fault rather than himself. Every now and

and again his lines speak to us, intimately, personally, sympathetically, as if he were writing of our own peculiar case, though too often they are suddenly withdrawn into an obscurity with which we have no part, or which seems to contradict our sudden recognition. He is very elusive, suddenly awkward when we expect him to be mellifluous, talking to himself when we expect the continuance of a clear strong voice. Strange obscurities, asides, super-sensitive observations, cerebral introspections, too-dimly-wrought suggestions, uncertain logical connections, blur some of his most sensitive passages. Many of his virtues and vices seem to realize combination in such a poem as *The Sunset*—though it has rather more energy of movement than is generally characteristic of him:

> It would be good, now,
> To leap upon a horse,
> And ride like a fond, romantic fool,
> Into the sunset where the kings carouse,
> Clinking their cups to fabulous women's eyes,
> Their swords thrown steaming on the blood-red skies.
> For reason at its best is a sorry tool;
> My fingers tire of it. For better or worse
> I would clutch something sharper; knit my brows
> On some insaner problem of the soul,
> That has no answer hitherside the moon.
>
> Oh moral priest; Oh counter-out of tills,
> Have you not sometimes longed
> To seek the Whore of Babylon, and croon
> A lovesong in her bosom; then ride on
> To hell, and snatch Boccaccio's quills
> To write some pleasantry against the dead,
> Till all the way to Paradise is thronged
> With crowds of wanton laughter?
>   So have I done,
> Rebel of virtue for fair virtue's sake,
> Striving to put my handprint on the sun,
> That I may touch the splendour, and awake
> From righteousness, and find an empire won,

> A kingdom of sufficient enterprise
> To keep the music and its makers fed
> Until the maddening sunset leaves the skies,
> And we are citizens again,
> Creeping upon the plain,
> Moral, benign, with souls quite safely dead.

The man is at strife with himself, for the arrows of the flesh strive against the shield of the spirit. And earth strives with heaven, the amorphous with the exquisite, and fine lucidity with obscurity. Figure of speech against figure of speech, and pure sensation gives way before an assertive intellectualism. Much of his verse, like John Freeman's, rustles elusively, and goes with dreaming feet over a carpet of fluttering leaves. After all, is there not a touch of something in him which is suggestive of Rilke? And has he not, perhaps, been too frequently under the domination of that very modern mental philosopher and psychologist, Freud? He has probably put much of his best self into his novels, so that his poetry, like Meredith's, is an incomplete aspect. . . . He is at his best when he is speaking of frustrated love or contemplating Nature from a hammock under the trees.

Very opposite to Richard Church, though not entirely opposite to Humbert Wolfe, is Roy Campbell—that post-War thunderbolt dropped into the camp of lyrical timidity and convention. He has, however, rather more in common with Redwood Anderson, particularly in his energy and rhetorical impulse. He has sonority and plangency, and his poems abound with powerfully cut images. He has also something in common with Siegfried Sassoon, and frequently employs the same rhythms, though his satire for the most part is less oblique. Unlike Siegfried Sassoon he has now and again been influenced by the French Symbolists, particularly Rimbaud—whom he is not entirely unlike in human character. So in some of his verse one can expect not only superabundant colour and strange imagery but also a certain amount of oddness and obscurity—though this last applies to his latest book, *Mithraic Emblems*, more than any of the others. The English poets of incisiveness and clarity such as Pope and Dryden have influenced him as well as the French poets of suggestion. Also, he has Byronic passion and fluency, and has probably read Byron with much appreciation. His latest book, *Mithraic Emblems*, is a hotchpotch of all things, and though it contains much that is memorable and fine, it is the least disciplined of his riper work and shows a good deal of confusion in the mystical tapestry—though it throws light on Mithraism.

His first book, *The Flaming Terrapin* (1924), written in his late teens, prompted A.E. to say of him:

> No poet I have read for many years excites me to more speculation about his future, for I do not know of any poet who has such a savage splendour of epithet or who can marry the wild word so fittingly to the wild thought.

It was a remarkable performance for a mere boy; but it showed a common youthful weakness—letting drive into the dark without any clear eye on the ultimate purpose or goal. It was very nearly pure poetry, but abounded with nonsense. After that he began to discipline his great powers, and in *The Wayzgoose*, a long satirical poem in the manner of Pope or Dryden, 'guyed' amusingly, if not effectively, nearly all the white inhabitants of the South African colonies:

> Attend my fable if your ears be clean,
> In fair Banana Land we lay our scene—
> South Africa, renowned both far and wide
> For politics, and little else beside:
> Where, having torn the land with shot and shell,
> Our sturdy pioneers as farmers dwell,
> And, 'twixt the hours of strenuous sleep, relax
> To shear the fleeces or to fleece the blacks.

A later book, *Adamastor* (1930), is so far his best—South African verse, if you like, save that the poet being of Scottish descent continually bears witness to something northern in his vigour. Abounding in energy, his verse roars and thunders and vomits aggression rather than wraps us round with heavily scented African somnolence. If a crude concrete comparison be permissible it is Ben Nevis in eruption, yet wind-raked by gales from the sea, with a travelling menagerie of zebras, buffaloes, leopards, baboons, antelopes, and cobras let loose on the slopes. But such a poet could hardly be expected to strike a really popular note. The derisive *Song of the People,* a savage plea for more individualism, makes half a dozen things clear. The poet is only at one with the spirit of Revolution in that he hates fraud, sham, pompous triviality, and insincerity. He is the individualist of democracy. But as regards the herd mind he is scathing, and almost too close a bedfellow with Nietzsche. Democrat, Roy Campbell may often have declared himself to be, but it does not alter the clear evidences, that as regards his natural leanings his mind is that of the aristocrat; though every interested reader will feel that like so many of his kind he is at one with farm labourers, honest vagabonds, navvies, miners, and fishermen, all who are unspoiled by our machine civilization. His independent and aloof attitude comes out in such beautiful and impressive lines as:

> There is no joy like theirs who fight alone,
> Whom lust or gluttony have never tied,
> Who in their purity have built a throne,
> And in their solitude a tower of pride.

While such a magnificent but sombre creation as *Tristan da Cunha* (one of the few really spacious poems in modern literature) is laden with stanzas which assert his own individuality knit with the arts of Milton and Byron, such as:

> Your strength is that you have no hope or fear,
> You march before the world without a crown,
> The nations call you back, you do not hear,
> The cities of the earth grow grey behind you,
> You will be there when their great flames go down
> And still the morning in the van will find you.

While, in another key, the last lines of *African Moonrise* (concerning a noisy dog which disturbed the night) express something of the same spirit of proud sympathy, though blent with swagger and mockery:

> Sing on, lone voice! make all the desert ring,
> My listening spirit kindles and adores . . .
> Such were my voice, had I the heart to sing,
> But mine should be a fiercer howl than yours!

But swagger and mockery have always been two of the half-dozen driving forces of Roy Campbell's art, and are as constituent of his virtues as his vices. Other vices are only too plain, for he is hag-ridden by an egotistical and undisciplined imagination. Even his greatest poem, *Tristan da Cunha*, is not free from blind driving, while *The Albatross*—a poem heavily laden with the jewellery and golden ore of Symbolism—turns terrific swashbuckler somersaults as it flies. And yet how good it is, weighted with things of this kind:

> I had been dashed in the gold spray of dawns,
> And hit with silver by the stars' faint light,
> The red moon charged at me with lowered horns,
> Buffalo-shouldered by the gloom of night.

He gets much pleasure out of the continually recurrent colour red, and also out of allusions to charging horns—in particular bull-fighting. During recent years he has lived much in the south of France, where he has played a prominent part in all sorts of sports, including bull-fighting. The biographical notice in Maurice Wollman's anthology, *Modern Poetry: 1922–34*, says of him:

Razeteur and professional lancer in La Joyeuse Lance (champions of the Mediterranean in Les Joûtes Nautiques, 1929–31). Took three cocardes in the Arena at Arles and Nîmes, 1921. Won the cocarde at the grand taurine gala of Istres, 1931, fighting and throwing the bull single-handed without the aid of cape.

And the 1937 *Who's Who* tells us that his last address was at Toledo in Spain, that he won the steer-throwing for Provence, that he is a bull-fighter both on foot and on horseback, and that his recreations are poetry, horses, cattle, drawing, and the guitar.

If one cared to liken to him to some wild animal it is the antelope or some other species of South African deer that one would call to mind, rather than the bull. He has speed (often immense speed), nimbleness, elasticity. His verse goes forward like a railway train or motor car, and with none of its joints clanking. Even in those old-fashioned rhythms in which he chooses to express himself, there is no doubt about the nimbleness and litheness, though they rush rather too monotonously in a tearing straight line. But it is remarkable how good a medium he has made out of such outworn things as anapaests in his poem, *The Palm*.

Perhaps as a satirist he has overstepped himself. One of his later books, *The Georgiad*, though often amusing and clever enough, is very uncompromising. Sir John Squire and the Georgians, Humbert Wolfe, and others come in for some ferociously hard and deep stabs. In *Mithraic Emblems* the modernist poets, though also assaulted, have been thrust against with rather more moderation. Certain of the lines, too, pin this absurd New Age, with the most rebellious of recent poets thrown in on the top of it:

> The sky had been reformed. There was no moon,
> The Sun resigned before the afternoon,
> The morning got the sack for being late,
> And daytime had been voted out of date;
> The stars were scrapped by order (for their fires
> Had had some sort of dealing with our sires
> But overhead more orderly to show
> A roof of patent globes was seen to glow,
> Not flung in gay disorder through the skies,
> But parallel and of a standard size,
> With numbers on them, written large and plain,
> And holes between them—to let in the rain.

That is moderate, for, generally speaking, Wolfe and the more caustic Sassoon are gentlemanly satirists in comparison.

A more recent satirist, but with closer affinity to Humbert

Wolfe than Sassoon or Roy Campbell, though he uses the heroic couplet of Pope and Dryden in the orthodox manner of Roy Campbell (see its curious individualistic changes in Humbert Wolfe's *News of the Devil*), is Gerald Bullett.   But his verse-story, *The Bubble* (1934), about the modern literary world is perhaps more a *jeu d'esprit* than satire, though it contains some satiric passages.   It does not really represent the modern literary world, being a genial caricature, and indeed somewhat frivolous caricature of it, rather than a mordant revelation, and indirectly raises the question—when is caricature satire, and to what extent can satire be really effective as complete caricature?   The poem has not been entirely understood, for though it appeared to be satire it had no particular quality of indignation or disgust in it.   Similar to *The Bubble* and yet violently different is Robert Nichols's *Fisbo* (1934), which probably sprang out of Roy Campbell's *Georgiad* (which in its turn sprang out of Pope's *Dunciad*).   But *Fisbo*, though the theme is not unlike, is a much longer, more diffuse, and more ambitious poem than *The Bubble*, and is mainly satirical, sometimes savagely and painfully satirical, and completely scourges the insincerity of fame-hunting poetasters and opportunist critics and reviewers.   Robert Nichols, though a good Elizabethan, and at one time a passable Georgian, shines in that kind of thing, but Bullett shines better as a pure lyrist, contemplating Beauty, Love, and Nature in the old manner (see his *Poems in Pencil*), with only slight impacts coming from the modern poets:

> Because I love her
> The sky is dark above her.
> Because I find her fair,
> There is menace in the very air.
> A single leaf of the tree
> Is not more frail than she,
> Whose every breath
> Draws her, because I love her, nearer death.

He seems to have drawn some of his verbal inspiration from the Carolines and Elizabethans.   He is a very careful craftsman and parsimonious in his output—which is all to his good, for though over forty, he is at present only at his beginnings as regards verse, and for the moment more important as a novelist than a poet.

Another finicking poet, and also rather recent, is the pastoral poet, Andrew Young. But his output is much larger than Gerald Bullett's, and it has rather more in common with Modernism. His prime literary roots, however, seem to be in Edmund Blunden, Edward Thomas, and the American pastoral poet, Robert Frost. But he is rather more condensed and lyrical than Blunden, and though he has not the clarity and warm feeling of Edward Thomas, his metrical forms are more studied, and are associable with Walter de la Mare's. He appears to live very close to Nature, though he is not always completely successful in translating his impressions. For instance, in a poem addressed to the river Dove, he speaks of an angler as 'a legless trunk wading your water.' But the association is surely with the trunk of a tree, which has no legs at any time, while as regards the angler he rarely wades more than two or three inches above the knee, the tops of his legs visible and moving. Andrew Young is more successful in couplets and short stanzas than in whole poems, some of his couplets being remarkable for their sensitiveness of construction and felicity of image, as in:

> Not by those high fells where the forces
> Fall from the mist like the white tails of horses,

Or:

> A cuckoo called his name
> Behind the waving veil of dismal rain.

Or:

> And single stars I saw
> Crossing themselves in awe.

Sometimes, however, he hovers between the startlingly good and the alienating, as in:

> You are as white as sin
> To your black kith and kin.

Andrew Young's chief faults seem to be preciosity and an oddness of image and association which are perhaps due less to the Modernists than to strong contacts with the Jacobean and Caroline metaphysical poets. But his virtues are much in excess of his faults, and in his hypersensitive, but dour way, he rivets the attention as a very important poet of Nature.

But the number of older poets standing outside the Georgian encampment (indeed a few of them were rather too late for it) who have no or little affinity with the extreme modernists, but who really demand a special book to themselves, is very nearly uncountable. They include nearly all the women poets (of whom more anon), and besides those already summed up, such names as Lazarus Aaronson, Claude Colleer Abbott, H. H. Abbott, Clifford Bax, F. V. Branford, A. E. Coppard, R. C. K. Ensor, Lord Gorell, Louis Golding, John Gray, R. Rostrevor Hamilton, Aldous Huxley, Julian Huxley, Frank Kendon, F. L. Lucas, P. H. B. Lyon (the head master of Rugby School), Hugh MacDiarmid, F. O. Mann, R. L. Mégroz, Edward H. W. Meyerstein, Edwin Muir (not to be confused with Kenneth Muir, a younger poet), Huw Menai, Wallace B. Nichols (not to be confused with Robert Nichols), Alan Porter, Edgell Rickword, Geoffrey Scott, Horace Shipp, Henry Warren, Charles Williams. None of them is over sixty-two, and none more than a few months under forty, while two or three are already dead.

Some of them, such as Edwin Muir and Edgell Rickword, are rather hard nuts to crack, in that, while being vigorous disciples of the formalists, they are brain-racked, and seem to stand between two camps. Edwin Muir has probably been much affected by Freud, while Edgell Rickword has certainly come under French influences, and like Roy Campbell seems to have partly fallen under the spell of Rimbaud (though I believe his literary debt to Rimbaud is considerably greater than Roy Campbell's)—while he has also written a very interesting book about him. R. L. Mégroz (whose own poetry is more or less submerged under his books of criticism) seems to think that Rickword has been somewhat influenced by Francis Thompson; but he hits the nail more soundly on the head when he calls him 'a saturnine dreamer.'[1]   Much of Rickword's verse is certainly very dreamy and very saturnine, and one of his frequent dreams concerns the beginnings of the universe and the first ascents of primitive man—but not with any optimistic eye on the present.   An even more depressing pessimist than Thomas Hardy (but with whom, of course, he has little in common), he contemplates with both disapproval and cynical resignation many of the shattered values of this post-War age:

> the sabotage of all the delicate tools,
> the swift insidious wheels, the quiet machines
> where the cramped mind weaves endless slave designs.

The new art, the new thought, are both of them loathly, but the old pre-War art as carried on by its present-day votaries is a manifestation of 'the cramped mind' which 'weaves endless slave designs.'   An Ishmaelite between two worlds, he goes on to speak of

> the death dance on the tight-rope of the will
> taut over chaos crammed with serried masks.

But he can sometimes be a poet of pure beauty, as in *The Tired Lover*, where he turns Gautier's Parnassian lyric *Chinoiserie* into a lyric of very deft suggestive symbolism—applicable to his own case and those of his own war-weary fellow soldier-poets.   He is, I am inclined to think, the only complete and satisfactory English Symbolist, though some of his symbolism seems rather too out of the way.   Though quite independent, he is not entirely unlike W. J. Turner, and, like Turner, he has been affected by Baudelaire.   Unusual sensitiveness to things physical, indeed almost morbid sensitiveness, renders some of his verse rather unseizable, while he sometimes translates a general natural effect into a curious human symbol,

[1] See Mégroz's critical study, *Modern English Poetry: 1882–1932.*

K

(as in *Moonrise over Battlefield*), which is the painter's job rather more than the poet's:

> After the fallen sun the wind was sad
> like violins behind immense old walls.
> Trees were musicians swaying round the bed
> of a woman in gloomy halls.
>
> In privacy of music she made ready
> with comb and silver dust and fard;
> under her silken vest her little belly
> shone like a bladder of sweet lard.

He is quite clearly not a satisfactory traditionalist, though tradition triumphs in his form.

Edwin Muir's intellectualism, on the other hand, works best inwards rather than outwards, and is philosophic and contemplative rather than nervously impressionist. But though up to the present he also has moved too much in a dream world, and has been too little in contact with real life, he seems to be developing along more forcible lines. A very recent poem, *Letters*, in the *London Mercury* (November 1937), shows him free of most of his vagueness, so that without yielding an inch of fundamentally intellectual ground he speaks to us with the tongue of lucid passion. His two most recent books, *Variations on a Time Theme* (1934) and *Journeys and Places* (1937), are very uneven in content, though generally excellent in technique. Occasionally his technique is not entirely unlike that of Peter Quennell, a younger poet with a much smaller output, who in his second book seemed to show some influence coming from the French Symbolists (but who, strange to say, started his literary career as a nature poet and got into the final issue of Edward Marsh's pastoral caravan). But Edwin Muir also employs old Scottish ballad forms, which he handles with exceptional mastery. Unfortunately for the average reader, many of his poems say something quite other than they at first appear to say, are, in fact, Surrealism, but Surrealism masquerading as traditional thought and conventional narrative. He is bound hand and foot to the Past, and yet he distrusts and fears the Past and strives against it. At any rate, while admiring the old stock-in-trade with a part of his being he seems to feel that in doing so he is a traitor to his whole being, to say nothing of his friends. He was born and bred in a place which he says he no longer recognizes, and yet he cannot walk out of it. The resultant poem is often extraordinary, and not a little painful. Take, for instance, *The Town Betrayed*, with its ultimate anti-Romantic stanzas (anti-Romantic in content, not in form):

> There our ancestral ghosts are gathered.
> Fierce Agamemnon's form I see,
> Watching as if his tents were Time,
> And Troy Eternity.
>
> We must take order, bar our gates,
> Fight off these phantoms. Inland now
> Achilles, Siegfried, Lancelot
> Have sworn to bring us low.

Edwin Muir ought to be treading in the footsteps of William Morris or G. K. Chesterton, but instead of that he is expressing his disgust with modern civilization in notes of icy despair, while he seems to be trying to spring out of the bed of a new morality, which, up to the present, no one has really formulated. He has, however, shown that he can avoid all that, and be profoundly meditative and finely communicative at the same moment.

Lord Gorell is the complete contrary of Edwin Muir; and if a person can be an anachronism, well then, Lord Gorell is an anachronism. He writes so entirely in the manner of earlier poets, such as Cowper and Wordsworth—and, in spite of his unhurried pace and rustic quietness, perhaps even Shelley—that he is difficult to assess. His thoughts and emotions are those of the common conservative man of sensitive intelligence and moral sympathy untouched by stunts and new literary movements, and unruffled by the disordered values of this new age. He is the normal imaginative man made vocal and delighting in poetry—expressed so exquisitely in:

> Lone midst the mountains, singing as a bird
> To Maker and to mate, lives Poetry:
> I, by the world applauded—or unheard,
> Her servant am, singing to Heaven and thee.

He has nothing in common with the Georgian pastoral poets except in the debt he shows to Wordsworth (for the Georgian technique or manner was generally very different), and no affinity with the Modernists save that in satirizing and parodying some of them he has shown a certain amount of knowledge of their existence. He seems to have much admiration for Greek poetry and to reveal Greek influences, particularly in his many long poems. But by no means all his simple verse has the beauty or vitality of the four lines quoted, though there is this to be said about some of the least impressive and most conventional, it often gives pleasure upon re-reading, and upon a second or third acquaintance to unfold a sensitiveness of thought or perception that at first seemed absent. Like Maurice Baring he delights in monosyllables, and makes use of a conservative vocabulary. But as with Maurice Baring his frequent threadbare words and phrases are apparently very carefully chosen; though, strange to say, he can be occasionally somewhat obscure. He has not always been too well handled by the reviewers and on one occasion answered them in this way:

> Grant it be
> Not pearls but shingle scraped from oozy bed—
> Still was it salved with labour and deep breath,
> Still was it his, his spirit's inner shrine,
> By God bestowed and humbly shared with Man:
> It called for kind, calm judgment, not for scorn. . . .

He has recently collected his poems of over thirty years into a volume of nearly six hundred pages. But the collection would surely have gained in strength and impressiveness if he had omitted about a third of the contents, and at any rate not included quite so much of his early work. Then such really good poems as *Apology*, *The Private View*, *Juventas Jactata* (satire), *On the Downs*, *Dies Irae*, *Chorus* would have come quicker under the eye. Because of the present state of the literary world I am tempted to quote the last in full:

> So shouted they in Babylon,
> 'A masterpiece! A rising sun!'
> Such was the cry in ancient Rome,
> 'A miracle! All people, come.'
>
> In Athens where the people came
> To hear the high dispute on fame,
> With worship shrill they raised to view
> The jewelled altar of the new.
>
> The wandering chorus, like a cloud,
> Now here, now there enwreathed the proud,
> And Beauty smiled and steadfast went
> In silence on her joy intent.
>
> The chorus sweeps, a wintry breath
> That flays the flowers into death—
> In Athens, Rome, and Babylon
> They were a moment and are gone.

Lord Gorell is something of a country-life poet, for at nearly all times his background is the English landscape; but more self-evident pastoral or bucolic poets are the two Abbotts, their language, too, quite conformable to the modern usage. Of the two, H. H. Abbott is the more detailed (after the manner of Blunden and Clare), but Claude Colleer is rather more forcible, and sometimes, indeed, a little brutal (after the manner of Thomas Hardy). They also both figure as translators. Claude Colleer Abbott has rendered into English many early medieval French lyrics, and H. H. Abbott a number of Anglo-Saxon riddles.

Frank Kendon, however, has still stronger affinities with the Georgian poets—particularly those who have commemorated the English scene—but he is a child of Nature more than most of them. Though too late for Edward Marsh's anthologies (his first book, *Poems and Sonnets*, was published in 1924), he was made prominent in a volume of rather similar collections by J. C. Squire. He has a really deep and sympathetic understanding of the countryside (there is certainly nothing of the week-ender about him), and when he was serving as a soldier in the East felt about things in this way:

> Oh, we speak not over much
> Of the strange lands we have seen,
> Our eyes were not for such
>   Very keen.
>
> And the brightest thing we knew,
> In a land of gaudy flowers,
> Was a daisy, tipped with dew,
>   English! Ours!

But while the technique of his verse does sometimes remind us of that of the Georgians, it displays many self-conscious devices of assonance or half-rhyming which are not common to them:

> I spend my days vainly,
>   Not in delight;
> Though the world is elate,
>   And tastes her joys finely.
>
> Here wrapped in slow musing
>   Lies my dark mind,
> To no music attuned
>   Save its own, and despising
>
> The lark for remoteness,
>   The thrush for bold lying,
> The soft wind for blowing
>   And the round sun for brightness.

> O tarry for me, sweet;
>   I shall stir! I shall wake!
> And the melody you seek
>   Shall be lovely, though late.

But others of Frank Kendon's assonance and rhyming experiments are as subtly and skilfully wrought as that, while he has also (in two or three of his poems) intermingled free verse with traditional measure. Though he is a lyric poet of distinction he has written two very long poems, *Tristram* and *A Life and Death of Judas Iscariot*, which are among the most notable narrative poems of this century. He seems to be at his best in verse-narrative, and even in his latest book of lyrics, *The Cherry Minder* (1935), his finest inclusion, *The Ends of Eden*, is really of the nature of a philosophic and religious tale.

The case of Henry Warren is more difficult to discuss. *The Times Literary Supplement* once said of him: 'Mr Warren's Muse is first cousin to Mr Blunden's.' But in the spring of 1932 Henry Warren may have considerably annoyed the Georgians, for he wrote of his 'unhappy volumes which (though like all genuine verse, they had their personal place and purpose) were so imitatively contemporary as to be mostly negligible, and certainly unworthy of the space accorded to them in reviews.' This interesting information was repeated by H. Ross Williamson in *The Bookman* of September 1932. . . . The fitting thing to say of it is that it is too amusingly candid in any way to stand against him. Some of Mr Warren's lyrics, such as *Bean-Flowers*, are too good to pass over entirely. Though he may at one time have repented of his 'unhappy volumes,' he has also, to-day, I believe, equally repented of his slighting of them. He is a very genuine pastoral poet, though to-day he is developing along somewhat other lines, his new poems being stronger and more contemplative.

Another nature poet almost as elusive to the critic as Henry Warren is Huw Menai. He has told us that he has been rather more attracted to Wordsworth than any other poet, and that the impacts of the War started him writing verse. He was born at Carnarvon, and from five to twelve was taught at 'the Ragged School,' and, in order to help his mother hawked fish, sold newspapers, and delivered parcels. He has also been a beer-bottler, a bookseller's packer, an unloader of ships' cargoes on the quays, and for some months was down a mine. During some part of his haphazard youthful career he went to South Wales, where he became an active Socialist propagandist, speaking at street corners and elsewhere, and wrote a weekly article for *Justice*. He also became a contributor to two other Socialist papers; and because of all this was denied employment in the mines and nearly starved. Considering his bitter handicaps, the metrical poise of some of his verse is a thing to wonder at, especially when it rises to the level of these entirely memorable lines:

> Though ragged all my garments are
> I still may gossip with a star,
> And that impartial dame, the moon,
> Will have her jewels about me strewn.
> And when her kindly work is done
> I find no snobbery in the sun.

A poet of large output who has yet to be more confidently judged is Edward H. W. Meyerstein. Besides lyrics, he has written many odes of a contemplative and religious character, and his prose includes a life of Chatterton. His verse, for the most part simple and intellectual, has been affected by neither Georgians nor Modernists. He stands very much alone.

As regards Frederick V. Branford and Aldous Huxley, they were included in Robert Graves's short list of 'malcontents from the Centre and Right . . . who have no great passion for revolution, and if the pinch came would defend no street barricades' (*Contemporary Techniques of Poetry*, 1925). Aldous Huxley has, I believe, well shown this side of himself in his novels; and Professor Geoffrey Bullough, in *The Trend of Modern Poetry*, says of some of his rebellious work (which, however, is cast into a completely traditional *mould*):

Pieces permeated by a typical world-weariness, an irony which played impartially over the mysteries of religion and the mysteries of the digestive organs, an introspective wit playing upon his own foibles as well as other people's in a shoulder-shrugging recognition of an all-too-common humanity (*Social Amenities*). Mr Huxley deliberately embarked upon a poetry of disgust. . . . Mr Huxley's attitude—that of an observer aspiring in vain to a lofty detachment —became prevalent after the War.

But Frederick V. Branford is not to be dismissed so easily, in that, though also a detached observer, he is shackled by no such unyielding pessimism. The biographical notice in Maurice Wollman's *Modern Poetry, 1922–34*, says of him:

Totally disabled while serving with the R.N.A.S. on the Somme. Only since 1932 has he sufficiently recovered to make any statements of his aims and methods.

He has acknowledged something of a debt to Francis Thompson; and he has also, one would deduce, been influenced by John Milton. He writes in the grand manner, and his eyes are continually cast upon vast horizons. He has something in common with J. Redwood Anderson, though he is rather more reminiscent of convention.

A very opposite poet to Mr Branford is Charles Williams, who is, generally speaking, very philosophical or theological, and slow in establishing contact with his reader. He is a crabbed, rough, and difficult poet, and apparently very much under the spell of John Donne. Of his early sonnet sequence, *The Silver Stair*, Mr A. C. Ward in his *Twentieth-Century Literature* (1928) wrote very flatteringly and declared it to be one of 'the few examples of sustained love-poetry in the twentieth century . . . a series of sonnets comparable with the *Sonnets from the Portuguese* in imaginative quality, though more intellectualized than Elizabeth Browning's.' Charles Williams has also written many blank-verse plays, where the influence of the Elizabethan dramatists (and, I believe, also Lascelles Abercrombie) is paramount. Latterly he has shown himself inclined to follow in the train that walks behind

* K

T. S. Eliot (see his recent church play, *Thomas Cranmer of Canterbury*).

Another Eliot admirer is the Scotch poet Hugh MacDiarmid. But his politics are Communist (see *Second Hymn to Lenin*, the title of one of his books of verse) and the majority of his best verse is in the Scottish vernacular. Some of his verse is too propagandist to be discussed as poetry, but in his suggestive and imaginative Gaelic-toned lyrics, he strikes a note which is original to himself:

> There was nae reek i' the laverock's hoose
> That nicht—an' nane i' mine;
> But I hae thocht o' that foolish licht
> Ever sin' syne;
> An' I think that mebbe at last I ken
> What your look meant then.

He seems to be the centre of a special Scottish school, and as such really cries out for a special chapter. One of his books bears the hypnotizing title, *A Drunk Man looks at the Thistle*.

Among poets who have published little, but whose volumes attract the critical sense, Alan Porter and Horace Shipp invite special mention. Alan Porter has published only one volume, *The Signature of Pain*, but in its distilled combination of the old and the new, of conservative form and feeling stretching elastically into the arms of a progressive, but sane intellectualism, it is unique among modern volumes. *The Times Literary Supplement* and other reviewing journals gave it a prominence which they do not often allot to a first book by a new poet. And Richard Church wrote of it in an introductory poem:

> Ah! What relief in this uneasy age
> Of pseudo-this and pseudo-that, to find
> One human being who is well-defined,
> Who, without apeing priests' or prophets' rage
> Burns with such frenzy as no mortal can
> Except he understands man's fraud on man.

Others, including Edmund Blunden and W. Force Stead

(Yeats's only religious poet), joined in with similar rhymed eulogies. And L. Aaronson (also a poet of distinction) added to the chorus of praise with:

> This is in praise of poetry, not my friend . . .
>
> .   .   .   .
>
> The verses he has forged through many days,
> Ceaseless in diligence yet bold in dream,
> Wedding deep fantasy with the closest scheme
> Of lean athletic architectural mood,
> In long sustained bright learned solitude.

As regards Horace Shipp, his later voice is not entirely unlike that of Humbert Wolfe—but as both of them are of Italian extraction, the cause may be partly other than that of influence. Both his slim books, *Hecuba in Camden Town* and *Palimpsest*, contain verse of good quality. One of the chief contents, *After Eden*, is a fine example of condensed tale-telling, and in *Hecuba in Camden Town* he shows what a virile and musical thing free verse may become in the hands of an artistic imagination:

> Camden Road
> moves on its way of dull indifference,
> or stops and stares, and smiles and passes.
> Overhead
> the clouds gloom, and the drab, brown smoke of chimneys
> sneaks from the houses, blurs and stains the sky.
>
> There is no light nor colour anywhere
> except this woman's grief—
> this gashed, slashed purple; lightning-riven passion.

It may of course be argued that such lines really resolve themselves into traditional blank verse, transformed and regulated by the pauses. But they do not as a complete whole fit into that framework, and I believe that good free verse (which best functions for purposes of satire) is always an intermingling of the traditional iambic measure with something more intimately conversational.

Horace Shipp has the eye of a painter (and in that he shows his affinity with the Pre-Raphaelites) united to a sufficiently sensitive spirituality. His greatest fault is an unpleasant trick of repeating words of weak and sugary significance:

> That night he tasted of the tree of knowledge:
> its sweet, sweet fruit; its bitter-sweet, sweet fruit.

But we have little to judge him by save a small output of early work, and like several others in this chapter, he has shown himself a poet of promise rather than of actual fulfilment; while others, such as A. E. Coppard (a brilliant writer of short stories showing the influence of Maupassant) and Louis Golding (a very successful novelist), are more famous in other spheres of work.

CHAPTER XVI

THE WOMEN POETS OF THIS CENTURY

FOR the most part the women poets of this century defy classification, for they have collected in droves, schools, and cliques less than the men. Exceptionally few of them are Modernists, and only two, Fredegond Shove and Victoria Sackville-West, were included in Edward Marsh's Georgian groups; and though their individual output has for the most part been small, it has been characterized by a very charming and disciplined lyricism. At the outbreak of war in 1914, the chief recognized women poets of the century (though not all of them were actually living) were Mary Coleridge, Michael Field (the pseudonym for two ladies who worked in collaboration), Alice Meynell, Rachel Annand Taylor, Lady Margaret Sackville, Margaret L. Woods, and perhaps Anna de Bary, together with certain members of the Irish school, particularly Katharine Tynan, Eva Gore-Booth, and Dora Sigerson Shorter.

Michael Field was the pseudonym of an aunt and niece (Katherine Bradley and Edith Cooper) who spent half their time in mutual admiration and assistance of one another and the other half in writing poetry. While one created, the other corrected, deleted, and added (at any rate that is the general supposition), and their affection for one another was so intense, that they actually did seem to become one person, so that it is impossible to detect collaboration.

They died within a few months of one another (1912, 1913), and both of them, strangely enough, of the same disease, cancer. This closed a literary career of great industry in which over a score of verse plays and several volumes of lyrics passed through the press. Their springs were partly in the Yellow

269

Nineties, to which period they seem to half belong. Their poetry is characterized by passion, colour, and felicity of rhythm and word—the themes of Love and Death being chiefly dwelt upon. Though little appreciated to-day, it is not impossible that the name Michael Field may yet come to be classed with Christina Rossetti or Elizabeth Barrett Browning.

As regards the others, some of them might be classed under the heading of religious poets (in the more conventional sense of the word), particularly Mary Coleridge (but a very variable lyrist), Anna de Bary (who, I think, was the least known), and Katharine Tynan. Of these Mary Coleridge was hardly less popular than Alice Meynell, for a collection of her poems published in 1907, just after her death, had, before the War, gone into a sixth edition. Her poems, very short, are not merely characterized by beauty of form (though her form is rather more conventional than Alice Meynell's) but are also very interesting. In the majority of them there is a definite idea worked out with clarity and spontaneity to a lyrical climax. Sir Henry Newbolt, a much respected pre-War critic as well as poet, said of her work: 'Mary Coleridge, though legitimately descended from many poets, was the imitator of none. Her poems were the offspring of character not less than of intellect.' And Robert Bridges: 'It is their intimacy and spontaneity that give them so great a value. They will be her portrait, an absolutely truthful picture of a wondrously beautiful and gifted spirit, whom thought could not make melancholy, nor sorrow sad.' She is rather more crystallized and tangible than Alice Meynell, and less clogged by sentimentality than Katharine Tynan. Her best-known and most beautiful lyric, *Our Lady*, I think more perfectly voices, in its opening stanzas, the Socialist origins of Christianity than any other poem in the English tongue:

> Mother of God! no lady thou:
> Common woman of common earth
> Our Lady ladies call thee now,
> But Christ was never of gentle birth;
> A common man of the common earth.

> For God's ways are not as our ways.
> The noblest lady in the land
> Would have given up half her days,
> Would have cut off her right hand
> To bear the child that was God of the land.

Another poet of the old school with a variable voice was Rachel Annand Taylor—a very passionate romantic with an occasional touch of real magic in her finger-nail, as in:

> We crazed for you, aspired and fell for you;
> Over us trod Desire, with feet of fire.
> Ah! the sad stories we would tell for you,
> Full of dark nights and sighing
> While—you were dying,
>   Chrysola.

And an equally fluent poet (but with fewer tendencies in the direction of rhapsody) was Margaret L. Woods, a dramatic as well as lyrical poet with a large output. Her language, to-day, sounds a little outmoded and her general stock-in-trade too conventionally Victorian, though some of her lyrical verse, such as *To the Forgotten Dead* and *Good Friday Night*, quite certainly have the quality of real greatness. But her strongest powers seem best displayed in her blank-verse dramas. . . . In contradistinction, a more restrained artistic voice is that of Lady Margaret Sackville, who seems to come midway between the Georgians and the poets of the Yellow Nineties. But she has fewer inclinations in the direction of decadence than the poets of the Yellow Nineties, while she seems to have rather more grip on moral and intellectual subjects than had the characteristic Georgian poets of pastoral life—to which a remarkable sonnet, *To One Who Denies* (published during the War), will bear witness: [1]

[1] This poem, which definitely belongs to a past phase, is not in any way a contribution to the post-War elasticity of mind which tends to put everything new, however outrageous, upon a pedestal of reverence. And at Lady Margaret Sackville's special request I have made one slight alteration, and substituted 'Pasteur' for 'Darwin.'

Old friend, I greet you! You are still the same:
You poisoned Socrates, you crucified
Christ, you have persecuted, mocked, denied,
Rejected God and cursed Him—in God's name.
You gave monotonously to the flame
All those (whom now you honour) when the new
Truth stung their lips—for fear it might be true;
Then reaped where they had sown and felt no shame.

Familiar voice, old adversary—hail!
Yesterday's fools are now your gods. Behold!
The generations pass and we can wait.
You slandered Pasteur, Florence Nightingale;
Now a new splendour quivers in the cold,
Grey shadows overhead; still you are late.

Lady Margaret Sackville, however, like Margaret L. Woods
and others, has also published since the War. She is often a
poet of pure beauty, one of the very best, and really ranks
among the first half-dozen of living women verse-writers.
Any inclination that she may have had in the direction of
wordiness has completely left her, for she has, since the War,
published much verse of epigrammatic shortness and texture.

Between the outbreak of war in 1914 and the present date,
an enormous number of women poets worthy of attention have
floated into the public consciousness. To what extent this
has been due to the emancipation of women, and through it
a liberation of their artistic gifts, is not quite clear; but certain it is that there are so many of them that in the compass
of a short chapter it is impossible to deal with all of them
quite justly and in their right proportions. Two of them,
Victoria Sackville-West and Ruth Pitter, both of whom won
the Hawthornden prize for poetry, compete for first laurels
as the most important women poets of the day, and though
a best seller among them has been Edith Sitwell, other
qualities than those of artistic excellence have been conducive
to her popularity.

Very few readers were aware of the existence of Ruth Pitter
until the appearance of Alida Monro's anthology in 1933

(*Recent Poetry : 1923–33*), when many readers grouped her among the more baffling of the modernists. But this was not the real Ruth Pitter, rather was it a ragging creature with her tongue in her cheek. . . . It is true that *Digdog* (one of the contents) was included in her *Mad Lady's Garland*, but there in its context it could be sufficiently understood, while as a detached poem it seemed to pass the limits of tomfoolery.

Ruth Pitter's first book of verse was published in 1920, her second in 1927, her third in 1930. No response of any consequence from either public or critics. But with her fourth, *A Mad Lady's Garland*, which contained a glowing preface from Hilaire Belloc, and was further supported by A.E., De la Mare, and others, came the beginnings of her fame. Here was a strong masculine voice, at any rate a voice that spoke with that creative completeness that has always been associated with male art rather than female, and with so much classical shape and restraint that one is almost tempted to speak of her as the first woman classicist. Of her *Mad Lady's Garland*, A.E. wrote: 'I would shrink from the grotesque poetry in *A Mad Lady's Garland* with all the shuddering with which we remove ourselves from the vicinity of cockroaches or earwigs, only Miss Pitter makes the creatures of her fantasy —spiders, fleas, cockroaches, worms, mice, or whatever else —speak so classically, and with so exquisite an artifice, that I am stayed to listen to them, and admit into my house of soul thoughts I would have closed the door upon if they had not come dressed in so courtly a fashion,' succinctly describing as well as eulogizing the contents of the book—which, however, can sometimes be identified with the symbolical, so that some of these animals and insects of hers seem to be people, and not necessarily unintelligent creatures whom Ruth Pitter has endowed with human thought. But the classical features of her verse are more to the front in a later book, *A Trophy of Arms*, which tempted James Stephens to a comparison with the middle period of W. B. Yeats: 'Were I asked—Who is the poet now best using the English language? I should answer, W. B. Yeats—considered as from ten years ago; and were it further inquired—Who is the next, the companion poet to that fine artist? I should answer, Ruth Pitter.' Be that as it may, there is no doubt that Ruth Pitter shows unusual power and skill in her medium:

> Your thoughts are vast, yet shapeless things,
> And never done, like Babel tower:
> But to its life this spirit brings
> Completeness, like the five-leaved flower . . .

which might also be taken as definitive of Ruth Pitter's own lyrical personality in comparison with many of her contemporaries. But as regards her medium she walks in borrowed garments. There is nothing particularly new or original about her form, and even that stanza and the whole movement of the poem from which it is taken will, in its texture, remind many readers of Gordon Bottomley's *To Iron-Founders and Others*. Her triumph lies in the exactness (yet freshness) with which she applies her words to a deeply imaginative and spiritual outlook upon her life. Like a true poet, she rarely lies or distorts. And if sometimes her revelations are formulated in rather too difficult or obscure speech, she more often communicates by a swift simplicity:

> I cast away, I cast away
> Things childish, and am not forlorn;
> But she had better have died, the day
> She stood so fair beneath the thorn.

During the War years and immediately following them Ruth Pitter was not in evidence. But well to the front was Muriel Stuart — her first poems published in the *English Review*, and her first book, *Christ at Carnival*, published in 1916. She seemed something of an overflow from the Yellow Nineties, a sort of female Dowson with a dash of Keats, but united to something considerably more pedestrian than either, and very individually herself. She was, in particular, a poet of physical passion, expressing, too, all the disillusionment that comes from it. She was sometimes no perfect artist;

but in nearly every instance, however much she reiterated, varied, or avoided her central theme, the sincerity and strong emotionalism of her verse belaurelled her with special distinction, and drew from Thomas Hardy the remark that at its best it was 'superlatively good.' The theme and treatment of some of her most characteristic poems—among them *The Bastard* and *The Centaur's First Love*—put her into the company of D. H. Lawrence, whom she might very well have preceded, so little does she reveal any actual influence. She is in some of her earlier verse, like Lawrence, a poet of the generative forces of earth, of that dark creative passion which defies human law and convention and goes its own way to its fulfilment or undoing. Latterly, as is quite natural, and following a perfectly logical development (especially as in her childhood 'she lived a free life in the woods and fields,' and is sprung on one side 'from hard-riding West of England squires') she has donned, if not very completely, the garments of a nature or pastoral poet. But it is in such a poem as *Mrs Effingham's Swan Song* that she reveals her most characteristic qualities and strikes her most moving note:

> I am growing old . . .
> I was not always kind when I was young
> To women who were old, for Youth is blind—
> A small, green, bitter thing beneath its fragrant rind,
> And fanged against the old with boisterous tongue—
> Those whose poor morning heads are touched with rime,
> Walking before their misery like kings.
> I did not think that I should feel such stings,
> Or flinch beneath such arrows, but now I know.

But in 1916, the year which saw the publication of Muriel Stuart's first collection, appeared Charlotte Mew's famous volume, *The Farmer's Bride*. She was already approaching her fiftieth year, so we may take it that these original and fresh-flavoured poems were in the nature of a small selection, and the ripened grain left out of much sifting. Her second volume, *The Rambling Sailor*, appeared in 1929; but further expectation had been cut short by her sudden death from her own hand in a nursing home just before its appearance—the final gesture of a very troubled unhappy life. She has an exceptional gift of narration (if sometimes too condensed) and her best poems are poignantly beautiful and very haunting, and these notes are intensified by her preoccupation with death and disaster. One can almost identify her with the unhappy fairy of her poem, *The Changeling* (in *The Farmer's Bride*), the only completely satisfactory poem of its kind in English literature:

> Toll no bell for me, dear Father, dear Mother,
>   Waste no sighs;
> There are my sisters, there is my little brother
>   Who plays in the place called Paradise,
> Your children all, your children for ever;
>   But I so wild
> Your disgrace, with the queer brown face, was never,
>   Never, I know, but half your child!

But it cannot be judged in selection, and to get its real flavour must be read through to its catastrophic conclusion:

> Black and chill are Their nights on the wold;
>   And They live so long and They feel no pain.
> I shall grow up, but never grow old,
> I shall always, always be very cold.
>   I shall never come back again!

It is interesting to compare the poem with Margaret Woods's *Changeling*, where it is the mother that speaks, whereas in Charlotte Mew's evident answer to it (there are obvious parallels, even in the language) the child explains why, to her intense regret, she has been such a naughty little girl.

Another poet not very distantly removed from Charlotte Mew, is that fine pastoral novelist, Mary Webb, who spent most of her life in the country, and therefore in external appearances lived much closer to nature than Charlotte Mew —who spent most of her life in the heart of Bloomsbury.

Still, her affinity with Charlotte Mew is not really very close, though it is certainly shown in such suggestively beautiful lines as:

> She was born and bred with the birds,
> Their words were her words.
> For she was come out of the earth and water;
> From lily leaf and ash bole.
> She said, 'I am the moaning forest's daughter,
> A tree hath my soul.'
> She slipped away between sunset and moonrise,
> Between town-hall and steeple,
> Back to her own people.
> Who knows where she wanders, where she lies?

Another of the poignant poets, and with a rather closer affinity to Charlotte Mew in that she is quite as much a poet of sorrow, is Mary Morison Webster—who has not yet received a quarter the attention which is her due. Her best poems are characterized by much depth of feeling united to precision of form, as in:

> Lord, who gavest this grief to me,[1]
> See, from out its bitter Tree,
> How, all night I sing to Thee.
>
> Though my heart with anguish break,
> Out of sorrow, for Thy sake,
> I, Thy Bird, do sweetness make.

But she is not exactly a religious poet. The religious note has been struck more forcibly by Fredegond Shove—who has strong affinities with Christina Rossetti. Very few people were aware of her existence until the inclusion of some of her lyrics in Edward Marsh's fourth Georgian anthology. One of them, *The New Ghost*, was not only one of the best half-dozen

---

[1] This is the prefatory lyric to Mary Morison Webster's third volume of lyrics, *Alien Guest*. All her volumes, like Charlotte Mew's, were published by the Poetry Bookshop.

poems in the book, but the only completely 'religious' poem in the series. She almost seems to distrust her art (or something conducive to her art) as an alienating force which may ultimately move across her vision of God and her duty to mankind, for one of her books, *Daybreak*, opens with a very powerful renunciative *Liturgy*, of which the first lines may be taken as typical:

> O deliver me, deliver me from my own self,
> From treachery, from fear, from hate;
> It seems so long that I have been laid upon the shelf
> Like a broken cup or a too, too brittle plate;
> Take me, O take me; wash me with your beams;
>   O good Lord, deliver me,
> Deliver me from the horror and from the dishonour of my dreams;
>   Set me free.

As regards Frances Cornford, though she has written one long poem, *Death and the Princess*, a morality play, her poems are generally short, and her notes variable, ranging from lyrics written through the eyes of a little child (and done with remarkable psychological rightness) to meditations on Death, Cambridge, and Nature. Her best-known lyric, *To a Fat Lady seen from the Train*, is an indulgence in light satire, and her most perfectly musical stanza is:

> I ran out in the morning when the air was clean and new,
> And all the grass was glittering, and grey with autumn dew,
> I ran out to the apple tree and pulled an apple down,
> And all the bells were ringing in the old grey town.

Not only Frances Cornford but nearly all the recent women poets have been influenced by the Georgian Pastoral movement, none more so than V. Sackville-West, who in 1926 published a modern Georgic, *The Land*, which would have made her the central figure of the Georgian Pastoral school if the front place had not been so firmly held by Edmund Blunden. In this book of the four seasons, Winter, Spring, Summer, Autumn, she tied herself closer to the first James

Thomson than any other English poet, though the technique
of her verse was Georgian rather than Thomsonian:

> I sing the cycle of my country's year,
> I sing the tillage, and the reaping sing,
> Classic monotony, that modes and wars
> Leave undisturbed, unbettered, for their best
> Was born immediate, of expediency.

But classic monotony is not the feature of her abundant
lyrical verse, which ranges from the pastoral to the human
and philosophic.

A more curious nature poet (one cannot quite call her
pastoral) is Lady Dorothy Wellesley, who touches fingers with
the Modernists, and comes midway between the Georgians
and the Modernists (forming almost a connecting-link). And
yet another is Sylvia Lynd—who, however, stands much closer
to the Georgians, so close, indeed, that many of her admirers
have been puzzled to account for her absence from Edward
Marsh's caravan. Sylvia Lynd is one of the truest of poets,
for she has a quick eye, a sensitive perception, and a technique
which expresses exactly what she wants to say. Not entirely
unlike her is Stella Gibbons, of whose first book, *The Mountain
Beast*, Edward Shanks wrote: 'The best book of verse I have
read since Blunden's *Waggoner*.' But Stella Gibbons is rather
less detailed in her recordings of natural phenomena than
either Blunden or Sylvia Lynd.

Another pastoral writer, Eiluned Lewis, is rather more to
the front in prose than in verse, but her very sensitive study
of child-life in the country, *Dew on the Grass*, would set her
among the poets even if she had written no verse.

Two others who seem to come into the pastoral circle are
V. H. Friedlaender and Teresa Hooley, though their notes
are very variable. Moreover, they are both emotionalists who
walk rather too near the edge of the precipice of sentimentality,
and they both indulge their occasional indignations in satire.
Teresa Hooley was once somewhat too depreciatingly called
by Edith Sitwell 'a soprano crooner,' though it is true

that the elbowing intrusion of her sex tends to thwart her intention as an artist. But Miss V. H. Friedlaender—who is also known as a weekly critic of her contemporaries—has rather closer perception of herself, and therefore in her lyrical moments shows a greater self-restraint, exemplified in such a stanza as:

> Lock the door of your heart
> On hope as on despair;
> Before your spirit can take flight
> There must be quiet there.

Then add to them the Yorkshire poet Dorothy Una Ratcliffe, who can turn out a good robust lyric in dialect, or write delightfully of the Yorkshire dales, and the English feminine pastoral company is very nearly complete.

But the lyrical company is by no means complete, for it further includes Margot Robert Adamson, Marion Angus, Stella Benson, Gwen Clear, Nancy Cunard, Elizabeth Daryush, Joan A. Easdale, Eleanor Farjeon, Yvonne ffrench, Viola Garvin, Jean Guthrie-Smith, Robin Hyde, Violet Jacob, Everest Lewin, Lilian Bowes Lyon, Rose Macaulay, N. K. McCausland, Orgill MacKenzie, Katherine Mansfield, Eva Martin, Phyllis Mégroz, Viola Meynell, Susan Miles, Margaret M. Radford, Grace Rhys, Madeleine C. Rock, Margot Ruddock, Blanaid Salkeld, Ruth Manning Sanders, Jean Smith, Jan Struther (Mrs Joyce M. Graham), Pamela Travers, Iris Tree, Evelyn Underhill, Sylvia Townsend Warner, Anna Wickham.

The latest comer is N. K. McCausland, whose recent volume, *The Legendary Shore*, is as spontaneously wild and intellectually imaginative as anything ever turned out by a woman, and, if imperfect, is at least a volume of great promise.

As regards Viola Meynell, she is a daughter of Alice Meynell, and though different from her in manner, she deserves at least a leaf from her mother's laurels. Her *Arab Love*, a powerful and beautiful poem, is as interesting in content as it is compelling in its musical, flexible rhythms.

Rather apart from any of them is Evelyn Underhill, a distinguished prose writer on religious mysticism, and a poet of religious mysticism, who occasionally establishes a dim relationship with A.E.

One of the most original is Susan Miles, who has chiefly distinguished herself as a poet of free verse, and free verse, strange to say, which though it may be often prosy, avoids some of the deepest pitfalls of the Modernists and Imagists, and is nearly always readable, compelling, and interesting. But in the second part of *Dunch*, and in two other little books, she has also shown how good she can be occasionally as a traditional formalist, although in such verse her peculiar critical imagination has felt itself too shackled; and so she has turned to free verse (which perhaps should rather be designated 'prose-verse') for expressing a completer vision of life as she sees it. But her own preference to-day is for her metrical verse, while she is probably best known by her very long, very strange and highly poetical novel, *Blind Men crossing a Bridge* (which really, I think, ought to have been written in blank verse instead of rhythmical prose).

A very original and meditative poet is Elizabeth Daryush, a daughter of Robert Bridges, and somewhat influenced by him, her quality at its best shown in such an irregular sonnet as:

> If your loved one prove unworthy, why then,
> by this much you 're the freer: if the block
> to which you 're bolted warp and shrink away,
> why then, it only gives you further play,
> makes life rough for you, of course, with its knock
> and rattle, with defection's loud sudden
> jars, but your own quiet integrity,
> tried thus the more, has but more room to be.
>
> So says one truth, but soon says another:
> Now in your soul-tissues a wrong sap stains
> the white rose that you were; your heart sustains
> the wild-thorn traits of your grafted partner:
> when the mistaken marriage mortifies,
> it 's your own branch and stem and root that dies.

But she is frequently a difficult poet whose meaning escapes us just as we seem to have captured it. It is strange, especially in consideration of her fresh and careful use of words, that she has not achieved greater popularity. Margot Ruddock, a new and very young poet whom W. B. Yeats has recently highly praised, has some affinity to her, though Margot Ruddock is less disciplined, and seems to write rather more out of her subconscious being. Moreover, at present Margot Ruddock is a poet of promise rather than actual achievement. But Elizabeth Daryush with her distant traditional roots in John Donne and Shakespeare's sonnets is a matured poet for the serious consideration of maturity, and she is all the more to be extolled in that she has so modestly labelled her various books, and called the contents not poems, but 'verses.' There is nothing stationary about Elizabeth Daryush either, for her powers are very much on the upgrade, her verse more and more crystallizing and ripening. (See, for instance, her recent book, *The Last Man*, published by the Oxford University Press, 1936.) She is, in fact, a traditional Modernist—rather different from the older poet Blanaid Salkeld, whose recent tantalizing, though at moments really thoughtful and beautiful long poem, *The Fox's Covert*, seems to be a seventy per cent contribution to the subconscious, but with the concrete feature that its stanza is of a new kind.

Other intellectual poets—or semi-intellectual poets—are Nancy Cunard, Anna Wickham, Rose Macaulay, and Sylvia Townsend Warner. Nancy Cunard's first book, *Outlaws*, was published soon after the War, and though it contains a good deal of modernist feeling is in no sense modernist in form. It was very highly rated by George Moore, who wrote a long and enthusiastic review of it in the *Observer*, and ensured its temporary success. She is perhaps the first woman poet who prayed to God to be given a hard heart—though her demands were not entirely unreasonable, and one of the lines ('And make me suffer singly') seems to be touched with laudable unselfishness:

> Oh God, make me incapable of prayer,
> Too brave for supplication, too secure
> To feel the taunt of danger! Let my heart
> Be tightened mightily to withstand pain,
> And make me suffer singly, without loss.

A later book, *Parallax*, is based on Eliot's *Waste Land*, but if less suggestive, it is rather more comprehensible than *The Waste Land*. Her other books are *Sublunary* and a large anthology of negro verse called *Negro*, which is the fruit of her social activities on behalf of the oppressed negro.

An intenser lyrical note with occasional colouring from the old Border ballad has been struck by Sylvia Townsend Warner—where poetry is often bedfellow with wit. She condenses, concentrates, and likes to contrast and associate and turn two aspects into one. Sometimes she trots out a very startling stanza:

> Christ, here are nails,
> Once driven in, will never lose their hold:
> Forged at Krupp's, Creusot's, Vickers', and tipped with gold
> Pen-nibs that signed the Treaty of Versailles.

In her technique, particularly in *The Espalier*, she sometimes reminds one of Humbert Wolfe. She is pastoral, anecdotal, meditative, folk-lore susceptible—all kinds of things — and her lyrical output has been considerably larger than is generally realized. She has also written one long narrative poem, *Opus 7*.

But Anna Wickham is more difficult to pin, and her lines *Self-Analysis* perhaps explain why she has so frequently eluded the anthology hunter, who seeks for definitiveness in the general output, and repose in the special poem:

> The tumult of my fretted mind
> Gives me expression of a kind;
> But it is faulty, harsh, not plain—
> My work has the incompetence of pain.
>
> I am consumed with a slow fire,
> For righteousness is my desire;
> Towards that good goal I cannot whip my will,
> I am a tired horse that jibs upon a hill.

But some of Anna Wickham's poems (most of them very short) are transparently lucid from start to finish; others seem contradictory or confused. Pain, love, hate, marriage, frustrated efforts in the direction of righteousness, frustrated efforts in the pursuit of beauty are among her themes. Her vision is sometimes somewhat odd or inhuman, even very violent, at other times naïvely simple.

Rose Macaulay has some tenuous affinity with Anna Wickham, but rather more with Sylvia Townsend Warner, though her handling of rhythm is very different. Wit, as in each of them, is one of her leading characteristics. But though she is sufficiently disciplined, it is not always easy to know exactly what she is driving at, and though she has been called a mystic, her mysticism is not quite of heaven—at any rate, not of the nature of such a poet as Francis Thompson. She is a very fluent, musical, and interesting poet, and sometimes produces exceptionally fine metrical effects—as in her poem, oddly misnamed *Farmer's Boy*:

> It is a naked country, without trees;
>   Scourged by winds from the seas;
>   Bald and bare;
> Harsh with sounds that drive like stones through the air . . .
>   (They do say
> There were forests here once on a day;
> But the great wars stole them away.)
>
> And when I walk at noon upon the bare,
>   The beaten ridge, where
>   The grass grows,
> Where once (they say) the pines climbed in rows,
>   I do hear
> A singing like to harps in my ear,
> And like a ship at sea the wind goes.[1]

The best of it is pure magic. But magic, particularly haunting magic, seems to occur frequently in the voice of the lesser

---

[1] At the request of Rose Macaulay a middle stanza has been omitted, and two slight changes made in the final stanza.

poets who are of the feminine gender.   It is abundantly present
throughout Eva M. Martin's *Flight*, beginning:

> The silence lay in the trees
>   As in a cup last even;
> Each tree stood like an emerald flame
>   Striving up to heaven,

and in Madeleine Caron Rock's exquisite violin lyric,
beginning:

> When Starra plays her violin—
> There's dancing sunlight on the river . . .

and in Phyllis Mégroz's *Silver Bride* (one of the most beautiful, if painful lyrics of this century), with its haunting
refrain:

> I am your thought made manifest,
> Possessing me you are possessed,

and in Violet Jacob's *Tam i' the Kirk*, which I sometimes think
an even better Scottish love-lyric than anything by Burns.
Though in this case perhaps 'poignancy' rather than 'magic'
is the bestowing quality, especially noteworthy in the last
stanza:

> He canna sing for the sang that his ain he'rt raises,
> He canna see for the mist that's afore his een,
> And a voice drouns the hale o' the psalms an' the paraphrases,
> Cryin' 'Jean, Jean, Jean!'

The trouble in writing about the women poets is that their
output has often been so slight, and just as their limited
reading public is buoyed up to expectancy, they suddenly
stop short, so that no further volume is forthcoming. Violet
Jacob, who has been surpassed by Hugh MacDiarmid as a poet
of the vernacular, is probably complete and fulfilled; but such
is not the case with another Scottish poet, Orgill MacKenzie,
who after publishing (in 1930) sixty pages of unusually

promising verse, seemed to close down her shutters. True, she let you just see through the chinks of them by the light of two or three short poems which appeared in the press, but nothing was forthcoming with the metrical power and originality of *The Cormorant*. Another Scottish woman poet who demands attention is Margot Robert Adamson, especially as she was included in Professor Lascelles Abercrombie's miscellany, *New English Poems*. And yet another is Marion Angus, who has a special aptitude for turning out a fine romantic Scottish lyric. But very few of the Scottish poets have made themselves felt south of the Border, and not all the necessary names have been included in this book. Helen Waddell (a remarkably gifted translator of medieval Latin lyrics) is included by Mr C. M. Grieve in his preface to Benn's Augustan anthology of Scottish poets, though most of her friends are under the impression that she is Irish—which is surely her true nationality.

The smallness of output seems to extend to nearly every one of the women—which is partly what distinguishes them from the men poets, many of whom go on publishing after the light of inspiration has left them. Pamela Travers, a poet admired by A.E., has not yet issued a book, and most of her lyrics are buried in the columns of the *Irish Statesman*. And Viola Garvin, a well-known *Observer* critic, has left her delicate imagination hanging like a half-concealed spider's web from a corner of her prose, for she has only published one small collection of verse.

Then there is Grace Rhys (the Irish wife of Ernest Rhys), whose slender output of only thirteen poems was published after her death in a choice little book of verse and prose entitled, *A Book of Grace*. Her vision of approaching death is remarkably conveyed in the lines:

> What do you say to a Death's-head,
> That lives, an angel, in the bed;
>
> Lips drawn tight over rows of teeth
> In a smile so sweet it takes the breath?

Another poet whose lyrics were issued in a book collection after her death was Katherine Mansfield. But her best poetry went into her exquisite prose, and most of her verses are merely efforts of rich promise, too often written in free verse where the subject-matter demanded a more tightened musical form. But *Sleeping Together* is a really fine lyric to treasure and remember.

The output of Everest Lewin (Mrs E. H. Macdonald) is less slender, and she has written what in my opinion is the most exciting and moving sonnet of this century — rescued by Maurice Wollman for his *Modern Poetry, 1922–34*:

Where, in the labyrinth of all my days,
　I met you and I loved you, is forgot.
　There seems to me no time when you were not,
No road which separates you from my ways,
No cup I drink in which you may not share,
　No shelter where I build you may not creep
　From the cold wind: no house wherein I sleep
That is not empty if you are not there.

You are the thorn of cactus in my thought,
　You are the leaven in my bread of days,
　　You are the tameless tangle of my lot.
Though I have loved you, loathed you, chid you, sought
　You and condemned you: what is blame or praise?
　　There seems to me no joy where you are not.

As regards women sonnet-writers perhaps the most prominent next to Everest Lewin and Elizabeth Daryush is Yvonne ffrench, who has been influenced by the French Parnassians—Hérédia and others. Her content is almost purely pictorial, and her atmosphere tropical or semi-tropical.

Very different is Ruth Manning Sanders, a poet of very English strength and freshness, who has written some interesting and musical lyrics about people, some of them of a rather grim character. In particular, there is the little anecdote of the ungenerous hoarding old woman who when she was dead watched her rebuffed relatives trying on her much prized garments, and resenting it as only a soul bound for hell could resent:

> If I could rise, if I could speak,
> I'd curse the blood from my sister's cheek,
> And these dead hands to this dead breast
> Would snatch again all I possessed.

Jan Struther, a much younger and later poet than Ruth Manning Sanders, and younger and later than most of those here discussed, has so far published very little; but there is a rather remarkable quality of music, thought, and wit in most of her verse, so that she cannot be passed over. Probably as a wit—which tends to obscure her activities as a pure poet—Jan Struther is quite the foremost of the women poets. Some of her most recent verse seems to reveal some slight influence coming from the later Yeats, though I am not quite sure if it is present in this curious atom of philosophy:

> I do not envy lovers who are never apart;
> For not in the pin-point starry conflagration
> Of touch or kiss
> Deepest contentment is;
> But in the memory of delight, and its anticipation—
> The interstellar spaces of the heart.

Another of the recent arrivals is Lilian Bowes Lyon, who combines some of the effects of modernism with traditional impulses, even in her pastoral verse. But her first book, *The White Hare*, is finer than *Bright Feather fading*, for she is at her best when she is only dimly aware of the latest currents of change. She strikes her best note as a pastoral poet, especially when her pastoralism is touched with human passion. She is developing somewhat oddly.

A very young and undeveloped poet is Joan Adeny Easdale, whose first book, issued from the Hogarth Press in 1931, was a collection of verses written between the ages of fourteen and seventeen—verses of exceptional promise, two or three of which were sufficiently satisfying. Her later book, *Clemence and Clare,* is perhaps the better one to judge her by, but it shows her still too youthful and fantastical for any true assessment.

A poet standing rather apart is Robin Hyde, for she has lived most of her life in New Zealand, and her outdoor atmosphere is not always of this country. But some of her books of verse have been published in this country, and are of such a sappy quality that they excite attention. She is very fervid, emotional, and fluent, and writes out of a strong, spontaneous (though too thoughtless) urge. Her roots of form are quite manifestly in Robert Browning, though as regards the moderns she seems to be considerably aware of the existence of Humbert Wolfe; and, perhaps, of T. S. Eliot. The chief faults are obscurity and recklessness—insufficiently atoned for by her lush imagery and rich sense of rhythm.

But of the poets who have been here only briefly discussed, at least one of them, Lady Dorothy Wellesley, requires some further attention, partly because of the bulk of her output and partly because of the recent admiration and enthusiasm of W. B. Yeats. Probably of none of the women poets have so many different and contradictory opinions been delivered, while even some of the attracted feel bewildered in offering judgment. So perhaps it will not be deemed out of place if I give in full my review of her *Poems of Ten Years* (1924–1934), published in the *New Statesman* of 10th November 1934.

Lady Dorothy Wellesley is not an easy poet. Of all the post-War living poets who have combined quality with quantity of output she is probably the most difficult. She has been classed as a 'Georgian,' though, actually, she stands much closer to the Pan-Moderns. At least she is a connecting-link; and among the several influences operating upon her that of Gerard Manley Hopkins is distinctly paramount. The change of manner, which took place about the middle of her verse career, is very discernible in such frequent passages as:

> 'Here by the fireside I hear the bleating of lambs,
> Borne from the high fields docketed in Doomsday,
> Over by Quarry Shaw.

L

> And I know how they run, knock-kneed, getting the jim-jams,
> Distressed to their dams,
> Frenzied, frantic, knocking at the milk
> As ewe walks gently their extravagance to tease,
> Chewing a straw.'

She is diffuse and undisciplined, uses words strangely and some-times wrongly, trifles with nonsense, fumbles, mumbles, cultivates the obscure, and as soon as she gets going with a really beautiful rhythm drops it for some dingy prosaic whisperings—for she does, now and again, write beautifully. And she is hyper-sensitive, and has further aristocratic quality in that she occasionally uses fine phrases, and epithets of real felicity and power. Moreover she has an enormous vocabulary, even more enormous than Susan Miles in her recent novel, *Blind Men crossing a Bridge*. In this she not only creates the illusion of jostling Shakespeare, but also of using all the words in the dictionary. Those reviewers who have described her as a 'simple poet' probably wrote about her in their sleep, unless it is that sleep is the right state of mind in which to approach her; for if she can be classed and defined at all it is as a Dream-poet. It is not merely that she is somewhat illogical and can rarely visual-ize quite clearly, but she is so obviously immersed in a dream world, continually given to fantastical day-dreaming, the repro-duction of night dreams, or groping back to a habit of mind as it was in her bizarre, kaleidoscope childhood:

> 'Here the deep-sea conger himself nosed a wild daffodil;
> The tiny sea-horse, alert, grappled the eglantine,
> And a flight of fishes perched on a cherry bough.'

Moreover, she does sometimes, quite successfully, arouse a dream-state of mind in a reader; and here her erratic sense of sequence and muddle of imagery perform their right work. To what extent this is the result of the deliberate rather than the inarticulate it is diffi-cult to say: though some of it must be very deliberate. But it is a pity that she should mar such good poems as *Camels in Persia* and *Fishing* by phrases like 'a night scarce purple for many stars' and 'lovely the mercury, the flutter of the sea.' 'Drat her!' one may be tempted to respond, 'she beats round the bush like a ghost at the planchette. Why all this circumlocution, jumping of gaps, and oblique imagery?'

More definitely one might say of her that, when she gets away from profuse detail, she writes rather more with her nerves than with her heart and brain. Profound intellectual content there is little; religious and spiritual content there is even less (note, for instance, her curious pagan vision of Christ), and the creation of word-magic (the true mission of poetry) is continually shattered by her lack of simplicity and self-control.

But in strange contradiction to all of this, Lady Dorothy Wellesley is a Nature poet, and huddles nervously into the circle occupied by Edmund Blunden and V. Sackville-West. She writes long, learned, and informing poems about horses, seals, moths, birds, garden flowers, forests, lilies of the valley, snakes, fishes, shells, the Spring, and Primitive Man. If only there were less crowding of content and clearer delineation of image and scenery she might have got away with it quite effectively. Whether she is always correct about the vegetation and creatures which interest her, only the omniscient can say; but, when she turns the multitudinous sheep of the Yorkshire fells into the wild ponies of Wales and Exmoor, one is justified in feeling suspicious. At any rate she seizes continually upon the exceptional rather than the general, upon the remote or suggestive rather than the obvious, upon the blurred rather than the clear-cut, upon the dream rather than the vision, and upon the weird rather than the everyday. At present she wears her laurels round her neck, but it is not impossible that a future volume will elevate them to her head.

Since that day she has published another volume (a selection of her poems prefaced by W. B. Yeats), and because of W. B. Yeats's intense admiration of it, and the further prominence he has given to her in the *Oxford Book of Modern Verse*, I am perhaps right in suggesting that her laurels have now been elevated to her head. How long they are going to stay there is another matter, and to what extent my own criticism is exactly right is also another matter. I have, I think, overstressed the influence of Gerard Manley Hopkins upon her, and I have, perhaps, underrated her spiritual, emotional, and intellectual quality. Moreover, the volume, which approaches the nature of a collected edition, contains by no means all her poems, and at least a few of them (particularly some omitted earlier ones) are marked by lucidity and compactness of form and clarity of image. Perhaps, in some instances, it would be truer to say of her imagery that it is over-diffuse rather than muddled. But I think she has allowed the various verse fashions—from Georgian Pastoralism to Modernism—unduly to captivate or distress her, and that perhaps her most individual and best verse is yet to come.

CHAPTER XVII

NARRATIVE POETS AND NARRATIVE POETRY

Owing to the sousing spate of printed matter and the intrusion of physical science upon mental concentration and leisure, the predominatingly popular poetry of the century has been lyrical rather than narrative; and with the exception of John Masefield and Wilfrid Gibson, the poets who have mainly chosen to express themselves in narrative verse, especially narrative verse of length, have been pushed on one side for lyrists with a smaller and often slighter output. Masefield as a direct story-teller in verse seems to stand in relation to all other narrative poets (from Chaucer onwards) in the same ratio as Shakespeare stands to the dramatists, for he is big in his pedestrian way, very big; while Gibson has, at least, the prestige of Crabbe. But the position of others is not so clear. The unwieldy output of Charles M. Doughty[1] makes contemporary judgment difficult, especially as he chose to write his long epic poems in an outmoded Elizabethan and pre-Elizabethan speech, abounding with archaic affectations and often quite wrongly punctuated:

> Cædmon, for all he goeth in servile weed,
> Rough wadmel coat and sark of unbleached line;
> With galages on his feet; is he whom men,
> Master-song-smith, esteemed in English tongue,
> In his life-time. He úntaught, save of heaven;
> Makes canticles of the Lamb and Holy Faith;
> Which daily are sungen, in their Minster Church.

---

[1] Though he has not written many poems, his pages almost seem to equal in number those of Masefield. The twentieth-century poets with the largest output reckoned by number of lines seem to be Masefield, Doughty, Gibson, Alfred Noyes, and Sturge Moore.

Doughty has epic grandeur and apocalyptic vision, a huge romantic storehouse, and casts a revealing eye on the English countryside, but of the compression which goes to make verbal magic very little — considerably less, indeed, than Gerard Manley Hopkins, with whom he has some affinity. So he is not at all in the public eye, and his books are under glass cases, and entirely overlooked by that poet's advertiser, the anthologist—who concentrates on short lyrics and rarely detaches from long works. In any case Doughty is not easily detachable, though that does not entirely shift the blame for his neglect from the shoulders of the anthologist—who might at least have stimulated attention to him in prefaces. *Adam cast forth* (but lyrical drama rather than epic), *The Dawn in Britain*, *The Titans*, *Mansoul*, are golden names in the reader's ear, fairy works and literary legends rather than books for the shelf, and a closer contact has yet to be established between Doughty and the average reader, so that he may be set in a position where he can be more satisfactorily blessed and cursed.

The case is somewhat other with Laurence Binyon, but less so with Sturge Moore, both of whom have to be judged by their long poems rather than their short. Laurence Binyon has probably shown himself at his best in his fine renderings from Dante's *Inferno*; but in *Porphyrion*, *The Death of Adam*, *Penthesilea*, *Tristram's End*, and other narrative verse he lays claim to our attention as an original poet of consequence, though in a speech and technique which, in spite of its probable influence upon the Georgians, does not strike everybody as specially new. He seems to be a disciple of Matthew Arnold, and often writes in the grand heroic manner, sometimes reminiscent of Milton, as in *Porphyrion* (1898):

> Yet astonished and dismayed,
> Those sacrificers saw the victim smile
> Triumphing and incredulous of death,
> Even in anguish: pang upon fresh pang
> Rekindled the lost light, the perished bloom
> Of memory, and he was lifted far

In exaltation above death; he drank
Wine at the banquet, and the stormy thrill
Of battle caught him, and he knew again
The dart of love and the sweet wound of grief
In one transfigured instant, that illumed
And pierced him, as the arrows pierced his side.

But as a pastoral poet he also rouses our admiration and pleasure, and in this quality he can be finely represented by detached pieces from his long narrative verse as well as by complete lyrics:

A land of showers, a land of quivering trees,
A land of youth, lovely and full of sap,
Upon whose border trembled the wide sea.
Young were the branches round him, in fresh leaf
Luminously shaded; the arriving winds
Broke over him in soft aërial surge;
For him the grass was glittering, the far cloud
Loosened her faltering tresses of dim rain,

while in another place he speaks of

beauteous undulation mild,
Inlaid with silver estuary and stream . . .

which, I think, is one of the most felicitously condensed pictures of landscape in English poetry—in which speciality Binyon occasionally triumphs. Nevertheless Laurence Binyon's chief fault seems to be diffuseness—due to a continuous poetical urge which has driven him to write too frequently, or at too great length, so that only a few of his lyrics lay special claim to our everyday attention; while even his ode, *The Sirens*, which by some is judged his best work, is so long as to intrude upon the dominion of narrative poetry.

Diffuseness, again, is the chief fault of Lascelles Abercrombie's narrative and dramatic poetry. But he is also full of exuberance, while the form and movement of his verse take after the Elizabethan dramatists rather than Milton. Classical features which predominate in Binyon, and which push themselves also into Abercrombie's tapestry, are obscured under a ponderous weight of florid Romanticism—often tending to the fantastical or bizarre. But the features of sentimentality which are so frequently present in Romantic poetry—and from which Masefield has by no means escaped—are entirely absent from Abercrombie. He is, though a very sensitive and imaginative poet, an extremely hard-headed one, and much of his tough, tangled verse is too cerebral to permit of quick reading. He takes pleasure in out-of-the-way subjects— especially the weird, the mystical, the horrific, the macabre —and sometimes suddenly turns an interesting story into a web of philosophical speculation. Witchcraft, the end of the world, a legend concerning St Thomas, the death visions of a friar, the death of gods, Judith's murder of Holofernes, an assault on the Virgin Mary by a bramble (figurative, of course) are among many strange themes which he treats at length and from an individual angle. But his sweep is very broad, and his strongly impassioned series of love-poems, *Emblems of Love*, has probably had a good deal of influence upon the love poetry written since 1912. In another book one of his strangest poems gives a new imaginative account of the death of Peregrinus, 'a man notable when the Christian Church was young' and who 'having famously lived a wicked life, publicly burnt himself in Greece.' Peregrinus's act in the eyes of the early Christian Church was a madman's act of self-glorification, a sort of inverted diabolism; but Lascelles Abercrombie puts justifying words into the madman's mouth, and in his address to the multitude which has assembled to see his immolation, explains it as a sort of self-purification, and, through an intense worship of the higher self, leading to worship of the divine:

> It is well said, Be good and love mankind;
> But it is better said, Be beautiful
> And love yourselves; for this contains the other.
> How can you love what is not beautiful?
> I would have each man passionately in love
> With his own Self: see that it take no harm,

And let not the base breathing of the world,
The nuzzling friendship of such mouths as munch
Garbage, come tarnishing your silver thought.

. . . . . .

For none who love and honour their own selves
Would do the frauds, malices, sneakings, lies,
The huffing impudence and bragg'd lechery,
That cause the life of man to smear a scum
Over the world as if a sewer had burst.

Not all Abercrombie's intellectual musings are as simply
worded as that, for, to tell the truth about him, he is nearly
as intellectual as all of the Modernists put together, and
if, instead of being elevated to heaven for his great virtues
he were sent to hell for his vices and condemned to swallow
the Modernists wholesale, he would not suffer the slightest
inconvenience of indigestion.[1] Formless he is frequently, but
it is the formlessness of a poet who lets idea and philosophy
triumph over external shell, who, while remaining a poet, is
not always sufficiently alert to the necessity for glamour of
word and rhythm, and is in no sense due to any *deliberate*
cultivation of the amorphous or obscure. How good he can
be in crystallization, especially when ecstasy takes hold of him,
as in some passages of *Emblems of Love*, or when his eye is cast
on natural phenomena, is well exemplified in such lines as:

The sun drew off at last his piercing fires.
Over the stale warm air, dull as a pond
And moveless in the grey quieted street,
Blue magic of a summer evening glowed.
The sky, that had been dazzling stone all day,
Hollowed in smooth hard brightness, now dissolved
To infinite soft depth, and smoulder'd down
Low as the roofs, dark burning blue, and soared
Clear to that winking drop of liquid silver,

---

[1] That is where the Modernists really do intend themselves to be understood.

* L

The first exquisite star. Now the half-light
Tidied away the dusty litter parching
Among the cobbles, veiled in the colour of distance
Shabby slates and brickwork mouldering, turn'd
The hunchback houses into patient things
Resting; and golden windows now began.

The passage is from his narrative-dramatic poem *Witchcraft ;
New Style*—one of the most straightforward and condensed
of his poems other than the lyrics (of which he has written
very few), and with which it is interesting to compare Edward
Thompson's ballad-narrative poem *Thoughts on the Islip Witch*
that, proffering an entirely adverse and sceptical point of
view about witchcraft, sounds almost like a carefully worded
answer to Abercrombie's poem. But this is a comparatively
slight piece of work, for as a narrative poet Edward Thompson
must be judged chiefly by his *Thracian Stranger* (1929, but
written before the War), a poem of over fifty pages, written
in Popian rhymed couplets, a very crowded, decorated work,
which tells the story of Pentheus's opposition to Iaccus
(Bacchus) and which in spite of some heaviness and unevenness in the narrative, succeeds in making the story very much
alive. Here the religious and mystical calibre of the poet's
mind is assaulted by paganism, so that the poem (a very
thoughtful one) almost reads like an attack on Puritanism
—at any rate on the extreme austerities of Puritanism—though
in many inconsistent asides Edward Thompson dwells on the
extreme danger of flouting the decrees of heaven. . . .
Although the speeches are long and frequent the poem keeps
to the old-fashioned texture.

One of the distinctive features of twentieth-century narrative verse—continuously displayed by Lascelles Abercrombie
and others—is a tendency to drop into straightforward dramatic
dialogue, marking a considerable severance from the Tennysonian tradition, which demanded that the story should
be told continuously and with less emphasis upon the
speeches.

A rather different kind of narrative poet from Binyon and

Abercrombie—and one with an even larger output than either —is T. Sturge Moore. But he, too, has frequently used the dialogue form for narrative in poems which probably only in one or two instances have the real right to be called stage plays. His curious, crabbed, and yet dreamy style is really too self-consciously poetical to be very communicatively successful in either narrative or drama; and perhaps he shows himself at his best in such a silver-throated lyric as *The Dying Swan*, or in his verse for and about children, or in his adaptations from the lyrics of the Symbolists and other French poets. A longer poem, *The Gazelles*, shows him at his best, though this again is a long lyric rather than a narrative poem. Sometimes he is nearly as cerebral as Abercrombie, and is baffling in the extreme if we have to judge him by his really typical output. His longest poem, *Judas*, of more than a hundred closely packed pages, is a mighty piece of patchwork, as rebuffingly tedious and obscure in some places as it is interesting and attractive in others, for the artist in Sturge Moore is continually overpowered by the philosopher and religious muser, to say nothing of a mind which continually loses sight of the main theme to indulge in a riot of arabesque imagery and profuse poetical association. While his numerical output in verse challenges comparison with Masefield's, he is the complete opposite of Masefield both in selection and manner, and at times almost seems to touch fingers with the Modernists— whom in many ways he preceded. With few efforts in the direction of simplification he delights in telling Biblical tales over again—the stories of Saul, David, and Goliath, of Jonathan, of Absalom, of Judas, of Isaac and Rebecca (but by no means the complete list), and would lay claim to being an important religious poet if he were not so lacking in religious passion. At other times classical themes absorb his attention, and it is this intermingling of Classicism, Romanticism, and attention to modern detail (almost describable as Realism) which makes him so difficult to judge. Beautiful and sufficiently clear meditative passages are jostled by unwieldy masses of verse which any save his strongest admirers might condemn as mere verbosity. As with Charles Doughty, his narrative poems (when criticism wishes to illustrate his finest qualities) are not easy to select from, though perhaps the following will give some idea:

> There were the sullen rocks and basking tracks
> Which torrents trample twice a year; there were
> The tiny tongueless flowers; mute earth was there:
> But skies were distant radiant and serene.
> His hungry eyes communed with solitude;
> Yet found that arching confidence no friend,
> But something cruel; and the urgent wind,
> Insistent out of season, chafed his soul.

And, mingling his worst into his best, as he so often chooses:

> Yet, though Ezekiel saw bones come together,
> Some watching corpses, have seen phantoms rise . . .
> The solid releasing a faint soft filmy shape
> That life fused with it, making one of two
> As lovers yearn yet never can achieve.

Very different in his natural simplicity and straightforward-ness is Alfred Noyes, who before the War published a notable narrative poem called *Drake*. It was a very long poem for a young man, a thing of rich green promise rather than full-coloured achievement, but it was very wholeheartedly praised by prominent poets and critics. Swinburne called it a 'noble work' and praised it for its vivid colouring, while Sir Edmund Gosse responded in very much the same key: 'I have read it aloud, a book at a time; and then we have discussed and expanded it in our fireside talk. It is noble stuff to read aloud, so vivid, warm, and sonorous.' But something of such praise is critically best explained as the generous encouragement that it was thought necessary to bestow on the more ambitious work of a young man of great promise. As a lyrical poet Alfred Noyes has too often inclined to the robustious and easy, achieving a popularity that has not been quite in line with real fame. But of recent years his note has deepened and strengthened, and in a really imaginative work, *The Torch Bearers*, he has given

us the fulfilment of his early promise. These collected narratives, which describe the crucial and tragic events in the lives
of the great physical scientists, occupy over four hundred pages
of highly competent (and sometimes more than competent)
blank verse, and seek to justify in the light of the Christian
religion all that they have accomplished. Many of the narratives are curiously interesting, none more so than the account
of a meeting between Sir Francis Bacon and Doctor Harvey,
in which the great chancellor is painted—and probably not
entirely incorrectly—in very sombre colours:

> Gray's Inn,—a shadowy room, and smouldering there
> Like a strange jewel on one high-panelled wall
> A dark rich portrait by Sir Anthony More,
> English, but all Madrid in colour and line.
>
> Under it, hunched in a tasselled high-backed chair,
> A lean form, with a mean and shifty face
> Of empty craft, a green and viperish eye,
> And, round his neck, the Chancellor's golden chain.

It is interesting throughout *The Torch Bearers* to compare
Alfred Noyes's blank verse style and content with that of
Drake (1908) and notice the post-War increase of a mystical
and intellectual horizon and a more fastidious way with
words. It is interesting, too, to compare Noyes's *Drake* with
Chesterton's *Ballad of the White Horse* (1913), two very long
poems inspired by great historical figures—Chesterton's better
as a poem, Noyes's as a good tale, for Chesterton's narrative
dissolves into a series of incidents, the poetry rather overpowering the plot.

Alfred Noyes, Sturge Moore, Lascelles Abercrombie, Laurence
Binyon, John Masefield, Wilfrid Gibson, Charles Doughty—
these seem to be the prominent figures of English narrative
poetry (epic and otherwise) of this century. But to their
number should probably be added the name of Maurice
Hewlett, who in 1916 published a long Socialist poem of over
two hundred pages, *The Song of the Plow*, setting forth the

'history of the governed race from the date of the Norman Conquest, that successful raid made a conquest by the acquiescence of the raided, when foreigners acquired an ascendancy which they have never yet dropped.' Hewlett's point of view is similar to that of William Morris and G. K. Chesterton, particularly similar to G. K. Chesterton's, and is that the only full-fibred Englishman is the small peasant and farm labourer, and that he is still under the dominion of foreign tyrants:

> I sing the Man, I sing the Plow
>   Ten centuries at work, and Thee,
>   England, whom men not christen'd now
> May live to call Home of the Free.
>   Enslav'd, back-broken, driv'n afield,
>   Ask him I sing how this may be,
> Him that the slipping share must wield,
>   And wring his brow that others eat,
>   And see them fatten on his yield,
> And by his pain derive their meat:
>   Hodge, hireling for a thousand years
>   To whom the burden and the heat
> To reap in sweat the sown in tears
>   Must be, whatever else betide; . . .

The poem moves swiftly, if somewhat jerkily—a modern rhythm slightly imposed on by Middle-English rhythms, and the vocabulary affected by antique phraseology, and often plunging into grammatical awkwardness and unintelligibility. But if it is not a great poem it is very nearly a great poem— and this in spite of its frequent obscurity and archaic tangle —an epic of the downtrodden, with the whole of English history unveiled in its pages. But it unfortunately failed to leave its mark, for it was published at the wrong moment, during the middle of the War, when the popular esteem was hovering between war poetry direct from the battlefield and pure Georgianism—the pastoral lyric poetry of escape. And the mode of speech seemed odd, something that may now be almost identified with Modernism:

Dead or alive, King William frowns
  On mutiny or hatching plot,
  And serves the new king England owns,
The red-haired bully, blunderer, sot,
  Thick with curses, thick as his blood,
  Shot in the Forest, and well shot.
Shot ill or well, shot bad or good,
  That red king was his father's son,
  To keep in awe his robber brood; . . .

Viewed as a whole, the poem shows affinities with Doughty's creations, though the rhythm is much swifter.

Maurice Hewlett, like Laurence Binyon, is also prominent as a translator (though he was well known as a great romantic novelist before achieving a certain amount of recognition as a poet), for he has put the first twelve books of Homer's Iliad into fluent and soft-flowing blank verse—probably the best verse translation yet accomplished.

Another poet of 'heroic' dimensions is Katherine M. Buck, who in *The Wayland-Dietrich Saga* has written 'the world's longest poem,' a gigantic unveiling of myth and folk-lore and barbaric customs, an enormous work revealing wide and massive scholarship, and much knowledge of wild life in the country.

Narrative poetry—and of very ornate and exuberant texture—has also occupied the genius of the Irish poets:[1] W. B. Yeats, Austin Clarke, Herbert Trench, A.E.; from which even James Stephens has not been entirely exempt, though a short verse narrative of his, *The Lonely God* (the story of God's loneliness after Eden, as told by Himself), which was included in Marsh's first Georgian anthology, was suppressed by him, and not included in his *Collected Poems* of 1926. Perhaps James Stephens felt that it was of the nature of a short epic, a type of narrative with which he disagrees, for in the preface to his *Collected Poems* of 1926 he has written:

A revival of epic is not to be wished; nor, while the general mind is steeped in what is practically a new element, is such a revival possible. Epic will only deal with matured, with thoroughly

---

[1] Though some of this preceded the death of Queen Victoria.

absorbed, mental or spiritual cognitions. It comes at the end of an era, and is a summary, or a reduction to mythological form, of all that its era meant. We are at the beginning of an era, and who creates a new world must create a new art to express it. Already a large proportion of the writings that we call classical have lost their authority, and that not by being outmoded. It is not time but change that is consigning these to oblivion. Another mind than that they reckoned with is consigning them to oblivion, and thumbs may be turned down to all that could interest and excite the élite of only a generation ago.

However that may be, the natural epic poet has taken no notice of such discouragement; for in 1934 J. Redwood Anderson published *The Human Dawn*, which is of the nature of two short epics, *Paradise* and *Beyond Paradise*, which, if not interesting in themselves (and many will disagree), should at least be read for their new and original development of blank verse.

> Now had the gibbous moon
> into the dun smoke of the west gone down;
> only a few stars remained, vibrant
> white points, and they, speedily fading out,
> made way for gradual morning. All was still
> in the dim forest's wide protectorate,
> save for the sea-like and faint voices
> of orient blowings about Paradise;
> the profound woods stood up like malachite
> ramparts, while Eden with its pleasant places
> lay green among them. But now the first
> whistle of a bird sounded and the dawn
> came like a child, shy and barefooted,
> lifting the cedar's curtain to look through
> with grey unstartled eyes: earth stretched her limbs,
> while over the bent grasses a wind yawned.

Biblical themes have been otherwise used by R. L. Mégroz and Frank Kendon; and though these two poets have not exactly shown themselves disciples of Sturge Moore, their verse seems to have been touched with some awareness of his existence. In *The Story of Ruth : an Idyll*, R. L. Mégroz has retold the Old Testament tale, but filled in the obvious gaps. The theme and characterization of Boaz, Naomi, and Ruth are finely developed, the blank verse, though quiet and unassuming, is strong and elastic, and the atmosphere of Palestine and the period exceptionally well conveyed. It is quite evident that more than book knowledge went to the making of it, so that on turning to the foreword one is not surprised to read: 'I was still in the British Army when, in 1918, I began to write the poem, with no more than an army Bible and a borrowed atlas for raw material, but this, and memories of service in the Egyptian Expeditionary Force, proved better than all the resources of the British Museum Reading Room.' Isolated passages can give no particularly clear idea of the poem's rich living quality, and almost at haphazard I select:

> Singing next morning, Ruth hastened down the hill
> Past terraced vineyards, watchtowers, olive trees
> Wind-blown from grey to green to grey again,
> And saw the harvesters like clustered grapes
> Bunching wherever waved the barley. She
> Was timid then and watched, and hearing jeers
> Went like a field mouse fearfully, and came
> Unto another field where barns and doors
> For threshing spread beneath a terebinth
> Dark-towered above them.

It is strange that a poet who has so admired the Sitwells (see his book, *The Three Sitwells*) should be entirely free from their affectations and vices, and though Mégroz has written only a few lyrics of good quality, there is little doubt that three or four more creations on the level of *Ruth* would set him securely among the poets of prominence, and at any rate near the front rank of narrative poets.

Another Biblical theme, that of Judas, has been treated at much greater length (in over a hundred pages) by Frank Kendon, that sensitive lyrical poet of the countryside, who is equally good, if not better, in narrative. Here again is some first-hand knowledge of the East (where Frank Kendon also served during the Great War), and out of this and Biblical knowledge and speculation Kendon has sought to construct Judas's whole career from the childhood period, in a work ambitiously entitled *A Life and Death of Judas Iscariot*. Sturge Moore's *Judas* deals with the subject from the time of the betrayal, but though there are a few similarities, the poems as wholes are in no way to be compared, particularly as Kendon's is in direct narrative and the intellectual subtleties easy to follow, while it has much more of the stuff of real life and landscape in it than has Sturge Moore's. The subject is best treated from the standpoint of Judas's disappointment, and his frustrated ambition and bitter jealousy of the other disciples, working disintegratingly upon his love and admiration for his Lord—which is Frank Kendon's main solution. But Lord Gorell in a ten-page poem (relative to narrative) interestingly revives a theory, out of Victorian theology, that Judas was more or less under the impression that Christ desired the betrayal as a point of procedure from which to assert His power and establish His heavenly kingdom upon earth, when he, Judas, would be specially honoured for so daringly obeying his Lord's subtle commands—which is also suggested in the early part of Sturge Moore's very long poem. All three poets ignore hard primitive instincts of evil, and in this show themselves true children of modern intellectual sophistication.

But all these poems were preceded by Harold Monro's *Judas* (1906), a blank-verse creation of between twenty and thirty pages, and a remarkably imaginative piece of work for a very young poet (as Monro was at that time). It is interesting for many reasons; for Monro almost seems to identify himself with Judas (his objective verse was nearly always personal in a greater or less degree) and we have in it the beginnings of those terribly sombre, fatalistic elements which were slowly to disfigure his unique imagination. His poem is hardly to be compared with Frank Kendon's, though the two are not without parallels.

But Kendon's long poem does not entirely succeed; princi-

pally because he has partially destroyed the mysterious nature
of Christ by dragging Him into the blank-verse dialogue and
putting words into His mouth which are not too closely
paralleled in the gospels; though the poem in at least its
first half, and in its fine ending, triumphs as a blank-verse
narrative of very high quality.   In a later narrative work,
Tristram, Kendon has joined hands with Matthew Arnold and
Laurence Binyon, though he has treated the subject in his
own original way—in a long ballad poem divided into nine
cantos.   But he has not used the rudimentary ballad form of
Sir Patrick Spens and *Edom o' Gordon*, but rather that of *Kinmont
Willie* and *Hughie the Graeme*, while something in his technique
and the movement of his lines is faintly reminiscent of
William Morris.   But though the stark beauty of the old
ballad is not there in any continuity, such lovely stanzas as:

> The body will not wake again,
> The delicate senses will not wake,
> In their closed caves the eyes will waste,
> The hands will no more music make.
>
> .   .   .   .   .
>
> 'And can you forgive his lightness so?'
> 'Who am I to forgive?' said she;
> 'Love never forgives—is never wrong;
> Nothing divides us—except the sea!'

may suggest it, but the ear longs for more of them.   The
poem, however, is full of natural ballad lilts, strong stirring
music and the movement and red-hearted clamour of an
old world:

> But no brave knight could match his skill,
> No treachery darken his renown;
> Wherever with secret, shameful heart
> He lived, he rode his foemen down.
>
> .   .   .   .   .
>
> The pennon like a golden snake
> Rippled and flapped, but never replied!
> 'This is love's lowest cowardice!'
> Said Tristram.   Then to horse's side

> He clapped the blood-red spurs again,
> And down the hill went thundering,
> Wheeling to the gate of the castle,
> And called aloud for sight of the king.

Another narrative poem in ballad metre which invites special praise, 'though it is only forty stanzas long,' is Lord Alfred Douglas's *Perkin Warbeck*, one of the most gripping and finely woven of the verse tales since Tennyson. But for John Masefield it might have been very nearly the last of its kind, for the fashion of that sort of thing has declined since the high years of John Davidson, who was one of the giants of the short metrical tale in rhyme.

Two long verse tales written in heroic couplets, *Catherine* and *Columbus*, have come from the pen of that distinguished scholar and journalist R. C. K. Ensor. He has his own special views about narrative poetry, rather different from those of James Stephens; and in a very challenging preface to *Catherine* which treats of the decline of narrative poetry, he scourges the Georgian school, and accuses it of plotting the downfall of narrative by pushing the lyric unduly into the foreground; so that paragraphs in James Stephens's preface, which was written later, may have been prompted by Mr Ensor. Of the two poems *Catherine* is the more poetical, but *Columbus* tells the story of that great man's life with close attention to detail and apparently very sound knowledge and examination of all the facts.

Returning to Biblical poetry (but somewhat connected with Ensor's verse in texture), what would happen if Jesus returned to earth during these abandoned days has been treated at length by A. St John Adcock and Ruth Manning Sanders. Though Ruth Manning Sanders's poem (*The City*) is the more poetically imaginative, the closer to true poetry, St John Adcock's *Divine Tragedy* really gets down better to the probable facts. In this long narrative exploit written in heroic couplets reminiscent at its best of Pope at his simplest—though occasionally broken into shorter lines—St John Adcock has sought to strip away the deceptive moral garments and spiritually destructive conventions of the modern world, and occasionally rises to sustained passages of convincing irony and realism. Throughout the tale he avoids anything in the nature of religious symbolism, which is one of the leading characteristics of Ruth Manning Sanders's rather more poetically informed fantasy.

One of the longest of the century's narrative poems is Lord Gorell's *Spirit of Happiness*, a blank-verse epic (or of epic nature) in which classical influences predominate. In his volume of collected verse (*1904–36 : Poems*)—which contains other verse of narrative character—the title of the poem was changed into *The Silver Cord*, but in each instance he prefaced it with the beautiful escapist stanza already quoted in a previous chapter. Somewhat resembling it in texture and spirit (at any rate it belongs to exactly the same classification) is a long poem daringly published as late as 1936 by the Cambridge University Press—*The Story of Psyche*, by a young poet, Robert Gittings. Both Lord Gorell's and Gittings's creations are rather more occupied with content than external form; and so also are Hugh I'A. Fausset's shorter blank-verse poems *The Condemned* and *The Mercy of God* (the latter a story told in dialogue), which hold the attention from first line to last (the main thing for the artist's consideration in telling a tale in verse).

The oddest misfit in all the assembly of little-read narrative verse is F. O. Mann's Hogarthian book, *The Sisters* (oddly enough published by the Hogarth Press). Here is the full clear voice of Crabbe, not Crabbe transmuted as in the narrative poems of Gibson, but Crabbe richly derived, reincarnated, resurrected (apply what epithet you like), and used in crude short stories for the purpose of describing modern life—often very drab life—with a slight infusion of John Masefield's violence. In such passages, however, he is rarely at his best, and as an original poet (he is rather more brocaded than Crabbe) should rather be judged by such things as:

> She was a buxom lass with melting eyes,
> Exuberant in sapphire and in size,
> With dimpled cheek and sympathizing nose,

Her mouth a cherry and her cheek a rose,
Of pure good nature and quick laughter made.
She helped her father in the catering trade.

Or:

E'en as he stared, athwart the roof-tops high,
Sword-like descending from the fissured sky
Of heaped and livid cloud, one splendid ray
Lit on her brow and spilt in gold away.

Or:

Her furtive eye was hard and granite-green;
She seemed the skeleton of what had been,
With rag of soul enough to just contrive
The harsh mechanics to appear alive.

His power lies in his descriptive prowess, of human character
and surrounding scene, rather than in the technical quality
of his tales. As a lyrical poet he is often very rough and
uncouth, but his narrative verse cries out for more attention.
He is witty, ecstatic, sentimental, maudlin, grim, vulgar,
brutal, fluent, awkward, newspaperish, and occasionally a very
dog of doggerel—a strange mixture of good and bad, with an
out-of-date note of odd tenderness in some of his passages.
But though Mann has published several books, and Professor Lascelles Abercrombie remembered him in his anthology,
New English Poems (1931), very few critics seem to be aware
of his existence, probably owing to the fact that around John
Masefield and Wilfrid Gibson have grouped no schools.

But the list is by no means complete. Among many others,
Edward Shanks, Richard Church, John Drinkwater, Walter
de la Mare, and John Freeman have indulged their genius
in narrative verse. John Drinkwater's excellently told *Preludes*
—a volume of verse stories which, like Fausset's *The Condemned* and *The Mercy of God*, treat of the theme of love from
different angles, and which strangely enough appeared in the
same year (1922), but all probably influenced by Lascelles
Abercrombie's *Emblems of Love*—may yet be judged his best
book. And even the fine verse dramas of Gordon Bottomley
and other Georgians are sometimes more of the nature of

verse tales than stage plays if we consider drama from the standpoint of the popular stage, and the demands of the man in the street.

Relative to the lyrical dramas of Gordon Bottomley are those by Lady Margaret Sackville (*Bertrud*; *The Wooing of Dionysus*; *Tereus*; *The Return of Ganymede*), her restrained, but impassioned voice not often falling below this level:

> She is not woman—I could never bend
> My adamantine and imperious heart
> To stoop before a woman; thus she comes
> Clothed in mysterious powers I understand not.
> I have broken many women; I have not loved;
> I have broken many women; shall she break me?
>
> .   .   .   .   .   .
>
> Let no man
> Think I am awed by this fine, delicate flame
> Wherewith the gods assail me.

Directly relative to the long verse tales of Masefield is Clive Hamilton's *Dymer* (1926), a poem of a hundred pages written in Masefield's narrative manner, though the subject is allegorical rather than realist.

The output has really been very large, larger than these pages can fully embrace, and it is only owing to the immense vogue of the novel, and much incapacity in the brain of the average reader to respond to the demands of sustained rhythm (due largely to the changes induced by machinery and the cinema), that so many of the century's narrative poems are practically unknown.

CHAPTER XVIII

ELIOT'S 'WASTE LAND'[1]

ONE of the half-score most discussed books of 1930 was T. S. Eliot's *Ash Wednesday*. It is strange that a tiny work, which was not exactly prose, should have received so much attention. It contained only thirteen printed pages, and though sprinkled with beautiful passages, had evidently, save in fragments, been written to be understood by no one but its author. But critics and reviewers—ancient reasonables as well as Modernist sympathizers—wrangled over the thing like dogs over a bone, and then went on to talk about T. S. Eliot's earlier poem, *The Waste Land*. This was quite as it should be, because *The Waste Land* has had more influence on the verse of the last half-score years than any other long poem of note. An admirer, writing in the year of grace 1929 in one of our most reputable monthlies, expressed half the truth in a thorned nutshell when he said: 'It is natural, at this point of our inquiry, to ask help of the young. For Mr Eliot's work, particularly *The Waste Land*, has made a profound impression on them and given them precisely the food they needed.' More recently Mr Eliot's followers have gone further than that. Young enthusiasts have written about the poem as a 'landmark.' One of them went so far as to say 'that by the literary historian of 2030 *The Waste Land*

[1] This chapter was originally published in Seumas O'Sullivan's *Dublin Magazine*, in April 1933. It was written in 1930 or 1931 (I forget which year) but was rejected by every editor of the English literary press. I believe I was the first to point out not only that *The Waste Land* could be interpreted as a dream but that it also contained a certain amount of sheer nonsense, passages that were never intended to be understood. I have made some slight revision, and added a little, including some notes on quotations, published in *Everyman*. The contents of the chapter are similar to those of my satirical and parodying poem *Cinder Thursday* (Benn), published in 1931.

will be regarded in much the same light as Wordsworth's and Coleridge's *Lyrical Ballads* are to-day, as marking the end of one literary epoch and the beginning of a new one.' While in the same revered journal a reviewer of *Ash Wednesday* wrote, 'suddenly—*The Waste Land*, and it may be said with small exaggeration that English poetry of the first half of the twentieth century *began*.' If I suppress all names it is because I feel that by now many of Mr Eliot's most sensational admirers have somewhat changed their minds, and that at that time they allowed criticism to give place to literary journalism.

For surely Mr Eliot never intended *The Waste Land* to be taken quite so seriously, at least not quite so constructively, especially as it exhibits too many of the features of a hoax. At any rate a hoax and earnest are strangely, hypnotically, and bafflingly blended. It is as if Mr Eliot were saying: 'Take this, you fox-terriers; it's all you are worth. Here's a bone for a dog.' If *The Waste Land* means anything to me in relation to 2030 it is that *The Waste Land* will be truly a waste land, unknown and unhonoured, leering out of the darkness at all other English poetry, which will be equally unknown and unhonoured. For surely, only in that way can *The Waste Land* mark 'the end of one literary epoch and the beginning of a new one'—the age of the supremacy of prose, particularly of prose which shall combine expression of excessive realism and machine-made thought with the skeleton incompleteness and nebulous aura of intuition. The serious way in which this sardonic jest and frightfully clever literary medley has been received and treated, is proof enough to me that the desiccation and disintegration of poetry have definitely begun. *The Waste Land* has a certain bony virility and hypnotic strangeness of suggestion (otherwise, of course, it couldn't have continued); so that the transmitted sound of some of it may bring stiffening into the work of a few other poets—often, it is to be feared, to their disadvantage. Beyond that it has little importance except as a gesture of mockery and disillusion, and contempt for the reader and critic; no value except as the banner of present-day war weariness and spiritual barrenness—one might almost say mental and moral degeneracy. It is in this last characteristic of decadence, that it is, of all our literature, the completest condensed expression of the feelings, thoughts, attitudes, activities, and tendencies of the present age. High praise, and yet most damning praise. And as the rhythm of modern life is so mixed and jarred, and full of dissonances and artificial derivations, you do, of course, find the expression of all this in the rhythms and movements and quotations and kaleidoscope patterns of *The Waste Land*—which is suggestive of gramophone groanings, wireless adjustings, machinery buzzings, fog-horn explosions, cinema clackings, motor traffic, underground traffic, street wanderings, the tarred road, comic opera, jazz, typewriter clickings, and sandwich-paper rustlings. The poem is a waste land in its methods, in the way it says and does things, even more than in what it actually pretends to say—which is, perhaps, that western civilization is coming to and end. . . . Though, personally, I'd rather drive a pony and trap round the crater of Mount Vesuvius (as I have so often done) than emulate T. S. Eliot by driving a motor car in hell.

Mr T. S. Eliot, though not of Oxford or Cambridge, is a man of considerable learning, a notable critic (if somewhat eccentric and overestimated critic), and *at his best* a poet in a cellar, and a rather good prose-writer. Considering all this, for many long months I took the poem quite seriously. But certain defects in it were a little too apparent. Either everything a man had learnt at school and the university was utterly wrong or Mr Eliot was a stammering pretentious man of genius, lacking the rudiments of solid education. In course of time the microscope revealed nearly everything that could be revealed. This is what I brought together on the table-cloth: (*a*) Bad grammar of both sense and syntax. (*b*) Absurd punctuation—which very often amounted to no punctuation at all. (*c*) Things upside down. (*d*) Disconnected thought, disconnected landscapes of thought, feeling, and ocular scenery. (*e*) The life of a man asleep, particularly of one suffering from a nightmare, rather than the life of one actively conscious. (*f*) An enormous number of tags, phrases, sentences, and echoes from other poets. (Though Mr Eliot has confessed to most of these in supplementary notes.) (*g*) The use of wrong epithets. (*h*) The queerest crudities of construction. (*i*) In at least two instances excessive coarseness of content. (*j*) An unpoetically assertive, if not pretentious, use of French and German. (*k*) Too many borrowed backgrounds; nearly as many as in all Milton's works put together.

The following passage will reveal some of these idiosyncrasies.

> A rat crept softly through the vegetation
> Dragging its slimy belly on the bank
> While I was fishing in the dull canal
> On a winter evening round behind the gashouse
> Musing upon the king my brother's wreck
> And on the king my father's death before him.
> White bodies naked on the low damp ground
> And bones cast in a little low dry garret,
> Rattled by the rat's foot only, year to year.
> But at my back from time to time I hear
> The sound of horns and motors, which shall bring
> Sweeny to Mrs Porter in the spring.
> O the moon shone bright on Mrs Porter
> And on her daughter
> They wash their feet in soda water
> *Et O ces voix d'enfants, chantant dans la coupole !*

Disconnection, oddity, insufficient punctuation, plagiarism —they are all so apparent! What at first is not quite so apparent is the false and muddled grammar of sense and syntax in such a passage as:

> Musing upon the king my brother's wreck [1]
> And on the king my father's death before him.

A teazing example of mispunctuation is the full stop instead of comma after 'him,' because, surely, the man was musing upon the 'white bodies' as well as the other things. A not

---

[1] This line is an altered line from *The Tempest*.

very apparent (though actual enough) instance of a wrong epithet is the use of 'low' before 'dry garret' because, of course, although a garret is never lofty, it is at the top of a house and is in no sense a cellar, which the words 'bones' and 'cast in' seem to imply. This use of wrong epithet is nothing like so prominent or frequent as the other anarchies, but it occurs several times, nevertheless. In the first part of the section, entitled *A Game of Chess*, a passage more consistent and Elizabethan in form than the introductory part of the poem would lead us to anticipate, we get:

> Glowed on the marble, where the glass
> Held up by standards wrought with fruited vines
> From which a golden Cupidon peeped out . . .

Just as we are beginning to admire the first twenty-eight lines we discover that they are full of confusion, that very little is clear to the senses, and that 'fruited vines' ought to be 'metal vines' or 'mahogany vines' or something like that, since the vines are manifestly devoid of natural life. While towards the end of the poem an extraordinary, but not too apparent, instance of an inversion, or thing upside-down, occurs in:

> We think of the key, each in his prison
> Thinking of the key, each confirms a prison.

For surely it is the prison that confirms the key, and not the key the prison. Keys lock and unlock other doors besides prison doors.

Most of *The Waste Land* cannot be understood, because *it was never meant to be understood*—except in patches (two or three of them, certainly, of some length). A man does not understand his lonely night of bad dreams, his disconnected bedroom panorama of sensations, mental pictures, broken, twisted images floating down into a tunnel of nightmare horror and dread. T. S. Eliot has thrown all literary discipline and discretion to the winds, and while he has actually created something (created the Disintegration of Creation), the midnight hour of one who has lost touch with God, or the delirious afternoon of one who is parting from his reason, he has blotched and stifled Victorian and Georgian poetry to an extent that is very disturbing. Had Mr Eliot labelled his poem, 'A Nightmare,' or 'My Neighbour's Inceptions of Lunacy,' or 'A Tale told by an Idiot . . . signifying nothing,' or 'A despairing Night of sleeping Unrest' the poem might have been accepted at its true value. But his methods and intentions were not at all clear, and so a certain section of the literary world has only too willingly allowed itself to be hoaxed. Just because the poem was impossible to understand, it was believed by many admirers to be intensely intellectual and imaginative. How Mr Eliot must have laughed! And yet it is equally probable that he has been more worried about it than amused—which certain sentences in *Ash Wednesday* seem to proclaim.

But it would be untrue to intimate that *The Waste Land* contains no poetry whatever. Indeed, it contains three or four remarkable passages, as, for instance, the one beginning:

A woman drew her long black hair out tight,

and ending with:

And voices singing out of empty cisterns and exhausted wells.

But through that flare of sombre beauty (almost reminiscent of Dante) Mr Eliot makes a gesture by which he seems to have intended giving himself away; as also in the following passage, near the end of the poem:

Datta : what have we given?
My friend, blood shaking my heart
The awful daring of a moment's surrender
Which an age of prudence can never retract . . .

As also in this passage, near the beginning of the poem:

A heap of broken images, where the sun beats,
And the dead tree gives no shelter . . .

As also in the final passage of the first section of the poem, though chiefly in its last line (quoted from Baudelaire):

You! hypocrite lecteur! mon semblable—mon frère!

As also in several other passages. But those readers who were not blind, for some reason or other (perhaps because of their shackling sophistication) seem to have made up their minds not to give the show away. Mr Eliot insults his reader by calling him a hypocrite, but all the time advancing behind the shield of quotation, thinks to put a bandage round the wound by associating the poor fellow with himself. 'The awful daring of a moment's surrender'—probably in committing this strange medley to print. The ordinary reader who is prominently a fool won't be able to see, and the intellectual reader who is prominently a hypocrite, or something equally unpleasant, will put his tongue in his cheek, or keep silence. While, of course, mixed up with those two are the sheep who are out for any profit they can get. So perhaps 'the awful daring' was no real daring after all. Is it not evident, Mr Eliot *seems to say*, that the light and courage of the human mind have long since been routed and put out? All that is left is a *Waste Land*. Yes, in a way, Mr Eliot is and has been well justified, and deserves, at least, a crown of thorns. He has spoken in his strange ironic idiom and definitely revealed something. But how difficult to praise at all, or to entirely damn. For he is one of the least desirable and yet most necessary activities in creation—*a practical satirist*. And like so many practical satirists he refuses to be a good English schoolboy and 'own up.' There are two sides to every penny, of course, and an artist is often this and that in spite of his intentions, but not necessarily what you want him to be.

The Waste Land, apart from its influence, has been very much overrated, for it is no more than the skeleton of a great poem, something which Mr Eliot did not clothe with flesh and raiment. So it takes upon it the appearance of an act of sabotage—a Creation of Disintegration. Another explana-

tion is that he cut it down from a much longer poem, tele-
scoping or dovetailing or jamming into one another the
isolated fragments of what he chose to rescue, with a glittering
eye all the time on the baffling and ridiculous; again an act
of sabotage, the destruction of his own poem, believing that
this moon-stricken generation is worthy of nothing better.

But a more charitable explanation and interpretation of the
poem is that it is a dream. We all frequently dream in this
way, and, indeed, a few people dream in no other way. The
dream is nearly always kaleidoscoped—not one dream, but
half a dozen—disconnected, muddled. But, to the dreamer
while he is in a state of dream, all is actual and natural.
Interpreted in this way, the poem takes upon it the hues of
real creation. It is the dream, the nightmare of an oppressed
melancholy scholar, who, though he may not have eaten too
much supper, has at least gone to bed with a vision in his
head of the approaching disintegration of European culture.
The difficulty always is to make the dream as real and communicable to the waking as the sleeping mind—and Mr Eliot
has definitely succeeded in doing this. In fact, he is the first
writer in English literature who has ever done anything of
the kind. And it has hypnotized and convinced in a wrong
sense every reader who aesthetically and intellectually has been
fast asleep.

The only snag in this interpretation occurs when we realize
the number of quotations which *The Waste Land* contains
from other poets. At any rate the idiosyncrasy constitutes a
slight defect. Though such lines might naturally come to a
scholarly mind during a state of dream, they would not come
in such quantities.

These quotations raise an interesting question: To what
extent was Mr Eliot aware of them when he wrote the poem?
Probably not entirely. At any rate, when he had finished it
he appended the necessary notes and pointed out that he was
not an unconscious plagiarist.

It has been said that Mr Eliot has always been aware of his
plagiarisms. Perhaps he has, or hasn't. At any rate they

occur in other poems without appended notes. For instance, the tiny volume entitled *Prufrock* contains these lines:

> Upon the glazen shelves kept watch
> Matthew and Waldo, guardians of the faith,
> The army of unalterable law;

the last being from George Meredith's sonnet, *Lucifer in Starlight*, which terminates with:

> Around the ancient track marched, rank on rank,
> The army of unalterable law.

The tiny volume entitled *Poems* (1920) contains the lines:

> The hippopotamus's day
> Is passed in sleep; at night he hunts;
> God works in a mysterious way—
> The Church can sleep and feed at once;

the third line being nearly the same as Cowper's

> God moves in a mysterious way.

A correspondent named William Addison pointed out the following in an issue of *John o' London's Weekly*. The obscure poem *Gerontion* commences with:

> Here I am, an old man in a dry month
> Being read to by a boy, waiting for rain.

But on page 142 of *Edward FitzGerald*, by A. C. Benson, the author introduces a FitzGerald letter with these words:

Here he sits, in a dry month, old and blind, being read to by a country boy, longing for rain.

But though I have often been transfixed by impressive lines which seem to me familiar, but which my ignorance will not allow me to place, I have more often been conscious of strong echoes rather than direct borrowings from other writers. For instance:

> The couched Brazilian jaguar
> Compels the scampering marmoset
> With subtle effluence of cat;
> Grishkin has a maisonette;

> The sleek Brazilian jaguar
> Does not in its arboreal gloom
> Distil so rank a feline smell
> As Grishkin in a drawing-room.

which are in part reminiscent of Baudelaire's poem *Le Chat*, especially the lines:

> Je vois ma femme en esprit. Son regard,
> Comme le tien, aimable bête
> Profond et froid, coupe et fend comme un dard,
>
> Et, des pieds jusques à la tête,
> Un air subtil, un dangereux parfum,
> Nagent autour de son corps brun.

The same book also contains the lines:

> I was neither at the hot gates
> Nor fought in the warm rain
> Nor knee deep in the saltmarsh, hearing a cutlass,
> Bitten by flies, fought.

which are reminiscent of Masefield's pre-War lines:

> The town begins on the sea-beaches,
> And the town's mad with stinging flies,
>
>   .   .   .   .   .   .
>
> There's sand-bagging and throat-slitting
> And quiet graves in the sea slime,
> Stabbing, of course, and rum-hitting.

But such kind of rewriting is probably permissible, though open to censure when it gets too close to a living or very recent poet. Flecker did it on several occasions, especially if he thought there was sufficient distance of time between him and the poet admired. A correspondent in *The Nation and the Athenaeum*, Edward G. Browne, pointed out that many lines in his noted *War Song of the Saracens* were direct translations from the Arabic. But in Eliot the thing occurs rather too frequently, so that my spasmodic pleasure is continually spoilt

M

by its being transferred into an unseen connection. I am always suspicious when I meet with a striking line or passage that it is not Eliot's own, and while reading *Ash Wednesday* I was several times transfixed by something which I felt I knew, but could not place—something which sounded like Malory.

Fortunately for modern poetry it has been rather shy of direct plagiarism. Otherwise it has attached far too much importance to Eliot, particularly in regarding him as the first letter of a new sentence rather than a heavy full stop, an inspired disconnection from which to write anew.

Surely it is chiefly as a satirist that we ought to judge Eliot. The company is a rather large one. (See, for instance, *Whips & Scorpions*, an anthology of modern satiric verse collected by Sherard Vines.) It includes Hugh MacDiarmid and W. J. Turner besides those already written about. But Eliot is not derisively voluble, like most of them. Being afraid of spilling his inky cup of tea he gives way to the most extraordinary antics to avoid it. The equally thrifty Sassoon takes matters more calmly.

CHAPTER XIX

MODERNISM IN POETRY

THE beginnings of what is known as Modernism in poetry are pre-War. I suppose the real author of Modernism was that Italian showman and disordered genius, Marinetti. He was the prophet of Futurism in verbal and pigmental art, with its gospel of speed, hard lines, strident rhythms, jarring full stops and lightning recoveries. Mathematic intruded upon logic as the prop of art, and the modern worship of the machine found expression in interesting, but irritating forms, from which such things as individual immortality and the deeper needs of the soul were entirely divorced.

In the *Figaro* of 20th February 1909, Marinetti published an exposition of the aims of Futurism, from which Harold Monro in his quarterly review, *Poetry and Drama*, of September 1913 (issued from his famous Poetry Bookshop), quoted the following:

We will sing the love of danger, and the habit of energy and fearlessness.

The foundations of our poetry shall be courage, audacity, and revolt.

We announce that the splendour of earth has become enriched by a new beauty, the beauty of Speed. . . .

All beauty is based on strife. There can be no masterpiece otherwise than aggressive in character. Poetry must be a violent assault against unknown forces to overwhelm them into obedience to man.

We will sing the great multitudes furious with work, pleasure, or revolt; the many-coloured and polyphonic assaults of revolution in modern capitals . . . stations, those ravenous swallowers of fire-breathing serpents; factories, hung by their cords of smoke to the clouds. . . .

Harold Monro partially approved; and in the course of his introductory article recorded his own principles—which were clearly to become the principles of two or three of his Georgian colleagues, and must have had some bearing upon the general development of Georgian poetry (though Georgian poetry entirely rejected the stridency, rhapsody, formlessness, and machine 'motives' of Futurism):

The first principles of *our* Futurism are:

(1) To forget God, Heaven, Hell, Personal Immortality, and to remember, always, the earth.

(2) To lift the eyes from a sentimental contemplation of the past, and, though dwelling in the present, always, *to live*, in the future of the earth.

In the same issue of *Poetry and Drama* appeared a number of very sympathetic renderings of Futurist poetry (adapted from the Italian by Monro himself), some of which do not sound very far away from Walt Whitman, especially such passages as:

We race.
We rise.
We must sing a new song of our speed,
We must chant a new hymn of ascent.
Soon we shall make ourselves lungs of the sponge of the spaces
And wings of the plumes of the clouds.

But in others there is such a fury of abandon and destruction of the normal that our ears are deluged as if by the ravings of madmen. Allied with Futurism were both Cubism and Vorticism, especially Vorticism—which is probably Futurism driven to its logical conclusion.

Apart from Futurism, but presently to timidly join hands with it in its production of Modernism, was the Post-Impressionism of the French and Belgian painters, and the dynamic patternings of the French Symbolist poets (Mallarmé, Rimbaud, etc.), which could be artistically injurious or salutary according to the way you swallowed them.

I believe that the first Modernist poets of consequence taken notice of in this country were pre-War, and were Ezra Pound and Ford Madox Hueffer (he now calls himself Ford Madox

Ford), but neither of them, at that time, broke entirely from tradition, and some of Ezra Pound's pre-War verses are very captivating.

Also rather apart from Futurism, and yet to ally itself with it in its use of free rhythms, was Imagism. It also owed much to Japanese poetry—which, of course, got somewhat transformed in translation and encouraged the breakdown of conventional English forms.

Then there was the free verse of the American poet. Walt Whitman, and everything else of Victorian times (though that was very little) which quarrelled with conventional law and order.

For at least a decade, the most important of all Modernist verse movements in English was quite clearly Imagism. But a few years ago it entirely fizzled out, principally because its chief constituent was one that recent Modernism has denied, i.e. clarity of image. True, it was art in rebellion, but in the centre of its rebellion was a shackling convention, so that it was a house divided against itself, and this division was finally shown in the wild caperings of some of its members. The thing that finally destroyed its tabernacle was the Cult of the Broken Image (which ended up in Contortionism), for except in the work of H. D. (Hilda Doolittle), Imagism was insufficiently supported by rhythm (basically metrical), which is really a manifestation of spirit, and without spirit nothing can long endure.

The first Imagist anthology was compiled by Ezra Pound and published in 1914. It contained pieces by the British and American poets F. S. Flint, Ford Madox Hueffer, James Joyce, Ezra Pound, H. D., Amy Lowell, Richard Aldington, and W. Carlos Williams.

The last Imagist anthology, which found it necessary to state that Imagism was ceasing to exist as a pure cult, even among its prophets, was published in 1930 with an introduction by Ford Madox Hueffer, and quite clearly shows how deeply Imagism had become entangled with Vorticism.

According to an American professor, Mr Glenn Hughes,

who has written a stout book about it (*Imagism and the Imagists*), Imagism was partly inspired by Greek poetry:

Hardness of outline, clarity of image, brevity, suggestiveness, freedom from metrical laws—these and other Imagist ideals could be drawn from Greek poetry as well as from Hebrew and Chinese;

which invites a considerable misunderstanding by over-condensation of statement, since *Greek poetry was very subject to metrical laws*. But he does occasionally show how the clarity of Greek poetry, the clear representation of its imagery and fine earthliness enter into some of the best work of the Imagists.

But this, of course, is not all. The actual precursors of the Imagists were, oddly enough, the French Symbolists, who were sprung from the loins of the Parnassians—a much easier starting-point of derivation to understand. In England the author of Imagism was T. E. Hulme, an aesthetic philosopher who was killed in the War and published only five short poems. The sponsor and promoter of Imagism, however, was probably Ezra Pound, though Amy Lowell, by her advertising methods a little later on, did more than any one to get the Imagists' work about and advance their ideals.

The most prominent of the Imagists are Richard Aldington, H. D., John Gould Fletcher, F. S. Flint, D. H. Lawrence, Amy Lowell, and Ezra Pound. But D. H. Lawrence expostulated that he was not an Imagist, and he seems to have been included owing to his prowess in coloured free verse and the sexual or physical quality of his imagination. That Anglo-American poet and art critic, John Gould Fletcher (who for a long time resided in London), is also a rather captious sort of Imagist. The reason for critical bewilderment must be fairly obvious, for he has a stronger mystical and religious sense than any of his colleagues, and continually shows inclination to escape from free verse into conventional metre and rhyme. I might almost have written 'therefore,' because all religious and mystical instincts tend to become pentecostally fiery or emotional and express their intensities in regular rhythms and word patterns (at any rate, where the

English language is concerned). But this is also a natural tendency in the work of H. D., who, though physical enough, is really too passionate and intense to be radically an Imagist. Her recent volume, *Red Roses for Bronze*, though alight with that Greek atmosphere and imagery which has characterized her other volumes, is at times downright rhapsodical, a riot of rose petals, but characteristically Imagist in such frequently occurring, chastened passages as:

> Then let me be a brother
> to your need,
> shoulder to steel-clad shoulder;
> let me take
> the helmet
> and the buckler
> and the greaves, Aristogiton,
> to your slender grace. . . .

Her Greek choruses are probably the best in twentieth-century literature, and she achieves very considerable vocal and platform effects by adroit repetitions of certain words and phrases:

> O which of the gifts of the gods
> is the best gift?
> this,
> this,
> this,
> this;
> escape from the power of the hunting pack,
> and to know that wisdom is best
> and beauty
> sheer holiness.

Imagism, strictly realized, seizes only upon the tangible and visual (i.e. the Earthly Image) and avoids any excess of emotion that is likely to take the mind away from what can be clearly seen, grasped, and contemplated. It is, therefore, at its most essential and narrowest a poetry of statement, a poetry of the mind and bodily sensibilities rather than of the soul, avoiding vagueness, transcendent symbolism, spiritual ecstasy, and stirring rhythms.

It made war on romantic falsity, that is, on sentimentality, and was more or less a poetry of physical sensibility. Perhaps Imagism as a self-conscious movement sought to achieve a poetry about things rather than about the poet's spiritual reactions to those things, in which strict sense, of course, it aimed at the impossible or almost impossible, so that most successful Imagist poems have to be recognized as poems of compromise, as semi-individualistic pictures of the finite. The Imagist attitude of anti-Romanticism was rarely completely expressed, and the original theories of Hulme only partially put into practice.

Though of recent years Imagism has been the battle-cry of a literary sect it seems necessary to remark that nearly all prominent poets, past and present, have at some time in their lives written Imagist poems;[1] for though the Imagist principles operate most easily in free verse, many a good Imagist poem has obeyed every conservative rule of form. And conversely, it also seems necessary to emphasize that the most prominent of the Imagists have in spite of their creed written verse which is by no means Imagist, a great deal in some instances — one of the reasons why Imagism as a coterie movement has by now quite betrayed itself and is practically dead.

While the most lovely and exquisite of this company of artists is the American lady H. D., and the most consistently Imagist the Englishman F. S. Flint, it is Richard Aldington who (as an Imagist) has riveted the greatest number of eyes in this country. Within his natural and self-imposed limitations, he has done some exceptional and curious work, and invited an attention which has swayed continually from unreasonable depreciation to over-estimation. Right or wrong, this Richard Aldington seems to have become the centre of the English group, and though his poems of pure or partial Imagism represent less than half his output in verse, they are

[1] Probably the greatest Imagist poet of all was Shakespeare.

of such a quality that they stamp him with its insignia from the outset. For instance, take this curious short poem:

> The chimneys, rank on rank,
> Cut the clear sky;
> The moon,
> With a rag of gauze about her loins,
> Poses among them, an awkward Venus—
> And here am I looking wantonly at her
> Over the kitchen sink.

Or this much more serious-minded fragment—freed, too, from that element of cynical humour or satire which ramps across some of Richard Aldington's pages:

> The ancient songs
> Pass deathward mournfully.
>
> Cold lips that sing no more, and withered wreaths,
> Regretful eyes, and drooping breasts and wings—
> Symbols of ancient songs,
> Mournfully passing
> Down to the great white surges.
> Watched of none
> Save the frail sea-birds
> And the lithe pale girls,
> Daughters of Oceanus.

But most of the Imagist poets have been harried by some sort of yellow devil. With nearly all of them it has been materialism, or some response or reaction caused by a too close regard of the mere concrete world. Surveying their work as a whole and disregarding the exceptionally good, one can say that while H. D. is passionately refined and resigned, Richard Aldington is often bitter or sensual, F. S. Flint morbidly frigid, John Gould Fletcher despairing, and Ezra Pound annoyingly superior or perverse. But their influence for good and ill, on traditional poets as well as eccentrics and border-liners has been considerable, and will probably continue.[1]   Professor Glenn Hughes, in his book on the Imagists, has remarked on the debt T. S. Eliot apparently owes to them, while I think that nearly every writer of free verse has at some time or other gone to school with them.   Richard Church, for instance, who generally writes in traditional metrical forms, has quite clearly modelled his free-verse book, *Mood without Measure* (1927), on the Imagist principles, and done it so well, with so much colour, clarity, and incisiveness, and with such close adherence to rules which the Imagists often violated, that I feel that Glenn Hughes's book is incomplete in not including him.

Unfortunately some of the Imagists gave way to fooling and parodying their own work.   Their frequent plunge from beauty and clarity into ugliness, obscurity, and eccentricity constitute some of the most amazing and awful contradictions in all literature.   William Carlos Williams sounds more like a new kind of verse-humorist than a poet, and the same applies to James Joyce (who, however, began his lyrical career as a strict formalist), while much of the later Ezra Pound is little better. Even Richard Aldington has written passages which will not allow of a moment's serious consideration.

But Richard Aldington is not developing that way, and his most recent verse, if sometimes rather more formless than he is capable of achieving and rather too strongly tinged with sorrow and despair, is full of warm feeling and imagination. Just as he was disintegrating he pulled himself up, and though little of his recent verse is metrical, it is probably saved from the worst features of formlessness by his continuous contemplation of the beauty of old Greece.   But the English poet who seems to have the most influenced him is D. H. Lawrence —not always to his good.

Imagism, I suppose, was too much of a stunt.   Its exponents had insufficient confidence in themselves and their aims.   They burned with no holy zeal like the Pre-Raphaelites, and found

---

[1] I have recently come across a little pamphlet of good Imagist verse, written as late as 1935—*Two Hours* by Clifford Bower-Shore, a young poet who combines spontaneous traditional movements with Modernism.

the free-verse line (so excellent for achieving clarity) pointing in all sorts of directions. When you write in free verse you are free of any known order of discipline; and when you are free of any known order of discipline you may land anywhere.

The Imagists were the natural opponents of the Georgians as well as the Victorians. They were equal enemies of both the Right and the Centre, and helped to prepare the way for the present domination of the Left-wing.

As can be seen, it was as much an American movement as an English one. So because the rest of the beginnings of Modernism had their origins on the Continent, we may almost regard the present condition of English poetry as an anti-British condition. But a certain dean of St Paul's, the Jacobean metaphysical poet John Donne, has also much influenced some of the Modernists (more often from his bad side than his very good), and of very recent years that ecstatic juggler and sentence smasher, the Victorian Jesuit priest, Gerard Manley Hopkins. Then to their outpourings add the domination of Sigmund Freud's psycho-analysis (again foreign) and the picture is pretty nearly complete.

No! not quite, for contemporary with the influence of Gerard Manley Hopkins came that of Rainer Maria Rilke, who, however, has done less damage, and perhaps would have done none at all if he had been read in the original German instead of in translations. But good should be said of the renderings of the *Duineser Elegien* by V. Sackville-West and Edward Sackville-West, which are nearly as subtly and finely worded as the original German—though they have escaped little of its obscurity.

What an array of primary sources!—Marinetti, the French Symbolists, the Dadaists and Surrealists, Walt Whitman, John Donne, Gerard Manley Hopkins, Rainer Maria Rilke, Sigmund Freud! Stirred together, in whole or in part, they seem to produce 'Modernism'.—though even the traditional poets have not escaped contact. Indeed, is there anything left save Modernism? And can any new poet get a hearing who does not admit himself of its ragged company?

Nearly all the old values and reverences have disappeared, and we are confronted by, what? Only the next century will be able to tell us plainly. The phenomenon has even made a member of the underworld lift up his hands in wonder. For what says Mark Benney in his lurid revelation, *Low Company*—that terribly candid autobiography of a burglar?

The truth was, I had conceived culture as meaning an intimate knowledge of Greek literature, familiarity with the works of Leonardo, the ability to appreciate Beethoven, and such-like acquirements. But here were real artists and writers who knew nothing about such things, or took them for granted . . . Joyce, Eliot, Rilke, Mann; Picasso, Gaudier, Wyndham Lewis; Keyserling, Spengler, Jung, Croce; Stravinsky, Bloch, Sibelius, Schönberg. These were the lords of the new culture; these had outshone the older artists, writers, thinkers, musicians till their work was reduced to the status of a clumsy child's ineptitudes. . . . The spirit of the new culture had one attractive feature: it justified, or seemed to justify, anything. Anything, that is, save the commonplace. It justified the *Café Vert*. It justified burglary. Whatever one did, Freud would excuse, Bloomsbury would approve. It was exhilarating. . . .

And then there is D. H. Lawrence, a writer of magnificent prose (both Imagist and rhapsodical) and indifferent verse, who has helped to open further flood-gates. A few of his poems have beauty of form, but for the most part they are slipshod or reckless pieces of work, and the critic, Hugh Ross Williamson, probably said the last word about him when he wrote in his *Bookman* editorial: 'He was not a great poet; he was not even a good one . . . and his poems are valuable chiefly as comments on his other work.'

Besides D. H. Lawrence and the other Imagists (and in two or three instances of stronger influential prominence), the chief recent or living promoters of Modernism have been T. S. Eliot, the three Sitwells, Laura Riding, and Gertrude Stein. To them should also be added Robert Graves, who commenced as a rather fantastical Georgian, and Harold Monro (now deceased), who found himself in the rather difficult position of Mr Facing-both-ways.

The Sitwells have clung together like black-currants on the same twig, and though they have many strong points of difference they have mutually helped to create what is known as 'Sitwellism'—which might also be termed 'kaleidoscope verse,' for they have produced by a lavish jostle of words something resembling that curious *changing* phenomenon caused by looking at bits of different coloured glass at the bottom of a tube (the kaleidoscope—a Victorian nursery toy), and moving it round and round. Osbert Sitwell, however, is primarily a satirist, and as a free-verse writer is obviously much indebted to the Imagists. In his thought he is the most lucid and compact of the three, and one continually gets the feeling that he is Modernist by too deliberate choice—a traditionalist astray; for in spite of his frequent formlessness he really belongs to that company which is headed by Siegfried Sassoon. To-day all the stress is laid upon Edith and Sacheverell, but it is quite possible that a later age will prefer him to them, especially as he has thrown a clearer light upon the follies and iniquities of the present time.

Sitwellism might aptly be compared with Euphuism, for it abounds with strange conceits, far-fetched figures of speech, fantastical allusions, imagination dishevelled and stifled under a play of a wild and riotous fancy; and though Edith and Sacheverell move in somewhat other realms than those of the Elizabethan, John Lyly, one can imagine a reincarnation of the man (which, of course, would submit to the peculiar demands of a later age) taking upon it a complexion not wholly unlike their complete or partial fusion. The future will probably reprint them only in books of criticism, for their verse has been a literary influence and curiosity rather than a thing of individual appeal, their best passages submerged under a mass of fruitless verbiage.

Both have assiduously overwritten themselves, for they have been under the tyranny of mere language. Manner and symbolism have been more important than inevitability of matter, the garment more to be desired than the body which it adorns, the tree-flower sweeter to the taste than the fruit which was to come out of it. They have stressed the surface of the lyrical sphere rather than the centre, the means of approach rather than the approach. Only they themselves can read their books from cover to cover.

From among important writings on the three Sitwells I would refer readers to R. L. Mégroz's bulky book, *The Three Sitwells* (Richards, 1927), and a chapter in Professor G. Bullough's more up-to-date volume, *The Trend of Modern Poetry* (Oliver & Boyd, 1934). For more destructive criticism I would refer them to an article by Geoffrey Grigson in the August *Bookman* of 1931 ('An Examination of the Work of Edith Sitwell'), and two articles in the *Everyman* issues of 1929 (28th February and 7th March) by Philip Henderson. This last is a young poet, half Modernist, half traditional, with an exceptional talent for writing lucid and virile literary prose; and because he has always had Modernist sympathies, his semi-destructive criticism of colleagues whom he might be expected to admire almost completely is, to say the least of it, well worth our serious attention. After pointing out that Sacheverell Sitwell's poetry is largely dependent upon echoes from other poets, and like Eliot's full of allusion (though I don't think in this connection that there are really many verbal echoes, as in Eliot), he goes on to say:

The greatest defect in Mr Sacheverell's poetry is not that he is incapable of writing a poem without entangling our brains in a mass of such allusion, but that his method depends for its effect upon obscurity and a confusion of our critical sense. And the obscurity of Mr Sacheverell is of a peculiar kind. It consists in his lyrical poems of a watery flux of semi-realized sensations and only half-embodied thoughts following one thick upon the other, inundating every clear impression. . . . This method is at enmity with the very purpose of poetry, which in its intellectual aspect alone should carry us further than the realm of prose by its synthesis and crystallization of intuitive thought and feeling. . . . Thus in *The Thirteenth Caesar* and *The Cyder Feast* we find this musical, aromatic technique of Mr Sacheverell at war with itself, defeating its own aims, and disintegrating our reactions by its very excess of subtlety. His sensibility, being extraordinarily acute and hyperaesthetic, has grown so absorbent, so much beyond his control that it floods his mind with a welter of delicate impressions that, without discrimination or selection, come pouring on to the page, apparently dictating to him their own direction and form. . . .

The truth is, that Mr Sacheverell Sitwell, though an indisputable poet and a very sensitive, cultured child of his age, has allowed himself to be badly entangled in some of the meshes of his sister's strange disorder, which, working upon his own natural tendency to diffuseness and formlessness, has resulted in an unwieldy mass of work through which only the most patient and determined can profitably paddle. He has no incisiveness, no continuous clarity; and in regard to his form, frequently hovers between uncertain blank verse and half-realized free verse or prose verse. For though he has a sensitive ear for the relative effects of consonants and vowels, his rhythmical sense is frequently quite out of touch with it. Frequently he gives one the impression of trying to write blank verse without being able to manage it, for contrary to all that his sister has written about him, he is a very indifferent technician, and the heavily brocaded and decorated garments with which he adorns the insufficient body of his thought and emotion are a muddle of ill-fitting curves and lapels, of topsy-turvy twisted sleeves and leg-holes and misplaced waistbands. When he is technically good, it seems to be more by accident or sudden unexpected inspiration than through the aid of any clear knowledge of what he is doing. In his rhymed verse he is equally unsatisfying and uncertain, so that, though he begins such a short poem as *Rio Grande* very magnificently, he soon turns away from his fine music and descends into metrical protoplasm:

> In the Rio Grande
> They dance no sarabande
> On level banks like lawns above the glassy, lolling tide;
> Nor sing they forlorn madrigals
> Whose sad note stirs the sleeping gales
> Till they wake among the trees, and shake the boughs,
> And fright the nightingales.

The passage certainly stimulates one to wish for more in the same key, but instead of continuing to give pleasure to the reader, Mr Sitwell's presently dwindles into this sort of thing:

> The noisy streets are empty and hushed is the town
> To where, in the square, they dance and the band is playing;
> Such a space of silence through the town to the river
> That the water murmurs loud
> Above the band and crowd together.

The phenomenon is characteristic and places Mr Sitwell among the artists who don't sweat, the careless poets who trouble themselves more about wildly chosen fine words and higgledy-piggledy imagery (but interwoven with passages of prosaic dullness) than consistent verbal music and disciplined patterns of effect. Otherwise he doesn't understand form, and is unable to fix his fluency into the compact physical framework which all great art demands. (Why in this connection has he entitled one of his books *Canons of Giant Art*?)

Through Mr Sitwell's pages move not only the imagery of the most fantastical of the Elizabethans, but also the forms and figures of rococo and baroque art. Nearly every kind of unusual musical instrument is mentioned by name, many kinds of strange fruit, trees, and flowers, while centaurs, salamanders, nymphs, fauns, satyrs, turtles, cobras, dolphins, maenads, shepherdesses, pierrots, unicorns, harlequins, ballerinas—all sorts of curious animals—ramp, crawl, rustle, and gallop through the diffusely poetical pages. Add to them the heroes and heroines of antiquity, with a suitable escort of gods and goddesses, and the uninitiated may get some idea of the too frequent preciousness of Mr Sitwell's art, and its removal from the human and everyday. Of course, classical themes and allusions ought not to render it 'precious,' but Mr Sitwell is obsessed by his external subject-matter rather than by his themes, so that for all his many sudden flashes of felicity and beauty, he does not, judged as a complete whole, sufficiently achieve his purpose.

Sitwellism started in the middle of the War, in 1916, with an anthology called *Wheels* (which continued until 1921), behind which Edith Sitwell was the principal driving and turning force. Besides the contributors Edith, Sacheverell and Osbert, there were others, including Nancy Cunard, Wilfred Owen, Iris Tree, Alan Porter, Aldous Huxley, and Sherard Vines. But much of the external work of these six poets had little strict relationship to Sitwellism, and Alan Porter was to move into a rather different atmosphere. A poem by Nancy Cunard set the name to this recurrent anthology, and the general outlook was delineated in her lines:

> I sometimes think that all our thoughts are wheels
> Rolling forever through a painted world:
> Moved by the cunning of a thousand clowns
> Dressed paper-wise, with blatant rounded masks.

But Nancy Cunard has always been a comparatively compact and lucid writer in comparison with Edith and Sacheverell, whose painted, paperish world has always been much too painted and paperish, their clowns and masks much too blatant and obscuring. The Sitwells are poets of despair (and in this they are true Modernists), but their expression of it is often very masked and oblique, so that, save for the satires of Osbert Sitwell and a few outstanding other things, like Edith Sitwell's *Gold Coast Customs*, one is often more aware of a stage of immense frivolity or quasi-mythological in-difference—a stage of gleeful dolls and cynical marionettes, of tumbling clowns and harlequins, of wooden horses be-stridden by nursery knights, and the veiled figures of an aloof antiquity—than anything relevant to the near present. Both Edith and Sacheverell have shrunk wearily from the con-temporary world of flesh and blood, and in its place set a world which has little relationship to the evidences of our eyes and ears, a world of unbridled and riotous fancy—not a world of deep insight or imagination. Sometimes they (especially Edith) seem to move in a country of the dead, an arena of

the fourth dimension. Sacheverell is really the more serious
poet of the two; but a large amount of Edith Sitwell's work
sounds as if written by an automatic pencil, a planchette
guided by a leg-pulling ghost. Some of it is complete nonsense, never intended to be anything but nonsense, never
intended to be understood at all or to communicate anything
clearly—a furore of disintegration, as nearly illustrative of
the disintegration of the speech of sensitive society as it is
of true poetry—in fact, extreme Modernism. Something of
which has been pointed out by John Sparrow in his important
book, *Sense and Poetry*, which includes passages from Edith
Sitwell among the frequent examples of nonsense verse.

It has been claimed that all the Sitwells, especially Edith,
have been much influenced by Baudelaire and others of the
French Symbolists. But rarely have these poets of superabundant imagery and suggestion let themselves loose with
quite such complete abandon. In her more disciplined and
serious moments (as, for instance, in *The Little Ghost who died
for Love*) she may remind us at times of Baudelaire (though
I think that there is a great deal more of the real Baudelaire
in Sir John Squire's *Lily of Malud*), but more often it is
Mallarmé, the most suspect and vague of the Symbolists,
with whom we would make the comparison.

Strange to say, she has written a very enthusiastic book
about Alexander Pope—whose ghost was probably very much
stricken with astonishment while she was doing it; for save
in her atmosphere of artificiality she bears no relationship
whatever to Pope, and her poetic method at all times has
been completely opposite to that of Pope. It is true that
Pope had no great vision, no wide eye on beauty or humanity,
but at any rate he had the gift of clarity and of assuming to
sympathize with what he did not deeply feel. He walked
with the moral and polite crowd, and voiced the feelings of
that crowd, for he was immensely conventional and the complete expression of the society of his day. He did not write
about that society so much as *for* it. But Edith Sitwell, though
veiled and oblique, when she touches society (she comes of a

very old and honoured family) is writing *about* it rather than for it. For has she not in this connection said:

This modern world is but a thin match-board flooring spread over a shallow hell. For Dante's hell has faded, is dead. Hell is no vastness; there are no more devils who laugh or who weep—only the maimed dwarfs of this life, terrible straining mechanisms, crouching in trivial sands, and laughing at the giants' crumbling.

So when her verse seems to have any clear application to our contemporary world she is manifestly writing about the maimed dwarfs of this life, about terribly straining mechanisms and the trivial people who have got stuck fast in trivial sands, with no intention at all to flatter or please a society which she has had the opportunity of viewing closely, and which, she seems to think, is representative of the upper world of to-day—expressed very oddly, but musically and power-fully, in such lines as these (from *Gold Coast Customs*):

> But those hardened hearts
> That roll and sprawl
> In a cowl of foul blind monkey-skin,
> Lest the whips of the light crash roaring in—
> Those hearts that roll
> Down the phantom street
> They have for their beat
> The cannibal drums
> And the cries of the slums,
> And the Bamburgher parties—they have them all!

Her world (when it is not an untranslatable world of sheer fantasy) is a world of rottenness and artificial glitter arched by the 'dark hairiness of bestial skies,' and beaten upon by all the trivialities.

But it is her untranslatable remote world of sheer fantasy which occurs the more often—when she writes continually in this way:

> Dagobert lay in front of the fire . . .
> Each thin flame seemed a feathery spire

Of the grasses that like goslings quack
On the castle walls: 'Bring Gargotte back';

But Gargotte the goose-girl, bright as hail,
Has faded into a fairy-tale. . . .

One of Edith Sitwell's most repeated devices has been her transference of sense values, which has helped to strengthen the incomprehensibility of her queer verse. So grasses 'quack,' light 'squeals' or 'creaks' or 'whines,' dew 'trills,' darkness 'grunts,' the sunlight 'hiccoughs'—evidences of one sense translated into terms of another; and about which she says in self-defence:

Our senses have become broadened, and cosmopolitanized. They are no longer little islands, speaking their own narrow language, living their sleepy life alone. Where the language of one sense is insufficient, they speak the language of another.

But this has always been realized, and poets in inspired and very vital moments have unconsciously or half-consciously made the transference. Did not Milton speak of 'blind mouths,' and Alfred Austin, in one of his very few good poems, write 'cloistered from deafening sight'? But that sort of thing never became a mannerism or a thing of continuous artificial deliberation. The reader was never before battered out of his wits by it.

Though the commencements of Sitwellism were in the middle of the War, the public was not particularly aware of it until a little later, about the years 1922-3. By that time, through the publication of their numerous books, backed by their united efforts of robustious self-advertisement, the literary world was beginning to be very conscious of their existence. Edith Sitwell had given out that in early youth she had taken an intense dislike to simplicity, morris dancing, a sense of humour, and every kind of sport except reviewer-baiting (see *Who's Who*), and Sacheverell Sitwell had said that one of his recreations was J. C. Squire. The reviewer-baiting was not merely confined to sallies against J. C. Squire and the Georgians, but was directed against all who disagreed with their aims and methods. They were out for battle, and when they got it, they complained, very amusingly, that they were persecuted. But while Osbert Sitwell was the most aggressive swordsman of the three, it was chiefly Edith who developed (or made pretence of) the 'persecution complex.' As regards this, Geoffrey Grigson has written that her later books are marked by a 'slum-like despondent sense of treachery.' But as the personal element rarely enters into her work, this rather applies to her general attitude to society and the reviewing world than to anything that she has actually written about herself in her strange verses.

But in spite of disapproval and dislike, about 1922–3, the daily and weekly press was beginning to pay a good deal of attention to the Sitwells; and censuring them as frequently as not. As an instance of the adverse article, take the one in *Cassell's Weekly* of 4th July 1923, headed 'A Literary Danger,' and subtitled 'Miss Edith Sitwell's Latest Experiment'—from which I will take some of the most moderate sentences:

The literary world is threatened with a new danger—the danger of Sitwellism!

One afternoon recently a number of people were invited to be present at the Aeolian Hall, in order to hear Miss Edith Sitwell, the poetess, create a new art—the art of Sitwellism. . . .

. . . Across the platform was stretched a curtain that represented a piebald face, one half white, the other crimson. Through the mouth came the end of a wooden megaphone, and through this came Miss Sitwell's weird voice, shouting to music such poetical gems as:

'Hell is as properly proper
As Greenwich or Bath or Joppa.'

And in this strain the unseen reciter continued. . . . The idea of this new art was explained in a prologue by Mr Osbert Sitwell. He pointed out that the main feature of his sister's experiment was the elimination of the reciter's personality, which was supposed to interfere between the art and the audience.

The disapproving writer also remarks (striking back with her own weapons) that most of her poems were proof of the fact that she was educated privately, had no sense of humour, and had taken an intense dislike to simplicity. Also that her audience was somewhat cracked-brained and eccentric in manners and appearance.

She was certainly something new. Nothing in English literature since Lyly's Euphuism had occurred in any way resembling her queer cult. But one virtue at least she has developed—the virtue of jazz. It is, possibly, a doubtful virtue; but she has somehow or other, developing from nursery and ballad rhythms, contrived to turn the orchestral music of jazz and its attendants into a new kind of jigging verse (see especially *Gold Coast Customs*). In this aspect of her art she has little affinity with her brother Sacheverell, who is not at all consistent as a verbal musician. But Edith Sitwell has clearly developed a *popular* man-in-the-street technique, a technique of cocktail modernity—though from which meaning is almost entirely divorced. As Professor Geoffrey Bullough says of her: 'In her fox-trots and polkas, rhythm is attained at the expense of meaning. Words exist as combinations of sound and accent; meaning is abolished. It is an exquisite art of sensations.'

But 'exquisite' is not always the right epithet of appreciation unless the tones of caterwauling be exquisite. For the title of her poem *Trio for Two Cats and a Trombone* might be put at the head of much of her other verse, for even its use of words is characteristic:

> Long steel grass—
> The white soldiers pass—
> The light is braying like an ass.
> See
> The tall Spanish jade
> With hair black as nightshade
> Worn as a cockade!
> Flee
> Her eyes' gasconade
> As her gown's parade
> (As stiff as a brigade)
> Tee-hee! . . .

In such abandoned moments vociferate all worried cats beneath
the moon of night though, often, it must be confessed, with
rather more force of inner meaning. And what, too, is one
to make of frequent lines like:

>   . . . country gentlemen, so countrified
>   That in their rustic grace they try to hide
>
>   Their fingers sprouting into leaves; we see
>   Them sweet as cherries growing from a tree—

where she really does put forth a meaning, and then destroys
it by suggesting that leaves grow out of cherries.

The truth is that she frequently throws her words about
anyhow, concerned only with a general effect of rhyme and
glitter—which only breaks away from conventional rhythm
(how technically conventional is at least fifty per cent of her
music!) when she is trying to reproduce the tones of such
modernities as fox-trot and jazz. In the rhythm of jazz she
has in at least one of her poems, *Gold Coast Customs*, been very
successful; and it is pity that such an adroit performance—
one, too, that contains more reality of passion than anything
else she has written—should not have been reduced to greater
symbolical simplicity, and freed in revision from its frequent
outbursts of incommunicable nonsense. Regarded from the
standpoint of its unconventional rhythm it has, it is true, a
technical basis resting upon a certain hackneyed form of the
old ballad, but its many variations and skilful adaptations,
through which beats a rattle of knuckle-bones and primitive
drums, compel our admiration, especially as the poem really
does set the pulses stirring.   And in some of her other poems,
she does, every now and again, fling down the short magical
passage, the counter of enchantment—though how difficult
it is to find a poem with any real unity, any obvious right
of independent existence!

Negroism (i.e. jazz), Euphuism, Vorticism, Imagism, French
Symbolism, Dadaism and Surrealism (offsprings of French
Symbolism in its decadence and decline), Cubism (I think a

great deal of Cubism) enter into the work of Edith Sitwell, and though her two brothers are rather less than she, the poets of many Isms, neither of them exist quite independently without some of them.

The three Sitwells have trodden the dust, and in the process kicked up great clouds of it, intermingled with the almost equally obscuring gold and silver powder from their moth-like wings (for they have neither the wings of birds nor butter-flies of day). For all their profuse self-advertisement and the amount of attention which the public has at different times bestowed upon them, their real importance is in the rear of their fame and notoriety. They are no more the equals (in combination) of three such poets as W. H. Davies, Masefield, and Lascelles Abercrombie (in combination) than John Lyly was the equal of Shakespeare; for while they possess in super-abundance the glittering superfluities of poetry, they are very frugally endowed with those strange and baffling essentials which go to make it a thing of consolation or permanent bewitchment. They have helped to prepare the way for the disintegration of poetry as much as for its nourishing—and that is no peacock feather in their coloured hats.

But the chief promoter of Modernism in England has been the American, T. S. Eliot, who came over to this country and got himself enrolled among the English poets. In Eliot's verse have been found all those ingredients of despair, obscurity, and post-War fatigue and defeatism which are deemed so essential to the poetic armoury of to-day.

It is not quite clear when Eliot first wrote his early poems, for his first volume of *Collected Poems* was dated 1909–25, while the initial poem, *The Love Song of J. Alfred Prufrock*, was dated 1917. According to this, a first draft of *The Love Song of J. Alfred Prufrock* may belong to the date 1909—which con-siderably precedes the War. At any rate, after about 1922, a few years after the close of the War, this country as well as America was very aware of his existence. He began to be timidly discussed, and according to a variety of critics he has been influenced by the French Symbolists and Surrealists,

by the Imagists, by John Donne, by some of the Old Testament poets (such as Ezekiel), by Dante and the later Elizabethans. In fact, many of the famous and notorious poets
of suggestion and nonsense, as well as a few of good sense,
have got into his melancholy, rat-infested cupboard. In spite
of reiterated affirmations of criticism, his debt to the Elizabethans is surely very slight, for he scarcely ever suggests them,
save in deliberate quotations, and with blank verse he seems to
have no real skill. As regards his content and the arrangement of his words he is not only a poet of aloof and recondite
intellectualism (but quite removed from the academic solidity
of Robert Bridges and Laurence Binyon), but also a versifier
of bewildering nonsense—in fact a Dadaist.

But what is Dadaism?

It is a French movement sprung out of the loins of the
most obscure and disintegrating of the French Symbolists
(such as Mallarmé) and is different from Surrealism only in
that it never tries to be anything at all, while Surrealism does
now and again make some real attempt to explore the
country of the subconscious. Dadaism was an expression of
nihilism and disgust, and a movement to bring notoriety to
its promoters, who expressed themselves down every by-way
of perversity and disintegration. The company of poets (if
you can call them poets) was known as 'Dada'—the origin
of the term a little obscure. 'Dada' in French is a child's
nursery term for a horse, but in an article in Seumas O'Sullivan's *Dublin Magazine* of October 1935 by A. J. Leventhal,
the suggestion is thrown out that Synge's *Playboy of the Western
World* inspired it:

It was almost on the eve of the War that the *Playboy of the Western
World* was produced for the first time in Paris. The idea of an Aran
parricide calling forth the plaudits of red-skirted island colleens
stirred up among a section of the audience responsive sympathy
even if they had not learned the new Freudian jargon that translated every prejudice, *idée fixe* or *tic* into a complex, and though it
was later that Oedipus was invoked to explain the particular complex involved in Christy Mahon's attack on his da, yet they felt

here was the Mene Tekel Upharsin—a burning signpost. They left the theatre to meditate as to how they should fashion the literary boy that would beat their overbearing papas into submission.

But their papas (or dadas) were more than the flesh-and-blood Philistines and moralists. There was the whole body of Art, a very large abstract dada, to contend against. Murder, of course, will out, but for a time the assassins seemed to have it entirely their own way. So they murdered form, colour, propriety, syntax, the sentence, logic, and suggestion (even the Symbolists had become traditionalists). Their contention, when they were attacked as German barbarians (the movement started in Paris during the War), that the boy-poet Rimbaud was their inspirer, hardly permitted of examination, for though Rimbaud had invoked the gods of destruction and violence, and committed all civilization to the flames, his poems often burn with great power and beauty, and though his symbols may be difficult, his form is beyond reproach.

That Greek-minded poet, F. L. Lucas, commenting on Dadaism and Surrealism in his brilliant book, *The Decline and Fall of the Romantic Ideal*, sees little difference between Dadaism and Surrealism, and says:

The Dadaists gave soirées where persons danced dressed in stove-pipes or announced that they would pull their hair out in public; or they held exhibitions to which the entrance led through a public lavatory, while hatchets were provided for the public to attack the exhibits, and a young girl, dressed as for her first communion, recited obscene poems. . . . In 1922, Dada, amid much tumult, died in giving birth to Surrealism. Where Dada had been a negative rebellion of adolescent whimsicality, Surrealism set out to release the Subconscious. . . . But, though it had acquired a theory for its infantilism, the new movement seems to differ little in practical results from the old.

But 'whimsicality' is almost too polite a term for a movement which behind all its fooling (and some of it rather obnoxious) was an expression of real disgust against a capitalist civilization which for a long time had been running off the lines and finally caused the War. The promoters of Dadaism, it is true, sought personal notoriety, thirsting to get themselves into the limelight; but behind Dadaism was the self-suicide of a universe. It was a muddled expression of defeatism, a vociferous inane witness to the leper body of western culture (or at least to some of its limbs). The inside of the sepulchre was full of dead men's bones, and Dadaism picked out all the mouldy fragments and cynically flourished them in the face of the respectable. Dadaism is not Art—which always, in some form or other, aims at the giving of pleasure—but a negation of Art, an apotheosis of contempt. It began badly and it went too far. An intellectual city like Paris could not tolerate it for long, and Dadaism passed on.

Its home now seems to be both England and America (Hitler has got rid of it in Germany—one of the few good actions of Fascism), though most of us first became acquainted with it from America. Gertrude Stein, the most prominent of the American Dadaists, has written many things like this:

> A little a little one all wooly or in wool
> As if within or not in any week or as for weeks
> A little one which makes a street no name
> without it having come and went farewell. . . .

And Laura Riding, another prominent Dadaist (whose name for some years, through the Seizin Press, has been connected with that of Robert Graves), things like this:

> By after long appearance
> Appears the time the all the time
> Name please now you may go.

And things like this (repeated monotonously, though with slight variations, through several pages):

> What to say when the spider
> Say when the spider what
> When the spider the spider what
> The spider does what
> Does does dies does it not. . . .

While Robert Graves, a fine poet who has recently involved himself in far too much obscurity (too remote from his very early influence, John Skelton), wilfully puts himself into the new movement with several strange poems, one of which seems to try to tell us who were the parents of Dadaism (the quoted lines only six of twenty-eight):

> His mother was a terrier bitch,
> His father a Dalmatian,
>   Guessing black or white,
> Not black because white
> Because black because white;
> Not white because black . . .

Something between a third and three-quarters of Laura Riding's collected poems (which she derisively calls *Poems : A Joking Word*, and introduces by a preface of extraordinary and seemingly deliberately confused prose) is a manifestation of plain Dadaism. But sometimes her Dadaism compromises (in its least disintegrating moments Dadaism can momentarily hold the attention, or even entrap the innocent and credulous through the introduction of symbols, or by means of some feat of technical adroitness) or passages of nonsense jostle occasional passages of plain sense—such cynical outbursts as:

> If there are heroes anywhere
> Unarm them quickly and give them
> Medals and fine burials
> And history to look back on. . . .

Or lines of more philosophical (though questionable) content break through to make us wonder if she is not a philosopher who has lost her way, such lines as:

> There is much at work to make the world
> Surer by being more beautiful.
> But too many beauties overwhelm the proof.
> Too much beauty is Lethe.

It is true that such lines have a prose movement, are mere prose cut into short lengths. But Dadaism has broken every law, including those of metre and rhythm; while as metrical expression it probably more often approaches the nursery rhyme than the slowly evolved rhythms of culture. . . . Listen to the prattlings of a half-articulate baby, a child of two or three, saying 'dada' mingled with every word and phrase that takes its fancy, and one of the possible origins of Dadaism steals upon the intelligence. Dadaism was so disgusted with everything that had gone before, that it would begin language over again and lend to it the fresh and foolish vigour of the nursery. Which is perhaps what Laura Riding had in mind when she wrote:

> Many gentlemen there are born not babes.
> They will be babes, they will be babes
> In the shades.
> They will dribble, they will babble,
> They will pule in pantomime
> Who were not babes in baby time.

Dadaism has very visibly enmeshed many of our youngest and most recent poets, and careful examination of the verses of W. H. Auden seems to point to a strong influence coming from Laura Riding—who preceded him by many years.

But Eliot, the chief contemporary influence on recent modern poetry, is also a partial Dadaist, though of recent years he seems to have been breaking himself free. But what is one to make of such lines as:

> When I lay bare the tooth of wit
> The hissing over the archèd tongue
> Is more affectionate than hate,
> More bitter than the love of youth,
> And inaccessible by the young . . .

which are taken from one of his very latest publications; and even more dadaistic (especially if you judge the poem as a whole—for that is only a third of it) than anything in *Gerontion* or *The Waste Land*? For the dense obscurities in some of his poems there is possibly something good to be said, and even for this passage, from *Ash Wednesday*:

> If the lost word is lost, if the spent word is spent
> If the unheard, unspoken
> Word is unspoken, unheard;
> Still is the unspoken word, the Word unheard,
> The Word without a word, the Word within
> The world and for the world;
> And the light shone in darkness and
> Against the Word the unstilled world still whirled
> About the centre of the silent Word . . .

which combines Dadaism with the more suggestive methods of French Symbolism (in the above by means of semi-nonsense creating the idea of the creation of the universe—'in the beginning was the Word'), seeking to really convey something. But too often Eliot merely tantalizes and mystifies, so that there occur moments when it is difficult to know whether he is really trying to express himself or deliberately fooling and bamboozling the reader with hypnotic gibberish. . . . There is at least one passage in the lucid *Murder in the Cathedral* which gets rather too close to the witch's cauldron, so that it seems improbable that Eliot ever intends to break entirely free. Judged by some of the work which originally made him famous, and a number of adverse remarks from his not-too-adverse critics, Eliot is a glorified Dadaist, a serious writer of nonsense verse, a satirist sharpshooter who aims at the target that he may miss it. But the other side of criticism has been taken rather more notice of, chiefly voiced by Hugh Ross Williamson in his book, *The Poetry of T. S. Eliot*; and in an expressive sentence by that fairly reasonable critic, I. A. Richards:

Some readers find in his poetry, not only a clearer, fuller realization of their plight, the plight of a whole generation, than they find elsewhere, but also through the very energies set free in that realization a return to the saving passion.

And the golden-tongued and unusually reliable Desmond MacCarthy has ingeniously compared him with Robert Browning—surely his very worst slip from the impregnable azure of 'Affable Hawk.'

To what extent Eliot's religious dramas, *The Rock* and *Murder in the Cathedral*, are really to be taken seriously as expressions of Anglo-Catholicism I do not know; but it is odd that they should come from the author of such a poem of bitter mockery as *The Hippopotamus*, untranslatable, it is true, much of its inner meaning veiled behind verbal nonsense, but nevertheless clear enough in its last two stanzas as no flattering comment on either Christianity or the Church:

> Blood of the Lamb shall wash him clean
> And him shall heavenly arms enfold,
> Among the saints he shall be seen
> Performing on a harp of gold.

> He shall be washed as white as snow,
> By all the martyr'd virgins kist,
> While the True Church remains below
> Wrapt in the old miasmal mist.

But French Dadaism made chaste maidens compromise with obscenity, so that you may terminate at the opposite from where you began, and ending in virtue or disgust suppress nothing of what precedes. Dadaism is every kind of wilfulness expressed in disintegration and unsolvable forms and movements.

But hear what one of the oldest of our critics, Mr G. M. Young, has said about Eliot in his recent book, *Daylight and Champaign*:

If I am right, then there has been in our day not a development, but a catastrophe, a gash at the root of our poetry, to which I can recall no exact parallel in literary history, and that a poetry with traditions so tenacious as ours should surrender at first sight to the first man who thought of translating French *vers libre* into broken-down Elizabethan stage verse seems to me, if it turns out to be true, to be one of the oddest things on record. Yet this I understand is the claim made for Mr Eliot, the Sinon by whose wiles the Wooden Horse was received into the fortress.

But that is by no means the whole of Eliot. He is too hypnotizing for only that. He is an actual poet, but is immensely wearied by the old forms and lyrical good manners, and while half-heartedly seeking new forms which shall be expressive of the jarring machine environment which envelops him, finds himself formulating a full stop, and then moving into an impasse of troubling darkness, which he can sometimes make tolerable only by an indulgence in sour laughter. He is a tongue-tied poet, and he is tongue-tied because he is suspicious of every popular poet of consequence who came before him. His background is mistrusted, insecure, and unprovocative, for he feels that the old reserve platform of eagles and trumpets has been hacked away by the War. In his desiccated despairing brain he continually hears something like a witch's incantation, which in its intermingling of sense and nonsense seems expressive of the unutterable dark things which he wants to say. So we often get in his verse a rattle of knuckle-bones and words uttered for the mere sake of words rather than for those lucid ideas and impressions for which civilized speech exists. In regard to some of this, G. W. Stonier in his stimulating and intellectually suggestive volume of essays, *Gog Magog*, writes with some measure of truth, but in much too flattering terms of defence :

Eliot is the poet of inhibitions, perhaps the only considerable poet who ever lived in whom the inhibition against writing poetry has been supremely powerful. His mastery of this strange situation is indeed extraordinary. Not to be free to write poetry, and yet to hint magnificently at it; to be master of the final flat phrase, and yet to suggest new beauties, and to obtain a new echo from the old ones; to come at the end of a movement (Symbolism) completing its decline, and yet to inaugurate a new movement in literature— to have done all this with a finality and finish which can be paralleled in few other writers, ancient or modern, is a very remarkable achievement. . . . Eliot is a defeatist, *fin de siècle*—end of all the ages! . . . In his strange, sweating, puritanical, bone-rattling way he is trying hard to be an Elizabethan—a later Elizabethan. . . . As a poet he feels infernally old.

The chief of living poets who has influenced Eliot is Ezra Pound—who is, indirectly, as much the author of Modernism as any one else. But Ezra Pound never had much to say, and has always been an experimenter in technique rather than a poet of any solid revealing shape or developed content. His curiously disintegrating mind comes out in his recent anthology (*Active Anthology*) and in his extraordinary letters and prose writings nearly as much as in his post-War cantos of enormous incomprehensibility. In a recent letter to the *Observer* he wrote: 'The truth is that English criticism would have gained considerably had Palgrave been strangled in his cradle'—a characteristic statement which suggests only too clearly the platform upon which he stands. . . . He is a disinherited intellectual, a scholar and linguist who has lost his way—turning in upon himself, and then outwards upon the culture which nursed him. He writes with his head in—is it the coal-scuttle?—and adds to his obscurity and aloofness by tagging his verse with scraps from foreign languages —which element of pretentiousness Eliot has been only too ready to take over from him.

But that is by no means the whole firework display, and among Modernist poets who have stood critically aloof while at the same time remaining Modernist, Sherard Vines may be taken as an outstanding example. One of his books was curiously enough named *Kaleidoscope,* and in another, *The Pyramid,* perhaps he wishes to suggest that the stony edifice of civilization has culminated in a point, beyond which there is no development. He is at present the professor of English literature at the University College of Hull, and was for many years an English professor in Japan. Japanese art and Japanese landscapes intrude upon Baudelaire, Rimbaud, and something seventeenth century—and though he has some affinity with both Edgell Rickword and Edith Sitwell, his voice is more

N

intrinsically his own than is the case with so many of the Modernists. His hard intellectual, and yet not unflexible rhythms are worth studying for their technique alone, and, though he is frequently difficult to understand, his intellectual and euphuistic exuberance does every now and again yield something upon which the mind can clearly seize. There is very little nonsense or pretence in Sherard Vines, though he is too hag-ridden by the War and its disintegrating aftermath, and he is no cheerful antidote against depression. But his finest and most compact lyric, *Day in the Desert,* is a little gem of its kind, and has the speech of enchantment:

> Along the dry coast of Arabia
> I heard the quail and the hard rattling tide.
> Distant, as untuned bells by a mere-side,
> Gaunt palm-fronds clanked, troubling the rare
> And bitter morning air.
> Then Azrael called to Ithuriel
> Flashing his brass wings yellower than sand;
> Ithuriel with a golden horn replied.
> Out of the resonant land
> Noon passed and evening died.

That is certainly very different from some of the new verse under discussion, which has even provoked the Vorticist artist Wyndham Lewis (a Modernist poet himself) to derision. For in his long and very strange poem, *One Way Song* (a book of over a hundred pages), it frequently appears as if he is both describing and parodying it—the description, however, more obvious than the parody in such a passage as this:

Again let me do a lot of extraordinary talking,
Again let me do a lot!
Let me abound in speeches—let me abound!—publicly polyglot.
Better a blind word to bluster with—better a bad word than none
  lieber Gott!
Watch me push into my witch's vortex all the Englishman's got
To cackle and rattle with—you catch my intention?—to be busily
  balking
The tongue-tied Briton—that is my outlandish plot!

And more obvious still in:

I sabotage the sentence! With me is the naked word.
I spike the verb—all parts of speech are pushed over on their backs.
I am the master of all that is half-uttered and imperfectly heard.
Return with me where I am crying out with the gorilla and the bird!

But he goes further than that, and out of the fog and vapour seems to suggest (in three magnificent lines) that Modernism is a movement of hypnotism, and the natural, if enforced, expression of the age:

We are not very rich in laurelled heads—
We are a little age, where the blind pigmy treads
In hypnotized crusades against all splendour.

What has recently happened is the sudden appearance of a bevy (or gang) of young poets (many of them under thirty years of age) who mingle Socialist politics with poetry and deny tradition. They advocate Communism as the new religion which is to reinvigorate poetry, and some of them are poets of disillusion and despair even more than their Modernist pre-decessors. Obscurity goes hand in hand with cacophony, and the joints of modern machinery clank and creak through their curiously inflexible periods. They have been praised, humoured, chided, and cursed, for there are, of course, good things in them as well as bad, and there are two aspects to every movement. But probably in this instance the adverse side of criticism is the truer side—its disapproval rather pithily, if uncompromisingly, put by Miss V. H. Friedlaender in one of her occasional inroads into free verse:

The young of to-day have decided
That poetry is not poetry;
Away with loveliness,
Away with music.
Let the lines roar like a traffic jam,
Stutter like a machine gun,
Let them be as monotonous as ribbon development,

> Stark as pylons,
> Obscure as police traps,
> Garish as petrol pumps.
>
> Well, then, so be it:
> The poetry of beauty is out of fashion.

But I think that Miss Friedlaender is the spokeswoman for nearly all the women poets—whose sex makes them naturally traditional and conservative, so that they hold themselves aloof from Modernism. Among the most disgusted, Teresa Hooley looks forward to a blessed future:

> When these thin drippings, void of rhythm or rhyme,
> Have tricked down the drain like coloured scum
> That floats in gutters on petroleum.

And, from another point of view (and embracing all their obscurantist predecessors), Humbert Wolfe has scourged them in the most stinging lines he has ever put on paper:

> And therefore since I cannot hope
> to write a line like tangled rope,
> or make a noise like beating rugs,
> or slatterns emptying water-jugs
> upon the street below, I swallow
> my sense of failure, and, Apollo,
> now usher to your Lordship's House
> the perfect modernist—the louse.

They roar, they beat wool. But in my opinion they generally do neither. 'Beating' suggests steady rhythms; and roaring is quite out of fashion, and clearly not good Modernism. Roarers like Wyndham Lewis are outcasts even among the older poets, while youth pushes him aside in favour of poets of flatter texture like T. S. Eliot or (even flatter still) Herbert Read. Rather do they caw or groan—croakers and groaners when they are at their worst, and sablewailers at their most musical.

But it is necessary to take more careful stock of the situation. Youth seems to have little to look forward to, and finds itself imaginatively and spiritually bankrupt through the sins of its predecessors. It has some reason to be despairing and angry and feel that it owes civilization a grudge. Unfortunately it confuses national fathers and grandfathers with foreign predecessors, for the chief blame is to be laid at the doors of foreign countries—of Germany and Russia, who were the chief causes of the War. Even the lacerating, soulless effects of Capitalism, which it so writhes against, look like the tentacles of an American dragon. Comparatively few are really conscious of the entire significance of the European disaster, conscious of it with all the fibres of their beings, but those few are the hyper-sensitive, among whom must be reckoned the poets. So the poets, estranged from the past and sulkily unwilling to express themselves in the flexible and musical forms of their fathers, either nihilistically smash up all sense, sensation, imagery, syntax, and punctuation (occasionally downright sabotage), or set themselves struggling tortuously in the direction of a new vision, or seek to express what they already hold in new forms. But in regard to this last it has taken thousands of years to build up poetry to its present forms, so what they are trying to do in a single decade is to achieve the impossible. Moreover, though they are by no means off the lines as poets of Despair, they have forgotten that Despair can be immensely boring and rebuffing. It cannot hope to get sympathetic attention while it is inarticulate, which means that, when it is functioning through the medium of verse, it must express itself more or less as Shakespeare and Milton made it. Nevertheless Despair is a difficult theme for short poems unless it is softened into the fabric of grief or stoical anguish. In which respect that wonderful Irish poet, James Stephens, has written the most illustrating lines possible about it:

> And Egan Rahilly begins a verse—
> 'My heart is broken, and my mind is sad . . .'
> 'Twas surely true when he began his song,
> And was less true when he had finished it:
> —Be sure, his heart was buoyant, and his grief
> Drummed and trumpeted as grief was sung!

For, as he meditated misery
And cared it into song—strict care, strict joy!
Caring for grief he cared his grief away;
And those sad songs, tho' woe be all the theme,
Do not make us to grieve who read them now,
—Because the poet makes grief beautiful.

Despair, anguish, grief, sorrow must, of necessity, be translated into beauty of some kind. Their contemplation can become aesthetically possible only through some special dignity or glamour of words—which means that the poet has got to be lifted into spiritual exaltation during the process of creation —not merely intellectually pleased with what he is doing. Nor is it enough even, during the process of composition, to be poetical-minded. Equally essential is some special musical adroitness in the arrangement of the words. Poetry is largely a physical thing, one of the Fine Arts, and all Art worthy of the name is a sensuous thing and firmly fixed upon tradition. To change the figure, Art is a stream; but whether the artist is in the middle of the stream or merely in the outer edge of it is of no particular consequence (at any rate, that is his affair) so long as he is in the stream and not in a muddy backwash or overflow. The normally sensitive and imaginative reader (and poetry is a means of communication) gets his purest delight out of poetry when form and content are inseverably locked. Poetry is partly a matter of form, partly of intellect, partly of soul and inspiration. Never is it singly and solely dependent upon any one of these, but is a baffling blend, a sort of verbal magic or crystallized communication of enchantment; so that when it is quite right it seems to be neither new nor old, neither conventional nor unconventional, neither very peculiar to this age nor any other. In every age there is probably a 'Left Wing,' something distinguishable from a traditional 'Right-Wing' poetry, but away from their ages when poetry really is poetry, the estranging militant differences disappear, and the two walk side by side as friends.[1]

[1] Part of this paragraph appeared in an autobiographical essay, *Peering into Darkness*, which I published in *Ten Contemporaries* (Benn), a volume of bibliography by John Gawsworth.

These very new poets emerged (rather suddenly) from the country of T. S. Eliot, chiefly from his *Waste Land*, and their first united appearance was in Michael Roberts's miscellany, *New Signatures* (published 1932), shortly followed by *New Country*. After that, others came upon the scene, and now we are not entirely certain who is Modernist and who is not, especially as some of these wilful people are getting tired of the monotony of speaking through the same Communist and fog-stuffed trumpet, and have started developing along lines of their own. Moreover, it is rather early in the day to write confidently about any of them, even about that profusely advertised trio, W. H. Auden, C. Day Lewis, and Stephen Spender, save to remark that Auden and Day Lewis show too many technical influences coming from the bad side of Gerard Manley Hopkins, and Day Lewis and Spender some good technical influences coming from the later Robert Bridges (see, for instance, Spender's *Express*[1] and Day Lewis's *Story of a Flight*). None of them is free from Dadaism (or, at any rate, the extremest forms of Surrealism), though it is a minor ingredient in Day Lewis and Stephen Spender in comparison with Auden, whose verse until very recently seems to have excommunicated rather more than it has communicated—including, of course, the English language. But Dadaism is even more pronounced in several of the later comers, and though Rayner Heppenstall may possibly be free from it, his troubled intellectualism and over-confidence in the merits of obscurity help to push him deep into the circle of the incomprehensibles. One of the most promising, and quite the youngest of the company, is David Gascoyne, who claims to be 'England's only wholehearted Surrealist,' and others worth serious attention are George Barker, Julian Bell, William Plomer, Michael Roberts, Louis MacNeice, John Pudney, Richard Goodman, Randall Swingler, Norman Cameron, Ronald Bottrall, Rex Warner, William Empson, Lawrence Whistler, Clifford Dyment, A. S. J. Tessimond, John

[1] Unfortunately Spender's *Express*, though so fine in its development, terminates on an entirely false note.

Lehmann.   At their worst they are contortionist and defeatist (cold-porridge poets who go breakfasting on slag-heaps), or, like John Lehmann, who began as a good traditionalist, are now too far to the left in politics; but occasionally real poems are achieved, or fine passages are allowed to trickle on to the paper.   So there are doubtless some stars among them, though they delight in obscuring their own beams; and many of them have begun badly by indulging too much in inter-breeding and not assimilating the traditional background before rejecting it.   Such a one did not originally seem to be Louis MacNeice, though he has certainly not yet fulfilled the strong promise of his first book, *Blind Fireworks* (1929). . . . As regards the most prominent of the young Dadaists, I have omitted them from the list (as well as some others whose work I am not sure about or who have published very little), because Dadaism is a movement of nihilism and negation, and therefore, of course, has no future.

All those young poets have run in teams, and appeared together in the same anthologies, though there are some definite distinctions as regards form and content.   For instance, A. S. J. Tessimond is developing into a traditionalist of peculiar grace and enchantment, while Julian Bell [1] is as much a nature poet as he is a poet of Modernist disillusionment, his forms being as traditional as Tessimond's.

Another who is different, but more difficult to assess, is Clifford Dyment.   He has gone from moderate Modernism to an extreme *naïveté* of traditionalism—neither of which garments fit him very well.   He is a poet of promise, though he has yet more fully to find his own voice.   Lawrence Whistler, on the other hand, who preceded W. H. Auden as a winner of the King's Medal, has sometimes successfully fused opposites and antagonisms, though he is more often a careful and original traditionalist.

But outside the list there are other moderate Modernists, poets who have been influenced by the new movements and

---

[1] Since writing these lines news has come to me that Julian Bell has been killed in Spain.

yet held themselves aloof from intermingling, and whose work has not appeared in modernist anthologies. Such a one is Robert Gathorne-Hardy, who in his earliest verse was somewhat influenced by Eliot, and throughout has been more or less under the sway of John Donne. And latterly he has made translations from Catullus. But he is best known as a novelist, botanist, and student of country-life. He has written one of the few technically good modernist poems in publication, though in his second line the particle 'but' might, perhaps, be changed more effectively into 'then':

> We were together when the mountain broke
> In smoke, silent, with lightning laced, but shod
> With sound, with dull sound of rock-smitten ground,
> With shrill sound of escaping vapour shod.
>
> We were together when the mountain broke.
> Where were you when the smoke descended? Blended
> With sound of rebounding rocks I heard your words.
>
> We were together when the mountain broke
> The first time; from erupted rock our home
> Constructed rose. We were together when
> A second time the vapour cleared; appeared
> To each our home ash-seared and each to each.
>
> But for the first outburst had grown no home,
> But for the last no known security.

Another young modernist poet (Modernist because of his frequent free-verse forms) who has not allied himself with any company, is Philip Henderson. He also, in one of his best poems, has taken certain of the new motifs of thought and form (but with a contrary attitude as regards machinery), and, like Gathorne-Hardy, though with rather less originality, bound them into a more compact and musical shape than is usual with such verse:

> Why should we live on in this sick uncertainty,
> Fearing the continuance of our lives, or fearing
> The advent of a state that will harry solitude
> And stamp down all sensitive vision in the common mud?

* N

Is it that life runs at a more metallic speed
Than heretofore, elements of glory dimmed now
With a general mechanistic counterfeit
For earth, for air, for light and the living personality?

Is it that now we live in ever recurrent dread
Of horrible extinction falling from the skies,
Unimaginable death and useless agony
We shall be driven to grapple with and deal to others,
That those among us poor and hungry and without a home
Shall never again want food or house or money—
Blown to air, or one with the slow-crumbling earth?

How can we live, how, being citizens, collective ants
Feverishly undermining our own content,
Daily perverted by malicious print,
Blindly diverted with amusements that no longer amuse,
Smoke-confused, din-deafened, speed-blunted,
How can we, citizens, assert our right to live—
Offal of a system that must destroy us or decay?

One of the most promising of the latest comers is Frederick
Prokosch, who, of Austrian and Anglo-German parentage,
went from the Continent to America and is now residing in
England. There is a good deal of obscurity in much of his
work, but probably little of it is really intentional, and at its
best his verse is distinguished by glamour and opulence. He
has, perhaps, borrowed something from Rilke, but at his
most lucid he seems to have been influenced by Hugo von
Hofmannsthal (who, I have understood, was influenced by
Keats).

Very different is Kenneth Muir, who in 1933 published
from the Oxford University Press an unusually fluent book
called *The Nettle and the Flower*, some of which had already
been made use of by the B.B.C. Here again are to be found
influences (including some downright pastiche) coming from
the older poets, with interminglings from the new—all transformed into running rhythms (some of them very conversational), which make you want to speak the verse aloud. It

valiantly confronts social deterioration; and in its loud energetic rage, its fury of invective, and the way it heaves clearly visible bricks at everything stupid or rotten in modern civilization is unique among the newest verse—which generally chooses to attack abuses in undertones and tangled obscurities.

In the same year another young poet, Edward James, issued a book, *La Belle au Bois Dormant*, which in its longest poem seemed to show some restrained influence coming from the Sitwells (at any rate there are shadowy resemblances to them). Other poems united the modern and traditional, but the best thing in it, *The Song of a Girl*, is one of the best love poems of the century.

But there is a full score of young poets of some consequence who revere even less the new leaders; and specially worthy of mention (though they do not hang together) are John Gawsworth, Geoffrey Johnson, Robert Gittings, Hamish Maclaren, F. C. Boden, William Montgomerie, Frank Eyre, Stanley Snaith, Paul Selver, John Betjeman, Christopher Hassall, R. N. Currey, Bryan Guinness.

Bryan Guinness, who in his first book was inclined to be saturnine as well as chilly, is developing into a poet with unique powers of lucidity and visualization.

R. N. Currey has as yet published no book, but over thirty of his lyrics have appeared in the literary press. Most of them are characterized by scrupulous adherence to light forms, among which figure some excellent paraphrases from old French poets, particularly Charles of Orleans, while he has also attempted Villon. But the Villon spirit (at any rate at its most violent) is better conveyed by Paul Selver in a little book of strident satirical verses entitled *A Baker's Dozen of Tin Trumpets*. Satire, too, has also partly occupied the attention of John Betjeman, whose *Continual Dew* (1937) was unusually widely reveiwed. One of the left-wing poets has described his verses as 'full of the prejudices of the nineteenth-century bourgeoisie in their most corrupt and inverted forms' —a very unqualified judgment, particularly as he is often a poet of indignation against the bourgeoisie, and in his amusing but very venomous poem *Slough* has cursed and scourged a modern industrial town as it probably never before has been cursed and scourged. But *Continual Dew* has some dim affinity with Douglas Goldring's pre-War volume, *Streets*; while it is also probable that John Betjeman has read the shorter poems of F. O. Mann.

F. C. Boden, a budding novelist as well as verse-writer, who commenced life in the mine, has affinities with Huw Menai (an older poet with similar drab beginnings). And Stanley Snaith (whom I sometimes think is the best of the younger generation), links up with the older pastoral poet, Andrew Young, though he seems rather more conscious of the destructive inroads of machine civilization, which he sometimes assaults with such fine phrases as 'the silver strategy of flowers.' Another, and younger poet, with a close intimate eye upon the countryside, is Frank Eyre—an expanding traditionalist of small output, but solid promise.

Geoffrey Johnson, another frequent nature poet, is rather over forty years of age, but nearly all his recent published work was written before he was forty, some of it long before, showing in both form and content complete freedom from the Eliot movements. He is uneven, but he sometimes writes fine lines, striking phrases, and, at moments, he certainly has a very impressive technique. And of Robert Gittings, also out of the current mode, Frank Kendon has written praisingly for the Cambridge University Press, and added: 'surprisingly free from science, obscurity, Eliotism, or nightmare introspection.'

As regards Christopher Hassall, I cannot do better than quote from Siegfried Sassoon's strong praise in the *New Statesman*:

Christopher Hassall's work is of that kind which provokes an immediate emotional, spiritual response in readers sensitive to poetry. Unfortunately the criticism of poetry to-day has fallen largely into the hands of those who have no natural response whatever to the poetic. . . . Mr Hassall will probably be told that he is altogether behind the times, because he does not conform to the current cant of machinery-poetizing and so on. . . . On every page there are epithets of startling felicity.

Among the Scotch poets is William Montgomerie, one of whose books bore the strange revolutionary title, *Squared Circle* —not at all descriptive of its sufficiently traditional contents, though partially denoted in the sub-title, 'A Vision of the Cairngorms.' Another Scotch poet, Hamish Maclaren, was once a sailor and later a pedlar, and something of the quality of his work may be deduced from the title of his book, *Sailor with Banjo*, a collection of sailor chanties and songs of the open road, of the kind that was popular during the first two decades of this century, but nearly all genuine, as they are the outcome of real experience.

One of the very young poets of solid promise besides Clifford Dyment and David Gascoyne, is John Gawsworth (Terence Fytton Armstrong), who claims descent from a kinsman of Shakespeare's supposed Dark Lady of the Sonnets, Mary Fytton. He was born as late as 1912, and nearly all his verse, which was mostly published between the ages of eighteen and twenty-one, shows plain severance from modern movements. Though a child of London city, with the roots of his troubled consciousness in the pavement rather than the country soil, his verse, though sometimes awkward or savouring of preciosity, is free from the traffic of the town, and free from the Isms to which it has given birth. He seems to have largely imbibed the late - Victorian and Edwardian poets of passion and sugared speech, the poets of the Yellow Book period and just after, with preferences for Ernest Dowson and Richard Middleton. He is a very considerable throw-back, especially as he appears to cast a continuously admiring side-glance upon the Elizabethans. Young Modernists find him quite unattachable, and in the vivid and rather pugnacious preface to his verse anthology, *Known Signatures* (a 1932 publication, very obviously hurled at the head of Michael Roberts and his *New Signatures*), he has defined his standpoint and explained the necessity for upholding tradition. 'Yet,' he says, taking up the cudgels for youth against youth, and indirectly implying that he is very much ashamed of his green and tender years, 'youth will not agree. Judgment has not fled to brutish beasts, but to incompetents, it would seem. Men have boastfully lost their reason.' His standpoint has always been uncompromisingly the same. His volumes of bibliography have avoided the inclusion of every thorough Modernist save Edith Sitwell, and the same applies to his anthologies of short stories and other edited books and booklets. . . . As a 'bookman' he is pre-eminent, almost certainly the best informed of any under thirty years of age.

But, by the years 1948–9, who, reading the last paragraphs of this chapter, will find himself touching fingers with even a third of the young poets mentioned? More than half of them, modernists, semi-modernists, and traditionalists have gone forth with a ravening sickle and cut their corn before it was ripe. It has not been merely an affair of sending verse to the printer before it was sufficiently filed, but of including too many poems which were no poems at all and ought never to have seen the light of day. How few are the consistent exceptions in that varied company of youth! And even the conscientious artists among them, the apparent exceptions, may ultimately prove incapable of development. It is an age of haste, of rending hurry, of noise and stridency, of cruel and exacting demands upon the purse. Can poetry ultimately survive? It seems hardly likely, unless the instinct for withdrawal asserts itself in the face of the multitude, and the poet writes only for his own emotional satisfaction. And yet what is the multitude? Does it really trouble itself in the least to find out anything about poetry and art? Seemingly it believes what it is told to believe and accepts any kind of advertisement insistence as a sure signpost to the genuine article. The true poet has so much to contend against, particularly the hypnotizing influence of clique criticism and press advertisement. He needs to be reminded of what Schiller in ecstatic despair told his German contemporaries

—that the Earth was divided up and given away before the poet was thought of, and that all that is left to him is the Kingdom of Heaven. It is of no use attempting, as the newest Modernist attempts, to voice the feelings of the Age, this Machine Age, rectified by the aspirations of Communism. Or to half attempt, and then turn in on oneself, accepting and rejecting in an impotent zigzag of perverse fatuity and topsy-turvy despair. The Earth, even in Schiller's time, had been divided up and given away to the unimaginative; and to-day the general evidences are ten times more apparent. For consider the greed and silliness and barren faith of the community we call Society! And consider the soiled prospect which the proud wielder of capital is privileged to call his own — a landscape that is being carefully devoured by hungry brick and steel, where corrugated iron sometimes even replaces the thatch on old Elizabethan cottages, where a mean scrabble of vulgar residences defaces the flanks of down and moorland, where the trees are hacked away, and the song of the birds made silent. Defilement, ravishment, and decay! Tin cans and broken earthenware litter the pebbled beds of the mountain streams; and the tarred roads, to the accompaniment of yelling wireless and gramophone, and growing ever wider and more unnecessarily numerous, stab their stifling and destroying arms into the great spaces that should be green with trees and waving with wheat and barley. And yet all that is only the acutely visible picture of the conflict between cynical, disordered wellbeing and gasping, disintegrating misery and want; of a world in which honour is bought and sold and the slaves of Mammon have joined hands with the slaves of sham progress and acid utilitarianism. With such evidences of annihilating decline before the throne of Vision it is perhaps not too pessimistic to suggest that the soul is dying, and that the brain which heaven bestowed upon it for its nourishing and apparelling has been impotently caught in the tentacles of the machine, and in blind acceptance and without effort towards rejuvenation is dying alongside its disabled consort.

Perhaps the most alienating of modernist poetry (and there is far too much of the very alienating) is the picture and exposition of all *that*, and not the sensitive expression of either indignation or imaginative compromise. At any rate, in more ways than one, wire-plucking has deteriorated into mere 'wire-pulling,' and even the rose sought after only for its withered petals or its briers; so that the cultured man in the street, for whose delight Shakespeare wrote his great verse of wit and passion, and for whom even Tennyson was an invigorating stream in spate, is bewildered and rebuffed, walking in a cloud of complete darkness where the demands of genius and real talent cry miserably for his sympathy and attention.

And the difficulty of improving or changing matters, of any kind of wholesome and efficient action, has been rendered more arduous by a certain section of the intelligentsia (a minority section, I believe, but nevertheless one that works underground and receives far too much sympathetic attention) which has its roots in Oxford and Cambridge, sending out its strange missioners to schools and colleges which might advance better in the way of honest revolution if they had never seen the movements of their mouths. For with the power and influence of Russia before their dissatisfied eyes, they frequently assert that they are Communist or have strong Communist sympathies. But the adverse fact lies heavy upon their shapings; so that their Communism is obviously not Communism, being neither flamboyant red nor charitable pink, but a dismal grey. For the creature of their invention is opportunist and perverse, full of strange cerebral pride and Machiavellian exhortations, a twister of syllogisms and a murderer of grand Art and the English tongue. Defeatist and passionless, dropping pennies of strange wisdom into the hungry hats of the most socially and intellectually fortunate of the dissatisfied young, it ambles mumbling along its cacophonous by-way, with the skeletons of a thousand murdered values clawing distractedly at its Freudian coat-tails. And if many of these values have received the quietus that they deserved, how can we, with any equanimity, view the death of more than half of them, or accept the creature's contemplation of unnatural likes and contraries with the extended palms of our intelligence? For how strange are its declared and suggested associations! And how strange, too, its antemetics! Freud and Karl Marx! Freud against Jesus Christ! What, really, have the first two got to do with one another? And why in the name of all the seraphim should a psychologist and mental scientist get pushed forward with pretentious claims of wisdom and reform against the greatest of humanitarians and the most exalted of social and spiritual prophets? Even the name of William Blake has been taken in vain, for that saint of song and sincerity and most imaginative of all English painters has been invested with special eccentricity as an excuse for some of the most contemptible trivialities of Surrealism, though we can rather certainly suppose that if he were reincarnated and to-day living among us (with so many models of nineteenth-century excellence before his seeing eyes) he would be putting a greater discipline into work that his rational critics consider too formless and unintelligible. And because of this and that, and the great religious passion that infuses his creations, would be equally slighted and unhonoured, dwelling, perhaps, in even greater poverty and obscurity.

Where Truth is so desiccated and delayed, how can Song —'the rose upon the lips of truth'—speak with any fullness of reality to either the sons of God or the common man? Is it really surprising, after all, that nearly every established reputation is in the melting-pot, and that sham poets, and stammerers of baneful periods, have been hoisted over the heads of those whose lips are touched with the great transforming passion? Is it really surprising that the true singers of songs, the poets of ecstasy and purifying pain, should hesitate and grow bitter, feeling that all their inspiration and endeavour are little better than an 'expense of spirit in a waste of shame,' and that very soon the term Poet will be as odious to the average intelligence as Zany or Hypocrite. How little astonishing, too, that some imaginative and sensitive spirits, who might have written enduring music in a better age, should succumb to the general fashion and sin against themselves and their brothers by inflicting verbal meanness and assassination upon the groping emotion! The sin against the Holy Ghost is another matter, for real inspiration is not so easily deflected, and it is only charitable to suggest that the Holy Ghost never spilt itself into the souls of certain uncompromising Modernists who have perpetrated obscurities which upon examination reveal little save unscrupulous hoax and cynical fake. The uninspired writer may do what he chooses without fear of eternal damnation, especially if he is completely aware of himself as a good deal less than uninspired. But that does not alter the tragedy of all that has darkened the corridors. It takes genius or something relative to genius in the years before thirty to fly into the brick wall of growing custom; and it is only a hero or a saint who can come out of the impact intact, especially when he knows that his rebuffed or unrecognized music is twenty times better than that of his belaurelled opponent.

If I have exaggerated, is it not sometimes salutary to set free the lightning? And is it not only babes and perverts, hypocrites, and the weak of heart who really dread and hate the lightning? And is it not in the interest of every poet worthy of the name, whether he be young or old, to look more deeply into his heart and then outwards upon his confused surroundings, and more carefully examine the walls of his confinement?

INDEX OF NAMES OF PEOPLE

371

MADE AT THE
TEMPLE PRESS
LETCHWORTH

GREAT BRITAIN